REFLECTIONS ON THE WEEKDAY LECTIONARY READINGS

Roland J. Faley

PAULIST PRESS
New York/Mahwah, NJ

Cover design by Sharyn Banks
Book design by Lynn Else

Library of Congress Cataloging-in-Publication Data

Faley, Roland J. (Roland James), 1930–
    Reflections on the weekday lectionary readings/ roland j. faley.
        p. cm.
    ISBN 978-0-8091-4541-6 (alk. paper)
    1. Church year meditations. 2. Common lectionary (1992) 3. Bible—Meditations. I. Title.
    BX2170.C55F35 2010
    242'.3—dc22

                                                              2010003616

Published by Paulist Press
997 Macarthur Boulevard
Mahwah, New Jersey 07430

www.paulistpress.com

Printed and bound in the
United States of America

CONTENTS

INTRODUCTION

Not too long ago, Catholic men and women underappreciated the Bible. While every Catholic household had a copy of the Bible, it was rarely opened or studied. There was a sense that studying the Bible was a "Protestant" pursuit. Thankfully, that day has passed. Since the Second Vatican Council, Catholic familiarity with the Bible has increased significantly. In part, this has been due to the quality of biblical preaching, the contributions of literary criticism, and the better preparation of future clergy in understanding and explaining the scriptures.

This book gives a brief explanation of each daily Scripture reading from the Lectionary. In writing it, I am following in the footsteps of Carroll Stuhlmueller, CP, of happy memory, whose *Biblical Meditations for Ordinary Time* has been a standard for many years. I hope to continue his fine work.

Some readers will be familiar with my previous work, *Footprints on the Mountain*, a commentary on the Sunday readings. In some ways, the present work was a more difficult challenge than that previous one. In the Sunday Lectionary readings, there is at least one point of convergence, usually between the first and third readings. This is not the case for the weekday Lectionary readings, which were selected to give the reader or listener a broad overview of both the Old and New Testaments over a two-year cycle. While the Gospel reading remains the same for years I and II, the first reading changes depending on the year, and there is no essential link between this first reading and the Gospel.

The scriptures are closely linked with the term *Eucharist*, the Greek word meaning "praise." In our Catholic tradition, the Mass is the greatest praise that we can give to God, and at the same time it contains God's instruction for us on how to live. Just as the Mass focuses on our praise to God, the daily scriptures shed light on how that glory is to be rendered. It is my sincere hope that this collection of commentaries on the weekday Lectionary readings will assist Catholic men and women in drawing closer to God through the wisdom of his word.

Advent, Christmas, and Epiphany

MONDAY OF THE FIRST WEEK IN ADVENT

Isaiah 2:1–5 (Year I: Isaiah 4:2–6)
Psalm 122:1–2, 3–4b, 4cd–5, 6–7, 8–9
Matthew 8:5–11

Today's readings, coming at the opening of the Advent season, speak of a future of peace and serenity, an idea that figures prominently in Hebrew thought. For Isaiah, destruction and devastation are not final; when tragedy has ended, a faithful remnant will remain. In a word, God's saving plan will not be subverted by human wrongdoing. As the place of God's real presence among his people, Jerusalem is singularly sacred. On Mount Zion, the presence of Yahweh will again shine forth.

In today's psalm, it is toward this sacred mount that the people move in solemn procession.

At the same time, today's Gospel moves us away from too narrow a vision. The faith in a revealing God is not the exclusive possession of a single people. In Jesus it becomes available to the world. A Roman centurion, faced with the likely death of a servant boy, turns to Christ and asks for help even though he understands the prohibition against a Jew visiting a pagan home. Yet the centurion's recognition of the person Jesus is remarkable and evokes one of Jesus' most striking compliments. The child is cured. There are no ethnic or social boundaries for the new reign of God.

Today's readings carry us from the church to the marketplace. Zion was sacred as the place of God's presence. Jesus carries God into the everyday world of people with their worries and cares. He removes the anxiety of a foreign military man and brings health to a troubled servant. Our life has a similar rhythm. We need our quiet time in church, but we also cannot avoid the unexpected phone call from a person who needs our help or support. In fact, that is precisely where Christ centers his first commandment—in God and neighbor.

Points to Ponder

Our parish church: God's dwelling place
God's faithfulness
Antithesis: sin and holiness
Reign of Jesus: open to all
Humility
Concern for the sick

TUESDAY OF THE FIRST WEEK IN ADVENT

Isaiah 11:1–10
Psalm 72:1–2, 7–8, 12–13, 17
Luke 10:21–24

Jesus speaks of the prophets and kings who did not live to see the age of the messiah. Isaiah was one of these, and yet he gave a striking picture of that age to come. Today's first reading is an illustration of this. The final age will be one of restoration, and the imagery with which Isaiah describes it is unmatched. There will be harmony and peace that extend to the whole of creation, and the human being stands at the very pinnacle of restoration in this newfound friendship with the Creator.

The messiah, the royal descendant of David, stands as a model for Christians who hold public office, whether as mayors, governors, or judges. They should couple wisdom with understanding, upholding the law but always recognizing the circumstances of the people they govern. Their calling excludes arrogance as well as partiality. Above all, public office should never be used for personal gain. Corruption should never be tolerated, and all people should be seen as equal under the law. This is the "spirit" of counsel, strength, wisdom, and fear of the Lord.

In a special way, justice shall be accorded the poor; the voiceless shall find a voice. Nothing is more in accord with the spirit of reconciliation than this. It is easy for public officials to heed the wishes of their affluent constituents, or of people who represent powerful special interests, while ignoring the concerns of citizens who have no real power or wealth. If we really do live in the final age, the age of Christ, then our policies should reflect this belief. It is hard to believe that millions in this world, where plenty abounds for the affluent, live in miserable hovels, subsist on a limited amount of rice each day, and often succumb to deadly disease. In some developing countries, mothers watch as their infants waste away or feel compelled to let their young children work grueling hours so that their families can survive. Our Christian goal must always be a place at the table of plenty for all people, especially the most needy.

Today's psalm extols the actions of a God who will bring justice to the oppressed and abundance to the impoverished.

Points to Ponder

Justice in the age of the messiah
Humility and the acceptance of God
Cosmic redemption
The poor in God's sight
Praying for wisdom

WEDNESDAY OF THE FIRST WEEK IN ADVENT

Isaiah 25:6–10a
Psalm 23:1–3a, 3b–4, 5, 6
Matthew 15:29–37

Isaiah, the Advent prophet, speaks of the final age in very earthly terms: a festive banquet, good wine, and choice food. The use of this sort of language contrasts with our own engagement in God, which is often otherworldly and overly spiritualized. When it comes to many of the basic joys of life, we are a bit Gnostic, a bit inclined to see material goods as somehow evil. The fact is that we are very close to God when we enjoy the earthly blessings he provides. A dinner party with those we love may bring us as close to God as an extended period of silence.

This is why Jesus did not go about telling the disabled to be content with their lot. In today's Gospel, he restores speech, sight, and healthy limbs. We can only imagine what this meant to people who could not enjoy a beautiful landscape or hear the laughter of little children. Bodily health in this world is a good thing, something we properly strive for. The work of health care professionals, who seek to cure ailments and heal disabilities, is a noble one.

Jesus' providing of food to his hungry followers is an early eucharistic reference in the gospel text. Jesus takes the bread, gives thanks, breaks the bread, and gives it to his disciples. This is clearly the language of Eucharist: the Mass is our food for the journey. It too has a very human affect on our lives. Our day is a little brighter, and our step a little lighter.

Faith unquestionably conditions our outlook on life, and the Mass stands at the center of our hope and our trust. The miracles of Jesus changed many people's lives. The Eucharist does much the same for us. And for that we can only be grateful.

Points to Ponder

> God at the dinner table
> Death as transitional not terminal
> The health care provider
> Eucharist as our "daily bread"
> Spirituality and the joys of this world

THURSDAY OF THE FIRST WEEK IN ADVENT

> Isaiah 26:1–6
> Psalm 118:1, 8–9, 19–21, 25–27a
> Matthew 7:21, 24–27

When Hurricane Katrina struck the city of New Orleans and the Gulf Coast, it brought more than one truth to light. It showed the face of poverty in many people's fragile homes and living conditions. In addition, to many people of other nations, it showed how inadequately the world's richest country had provided for its most helpless. A similar impression was created in France a short time later when a rash of rioting and burning pointed up the frustrations of an ethnically diverse population.

Today the scriptures speak of faith, using the image of structures. They also reveal the true religious spirit so often found in the world's poorest, the "have nots" of society. The house that withstands a ferocious storm is one built on a firm foundation, whereas homes built on shifting sands will not survive. Here the translation to faith is an easy one to make. People solidly rooted in faith are aware of God's place in their lives—lives committed to the understanding of sacred truth and growth in appreciation of that truth. On the other hand, the "fair weather" Christian sees faith as a convention, a form of identification, an interesting tradition. There is very little cost to discipleship. It is a faith of shifting sands, a perishable house.

Why are the poor so privileged in the Bible? Doesn't experience show us that they are the people who suffer the most in life? Yet they stand out as the examples of trust. Not blinded by riches and worldly competition, the Lord remains their lot in life, and it is God who commits them to our care. Isaiah says that God humbles those who occupy high places. It is the poor who are ultimately lifted up. So often our experience brings us up against those who have so little and yet believe so deeply. The poor have much to teach us.

As the psalmist says today, "Better to take refuge in the LORD than to put confidence in princes."

Points to Ponder

> The lessons of the poor
> Trusting in prosperity
> The true meaning of faith
> The cost of discipleship

FRIDAY OF THE FIRST WEEK IN ADVENT

> Isaiah 29: 17–24
> Psalm 27:1, 4, 13–14
> Matthew 9:27–31

Advent is a season of hope. We relive the longing of Israel for final redemption, with our own eyes directed toward a future of justice and equity. The conviction is deep that our Redeemer lives.

Jesus gives sight to the blind men in today's Gospel. This is seen in the Isaiah reading as part of God's promise for the final days. But that reading speaks of other things as well, beyond the blind seeing and the deaf hearing. It marks the end of oppressive governments, of which we see more than our share today. How cruelly and inhumanly are the rights of the poor trampled underfoot! The age of the kingdom will also see the end of those who trumpet freedom and then, with arrogance, export their own brand of liberty, often secularist and morally offensive. The age of the kingdom will see an end of schemers and predators who lie in wait for the innocent and defenseless.

Isaiah also speaks of the judicial system in an age when honesty and truth will abound, when fraud and deception will be no more. A judge will be determined by his qualifications of learning and integrity, not by his political leanings.

Furthermore, and in a positive sense, it will be an age when children will be impressed by goodness and will see the presence of God mirrored in their surroundings. The word *awesome*, used so commonly by our youth today, will be the reaction to seeing lives lived in God's presence.

Yet, allowance is still made for mistakes. Error will lead to understanding. As the letter of John says, if we say we are sinless, we are liars (1 John 1:8). Good will and a change of heart make all the difference in the world.

We all suffer from blindness, but every positive step along the way moves us on the road to clearer vision.

Points to Ponder

> Moral blindness today
> Human rights for all people
> Imposing values on others
> Justice in the judiciary
> Correcting our mistakes

SATURDAY OF THE FIRST WEEK IN ADVENT

Isaiah 30:19–21, 23–26
Psalm 147:1–2, 3–4, 5–6
Matthew 9:35—10:1, 5a, 6–8

The Matthean Jesus had an earthly mission to the Jewish people. The disciples today are sent exclusively to the lost sheep of the house of Israel. It is only after his resurrection in Matthew that Jesus commissions his disciples to the world at large.

The Jews are closer to Christians than any other believers. While we lack agreement on certain basic issues, we share a common scriptural heritage and other shared beliefs. Unfortunately our parallel histories carry many scars. Christian attitudes toward the Jews historically made a contribution to anti-Semitism, even though, as Pius XI stated, we are spiritually Semites. Advent is a time for some honest soul searching. What strains of anti-Jewish feelings are present in our lives?

The lament of today's Gospel that the harvest is ripe but the harvesters few has a sobering ring in our time. In fact, it is a wake-up call. Certainly we must beg the master for more workers but also draw on our own resources to work toward a solution. In this country, the number of Catholics increases each year by the thousands, while the number of priests continually decreases. "Priestless Sunday" has become an all-too-common expression in parts of the country where this was never the case before. It is very likely that some important adjustments will have to be made in the future if we are to remain eucharistic communities.

But there is a bright sign to the "harvest question" as well. The word *ministry* was long applied only to clerics, but today its meaning has expanded extensively. Ministers of varied descriptions people our parishes today. With ever-greater clarity we see ourselves as "one body with many members," all making their contribution to the whole.

Surely, the needs of the harvest are not being completely met, but new laborers, now performing various functions, are rising to the challenge.

Points to Ponder

> Christian-Jewish relations
> The ministerial priesthood today
> The priesthood of the faithful
> One body: head and members

MONDAY OF THE SECOND WEEK IN ADVENT

> Isaiah 35:1–10
> Psalm 85:9ab and 10, 11–12, 13–14
> Luke 5:17–26

The question posed by Jesus in today's Gospel is a good one. Which is easier to do: forgive sin or restore health? It is easier to say, "Your sins are forgiven," because this requires no proof. But the truth of the matter is that it is *harder* to forgive sin because it is rooted in alienation from God. To restore spiritual health is the work of God alone. There are interesting features to the paralytic story. We can reflect with profit on the friendship of the men who carried the cot, gaining entrance only by bringing the man to the roof of the house. They demonstrated a real solidarity with their friend's suffering. What of our own concern for the disabled? Do we deal with them compassionately and with respect? How many of us have become annoyed when the only open spaces in a crowded parking lot are the handicapped ones? The truth is that we should offer a prayer of thanksgiving that public authorities are concerned about the less fortunate.

The paralytic was overjoyed with his cure. After years of suffering, his gait is lighter and his step faster. Yet the Gospels are keen on linking this miracle of Jesus with his power over sin. There is no greater satisfaction in being a minister of reconciliation than to see the relief of people in being unburdened of sin. They are lighthearted, with a joy that no one can take from them. Being a minister of the sacrament of reconciliation is not a dreary task, for it reveals the goodness of people.

Isaiah today speaks of both human reconciliation and the restoring of nature as well. In those final days, the desert, no longer parched, will be fully irrigated. Ponds and marshes will replace arid waste. In our time we have the means to hasten the day of redemption in turning deserts into verdant pastures. With the technology at hand, no people on this planet should live without food and drink. It is a worthy cause to bring repeatedly to the attention of elected officials. Since human need is the cause of God, we are called to look beyond our own concerns to those of a hungry and deprived world.

Points to Ponder

> The sacrament of reconciliation
> The meaning of friendship
> The needs of the disabled

TUESDAY OF THE SECOND WEEK IN ADVENT

Isaiah 40:1–11
Psalm 96:1–2, 3 and 10ac, 11–12, 13
Matthew 18:12–14

The first chapter of the second part of Isaiah announces a central theme. The time of captivity is past; the road to the homeland is made secure. Jerusalem stands at attention in welcoming her exiled sons and daughters. It is the word *comfort* that is most striking. The people had long felt desolate and abandoned in their sinfulness—without hope, country, or temple—and are now summoned to return home. Cyrus, the Persian king, will even assist the people in their resettlement and reconstruction.

It is a warm and comforting message, like the shepherd carrying his sheep back home. Comfort became visible in the face of a frightened infant in his father's arms in the wake of the 2005 Pakistan earthquake. The father had carried the child for miles over mountain passes to bring him to a medical aid station. He was near death. There was little life in his half-closed eyes. In a short time, with basic medical assistance, the child revived. By the time he was lifted by helicopter a few days later, his eyes were bright, and the comfort derived from his father's arms was palpable.

When people are deeply depressed, God is often their only refuge. We can never forget one of faith's strongest lessons.

Points to Ponder

The comfort of God
Cyrus—worthy of recognition
The lost sheep

WEDNESDAY OF THE SECOND WEEK IN ADVENT

Isaiah 40:25–31
Psalm 103:1–2, 3–4, 8 and 10
Matthew 11:28–30

There is more than one Christian paradox. One of them faces us today: Is the living of our faith easy or difficult? The truth is that it is both. To live the ethic of the Sermon on the Mount is to stumble every day. To avoid sin is more easily said than done. On the positive side, it is hard to "turn the other cheek" and "walk the extra mile." And in the marriage relationship, it might be easier to call it quits than to work things out. Yes, there are many days when the rocky road of Christian conduct presents more than its share of obstacles.

But there is the other side of the coin. Our psychological support is unmatched. The Advocate whom the Lord has sent us is the active symbol of God's love. Once we are convinced that we have been loved to death, all things are possible—and joyfully so. This is precisely what today's short Gospel tells us. In effect, the Lord says that we should simply turn to him and he will give us the strength to continue. The whole message is one of comfort and consolation. Christ recognizes clearly that we carry a "yoke," and no one is "yoked" with pleasure. To act as a Christian is frequently a "burden," but, fear not, says the Lord, "I will give you rest." The yoke will not seem that heavy, nor the burden unbearable. A deep faith in the Christ, who has first loved us, makes everything brighter and every day more cheerful.

I remember a paralyzed woman in Milan. Though confined to bed for twenty years, she was regularly visited by ministers of communion. During these eucharistic visits, her face radiated an incredible joy, and her conversation was as timely as it was good-spirited.

We all feel that our faith is severely tested at times. We may be bloodied but not bowed. Isaiah assures us today that as long as we run we will not grow weary, we will walk and not feel faint. There is a strong Advent message here. We never walk alone. As the psalmist says, the Lord is merciful and gracious.

Points to Ponder

Spiritual struggles
The consolation of faith
Perseverance
Reaching out to the weary

THURSDAY OF THE SECOND WEEK IN ADVENT

Isaiah 41:13–20
Psalm 145:1 and 9, 10–11, 12–13ab
Matthew 11:11–15

John the Baptist was unquestionably a remarkable figure. With his ascetical spirit and few if any "creature comforts," he heralded the approach of the final era and gave his life in defense of the truth by pointing out the moral failure of the king. Although he is primarily an Old Testament figure, the church did not hesitate to single him out for saintly honors as the forerunner of Jesus. As today's Gospel makes clear, he was not part of the kingdom of God in the sense that the apostles and other sainted figures were. In that regard, we citizens of the kingdom are more blessed than he.

The Old Testament figure, Elijah, was an early prophet who was taken to God without undergoing death. Jewish belief held that

Elijah was destined to return to die before the end of time. As the prophet Malachi states, Elijah was to appear before the final days (cf. Mal 4.5). The Gospel today sees John the Baptist as the Elijah figure.

Are we convinced that our life in God, as baptized citizens of God's reign, is an unparalleled gift? In the history of God's activity in the world, Christ stands as the pinnacle. In fact, history is divided into the era before Christ (BC) and after (AD). But more than that, he gives us new life, life in the Spirit, which is the door to eternity. It is precisely that which distinguished the baptism of John from that of Jesus. No honor, or award, or recognition in life surpasses that of Christ. Of course, all is not yet perfect. The church still suffers violence—the violence of infidelity, clerical misconduct, persecution, apostasy. But the forces of evil will not prevail. Christianity is an imperishable gift.

Isaiah today speaks of Israel's God as the redeemer. Bondage to freedom. Water not desert. Springs of water for dry ground. Trees and plants for wasteland. Yet it is all but a shadow of the great event, something beyond even the vision of John the Baptist. Christ for us, the source of our salvation.

Points to Ponder

> The figure of John the Baptist
> Prophetic courage
> The grace of the Christian life
> Joy in the midst of suffering

FRIDAY OF THE SECOND WEEK IN ADVENT

> Isaiah 48:17–19
> Psalm 1:1–2, 3, 4 and 6
> Matthew 11:16–19

"Sometimes you just can't win."
"If you don't like the message, then shoot the messenger."
"To get the desired idea across, put a 'spin' on it."

Some attitudes never change. What was true in Jesus' time is true in our time. Jesus' opponents would stop at nothing to trip him up, to catch him in a contradiction. They did not like John the Baptist, so they labeled his asceticism madness. Jesus' conduct, on the other hand, was not ascetical enough—eating and drinking in public made him dissolute at best. The best way to deal with an undesirable message is to slander the messenger.

Time, however, has proven the truth of the gospel message, and there is a lesson to be learned there. There are many times when the truth flies in the face of our own convictions. What is called for is quiet discernment, not instant rejection. Before we discredit what is said or who says it, honest assessment is called for. Often it seems easier to find a way out rather than face the truth.

At Jesus' trial, Pilate asked him, "What is truth?" It is a question that has broad currency in our time. From politics to commercial interests, we increasingly wonder what are the facts. Bending the truth to make it fit is all too common. There are times when churchmen in authority follow the same path. And to be quite honest, there are times when we do the same. We are inclined to bend the facts to make things appear in a better light.

The scriptures speak often of the primacy of truth. Jesus is referred to as the truth in John's Gospel. Today Isaiah tells us that the Lord will unfailingly lead us to what is good. It is a path that leads to a flowing river and dashing waves.

In an age of obscurity and doubt, where there are more questions than answers, we pray for personal transparency. What you see is what you get.

Lord, enable us to speak the truth in love.

Points to Ponder

The "spin" in modern life
The truth will sometimes hurt
Evading or manipulating the truth
Speaking the truth in love

SATURDAY OF THE SECOND WEEK IN ADVENT

Sirach 48:1–4, 9–11
Psalm 80:2ac and 3b, 15–16, 18–19
Matthew 17:9a, 10–13

Elijah is an Advent prophet; he played a key role in Israel's hope for the future. As Sirach states in today's reading, Elijah was taken to heaven in a whirlwind without undergoing death, and it was expected that he would return. That return became identified with the end of time. The Matthean Jesus clearly sees John the Baptist as Elijah, coming as he did at the dawn of the messianic age and calling for a change of heart.

But it was an appearance that turned out to be more chilling than thrilling. Finding his message unacceptable, John's opponents made him pay a dear price for speaking the truth of righteousness. His head was served on a platter to the illicit wife of a sensuous king.

And it was no different in Jesus' case. The path of suffering and death was already laid out for him. An inglorious outcome for one who had come with a message of respect, concern for others (especially the poor), and an embrace for people of every station in life. It is all very ironic. John and Jesus sentenced and killed because of the truth. It is a lesson in life that has been too often repeated.

Violence begets violence. Yet humanity has not learned the lesson. Conversation and dialogue is the only answer to disagreement. Catherine of Siena bridged an ecclesiastical impasse by convincing the pope in France to return to Rome rather than remain in exile. The Christian crusaders went to the Holy Land with scimitars and swords to retake the holy places. Francis of Assisi took another strategy and made a personal visit to the Muslim sultan to attempt a solution.

Peace often comes at a dear price. But peaceful conversation is worth much more than violence. Is not the same true of family disputes and disagreements? What is gained by hostility and aloofness? Only greater pain, and the realization that Christianity calls for something more.

The return of Elijah was viewed as a time "to turn the hearts of parents to their children." Too many families suffer from alienation. Elijah, John, and Jesus were reconciling figures who wanted only to speak the truth. They offer us food for thought.

Points to Ponder

> The person of Elijah
> John the forerunner
> Jesus the liberator
> Family harmony
> Harmony versus hostility

MONDAY OF THE THIRD WEEK IN ADVENT

> Numbers 24:2–7, 15–17a
> Psalm 25:4–5ab, 6 and 7bc, 8–9
> Matthew 21:23–27

In today's reading from Numbers, the pagan seer Balaam summarizes the role of the prophet as "one who hears the word of God." Hence, as much as he may have wanted to speak against Israel, he can only proclaim a future of harmony and peace.

In these terms, Jesus is clearly a prophet in his own time, since his career is wholly centered in the word of God. He was not self-directed, but, as he said repeatedly, he lived only to do the will of the One who sent him.

That being the case, the question raised by his opponents in today's Gospel admits of a very simple answer. His authority is derived wholly from God for whom he is an emissary. But it was an answer that would certainly fall on deaf ears. Even though the crowds followed after him, the chief priests and elders were of a different mind-set. For them this was a man who healed on the Sabbath and did not hesitate to set aside precepts of the law. Such authority could hardly come from God.

Jesus sees the futility of a direct answer and responds by presenting his opponents with a dilemma regarding the authenticity of John the Baptist's ministry.

There is a lesson here on duplicity and evasion of issues. If something is a matter of conviction, then we stand by it at all cost. Matters of controversy, on the other hand, admit of differing points of view. What we want to avoid at all cost is any form of subterfuge. Jesus' question to his opponents admitted of a simple up-or-down answer. What he got was no answer at all. In the face of duplicity, Jesus refuses to speak and play into their hands.

Paul was accused of vacillation by the Corinthian community. His rebuttal is interesting (2 Cor 1). He claims that, contrary to their assertion, he is not both "yes" and "no," any more than was Christ himself. Christ was an unequivocal "yes" to God, and such was the stance of Paul as well. Paul did not "waffle" before God or the Christian community. Like Balaam, he was one who heard what God said.

At times, we talk around issues and remain "politically correct." To equivocate endlessly is to be spineless. Let us speak the truth in love, whether it be "yes" or "no."

Points to Ponder

> Honesty of character
> Strength of conviction
> Equivocation
> Our "yes" to God

TUESDAY OF THE THIRD WEEK IN ADVENT

Zephaniah 3:1–2, 9–13
Psalm 34:2–3, 6–7, 17–18, 19 and 23
Matthew 21:28–32

There are two lessons in today's readings. The first is "Pride comes before the fall." The second is "It is never too late." Despite their obstinacy, God's people were never rejected. As Zephaniah states, even though the obstinate multitudes would be displaced by peoples of other nations, a remnant would always remain. These are the good and faithful people, few in number but humble of heart. In other words, the plan of God, while suffering many setbacks, is not to be thwarted; the remnant is the carrier of the promise.

In the story of the two sons, the allusions are clear enough. The self-sufficient and self-righteous people, the ones claiming fidelity to the promise, prove to be inflexible in their outlook. Supposedly ready and willing, they remain opposed to Christ and refuse his invitation. They agree to go into the vineyard but never actually go. But the unwashed tax collectors and sinners, whose initial response is clearly inadequate, subsequently see the error of their ways and respond to Christ. Their original "no" becomes a "yes."

Despair is a word that should have no place in our vocabulary. God's forgiveness is as close as a change of heart. It is never too late. Many Christians of exemplary life have at some time in their life touched bottom. They know what it is to be touched by God's goodness. Self-righteousness, on the other hand, is a great danger. This is to make God over into our image. It is rooted in pride, the greatest obstacle to the acceptance of God's will.

Points to Ponder

> God's forgiveness
> Pride as the great obstacle
> Humility, the direct line to God
> Turning one's life around

WEDNESDAY OF THE THIRD WEEK IN ADVENT

> Isaiah 45:6c–8, 18, 21c–25
> Psalm 85:9ab and 10, 11–12, 13–14
> Luke 7:18b–23

Today's Gospel brings to mind the story of the parish in the American Southwest that had gone through three pastors in one year, much to the frustration of the parishioners. When Pastor

Number Four arrived and, a bit nervously, greeted the congregation after Mass an elderly lady approached him and asked, "Are
you the one who is to come or shall we look for someone else?"

On a more serious note, the scriptures today address two
important features of our human existence. Jesus defines his messianic mission in terms of alleviating human need. Sight for the
blind, mobility for the lame, sound for the deaf, and justice for the
impoverished. These needs are met in our time by professionals
in different sectors of society. They are present in emergency and
operating rooms, in hospice care and medical relief programs.
They work the halls of Congress. They bring hope to the med-
ically disadvantaged. Yes, for many it is a livelihood, but one with
a strong ingredient of human compassion. And how do we bring
good news to the poor? Through shelters for battered women or
homeless people. We think of the owner of a major corporation,
one of the wealthiest persons in the world, who has channeled billions of dollars into fighting disease in impoverished Africa.
Whether conscious or not, this is the work of the gospel.

But there is a second feature in today's reading from Isaiah.
The Lord speaks of his creating the earth not as some kind of
wasteland, but as a place that will be lived in. Unfortunately, this
well-designed universe, which is our home, is in our time on a
track toward becoming a wasteland. Global warming, pollution of
the atmosphere, environmental destruction—these are a number
of the ways in which commercial interests and our own selfishness
contribute to a gradual disintegration of the world we leave to our
children as an inheritance.

The word speaks to us of many things, and not things that
are irrelevant. These are biblical issues that should concern us.
We owe gratitude to those who work for the good of others. And
there may be some way we can share their task.

Points to Ponder

> A mission to the sick
> Thinking of the disabled
> Our concern for the poor
> Environmental issues and the gospel
> Jesus: a different type of messiah

THURSDAY OF THE THIRD WEEK IN ADVENT

Isaiah 54:1–10
Psalm 30:2 and 4, 5–6, 11–12a and 13b
Luke 7:24–30

The film *The Squid and the Whale*, while probably not suited for a general audience, illustrates tellingly the tragedy of divorce. Not only is it painful for husband and wife, but its effect on children is often devastating. Quite aside from its religious implications, divorce wreaks havoc on human lives and on society in general.

In the scriptures, Yahweh is often depicted as divorcing his faithless wife, Israel, but, as in today's reading, he inevitably takes her back after her pain has been endured and her punishment completed. Such a divorce, while unquestionably metaphorical, points up the tragedy of sin and a wanton disregard for God's will. Separation causes great pain and is an apt illustration of the price of sinful conduct.

Yet Yahweh's separation is never definitive. He wants desperately to restore the marriage and bless it by siring many offspring. When speaking of marital happiness in Hebrew culture, the blessing of children tops the list. Today Isaiah speaks of a vast progeny and future growth as a people. Yahweh is the restorer and the provider simply because he is "the one who has compassion on you."

But God's mercy is ultimately broader than that. It is in the sending of his Son that the reign of God has finally appeared. And it far surpasses anything that the prophets had envisioned. Even the forerunner of the Lord, John the Baptist, who never experienced the risen Christ, was not a member of the kingdom. That is what today's Gospel tells us, and it offers much food for thought.

The two thoughts can be paired in today's readings: divorce and the Christian life. For two Christians to stand before God and promise fidelity unto death is a profound commitment. Difficulties do arise and may become so severe that separation is the only answer. But it is always a move taken in grief. Yet we should never underestimate the power of grace. It often accomplishes the unimaginable. "I am truly sorry." "I ask forgiveness."

"I do forgive you." "Let's work this out." These are sentiments that when spoken sincerely and resolutely can often avoid marital shipwreck.

Points to Ponder

>Blessings of married life
>The tragedy of divorce
>Kingdom of God and John the Baptist
>Marriage preparation

FRIDAY OF THE THIRD WEEK IN ADVENT

>Isaiah 56:1–3a, 6–8
>Psalm 67:2–3, 5, 7–8
>John 5:33–36

Sacred time and sacred space are essential. But whatever happened to Sunday observance? Some say, "I'm simply too busy. What's wrong with me cutting my grass on Sunday?" There's nothing wrong with cutting your grass, but what about God? The purpose behind the Sabbath, spoken of today by Isaiah, is to put God at the center of our life, with much of the rhythm of daily life set aside. The day is "profaned" when our human concerns take precedence over God. Sunday is a time to recognize our total dependence on our Creator. He is the source of our life and our livelihood.

The ancient Hebrews made their way to the temple in order to stand in the "house of prayer." The same reasoning leads us to our own parish church each weekend. It is there that we as a community lift our hearts in prayer in recognizing the sovereignty of God.

Why is it that some people take Sunday liturgy so casually? Why does Sunday become no different than any other day? This is all a part of God being left out of life. It begins with our gradual surrender to all those things that are passing away. False gods are present today—prosperity, commercialism, unbridled ambition—and the danger is we may not realize that we are guilty of idolatry. The Romans had it right: *Caveat emptor*. "Let the buyer beware."

John the Baptist was an ascetic. His diet was wild locusts and honey. His clothes were of rustic camel's hair. And he was fully alert to what God was doing. The evangelist calls him a "shining lamp" illuminating God's realm. The future was to bring an inextinguishable light in the life and works of Jesus. Now the torch has been passed to us, but it can be dimmed in our hearts, maybe even extinguished, by the passing concerns of the world.

We need our Sunday as surely we need our church. Both are concrete reminders of our origin and our destiny. We are pilgrims on a journey. Our vision must not be blurred. We need our time for reflection and our time for thanks. Sacred time and sacred space, proposed by Isaiah, will always be essential for us.

Points to Ponder

> Sunday observance
> The parish church
> Community and private prayer
> Values for our young people

DECEMBER 17

> Genesis 49:2, 8–10
> Psalm 72:1–2, 3–4ab, 7–8, 17
> Matthew 1:1–17

Some people enjoy tracing their family trees. Others would just as soon leave the past alone. In some cases, we find an illustrious ancestor, a real credit to the family line. In others, there are skeletons in the closet who might just as well stay there. In biblical times, genealogies were common in tracing family lineage, and the Old Testament has any number of them. Today's scriptures give us the genealogy of Christ himself.

This genealogy, more popular than strictly scientific, underscores Jesus' Hebrew and royal lineage, as a descendant of David. It has more than its share of unsavory characters. Most of the kings of Judah, who are listed, are dismissed in the Book of Kings as men who did evil in the eyes of God. They were characterized by idolatrous and licentious conduct. Only Hezekiah and Josiah receive high praise. But it is encouraging to note that sinners are not discarded or disowned in Christ's family tree. After all, it was for the sinner that Christ came. Sin may have been a *felix culpa* or "happy fault," but it was still a fault, and Christ confronts it directly. He took the weight upon himself and made us all free.

We can all take courage from the fact that Christ did not turn away from human misconduct. In fact, it was for this that he came. It is truly unfortunate to feel so broken because of our mistakes that we feel excluded and without hope. The prophet promised that those sins as red as scarlet would become white as snow. Human justice—which is often about retribution, even if that means execution—and divine mercy are poles apart. The mercy of God can reach the darkest recesses of any prison cell block.

In Christ's genealogy there are five women: Tamar, Rahab, Ruth, Bathsheba, and Mary. They have one thing in common: they conceived and bore children under unusual circumstances. None more so than Mary, whose son was fathered by God himself. So while Christ took upon himself the full weight of human weakness and sin, he was still God's only Son.

The meaning of Christmas is found in a genealogy: Jesus, God, and man, for the salvation of the world.

Points to Ponder

> Forgiveness and the weight of guilt
> Upholding Christ as God
> Appreciating our forebears
> Justice and mercy
> The death penalty

DECEMBER 18

> Jeremiah 23:5–8
> Psalm 72:1–2, 12–13, 18–19
> Matthew 1:18–25

Government is a noble profession. The fact is, however, that it often disappoints. Advent points to the arrival of a new and different government, the reign of God, our heavenly king. It is repeatedly asserted that this future monarch will be just and will rule with wisdom. These characteristics appear clearly in the Jeremiah reading today. The repeated emphasis on qualities of honesty and uprightness only highlight the fact that these attributes were absent in kings of the past.

The era of the messiah was to be clearly God directed. The name given to the child of Mary is Emmanuel, "God with us." Jesus will be a king of a different kind. While presiding over a realm, he will be, as another prophet states, a king mild and humble, seated upon a donkey. This is a king who spent his life doing good while teaching what true goodness means. As our "window on God," this is a king who avoids any form of pomp or acclaim; he is the champion of compassion, forgiveness, and concern. These qualities in God were known to Israel in the past, as Jeremiah states today, when he brought his people out of Egyptian bondage and centuries later freed them again from the captivity of Babylon. But never was the nature of God more evident than in these final days, with the Word incarnate who gave his life that we might live.

To aspire to public office is certainly highly commendable. It has its inherent dangers—compromise of principles, graft, corruption in different forms. But it is always heartwarming to see men and women elected to public office who maintain a posture of faith and moral principle. In the face of temptation, such men and women stay their moral course. Public office is a chance to enhance the reign of God, especially in concern for the neediest people in society. It tells us that Emmanuel is still with us.

Points to Ponder

> Faith and politics
> The reign of God today
> Jesus as Emmanuel
> Jesus as son of Mary
> Joseph, the upright spouse

DECEMBER 19

Judges 13:2–7, 24–25a
Psalm 71:3–4a, 5–6ab, 16–17
Luke 1:5–25

The mother of Samson and the mother of John shared similar stories. With the passing of years, neither had borne children, to the chagrin of their husbands. In Hebrew society, a childless marriage was an immense misfortune; in children, family life was prolonged and life itself extended. In the home of these two women, there was no infant to be fed and cared for, to be bedded and clothed; no cry to break the still of night.

In the course of time and through the power of God, the tragedy was overcome. As happens in the scriptures, the future births are heralded while the child is still in the womb.

In our days of advanced medical technology, the childless marriage is not as common as at one time. In many cases it is dealt with by adoption, a very commendable step in the life of a childless couple. The child is raised in a warm atmosphere that might have otherwise been denied and is fully integrated into the family's life. Children are informed of their adoptive status without in any way diminishing their sense of belonging.

The strong desire for children that underlies today's readings also points up the tragedy of a procured abortion. To eliminate human life at any stage is tragic; it is even more tragic to destroy life in the womb when it is only beginning.

In the births preannounced in today's readings, two things are worthy of mention. First, Samson's mother is never given a name, although his father, Manoah, is mentioned repeatedly. The woman is simply the barren wife who has "borne no children." The reason for this is not clear; other women in the Bible, of lesser status, are regularly named. Samson's mother remains in the shadows, as happens frequently in today's society. The mother of an illegitimate child or the person who has been disgraced or violated and wishes to remain anonymous. They may be hidden but should not be forgotten. Every person has dignity before God.

Second, the Baptist was born into a priestly family. This may go a long way in explaining the strong sense of faith in his life.

The Christian community is called in scripture "a royal priesthood." Every family is part of that priesthood; an atmosphere of living faith is a harbinger of a future generation's sense of values. Or as the psalmist says today, "You who took me from my mother's womb, my praise is continually of you."

Points to Ponder

> Childlessness
> Adoption
> To call by name
> Christian values in the home

DECEMBER 20

> Isaiah 7:10–14
> Psalm 24:1–2, 3–4ab, 5–6
> Luke 1:26–38

"Ask a sign." King Ahaz in the eighth century BC is seriously troubled by the threat from the Assyrian Empire. The prophet exhorts him to ask for a sign of deliverance. He refuses. Nevertheless, a sign is given. The future birth of a special child will be a clear indication of God's presence, as the child's name itself will indicate. He will be Immanuel or "God with us."

We have no clear indication of who this child promised to Ahaz was. It may well have been his own son, Hezekiah. But this was a prophecy that proved to have a life of its own. There was another time of deliverance that loomed on the horizon, and it came to rest on a humble house in Nazareth and a young girl with a heart open to God. Not only will the child she bears be the expected descendant of David but also the Son of God. It would be a case of "God with us" in a most singular and exceptional way. God himself was to walk the earthly journey, our companion in life, the One who would give his life for our salvation.

Ahaz refused to ask for a sign, but Mary does not hesitate to ask the meaning of the sign to be given her. It is a secret long hidden in the heart of God. The child to be born of Mary was to have

God as father. Son of Mary and Son of God. But the consent of the young girl is required. What will it be?

A leap of faith into the unknown. Her response is a clear expression of the obedience of faith. Puzzling it undoubtedly was, but it is God who asks.

It so often happens in life. There are uncertainty, doubt, fear, and hesitation in the face of the seemingly impossible. It is obedience to which we are called time after time. Yet there is only one answer:

Be it done to me according to your word.

Points to Ponder

> The obedience of faith
> "God is with us"
> Reading the signs of the times
> Faith and doubt

DECEMBER 21

> Song of Songs 2:8–14
> Psalm 33:2–3, 11–12, 20–21
> Luke 1:39–45

There is a strong sense of movement in today's readings. In one, a young man, at the first stirrings of spring, runs to greet his beloved. Abounding in energy and absorbed in this forthcoming romantic encounter, he longs for the first glimpse of her. In the Gospel, the expectant mother of the Messiah travels with haste to the hill country to visit her pregnant cousin Elizabeth. The hand of God is present in both pregnancies at the dawn of a new era.

The Song of Songs contains some of the most beautiful poetry in the Bible. The strong love between the lover and beloved has vivid emotional, even erotic, characteristics. The songs center wholly on the love between two people and may well be derived from a Hebrew wedding ceremony. The love between the two is held together by strong human forces in the spring of the year when the attraction is said to be the most intense.

Unfortunately, in our time the beauty of human love often takes second place to the unbridled expression of sexuality. This is to exchange the noble for the tawdry. This strong attraction underlies the unity of marriage, the spirit of self-giving, and ultimately the birth of new life. The sexual component is noble, and the Bible does not hesitate to extol it as a God-given impulse. There is a context for our teaching on sexuality. What is good must be seen as such and set forth, especially for the young, in a positive way.

If Mary's response to the annunciation was the obedience of faith, her journey to Elizabeth springs from the charity of faith. Mary goes to Elizabeth, Jesus to John, the greater to the lesser. Elizabeth's greeting expresses her unworthiness, just as John in the womb accedes to the unborn Christ. Today we hear much about status, protocol, and political correctness. The Gospels have little time for such concerns. In her Magnificat, Mary will acknowledge God as the source of any recognition she might receive. As the whole discussion of honesty and humility unfolds in the scriptures, each of us is called to personal discernment.

Points to Ponder

Human love and sexuality
Preparation for marriage
The greater and the lesser
The importance of humility

DECEMBER 22

1 Samuel 1:24–28
1 Samuel 2:1, 4–5, 6–7, 8abcd
Luke 1:46–56

Anna and Mary bear striking resemblances. In the birth of their respective sons, the power of God is made manifest, inspiring each of them to raise their voices in praise to the Almighty. In Mary's case her hymn is the Magnificat, which is today's Gospel. The canticle attributed to Anna is today's responsorial hymn.

But there is also a real difference between the two. Anna was distraught over her sterility and had repeatedly asked God to gift her with a child. The favor was finally granted in her son Samuel. Mary had no immediate expectation of a child, although she was engaged to Joseph at the time of her election. She is advised by the heavenly messenger that she will have a son whose parentage she would share with God himself. It is the willingness of both women to see God as the source of their joy that is so apparent in today's liturgy.

In what is likely a hymn of the early church, adapted to Mary's sentiments, the Magnificat sets forth the basic virtue of the Nazareth virgin. The dominant note that is struck is the greatness of God at work in the order of redemption. But there is an added note here. Mary states that the God who is great has looked on the lowliness of his servant and decided to raise her up. She claims nothing for herself. She is simply a vessel that God has filled. Mary wants us simply to remember that "the Mighty One has done great things for me."

Our era of instant gratification and media hype finds new heroes for us at every turn. Since everyone is entitled to his or her "fifteen minutes of fame," the personalities range from academia to athletics. But as we sift through the daily news, it is well to remember that the forgotten people of our society often instruct the privileged. And we see a Christian response to misfortune in the people who contribute from their limited resources, volunteer in a soup kitchen, or work with battered women. The God who is mighty still calls on our Marys and Annas. God elevates the lowly and brings down the strong. But do we take notice?

Points to Ponder

> Yearning for a child
> Seeking God's will
> Responding to God
> The providence of God

DECEMBER 23

Malachi 3:1–4, 23–24
Psalm 25:4–5ab, 8–9, 10 and 14
Luke 1:57–66

Our redemption is near at hand. Advent draws to a close; Christmas is two days away. In our scriptures today, the spirit of expectation runs high. Malachi speaks of the return of Elijah to prepare God's people for the end, following which the Lord himself will repossess his temple. At the same time, the end is a mixed blessing. It will spell reconciliation and peace for some, as fathers and sons are reunited in a spirit of accord, while others will experience purification and refinement as the wheat is separated from the chaff, even among the priestly class. Though the grace-filled moment is offered to all, some will remain hard of heart and refuse to respond to that grace. The justice of God is a two-way street.

Elijah appears in the figure of John the Baptist. He is the forerunner of the Lord, preceding the latter's arrival in the temple (cf. Luke 2:22–38). His name itself is God given, as Zechariah and Elizabeth affirm. The name signifies "God's favor," a clear allusion to what the birth of Jesus would mean for the world. The infancy narratives are replete with signs: Mary's virginal conception, Elizabeth's delayed pregnancy, Zechariah's loss of speech. The signs rise to a crescendo in the birth at Bethlehem and its significance for the good of the world.

Conversion plays an important part in the Christmas message. Christmas for some people is like any other holiday, even though a bit more festive. Its true religious significance is largely lost. "Happy holidays" replaces "Merry Christmas." Others find their way to church only at this time of year, though even this minimal spiritual participation hints that something is stirring in their hearts. For others, the time speaks volumes, identified with John's name, God's great favor. The words of Titus resound: "The grace of God has appeared" (Titus 2:11). Yet gratitude never wants to disparage anyone. A change of heart can come at any moment. And when it does Emmanuel will be there to help.

Points to Ponder

> Christmas: "the favor of God"
> Gratitude versus lukewarmness
> Christian symbols of faith
> Family reconciliation

DECEMBER 24

> 2 Samuel 7:1–5, 8b–12, 14a, 16
> Psalm 89:2–3, 4–5, 27 and 29
> Luke 1:67–79

The feast that we celebrate tonight is, for the person of faith, the most important birth in world history. The promise goes back to Abraham, the sainted patriarch of the Jewish people, and it centered upon a people freed from fear and dedicated to the service of God. An era of peace and harmony stood on the horizon. This appears clearly in the hymn of Zechariah, read as today's Gospel. The prophets never lost sight of the descendant of David, who was to preside over this renewed kingdom of God.

The story of David's intent regarding the temple is an interesting one. He lamented the fact that he lived in luxury while the dwelling of God was nothing more than a tent. To end this inequity he determined to build a suitable house for the Lord, but his intention was thwarted. The construction of the temple, a political as well as religious tour de force, was to be the work of his son Solomon. Then, through an interesting play on words, God expresses his wish to build a house for David, a dynasty that would last forever.

But it turns out this house is not the royal house of David, with its many decadent kings, men who were nothing more than disappointments. Faith tells us that it was the descendant of David, born in Bethlehem of modest circumstances, who would become the king of promise in an everlasting dynasty. It is a theme that resonates in Handel: "He will reign forever and ever."

This recounting is more than a brief biblical overview. It is really God for us. As this plan unfolded through history, it was personal and directed. Christ is the new David, the predestined king of the ages. It is his example and his teaching that express his sovereignty and that directs us through life. Kindness over vindictiveness, honesty over corruption, moderation over excess, forgiveness over hatred. It is not an easy ethic, but it is positive and rewarding. He tells us that his yoke is easy and his burden, light. For the gift of our Savior king, we once again give thanks this Christmas season.

Points to Ponder

> God's promise
> David: both noble and human
> The king, meek and humble
> The Christian ethic and human values

DECEMBER 26—ST. STEPHEN

> Acts of the Apostles 6:8–10; 7:54–59
> Psalm 31:3cd–4, 6 and 8ab, 16bc and 17
> Matthew 10:17–22

On the day after Christmas, it may seem strange that persecution is our theme. St. Stephen is the church's first martyr, and his feast is celebrated in immediate proximity to the birth of the Lord whom he served. Not only was a Stephen a grace-filled person, he was also a skilled debater, with the result that his litigants proved to be no match for him. As happens all too frequently, disagreement turned to violence, with his opponents railing against Stephen. They finally killed him in a classic case of religious zeal gone berserk. Among the opponents is an interesting figure, the young Saul who will soon become Paul, the apostle to the Gentiles.

Early Christians fared no better than the protomartyr. The death of Stephen was an omen of things to come. Today's Gospel presents a picture of what transpired in the latter part of the first century. Cruel torture, public litigation, sharp family division. The followers of Jesus endured all of these things. But Jesus assured them of divine guidance and a future that is certainly theirs. Perseverance spells salvation.

Have this mind in you that was also in Christ Jesus—his reminder of Paul is clearly reflected in the death of Stephen. During his trial, Jesus assured his accusers that they would one day see the Son of Man coming on the clouds of heaven; so Stephen dies with a vision of this eschatological figure. Stephen, like Jesus, dies by surrendering his spirit to God.

The spirit of Christmas is not limited to ornaments and tinsel. Nor even to the peace and calm of the crèche. It is the assurance that the child came to suffer that gives us hope, and so, like Stephen, Christ's surrender must be our own. As we pass through this valley of tears, we are certainly called to suffer. But with Christ's sentiments as our own we shall surely prevail. And the true spirit of Christmas will never be lost.

Points to Ponder

> Religious division
> Family division
> Christ the model of tolerance
> Paul's conversion
> The assurance of heaven

DECEMBER 27—ST. JOHN

> 1 John 1:1–4
> Psalm 97:1–2, 5–6, 11–12
> John 20:1a and 2–8

John the Apostle, one of the original Twelve, was the brother of James and the son of Zebedee. At one time he was identified as the author of the fourth Gospel; that position is not widely held today. The author of the Gospel is simply said to be "the disciple whom Jesus loved" (John 21:20), but nowhere in the Gospel is that disciple identified.

The feast today, however, honors John, one of the apostles, one who certainly lived the life of discipleship. In today's introduction to the first letter of the author John, the disciple is said to be one who accepts the reality of Christ, who believes that he is truly God's Son who has appeared in the flesh. He was a man in the fullest sense of the word. At the same time, as today's Gospel makes clear, the believer is convinced that the tomb was empty because Jesus had risen and had gone to the Father.

Moreover, as the Gospel of John describes him, the "disciple whom Jesus loved" is the one who rests his head on the chest of Jesus, stands at the foot of the cross, is entrusted to Mary, runs to the tomb on Easter morning, and recognizes the risen Christ on the lake shore. In short, he is the true believer who never falters and never abandons the Lord. While we know little about the Apostle John, we hardly err in seeing many of these qualities in him.

Early Christianity saw the emergence of heterodox groups who were qualifying their belief in the God-Man. Some claimed that he was not truly man but only appeared to be such. Others recognized his manhood but not his divinity; he was the best of all possible men but that and no more. Orthodoxy has consistently taught what the writings of John the Evangelist express: Christ was God in the flesh.

At times we find it difficult to be the faithful disciple. We are prone to avoid the difficult choice that often leads to the cross. We practice our faith but hardly run to the tomb. We view the shoreline of life from various angles but do not always see the Lord in what transpires. There is a real lesson in today's readings. To remain true to Christ throughout life is not an easy path but becomes possible with the conviction that Christ alone is truly the way, the truth, and the life. In the words of Isaiah, it means "to run and not grow weary."

Points to Ponder

Jesus, true God and true man
The beloved disciple, resting in Christ
The beloved disciple, standing at the cross
The beloved disciple, running to the tomb
The true disciple, "It is the Lord."

DECEMBER 28—THE HOLY INNOCENTS

1 John 1:5—2:2
Psalm 124:2–3, 4–5, 7cd–8
Matthew 2:13–18

Interpreting the birth of Jesus and the visit of the Magi as a threat to his royal position, Herod orders the death of all male children in Bethlehem under two years old. Matthew is keenly interested in pointing up likenesses between Jesus and Moses and draws here a striking parallel to the pharaoh's order to destroy the Hebrew male offspring at the time of Moses' birth in Egypt.

The death of innocent children, whether in biblical times or our own, strikes us deeply as a real injustice. It is a grim fact that children continue to be subjected to barbarous deaths. In very recent times, from the former Yugoslavia in Europe to Rwanda in Africa, ethnic cleansing has made victims of helpless women and children. In the troubled Middle East, suicide bombers indiscriminately take the lives of innocent people, including children. And, despite all the talk of limited tactical strikes, war takes the lives of all too many noncombatants. The fact is that children are often the first to perish.

In addition, today's feast reminds us of the innocent lives that are taken through abortion. Today more and more voices are being raised on behalf of the voiceless. Whatever the reason for an abortion, it is the innocent who suffer. It is not a sectarian issue; it is a human one.

We cannot pass over the reading from John's epistle without touching on one of its issues. Life in the Spirit is granted through initial recognition of sin and guilt. But today's reading makes clear that even after baptism, sin frequently occurs. In such a case our heavenly Intercessor stands with us in seeking forgiveness. So much emphasis in the New Testament falls on initial justification that we are often led to wonder if there is a "second plank after shipwreck." The answer is an unequivocal "yes." Even with the best of intentions, we all stumble along the way. While not rejecting Christ, we do not always live up to what he asks of us. It is good to know that the helping hand of Christ is there to lift us up.

Points to Ponder

The death of innocent children in our day
The child in the womb
Violence in the world today
The sacrament of reconciliation

DECEMBER 29—FIFTH DAY OF CHRISTMAS

1 John 2:3–11
Psalm 96:1–2a, 2b–3, 5b–6
Luke 2:22–35

Simeon was a pious and just man, now advanced in years, who devoutly fulfilled his temple responsibilities. He had been assured that he would live to see the messiah before he died, which, as a devout Jew, he longed to do. In today's Gospel he meets the parents of Jesus, who had come to the temple for the presentation of their child. As Simeon embraces the child, he praises God for this gift, which is to be the "light for the revelation to the Gentiles." But there are shadows on the scene as well. Jesus is destined to be a cause of division, and his mother will not escape the pain of that division.

Simeon lived to see the light. And it is John who today spells out the meaning of the symbolic light and darkness. To accept the truth of Christ is to embrace the light; to reject him is to walk in darkness. And what does it mean to accept the light? First of all, says the epistle, it means to pattern our lives on his, to live as he did. And second, it means to love one's brother and sister. To walk in darkness is to see the Christ event as meaningless and to live with a spirit of hostility to others. Yes, this teaching is repeated over and over again in John. But the fact remains that it is the heart of the Christian message.

Christmas is a feast of lights. It appears on Christmas trees, candles in the window, tree-lit streets. But does it really speak to us of the light of the truth that Christ brought into the world?

Our life today is overcast by the clouds of darkness. Living for the moment, the cult of affluence, lustful promiscuity—all play their part in modern culture. And this is only magnified in the world of politics and government. There is the expanding chasm between rich and poor on a global scale. There is the desire to use other countries for our own selfish ends. In our own country, there is the marked separation between the "haves" and the "have nots," so evident when disaster strikes.

Yes, the light is ours. But it is not to remain hidden under the basket. It is to shine forth in our own life and conviction and find its way to the marketplace, the boardroom, the ballot box, and the halls of Congress.

The tinsel of Christmas will pass, but its True Light must prevail.

Points to Ponder

> Christ the fulfillment of promise
> Lifelong dedication
> The unity of the Testaments
> The darkness of our times
> The light of Christ today

DECEMBER 30—SIXTH DAY OF CHRISTMAS

1 John 2:12–17
Psalm 96:7–8a, 8b–9, 10
Luke 2:36–40

Growth comes in different forms. Returning with his parents to Nazareth, Jesus grows in stature, in intelligence, and, above all, in faith. Anna, too, experienced growth in her life. In the presentation account, she appears in the temple together with Simeon. Widowed after seven years of marriage, she grew into her eighty-four years by a life of faithful prayer and fasting. It was a steady, sustained growth, culminating in her encounter with Jesus the Messiah.

The letter of John today looks at Spirit growth in fathers and sons. The father, as the elder, has been gifted with a faith experience of Christ, hidden from the ages and now revealed: God's son in the flesh. This is the cornerstone that, once accepted, leads to a growth in faith and love. John then addresses the sons, or children, whose lives have been involved in the struggle, conquering evil not with a single blow but by facing the daily challenge.

The elderly and the young face a common crossroad: one fork leads to growth and the fullness of God; the other, to chaos and destruction. John summarizes the choices. One may follow the enticements of a world that is passing away; it offers affluence, entrapment, sexual license, and corrupting forces. But it is inevitably misleading. Yet, put quite simply, true growth lies in taking the other fork, the route of Jesus and Anna, that of doing God's will.

Choices face us every day of life. It may appear gratifying to choose the wrong path. But the right choice leads to a clearer vision, one that grows within us. It is the way of God. As Paul says, "When I was a child, I spoke like a child, I thought like a child, I reasoned like a child...; when I became an adult, I put an end to childish ways" (1 Cor 13:11).

Points to Ponder

Life in widowhood
Christian growth
Wrong choices
The right choice

DECEMBER 31—SEVENTH DAY OF CHRISTMAS

1 John 2:18–21
Psalm 96:1–2, 11–12, 13
John 1:1–18

The prologue to John's Gospel, read at today's Mass, offers four points for our reflection. First, it highlights the eternity of Jesus Christ. In fact he is actually called God, an unusual designation in the New Testament since "God" was initially seen as applying only to Yahweh. In his eternal Godhead, Jesus is present with the Father in the whole process of creation. In fact, as God's wisdom, he is the blueprint that guides the whole creative process.

Second, Jesus enters the world as the life giver; he confers the Spirit, described variously in John's Gospel as light, life, or water. It is the Spirit that lifts humans to a whole new plateau of existence; it is life in God. If the law given to Moses was a gift, the life of the Spirit is called simply "grace and truth."

Third, Jesus came in the flesh. Contrary to some of the thinking within the early Johannine community, he was not simply an apparition or vision. To those who looked with disdain on anything human or material (perhaps those identified with the antichrists of today's epistle), there was only one response. "The Word became flesh and lived among us" (John 1:14). He was man in the full sense of the term.

Finally, John the Baptist was not the light, as some may have suggested. He had a clearly subordinate role as the forerunner, the one who prepared the way of the Lord. There is some New Testament evidence for a strong advocacy of John's baptism, perhaps because Christ himself had received it. The Gospel of John, however, is clearly interested in setting the record straight.

While John is rich in its very positive approach, it has a very distinctive apologetic. It wants to uphold the eternity of Christ while never losing sight of his humanity. He is the savior and life giver in a way that far outdistances anyone from Moses to John the Baptist. When we consider all that the term "Jesus Christ" connotes, it is not surprising that there were some failures in articulating the Lord and his mission adequately in the early years of the church's life. But error often leads to gain—in this case, a clearer expression of belief. The prologue to John's Gospel, even with its soaring beauty, serves a very practical purpose.

Points to Ponder

> Jesus the eternal Word
> Jesus as true man
> The subordination of the Baptist
> The gift of Spirit life

JANUARY 2

1 John 2:22–28
Psalm 98:1, 2–3ab, 3cd–4
John 1:19–28

The liturgical readings from the feast of Mary, the Mother of God (January 1), to the Epiphany draw on the Johannine literature in pointing up the deeper significance of the Christ event. Today's readings stress the importance of the truth, with Christ as its noblest expression.

A *lie* is defined as a lack of conformity between the mind and reality. Objective facts say one thing and, for a variety of reasons, the person says another. This may be called *equivocation, obfuscation, deception*, or simply a *lie*. When John's epistle was written, Christians were separating themselves from the faith community as well as from the truth. In denying that Christ was truly the Son of God, they were declared antichrists. In so saying and professing, they sinned against both Father and Son. The charge against them is strong. They deny the truth and are nothing more than liars.

The authentic Christian remains strong in his faith affirmation. That person stands in the truth, anointed in baptism, and destined for eternal life. If we remain in the truth, evil will have no hold on us. We are well prepared for the fullness of God that will come at the end of the road.

John the Baptist was a celebrated preacher and end-time prophet in his day. But, as in today's Gospel, he makes no exaggerated claims. He speaks the truth. No, he is not the messiah, nor Elijah, nor the expected eschatological prophet. His baptism is one of conversion administered with water. Yes, there is one coming after him who will far exceed him in his person and his ministry. There is no equivocation, no duplicity. He states it as it is and merits the praise of Jesus. No one born of woman was greater than he.

The truth in our time is evasive. People in government distort the truth in what is referred to as the "spin." CEOs of major companies face incarceration for the deceptive use of funds for their own personal gain. Sadly, we have seen examples of the evasion and concealment of truth within the church itself to the detriment of members of the faithful.

In our daily lives, we may be inclined to alter the facts for reasons of pride, personal interest, or embarrassment. The truths of faith are, of course, paramount. But truth is not selective. It seeks objectivity and candor in all instances. In the spirit of gospel transparency, let our answer be "yes, yes" or "no, no."

Points to Ponder

The truths of faith
Truth in daily life
Truth in society
Distortion of the truth
The limited claims of John the Baptist

JANUARY 3

1 John 2:29—3:6
Psalm 98:1, 3cd–4, 5–6
John 1:29–34

Two words of great significance appear in today's scriptures: *lamb* and *children*. John the Baptist recognizes Jesus as the Lamb of God. At every Eucharist before the communion, the celebrant raises the host and says, "Behold the Lamb of God." The background to the image is found in two evident sources in the Old Testament. The first comes from the Passover ritual celebrating the liberation of the Hebrews from Egyptian bondage (Exod 11–12). In order that the Hebrew children not be slain by the avenging angel, the Hebrews were to sprinkle the blood of a newly slaughtered lamb on their doorposts. The lamb then became a symbol of deliverance in the Passover ritual.

The lamb appears again in the last song of the servant in the Book of Isaiah. The mysterious servant is about to undergo death in expiation for the sins of his people (Isa 53). He goes to his death humbly and submissively, like a lamb led to the slaughter. These instances serve as background to our understanding of Jesus as the

Lamb of God. Like the Hebrews in Egyptian bondage, we have been liberated from the slavery of sin through the blood of a lamb—Christ. And like Isaiah's humble servant, Christ with perfect submission hands himself over for our salvation.

In the Johannine writings, the author shows a marked preference for the term *children* in addressing his audience. It is used as a term of endearment for his own community members. Through Christian baptism we become part of the family of God. Father and Son are united by the Spirit of love, and that same Spirit is infused in us. This distinguished the baptism of Jesus from that of John. We are no longer outsiders, hired hands, or domestics. We now come in by the front door, are seated at the master's table, and are part of the family inheritance. This is reality, not wishful thinking. We are truly privileged to be children of God.

The lamb and the child are joined. If Christ had not become the Lamb, we would not be family members. Gratitude is the only motive for goodness. We are saved by God and then made his children. No Christmas present can match that.

Points to Ponder

> Jesus the Lamb of God
> Jesus servant of the Lord
> Jesus our Brother; God our Father
> Fellow Christians: brothers and sisters

JANUARY 4

> 1 John 3:7–10
> Psalm 98:1, 7–8, 9
> John 1:35–42

Today the epistle of John claims that the person who belongs to Christ cannot sin. This is in seeming contradiction to his earlier statement that we all sin and cannot claim that we are innocent (1:8). Here John speaks of a sinful way of life, not the occasional mishaps that befall all of us (5:16f). In other words, we set ourselves on the right course and strive to adhere to it. That is a sinless way of life. For John there are only two possibilities: to choose death and abandon Christ or to choose life and remain with the Lord on our earthly journey, occasional mishaps notwithstanding.

This all corresponds well with the call of the first disciples in today's Gospel. Two of them, one of whom is Andrew, ask Jesus, "Where are you staying?" The question can be read on two levels, one regarding Jesus' place of residence; the other, the divine indwelling. The truth is that Jesus "stays" in the Father and the Father in him. In "coming" and "seeing," the disciples are invited to a deeper life in God. Later, Andrew goes to his brother Simon and claims to have met the Messiah. The journey of faith has begun.

It is interesting to note that the first disciples are not said to be fishermen. In John there are no boats or nets; they are simply disciples of the Baptist, who pass from him to the Lord. In the synoptic tradition, Simon's change of name comes later. In John, Jesus calls him Cephas ("Peter") right away.

The passage from sin to grace, from Satan to Christ, is a matter of choice. But once undertaken, it represents a complete transition. It is as different from a sinful way of life as darkness is from light. The Christmas season reminds us of what that choice has meant in our own lives.

We are often saddened when people dear to us no longer walk the path of faith, when the Eucharist and the other sacraments no longer have meaning for them. Yet prayer can work wonders, as St. Monica discovered after years of praying for her son St. Augustine. In our love for those whose faith has grown dim, let us never fail to bring them before the Lord. At the same time we are grateful to know where the Lord "is staying." We too dwell with Father, Son, and Spirit in the household of God.

Points to Ponder

> To come and see
> Staying with the Lord
> Dangers to faith today
> Love for the erring

JANUARY 5

1 John 3:11–21
Psalm 100:1b–2, 3, 4, 5
John 1:43–51

Nazareth was a nondescript, dusty trade-route town in northern Palestine's region of Galilee. Not only were there no expectations of a messiah from there, there were hardly any expectations there at all! Nathanael's question in today's Gospel is not surprising: "Can anything good come out of Nazareth?" The answer came to him from Jesus, who describes a moment in his life that this rabbi could never have known. In a profound expression of faith, Nathanael recognizes the Nazarene as both Messiah and Son of God.

Jesus' place of origin was not the only unusual thing about him. His teaching of unconditional love was equally remarkable and challenging. In today's first reading from John, the word *love* appears six times. It is seen as the sole criterion by which the Christian is recognized. Hatred brings nothing but chaos and disorder, as the life of Cain amply illustrates. With the murder of his brother, Cain unleashed a dreaded form of hatred. Hatred, however, can either express itself in actions or fester internally. And as the epistle makes clear, there are lesser forms of hatred: dislike, contempt, abuse, and rejection, to mention but a few. They have no place in the Christian life.

Christ has given the supreme example of love in his laying down his life for us. John does not exclude the possibility of a Christian having to do the same. But other forms of love are given prominence: peacemaking, sharing, and a sense of concern for others are a few of the examples cited.

We generally take our failures of unkindness rather lightly. But on the scale of things they are probably not that insignificant. There is no virtue in the scriptures given such prominence, no clearer sign of being a disciple of Christ. If we disregard the significance of our lack of charity, then the luster of Christianity will be lost. Do I have to make that unkind remark? Why can't I find room in my schedule for that person's need? Do I realize the pain my aloofness can cause?

"Behold these Christians," a nonbeliever once said, "how they love one another."

Points to Ponder

The faith of Nathanael
Forms of hatred
Expressions of love

JANUARY 6

1 John 5:5–13
Psalm 147:12–13, 14–15, 19–20
Mark 1:7–11

The letter of John today states that Jesus is the Son of God who came through water and blood. The blood is that of his redemptive death, a death that has given efficacy to the baptism (water) that he confers.

In today's Gospel reading from Mark, John the Baptist proclaims that he is not worthy to untie the sandal straps of the One coming after him. Jesus ratifies the baptism of John by going to the Jordan and being baptized by him. The account is brief and centers solely on the essentials. While it describes what Jesus receives at John's hand, the account is also a catechesis on the meaning of Christian baptism.

Our own baptism had singular importance as the moment of our incorporation into the life of the Triune God. That same Trinity is depicted as present when Jesus is baptized. Jesus enters the water; the Spirit descends upon him; and the voice of the Father acknowledges the Son as the one on whom his favor rests. In baptism, we too are given over to Christ in affirming him as God's Son. Here the Gospel scene is like a finely etched cameo pointing to our own baptismal immersion.

When we are baptized, we are called to march to a new tune. We are to live our lives in such a way that they would make no sense if God did not exist. We have quite truly "put on the Lord Jesus." We are clothed in him and are called to think his thoughts.

Unfortunately, in our time baptism often has more social significance than one that is truly religious. In many countries it is simply accepted practice, with little attention given to its deeper meaning. The person baptized must continue to grow in understanding and living the faith. The religious education of a child is a major responsibility of the parents; this cannot simply be relegated to a weekly catechism class. We come to love what we know, and in far too many cases that knowledge remains minimal. In any area of our lives in which we desire expertise, we grow in knowledge. It can be no different when it comes to our faith.

Points to Ponder

Water and blood
The Trinity at Jesus' baptism
The Trinity at our baptism
Our understanding of baptism today

JANUARY 7

1 John 5:14–21
Psalm 149:1–2, 3–4, 5 and 6a and 9b
John 2:1–11

When is a wedding not a wedding? When it becomes an end-time event. There is much more to the Cana wedding than meets the eye. When the wine supply is exhausted, Jesus creates more as a sign of end-time joy. He declines initially because his "hour has not yet come." It is only with his death and resurrection that the final period will be fully inaugurated. Wine is an end-time symbol of the new life that Christ provides with his atoning death. It replaces the Jewish purification water of the former era. Now is the time for the forgiveness of sin. We are to approach the forgiving Christ with a spirit of confidence and assurance.

Some sins are deadly; others are not. What is an example of a deadly sin? According to the teaching of John's epistle, to deny that Jesus is the Son of God or did not really come in the flesh would be deadly, since it is tantamount to denying a cornerstone of faith. A spirit of indifference to faith would be deadly, since faith is not a mere supplement to life or simply an addendum.

Unfortunately, in many lives in our time, the concerns of faith are often sidetracked or seen as peripheral. Our livelihood is certainly important, but it cannot become the be-all and end-all of our existence. Justice and honesty must be key values for us. To downplay justice is to put our faith on the "back burner." If our lives are reduced to secular values, we betray a precious heritage.

Hebrews says that Christ is God's last word. It doesn't get any better than that. There is only one era left, and that lies beyond the grave in eternity. We pray to remain faithful. The Cana event speaks of the end-time, the era in which we live. May any form of betrayal be far from our lives.

Points to Ponder

> Deadly and nondeadly sin
> Tasting the wine of God's love
> A "wedding" symbol of the end-time
> The presence of Christ in our lives

MONDAY AFTER EPIPHANY

> 1 John 3:22—4:6
> Psalm 2:7bc–8, 10–12a
> Matthew 4:12–17, 23–25

Up to this point in Matthew's Gospel, Jesus' time has been largely spent in Judea, with the emphasis falling on his Davidic credentials (Bethlehem). It is in the northern region of Galilee (Capernaum) that his ministry begins. The author employs the words of Isaiah addressed centuries before to the two northern tribes of Zebulun and Naphtali. In the early part of the first millennium BC, these two tribes were overrun by Assyrian forces and were largely decimated. When Isaiah spoke of the new era to come, he spoke consolingly to these two tribes and assured them of a brighter future. For Matthew, that time has arrived with the coming of Jesus.

Jesus' first preaching tour takes him through much of Galilee. While he is involved in preaching and teaching, the major emphasis here falls on his healing ministry. People with a variety of illnesses were brought to him. Jesus performs his wonders with a great deal of solicitude for people racked with pain. This inevitably attracts a large amount of attention, but Jesus' intention is clearly to bring help to those in need.

It is aptly said that a Christian is never more so than when he or she is assisting others. There are many people who do not believe that they have the strength to cope with another day. How meaningful it is for us to be present to them. Such acts of charity have immeasurable consequences.

The letter of John reminds us again today that to deny that Jesus Christ came in the flesh is to separate ourselves from God. This is but to say that there are certain truths of our faith that are immutable. The incarnation is one of them. Jesus was not merely a good man. Nor did he simply seem to be a man. As John states, "And the Word became flesh and lived among us" (John 1:14). This is the central belief of our faith.

Points to Ponder

> Homiletic helps
> The reality of the incarnation
> Healing the brokenhearted
> With faith, light has arisen

TUESDAY AFTER EPIPHANY

> 1 John 4:7–10
> Psalm 72:1–2, 3–4, 7–8
> Mark 6:34–44

The story of the loaves and fish has been heard so often that we might think it needs little retelling. But there is a single verse in the reading from the letter of John that gives meaning to the Gospels as a whole. "God's love was revealed among us in this way: God sent his only Son into the world so that we might live through him."

A real appreciation for that verse opens fully the door of Christian faith. In short, we do not live justly to win God's favor. God's favor was won before we were even conscious of it, and through no effort of ours. Since God's favor has touched us, our love is simply reciprocal. Many people see the Christian life as an endless effort to get somewhere. But the truth of the matter is that we are already there. We were the recipients of that love before we were even aware of it.

Today's Gospel, then, is a perfect fit. It is hard to escape the eucharistic allusions that can be heard in that narrative. As happens at each Eucharist, Jesus takes the loaves, blesses and distributes them. Of course, the event itself was not a Eucharist, but the evangelist reminds us that we are no less privileged than those people in the desert. At every Mass, we are truly nourished by the Lord as we feed on his sacramental body and blood. What greater sign of our being favored and loved?

What is vitally important is that we bring that love of God to others. To bring communion to the sick is a very singular ministry. In that act, the presence of Christ is complemented by our own charity in an outreach to the less fortunate (whether in sickness, poverty, or some other misfortune). Christ is telling us that where our feet go, he can go; where our eyes see, he can see; where our ears hear, he can hear. For this reason it is important to realize that God's love flows into us before it ever makes its return to God.

Points to Ponder

> God loved us first
> Eucharist as God's concern for us
> Ministering to the disabled

WEDNESDAY AFTER EPIPHANY

> 1 John 4:11–18
> Psalm 72:1–2, 10, 12–13
> Mark 6:45–52

Of the various difficulties present in modern society, one of the most prevalent is the fear of commitment. Engagement in an enterprise that will last a lifetime is very threatening. This is certainly true of marriage as well as other lifelong engagements. When the idea of lifetime commitment is presented, the response all too frequently is, "You mean, until I *die*?"

Our first reading today tells us that Christian love, when perfected, casts out all fear, and that includes the fear of failure as well. Today's Gospel finds the apostles still weak in faith and thus frightened and uncomprehending. They had witnessed the miracle of the loaves but were still lacking in understanding. Jesus now appears to them walking on the water of the lake, enters the boat, and allays their fears.

There is no denying that an atmosphere of fear is present in modern society. Antisocial behavior is all too common. People are afraid to be on the street at night. We teach our children at an early age to beware of strangers. The circumstances wherein we divulge a credit card number are very few, and never our Social Security number. The reasons for this are not unreasonable. Crime, unfortunately, is a fact of life today. Yet we cannot deny the fact that we are surrounded by many good and trustworthy people. There are times when we must step out in faith, even when the outcome is not certain. Where faith is strong, and accompanied by love, fear is cast out.

We must be clear. To give one's life for a worthy cause, as an act of love, banishes fear. The letter of John summarizes it well today. "God is love, and those who abide in love abide in God, and God abides in them."

Points to Ponder

> Weak faith and fear
> Strong love and courage
> The witness of a lasting marriage

THURSDAY AFTER EPIPHANY

1 John 4:19—5:4
Psalm 72:1–2, 14 and 15bc, 17
Luke 4:14–22

Upon returning to his home town of Nazareth and reading from Isaiah in the synagogue on the Sabbath, Jesus defines his mission. Those who are expecting an earthly monarch will have to look elsewhere. Jesus identifies himself with a God-directed mission to the poor and to those physically or socially handicapped. The promise of Isaiah, Christ asserts, is fulfilled in him. As the letter of John insists, the one who hates his brother or sister is far from God. Moreover, the One who comes as our teacher and guide must himself offer an example of unqualified love. It is this love to which Jesus points in this early synagogue visit.

While the reaction of his audience is initially one of admiration, it takes little time for the people of Nazareth to reject him. He becomes the prophet without honor in his own country. In the face of his extraordinary claims, the mood of his audience changes. Claims that do not meet people's expectations are more easily rejected than tested.

The calendar of Christian saints is replete with people rejected because of their honest gospel stand. One thinks of Archbishop Oscar Romero of El Salvador who was shot for speaking on behalf of the voiceless under a military dictatorship. It is often easier to be silent than to take a strong unequivocal position. One thinks also of St. Clare of Assisi, who wanted to give her life wholly to the gospel after the manner of her mentor and friend, Francis, but was strongly opposed by her own family.

In the face of important moral decisions, we may find reason to remain silent and undistinguished. But the Spirit emboldens us and moves us toward the hard decision. In today's responsorial, the psalmist prays for the king in words that could be applied to all of us. "Give the king your justice, O God." And to each one of us as well.

Points to Ponder

Speaking the truth in love
God's concern for the unfortunate
Taking an unpopular position

FRIDAY AFTER EPIPHANY

1 John 5:5–13
Psalm 147:12–13, 14–15, 19–20
Luke 5:12–16

Credence is derived from the credentials presented. We may be inclined to think of Christ's credentials as his miracles. And yet in many instances, when it comes to the miracles of Jesus, he counsels silence. The principal note of credibility that the Gospels set forth is the witness that the Father gives in sending his Son into the world in atonement for sin and then bringing him through his ordeal to the glory of the resurrection. Whoever believes in Jesus Christ hears that testimony. Whoever rejects that teaching makes of God a liar and has no life in him.

In today's Gospel, the cured leper is told to present himself to the priest in order to be restored to the community. Any form of leprosy, which included even skin disorders, excluded one from participation in the life of the community. Reintegration could only take place with the priest's acknowledgment that the disease was no longer present. While the teaching of Jesus went beyond the Jewish law, he was never indifferent to its prescriptions. He was a reformer, not an iconoclast. There are those who remain attached to practices that are no longer in the forefront of church life. These people deserve respect and reverence even when our religious mentality differs pronouncedly. Religious practice dies a very slow death. While we may not always share another's convictions, we can still appreciate his or her position.

The words of John today retain their overriding importance. Jesus Christ stands at the heart and center of our belief. He alone is the way, the truth, and the life. There is nothing this side of heaven that has greater importance than our single Lord and Savior. To believe in him with total conviction is to have eternal life.

Points to Ponder

> The Father's witness to Jesus
> Jesus' respect for the Law
> Eternal life begins now

SATURDAY AFTER EPIPHANY

> 1 John 5:14–21
> Psalm 149:1–2, 3–4, 5–6a and 9b
> John 3:22–30

The reference to Jesus' baptism ministry in today's Gospel is singular in the New Testament. At this early stage, this is evidently a reference to the same type of conversion baptism that John the Baptist administered. The Spirit baptism was a post-Easter reality. This pre-Easter baptism was a commitment to a profound change of life in anticipation of the final era. This activity of Jesus lent support to the ministry of John and endowed the latter with credibility as an eschatological prophet.

At the same time, the words of John are decisive. He was not the messiah and unhesitatingly deferred to Jesus, the one whose star was in the ascendancy, in the face of whose surpassing significance John can only decrease in importance. To defer to another is not always easy in life. We all seek assurance of our own worth and merit. But it is always the Christian thing to defer with dignity rather than chagrin and unpleasantness. John was not interested in accruing honor to himself. He may have been the groomsman but he was not the groom. There is a lesson there for all of us.

In the letter of John today, he speaks of different grades of sin. Not all sin was deadly; apostasy was obviously one that was. We are to pray for one whose sin is not death-dealing. It may well mean the regaining of Spirit life. Hence, it is always commendable to pray for ourselves and other sinners, since God's mercy is inexhaustible.

As our epiphany octave draws to a close, we are again given reason for gratitude. What Christ has promised has come to life in all of us. Baptism is our door to life. If we have faltered after that, God's goodness has touched us time after time. We are forgiven. Let us put the past behind us and move ahead. We now live a life that springs up to eternity. We have indeed been blessed.

Points to Ponder

Jesus' baptism ministry
John decreases and Christ increases
Praying for those in difficulty

Ordinary Time
Weeks 1 to 8

MONDAY OF THE FIRST WEEK IN ORDINARY TIME

Year I

Hebrews 1:1–6
Psalm 97:1 and 2b, 6 and 7c, 9
Mark 1:14–20

This annual cycle begins with Jesus' proclamation that the reign of God is at hand. What that fulfillment means is the theme of today's reading from Hebrews. Jesus, as God's "last word," stands at the center of the reign of God. As God's Son, he exists eternally, long before the end-time reign. He is the "blueprint" of God in the whole process of creation, as well as being the one for whom all things were made. Creation is from him and for him. Now, in time, he has atoned for our sins through his death and reigns in glory with the Father.

The response to God's goodness in Christ is discipleship. "Follow me."

The sacrifice of the first followers may seem slight—some nets and a few boats. But for them it meant giving up home and livelihood, not an insignificant thing in any age. A response to Christ is never effortless, but it comes from a grateful heart. Today's Psalm speaks of the Most High touching the earth and each one of us with his goodness.

Points to Ponder

Christ, the beginning and end of creation
Christ, God's blueprint
Christ and the angels
Disciples as fishermen
Christian community, a new family

Year II

> 1 Samuel 1:1–8
> Psalm 116:12–13, 14–17, 18–19
> Mark 1:14–20

The call that the disciples of Jesus received differs from that of Samuel. His life story begins in today's first reading. The Samuel story is an impressive one of a man who was singularly upright throughout his life. Born of a formerly childless marriage, he was the son of the faith-filled Hannah and a concerned father, Elkanah. He was raised within the precincts of a major sanctuary, in an atmosphere of piety and respect. In today's reading, Hannah pleads with God for a child. Her prayer is marked by perseverance, even as she bears the reproach of her husband's second wife. What is striking is the confidence of her prayer.

The disciples of Jesus on the Sea of Galilee respond to their call with a sense of immediacy. Their response is decisive, while Hannah's journey of faith lasted many years. For a Hebrew woman to be childless was little better than being accursed. The fulfillment of her call to be the mother of a prophet was slow in coming, but her longing never wavered. While we admire the sons of Zebedee for their resolute action, our hearts are with Hannah, for whom the call seemed so delayed.

Points to Ponder

> Parents' longing for a child
> The gift of a child
> Perseverance in prayer

TUESDAY OF THE FIRST WEEK IN ORDINARY TIME

Year I

> Hebrews 2:5–12
> Psalm 8:2ab and 5, 6–7, 8–9
> Mark 1:21–28

The reading from Hebrews today accords Christ total primacy in the created order. In his humanity, subsequent to his death and resurrection, there is nothing in creation that stands above him. He is the alpha and omega, the beginning and the end of all that has ever been or will ever be.

Yet, the author of Hebrews makes clear that Christ was made perfect through what he suffered. Without suffering, Christ would not have been completely human. With his suffering, he is like us in everything except sin. Suffering is always a bitter pill to swallow. But just as it was part of Christ's coming to glory, so too it is for us. The burden of sickness and distress plays a significant part in our offering to the Father. Paul even says that suffering endured for the sake of Christ's body, the church becomes part of Christ's redemptive suffering offered to the Father. Pain, then, is never worthless; it has a part to play in the plan of salvation.

In today's Gospel, Jesus' authority appears in the expulsion of the demon tormenting the man in the Capernaum synagogue. Onlookers are astounded. The demon's question to Jesus: "What have you to do with us?" may be better translated, "What do you have in common with us?" The answer, of course, is "Nothing." In fact, Jesus came to vanquish evil. Like the rest of creation, it too is subject to him.

Our baptism means that we have cast our lot with Christ, not with lesser powers. Victory will ultimately be ours, in spite of the pain and suffering that will be part of our earthly journey. When tempted, let us have nothing in common with evil, but put evil behind us and move forward.

Points to Ponder

> Christ's primacy in creation
> The offering of pain and sorrow
> Jesus confronts evil
> Dealing with temptation

Year II

> 1 Samuel 1:9–20
> 1 Samuel 2:1, 4–5, 6–7, 8abcd
> Mark 1:21–28

When Eli sees Hannah praying with great emotion at the temple, he mistakenly assumes she's drunk and reprimands her. Unfortunately there are too many Eli incidents in life. Under any circumstances, it is difficult to take unwarranted criticism from another. But when that criticism comes from a person in authority, especially a religious person, it is even more difficult to accept. All Christians, religious authorities especially, should think before they criticize, since circumstances may not always be as they seem.

It is interesting in the Gospels to note how circumspect Jesus is in his speech. He never descends to vindictive speech. He is a model of temperate speech and of spiritual outreach. When he is faced with blatant evil, he deals with it resolutely. When faced with a sinful woman, he refuses to accuse her and sends her on her way with a word of counsel.

Hannah eventually has a son, and he is well worth the wait. He is the upright and dedicated Samuel. Eli's original insult of Hannah, when he assumed she had been drinking, is long past. His final words to her are those of blessing and encouragement. But that original insult, based on a misunderstanding, still gives us pause. A lack of charity is often considered a minor infraction. But it bears remembering that it can do considerable harm.

Points to Ponder

Speaking the truth in love
The evil of rash judgment
Jesus, the model of charity
The wise exercise of authority

WEDNESDAY OF THE FIRST WEEK IN ORDINARY TIME

Year I

Hebrews 2:14–18
Psalm 105:1–2, 3–4, 6–7, 8–9
Mark 1: 29–39

The death of Jesus has set us free. We no longer live in bondage or in fear of what is to come. Hebrews advises us today that Christ himself was tested through his suffering and is thus in a position to help those who are tempted. His coming was first directed to his fellow Jews, the children of Abraham. We are not certain about who the original audience of the Letter to the Hebrews was, but it is likely that it was made up of Christians of a Jewish background, since so much of the letter points to a familiarity with Jewish life and cult.

In Mark's Gospel, early in his ministry Jesus visits the home of Peter and cures the apostle's mother-in-law. The structure of this brief account follows the miracle story form. There is a brief description of the illness (fever) and the action of Jesus ("grasped her hand, and helped her up"). Finally the completeness of the cure is underscored, when it is said that the woman waited on them. This service is described as a *diakonia*, the common term for Christian ministry. There may well be a deeper teaching here. We too have been cured of our alienation from God by the redemptive action of Christ. What remains for us is to respond in a spirit of Christian service. If we have been "graced" by God, then Christian service or ministry is a natural result. This is something of which we should be always mindful.

For Christ to be our high priest, interceding before God on our behalf, he first had to know what it means to be human. So too we who have been cured of our spiritual fever are called to express our gratitude in a spirit of service.

Points to Ponder

> The humanity of Christ
> Healing and service
> The "testing" of Jesus

Year II

> 1 Samuel 3:1–10, 19–20
> Psalm 40:2 and 5, 7–8a, 8b–9, 10
> Mark 1:29–39

When Samuel was called by God during sleep, he never thought of supernatural intervention. He could only conclude that Eli was calling him. The priest advises the young man to go back to bed and only grasps the truth of the matter after the third intervention. If it happens again, says Eli to Samuel, then respond, "Speak, Lord, for your servant is listening."

It is easy, and all too frequent, to confuse "hearing" with "listening," but there is a marked difference between the two. There are many things we hear in the course of a day without really listening. Listening implies attentiveness. We may hear background music playing while we work, but when we go to a concert we are definitely in a listening mode.

The life of Samuel, one of the Bible's most inspiring personalities, was one of complete adherence to God's will. Many biblical people have excellent qualities but often have feet of clay as well. We are all called to listen to God's voice but, in the cacophony of modern life, it is not always easy to discern God's will. In the Marcan Gospel today, Jesus sets forth an important principle. He is told that people were clamoring for him in the towns he had visited. But he had no interest in returning to ground that had already been plowed. He wants to visit neighboring villages that had not yet even been touched by the good news.

Rather than set out for new ground, we often prefer "the tried and true." Christ never surrenders to the attraction for popular acclaim. His life was short, and there was much to be done.

We do not know what the Lord may ask of us. Faith and trust will call us forward, often away from familiar ground. The church's expansive vision from the start moved her from Jerusalem to the far-reaching Gentile world. And of that, we are all beneficiaries.

Points to Ponder

> Listening to the word of God
> Responding to God's call
> Moving into the unknown
> Ecumenism challenges

THURSDAY OF THE FIRST WEEK IN ORDINARY TIME

Year I

Hebrews 3:7–14
Psalm 95:6–7c, 8–9, 10–11
Mark 1:40–45

We live in the moment of the great "today." It is the "today" of God's ultimate word to the world, the age of God's Son, Jesus. Every day of our life is a moment of grace. Israel's great "today" saw its people falter. Instead of being faithful to God during their desert sojourn, they revolted against him, for which they paid the penalty of not entering the promised land.

We are indeed blessed, but we often lose sight of the fact that we are living in the promised times. Nothing will ever exceed the gift of God that is his Son. We are blessed to be part of the great "today." We know that the gospel calls us to live honestly and uprightly in this world. Yet we see so much deceit and deception in our times. We know that every human life is sacred, and yet abortion on demand is a given in modern society. War continues with people dying for causes that remain blurred. It is easy for our hearts to harden and become insensitive.

Jesus performs a cure in today's Gospel and then enjoins silence on the beneficiary. But the beneficiary does just the opposite. He has received a great favor and been asked to remain silent. The cure becomes public at every turn.

As we live in the great "today," the psalmist asks us not to harden our hearts. Rather let us live a life of gratitude and openness to God. Let us walk a narrow line and avoid selfishness and licentiousness. We are now partners of Christ as long as we retain that confidence with which we began.

Points to Ponder

Israel's lack of fidelity
Fidelity and commitment
Living in the "today"

Year II

> 1 Samuel 4:1–11
> Psalm 44:10–11, 14–15, 24–25
> Mark 1:40–45

The Israelite defeat at the hands of the Philistines proved to be a critical moment in Hebrew history. Not only did they lose a large number of soldiers, but the ark of the covenant was captured by the pagan enemy. It represented an incredible loss.

The ark had great significance for the Hebrews. It was more than a symbol of God's presence; in a certain sense it "localized" the deity. While God remained invisible, with no one able to look on him and live, the fact is that he was believed to be truly present with the ark, which served as his throne or footstool. That being the case, the loss of the ark to a pagan enemy bordered on the sacrilegious. Fortunately it did not remain long in Philistine hands, but its seizure remained an inestimable loss.

At this point, the Hebrews felt bereft of guidance and security. While some of this may be attributed to rather primitive theological reasoning, it has interesting modern parallels, with the modern exclusion of God from the public arena. There is no doubt that our Constitution clearly calls for a separation of church and state. The government may not endorse any particular faith or accord it any precedence. On the other hand, our times are characterized by an exaggerated secularism that sees no place for religion in the public forum. This is not in accord with the long history of legitimate religious expression that is a part of or history.

Faith is an integral part of American history. Without impinging on the principle of separation, there is still room for religious expression in the public forum. The loss of the ark to the Philistines was tragic for the Israelites. So too the loss of religion from the public forum today represents an unwarranted loss as well.

Points to Ponder

The significance of the ark
The capture of the ark
Faith in the public forum

FRIDAY OF THE FIRST WEEK IN ORDINARY TIME

Year I

Hebrews 4:1–5, 11
Psalm 78:3 and 4bc, 6c–7, 8
Mark 2:1–12

"Let us strive to enter into that rest." None of us really knows what the experience of eternity will be. Various images appear in the scriptures, and that is what they are—images, a manner of expression or speaking. Rest is one of those images. The Bible sees rest very positively, such as the rest associated with the Sabbath or as the way in which God concludes the work of creation. Today's reading states that we are certain of entering into that rest if we persevere in our faith.

In Mark's Gospel, Jesus is often seeking to get some rest. Yet as the crowds press upon him, he is always reluctant to turn away. Today's Gospel is no exception. The people surround Jesus even to the point of blocking the door. Unable to reach him, the four men carrying the cot take the unusual step of digging through the roof to reach Jesus. Christ's reaction might strike us as unusual. The connection between sin and suffering was easily affirmed in first-century Palestine. Jesus simply states that the man's sins are forgiven. Since the forgiveness of sin was seen as only God's prerogative, his critics object. Yet Jesus does not back away. His power over sickness vindicates his authority over sin. If he can deal with the one, he can deal with the other. The man is healed and sent on his way, to the amazement of the onlookers.

We all pray for the grace to enter into the Lord's rest. We are confident of his great mercy that has repeatedly touched our lives.

We walk the glory road not because of our own abilities but because his goodness has repeatedly been felt.

Points to Ponder

Images of eternity
Entering into rest

The gift of forgiveness
Healed and continuing the journey

Year II

1 Samuel 8:4–7, 10–22a
Psalm 89:16–17, 18–19
Mark 2:1–12

No form of government is perfect. But most of us would say that, even with its imperfections, democracy is our preferred form of rule. At times we learn that our elected officials have feet of clay. But we would still be reluctant to abandon the system.

In today's first reading from Samuel, the people ask the prophet for a king. God acquiesces to their request, albeit reluctantly, since kingship will certainly prove to be a mixed blessing. The speech of Samuel is part of the antimonarchical strain in the Book of Samuel in pointing up the negative aspects of kingship. Confiscation of property, conscription, tithing—these are some of the less pleasant features of a future kingship. But nonetheless a king will be given to the people, even though the step represents an encroachment on the rights of Yahweh.

Jesus avoids at every turn any notion of a human kingship. It is emphatically not the purpose he is called to fulfill. He was so unlike a royal messiah that any chances of his being seen as a kingly figure were minimal. As the emissary of the Father, he forgives sin and cures disease.

In our own lives, there should be no confusion of allegiances. We cannot equivocate on the demands that God makes of us. In balancing the demands of God and Caesar, there is no doubt where our first allegiance lies. Yet we know full well that in living our daily lives we are at countless turns faced with the "rule of Caesar." The good order of society depends on it. We are not free to disregard taxes—even though we may work to reduce them. The ordinances of public safety bind us in conscience. In the great majority of issues, the Christian is a good citizen. But when our conscience prods us to raise our voice in objection, we should not fail to do so.

Points to Ponder

Morality in public office
Our responsibility in the social order
The "life issues"

SATURDAY OF THE FIRST WEEK IN ORDINARY TIME

Year I

Hebrews 4:12–16
Psalm 19:8, 9, 10, 15
Mark 2:13–17

A lack of appreciation for the Bible was once regrettably common among Catholics. The Second Vatican Council changed all that, ushering in the rise of biblical interest among lay Catholics. At first, some people wondered how Catholics would respond to workshops and lecture series on a contemporary understanding of scripture. But people responded very positively, and their love for the Bible has not diminished over the years. Hebrews today speaks of the penetrating power of God's word. It reaches the reflections and thoughts of our heart and enables us to hold a mirror up to our deepest human aspirations.

Jesus is God's gift to us. He now is present in the heavenly court, acting as our high priest, interceding for us in our weakness. We all wrestle with our weaknesses. But Christ was tempted just as we are. He is like us in every way, except that he did not sin. He is thus in a unique position to sympathize and help us in our inadequacy.

In the Gospel narrative, we cannot help but be impressed by Levi's willingness to leave behind his tax collector post—a position that was looked down upon by the people as being corrupt and sinful—and follow Jesus. It could not have been easy for Levi to leave behind his former associates and friends. Jesus dines with Levi and is criticized for it, since the law forbade a practicing Jew from association with public sinners. Jesus gives little heed to such precepts. Indeed, this is one of the things that makes his mission different. He comes into the world precisely to find sinners and the spiritually ill, not to avoid them.

If we would find time for scripture reading in our daily lives, we would certainly become more sensitive to God's will. It will also make us less judgmental in our dealings with others. It reminds us that no one is beyond the pale of God's love.

Points to Ponder

The love of scripture
Christian inclusiveness
Love for the sinner

Year II

1 Samuel 9:1–4, 17–19; 10:1
Psalm 21:2–3, 4–5, 6–7
Mark 2:13–17

"Looks aren't everything" is a common axiom. This is certainly the case with Saul. He is a man of remarkably good looks who is anointed by Samuel, at God's direction, as Israel's first king. In his life, he shows some remarkable traits. For example, he never shirks from his duty to defend his people from alien forces. Yet, in many ways he is not a faithful Yahwist. He turns violently on the young David, a member of his court, whom he sees as a threat to his own sovereignty and therefore a person to be eliminated. His repeated attempts do away with David are recorded in the First Book of Samuel. When Saul's son, Jonathan, becomes David's cherished friend, Saul is infuriated. It is only when Saul and Jonathan die in battle that the way is paved for David's ascendancy.

Saul, the anointed of God, is rejected as king. He is the son of disappointment. Such is not that unusual in life. It very often happens that a highly regarded person ends up as something less than expected. This can be a very painful experience. It reminds us that our primary hope must be placed in God, with the hope that the human components will work toward a positive outcome.

When Jesus calls Levi to follow him, he has a certain result in mind, a certain hope for Levi. Levi also has to move forward in faith, hoping to do the right thing. It is the same with us. We may not be sure of the outcome of a course of action, but, if the cause is right, we know that it is worth the effort. As the old saying goes, "It is better to have loved and lost than never to have loved at all."

Points to Ponder

Envy and the fall of Saul
Election and free will
Stepping out in faith

MONDAY OF THE SECOND WEEK IN ORDINARY TIME

Year I

Hebrews 5:1–10
Psalm 110:1, 2, 3, 4
Mark 2:18–22

Today's readings highlight two aspects of Jesus' life and ministry that did not follow the traditional pattern. The Letter to the Hebrews develops at some length the priesthood of Jesus. He stands now as the high priest interceding before God on our behalf. The difficulty with this idea lay in the fact that he was not a descendant of the priestly tribe of Levi, and he made no claim to priesthood in his earthly life. But Hebrews finds an interesting precedent. Genesis recounts the story of a pagan priest, Melchizedek, who makes a brief appearance as Abraham returns from battle and offers the patriarch some bread and wine (Gen 14:18–20). Abraham then offers tithes to the priest. Since Abraham shows honor and respect to this otherwise unknown priest, the Letter to the Hebrews sees Melchizedek as a type of Christ and develops this typology along various lines.

Then there is the question of fasting. While Jesus himself is depicted as fasting at the start of his ministry, it does not receive prominent emphasis as a form of mortification. To his questioners in today's Gospel, Jesus answers in terms of the wedding feast.

The age of the messiah was often seen as a festive time, like the time of a wedding. Fasting at such a time was seen as alien to its festive spirit. But the Gospel goes on to say that when the bridegroom is no longer present fasting will again be in order.

Today we designate the leader of the local congregation as a priest.

It is interesting to note that it is a term never used of any Christian ministry in the New Testament. The term is used exclusively of Christ, who is our sole mediator before God. Our local priests are sharers in that sole mediatorship of Jesus.

One heard much more about fasting in an earlier day than is the case in our time. Even devoutly religious people do not seem to accord it any real priority—if anything, we seem to be eating more! But fasting still has its value in helping us curb our appetites. It does no harm to cut back on calories in atonement for sin, whether our own sins or those of others.

Points to Ponder

> Christ our high priest
> Melchizedek as a type of Christ
> The role of fasting in our lives

Year II

> 1 Samuel 15:16–23
> Psalm 50:8–9, 16bc–17, 21 and 23
> Mark 2:18–22

Saul did not enjoy God's favor for long. Today's reading recalls an occasion when he incurred God's displeasure. The prophet Samuel makes it very clear that obedience is of greater value than sacrifice. Submission to the will of God takes precedence over ritual. In so many words, Saul is told that his days are numbered.

While Jesus has no argument with fasting, it is clear that the emphasis of his teaching falls elsewhere. It is always spiritual alertness that comes to the fore. This means to see my neighbor as brother or sister and to regard that relationship as preeminent, to the exclusion of my personal concerns. We can ask ourselves, which parables stand out most clearly? The Good Samaritan, the father and the prodigal son, the lost sheep, the lost coin. More than anything else, it is the recognition of the sovereignty of God and the needs of others.

Everything rotates around this basic principle.

We may feel a certain remorse for eating that chocolate cake during Lent. But God is more concerned about the person with whom I have not spoken for months. Or the shut-in who could use an occasional helping hand.

The Samuel story suggests that we not disregard what God asks of us. The Gospel at least suggests that we don't have to travel far to put Christ's teaching into practice.

Points to Ponder

Saul's disregard of God's will
Obedience better than sacrifice
Fasting in our lives
The Great Commandment as paramount

TUESDAY OF THE SECOND WEEK IN ORDINARY TIME

Year I

Hebrews 6:10–20
Psalm 111:1–2, 4–5, 9 and 10c
Mark 2:23–28

The author of Hebrews prays today that his listeners remain firm to the end. When God swore to bless Abraham with progeny, he swore by himself since there was no one superior to him by whom he might swear. It was a promise that penetrated the veil separating us from eternity. This upholds and verifies the lasting truth of what is affirmed by our high priest belonging to the order of Melchizedek.

In explaining why his grain-plucking disciples were exempted from the Law, Jesus refers to an incident from David's life. On one occasion when David and his men were hungry, they were permitted to eat of the holy bread that was reserved for the priests of the sanctuary. In other words, the law of necessity took precedence over precepts of ritual. Mitigating circumstances often alter the binding force of positive law.

Some people are very hesitant to allow anything to interfere with Sunday Mass. And this is generally commendable. But there are certainly circumstances when other legitimate concerns take precedence. The illness of a sick family member may make attendance impossible. We must let our conscience be our guide. Circumstances may clearly alter our ability to attend.

We must remember that Christ is our high priest, not our task master. He certainly understands that circumstances may alter a pattern of conduct. As Christ says, the Sabbath was made for humans, not vice versa.

Points to Ponder

We are Abraham's progeny
God is not unjust, remaining in service to his people
Letting a well-formed conscience be our guide
Sabbath for man, not man for Sabbath

Year II

1 Samuel 16:1–13
Psalm 89:20, 21–22, 27–28
Mark 2:23–28

The selection of David to be king took an unusual tack. Son of Jesse he was, but the last in line. A young sheep herder, he was untempered by experience, perhaps the least prepared of all his brothers. The standards of his selection were not human, but those of a God who makes greatness out of nothing. Saul had long since outserved his usefulness and was rejected as king. It is the tribe of Judah that will now be the standard bearer.

It is undeniable that on more than one occasion, David proved to be a disappointment. The candor of the Book of Samuel in recounting his misdeeds is refreshing. There is no attempt to gild the lily. But even with his human failings, David was a faithful Yahwist. He did not compromise God's sovereignty by introducing pagan cult. When he sinned, he asked for forgiveness with deep expressions of sorrow. When his son Absalom revolted against him, Absalom was killed—even if it caused the king no small amount of anguish. He wanted to see the temple built in Jerusalem, a task that was left to his son Solomon.

Many of us today have mixed feelings about the political arena. We have strong feelings about the presence of corruption and dishonesty. It was not much different in the time of the Jewish monarchy. The greater number of the kings proved to be disappointments. Yet they are still present in the genealogies as Jesus' ancestors. God went beyond human expectations. Once again God wrote straight with crooked lines.

Points to Ponder

> The selection of David
> David's character
> Importance of political integrity

WEDNESDAY OF THE SECOND WEEK IN ORDINARY TIME

Year I

> Hebrews 7:1–3, 15–17
> Psalm 110:1, 2, 3, 4
> Mark 3:1–6

Today's reading from Hebrews contains a categorization of Melchizedek as a type of Jesus. The name itself is explained in terms of the two Hebrew words *king* and *justice*. Melchizedek is said to be the king of Salem, translated as "king of peace." Both terms are applied to Christ, who is both king of justice and king of peace. Moreover, there is no mention of Melchizedek's geneal-ogy. Therefore, he is not a priest because he comes from a priestly line but rather a priest by divine appointment, like the Son of God, who, without a priestly lineage, is destined to remain a priest forever. Melchizedek also offers bread and wine, which is of sig-nificance to Christians.

What is clear is the intention of Hebrews to see Christ alone as priest of the new covenant. That has ramifications for all of us who live in Catholic and priestly communities. There are times in our lives when the parish priest goes beyond our fondest expecta-tions. His care for his people, his ready availability, his attentive-ness to liturgy and preaching. For such a blessing one can only be grateful. But somewhere along the path of life, there will be a pas-tor of a different ilk, perhaps more given to scolding than affirm-ing. Frustrated parishioners may ask, "What did we do to deserve him?" This is all part of the human face of the church. In moments of trial we must keep our attention fixed on Christ, our one high priest, who remains always the center of our lives. When things go adrift, we must return to Christ the first priest, who will never abandon us and will see us through the difficult days.

Christ claimed that it was always a good thing to express kindness on the Sabbath. It is well to remember that there are no limits placed on our ability to do good.

Points to Ponder

> Christ, king of justice and king of peace
> Church life: sometimes positive, sometimes not
> Doing good: anywhere anytime

Year II

> 1 Samuel 17:32–33, 37, 40–51
> Psalm 144:1b, 2, 9–10
> Mark 3:1–6

Most of us know the story of David and Goliath. We proba-bly learned it at an early age in our religion class. Who do you think is the true victor, David or the Philistine? The answer is

"Neither." It is God who is the hero. On the human level, Goliath has the upper hand in terms of skill and size. He scoffs at the shepherd boy who has been sent to oppose him. Yet he is felled by a stone from David's sling. David overcomes his adversary because God wills it.

When our favored team loses in football, we try to justify the loss. Our quarterback was injured in the first quarter. Or our team was affected by two preceding losses. Whatever the reason, the loss stands. In the biblical narrative, we are often invited to see the hand of God at work. And very often it is a case of God making greatness out of nothing. Human agents become secondary when the hand of God is in the ascendancy.

When Jesus appears in the synagogue, his opponents are already prepared to kill him. At this point in Mark's Gospel it appears to be very early for such a violent reaction. It should be remembered that, in assembling his material, the evangelist is not usually following a time sequence. What may have occurred later in Jesus' ministry is drawn here, where the context is a series of events dealing with opposition to Jesus.

For Jesus there is no doubt about the rightness of performing a good deed on the Sabbath. He does not hesitate to heal regardless of the reaction. Respect for Sunday rest is a good thing; to look upon it slavishly is not.

Points to Ponder

> The faithful David
> The caustic Goliath
> Attitudes toward the Sabbath

THURSDAY OF THE SECOND WEEK IN ORDINARY TIME

Year I

> Hebrews 7:25—8:6
> Psalm 40:7–8a, 8b–9, 10, 17
> Mark 3:7–12

Although Christ himself is sinless, he has taken sin upon himself. Today's readings highlight two aspects of his mission: the heavenly and the earthly. As our heavenly high priest, he is seated at God's right hand, ever ready to make intercession for us. Unlike the earthly priests who had to make repeated offerings for themselves and for the people, our present high priest has offered one lasting sacrifice, never to be repeated, by which he has established a new and lasting covenant.

In the Gospel reading today, we pass to Christ's earthly ministry. We find him at the center of a milling crowd with no place to turn for respite. People with afflictions try to touch him. He tells the disciples to prepare a fishing boat for him to avoid the press of the crowd. The demands of the people are prominent in Mark's Gospel. And yet Jesus resolutely faces his trials.

The readings underscore these two features of Jesus' calling, one eternal, the other temporal. Both offer food for thought. There are those moments when we turn to the heavenly Christ, our intercessor before the Father. We need those precious moments when we turn to our high priest with confidence.

At the same time we know what it means to be faced with pressing demands that can lead to fatigue and frustration. Yes, these are trials, but it is still wonderful to grow weary in the service of God and our fellow human beings. The demands will never be too great, for he assures us that his grace will always suffice.

Points to Ponder

> Prayer time in our daily life
> The one eternal sacrifice
> The demands of others on our time

Year II

> 1 Samuel 18:6–9; 19:1–7
> Psalm 56:2–3, 9–10a, 10b–11, 12–13
> Mark 3:7–12

As we continue our readings from the Book of Samuel, features of Saul's unsavory character come more and more to the fore. David's reputation as a warrior has increased, with the result that the people are giving him more acclaim than Saul. This infuriates the king, who sees it as a threat to his position. David himself has done nothing to merit such a negative sentiment. He is a faithful servant in the king's court.

The figure of Saul's son, Jonathan, stands in sharp contrast to that of his father. Knowing of his father's intention to kill David, he allays his father's fears, and David, at least for the moment, is free of worry.

Envy is a very destructive vice, tearing at the fabric of our own character and doing damage as well to the good name of others. We begin with the recognition that we all have gifts that complement those of others. Envy, instead of seeing the good in others, sets us on a collision course. It is repeatedly mentioned in the New Testament. It is the "green-eyed monster" of Shakespeare's *Othello*.

Friendship, on the other hand, is a great gift of God. Our true friends may not be numerous, but each one is a treasure. A friend, said A. J. Cronin, is one in whose presence it is not necessary to say a word.

We ask the Lord today to help us eradicate any shade of envy from our lives. At the same time, we pray for our friends and are grateful for all they mean to us.

Points to Ponder

> Saul's jealousy
> The friendship of Jonathan
> Gratitude for our personal gifts

FRIDAY OF THE SECOND WEEK IN ORDINARY TIME

Year I

> Hebrews 8:6–13
> Psalm 85:8 and 10, 11–12, 13–14
> Mark 3:13–19

The word *covenant* is probably not part of our everyday vocabulary. Its religious significance, however, is central to our understanding of church. The covenant is a bond between God and his people. We meet a number of covenants in the scriptures. The main one in the Old Testament is that made between God and the Hebrew people on Mount Sinai.

Today's reading from Hebrews indicates that the Sinai covenant has been replaced by the new covenant sealed in the blood of Christ. The former covenant had outlived its usefulness, repeatedly disregarded by the Israelites and violated by their conduct. Now the day of the new covenant, foretold by the prophet Jeremiah, has arrived. It is a covenant characterized by a deeply internal spirit, written on the heart, not on stone. Christ has not only forgiven sin; he has established a new bond between God and his people, one that potentially embraces every race and nation.

We are too inclined to think of salvation only in personal terms. But the fact is that we are saved as a people, which means that we cannot be indifferent to the welfare of our brothers and sisters. We are a community of the faithful, a fact highlighted as we gather together to celebrate Mass.

The apostles named in today's Gospel were the first ambassadors of the new covenant. Their message, as Paul indicates, was simple and direct: Be reconciled to God. Reconciliation stands at the very heart of Christ's mission.

Points to Ponder

The new covenant
The universal call of Christianity
A reconciling mission

Year II

1 Samuel 24:3–21
Psalm 57:2, 3–4, 6 and 11
Mark 3:13–19

Nothing seems more alien to the Christian spirit than violence; yet, today it seems to meet us at every turn. Innocent people are violated on the street and in their homes. It is offensive in many ways but certainly because the Christian ethic is clearly nonviolent.

It must be admitted that the Old Testament had a moral code that was in many ways different from our own. When the Israelites waged destructive war, it was often seen as part of God's plan. But there are moments even there when human dignity comes strongly to the fore.

In today's first reading, David, being pursued by the envious Saul, has an opportunity to kill the king. Urged on by his associates, David realizes that he has a matchless set of circumstances to dispatch the king. But he refuses to raise his hand against the anointed of the Lord. Such for him would be an act of sacrilege. So he spares the life of Saul, who then extols the magnanimity of David.

All of us at times become distraught in our personal relationships. But rather than strike out and hurt, we are called to withhold even the harsh word. Harshness, after all, is a form of violence. We remain opposed to the death penalty because it simply continues the violence of the crime's perpetrator. There are limits to justice imposed by a basic respect for human dignity.

The twelve apostles, listed in today's Gospel, were men of simple backgrounds, not illustrious by human standards. What was asked of them was faith and loyalty. Because of their positive response, in the main, they have been remembered through the ages. Our church is founded on the faith that they received and transmitted. For this reason, our faith is said to be apostolic.

Points to Ponder

Human dignity in our times
Respect for authority
Apostolic faith

SATURDAY OF THE SECOND WEEK IN ORDINARY TIME

Year I

> Hebrews 9:2–3, 11–14
> Psalm 47:2–3, 6–7, 8–9
> Mark 3:20–21

The author of Hebrews continues with his comparison of the former and present rituals. In the former dispensation, worship took place in one of two places: the outer sanctuary, where the greater number of sacrifices were offered, and the Holy of Holies, where the high priest sacrificed once a year on the day of atonement. On that very special day, the flesh of a sinful people was cleansed.

The risen Christ, however, has entered into the heavenly sanctuary, divine in its origin, offering not the blood of animals but his own blood, cleansing not the flesh but our sinful consciences. And in conferring the Spirit, he sets us on a footing to worship the living God. The author's lengthy emphasis on the superiority of Christ's covenant underscores the goodness of God in our lives.

Again, in typical Marcan fashion, the Gospel today underscores the demands of Jesus' earthly ministry. The pressures are continuous, and the demands of the crowd unrelenting. At this point the disciples cannot even get the food they need. The response of Jesus' family to this situation is terse and expressed in a way that the evangelists would generally avoid. The situation has led them to the conclusion that he is mentally disturbed. The conjecture may seem inappropriate, but it is a testament to Jesus' total self-donation.

Today's readings highlight the generosity of Christ in his earthly ministry and his role as heavenly high priest. We have argued that Christian virtue arises out of gratitude. The readings of the past weeks have made that very clear.

Points to Ponder

> The single sacrifice of Christ
> The pressures of Jesus' ministry
> The reaction of Jesus' family

Year II

> 2 Samuel 1:1–4, 11–12, 19, 23–27
> Psalm 80:2–3, 5–7
> Mark 3:20–21

David was blessed with a magnanimous spirit. His grief over the death of his closest friend, Jonathan, is easily understood. Saul, the king, had tried repeatedly to destroy David. But in the lament of David for both father and son, Saul is extolled as a mighty warrior, the glory of Israel. Women are reminded that it was Saul who made it possible for them to don fine clothing and gold ornaments.

Jonathan, on the other hand, was David's closest friend; more than a friend, he was a brother.

There is a Latin expression that goes, *De mortuis nihil nisi bonum*. "When it comes to the dead, nothing but good is to be spoken." It is a good rule of thumb. Conversation may easily take a turn to bring the dead up for criticism. Yet when we speak unkindly of the deceased, we point the finger at ourselves. They have no way of defending themselves, and we are often trying to put ourselves in a better light.

The bonds of friendship are not severed with death. Some friends in life, perhaps no longer with us, were always with us and never failed to be at our side. They cannot be forgotten and should not be.

What can be a greater sign of friendship than Jesus' dedication to the crowds who sought him out, to whom he and his apostles ministered even when they were tired and hungry?

Points to Ponder

> Respect for the deceased
> The gift of friendship
> The friendship of Christ

MONDAY OF THE THIRD WEEK IN ORDINARY TIME

Year I

Hebrews 9:15, 24–28
Psalm 98:1, 2–3ab, 3cd–4, 5–6
Mark 3:22–30

What is the sin against the Holy Spirit that cannot be forgiven? It is nowhere specified in the New Testament. The context will have to give us the key. Therein the opponents of Jesus maintain that he does good by the power of evil. The sin then would be to call light darkness or good evil. Since all sins can be forgiven, the dictum about this sin places it in the category of being most serious.

It was one thing for persons who followed Jesus to find his teaching unacceptable and walk with him no more. It was quite another to accuse him of being an instrument of evil. Jesus states clearly that if such were the case it would mean that he and Satan were working against each other. Satan then would have a divided kingdom, and his efforts would be lost.

Hebrews once more carries us aloft. Christ has dealt effectively with evil. He died once for all sins ever committed. Unlike the high priest of a former day, he does not need to offer atonement with animal blood year after year. But coming as he did, he offered himself once in atonement for sinful humanity. Now there remains only his return to bring to glory all those who have been justified.

Unfortunately in our days there is little discussion given to the question of sin. We tend to treat it as a matter of little consequence. Yet we have all found ourselves shipwrecked, or at least close to it, in the course of our lives. By acknowledging sin, we can put it behind us, fully aware that we are forgiven.

We live in the company of our heavenly high priest. We have every reason to be grateful to the God who has never left us.

Points to Ponder

The unforgivable sin
Being allied with evil
A once-for-all sacrifice

Year II

2 Samuel 5:1–7, 10
Psalm 89:20, 21–22, 25–26
Mark 3:22–30

By either ancient or modern standards, David had a long reign as ruler of an entire country: thirty-three years. As today's reading states, it was at an early stage that he captured Jerusalem, with the overthrow of the Jebusites, who held Zion, which became known as the city of David.

As disappointing as Saul had been, David began his reign on a very positive note. As we look at the long list of monarchs who followed, we only regret that the note of quality was not maintained. The fact is that, overall, the kingship in Israel and Judah was a monumental failure. Most of the kings were guilty of corruption that wreaked havoc among the Hebrew people.

Was it absolutism that caused the country's moral disarray? As Lord Acton famously said, "Power tends to corrupt, and absolute power corrupts absolutely." The breakdown in faithful Yahwism soon became eminently clear. There was the imitation of foreign courts, the importation of pagan brides, the introduction of pagan cult, and rampant commercialism. The major defeats that Israel experienced during the first millennium were explained in terms of religious infidelity and moral waywardness.

Who can deny that in our times we need to return to our moral compass? Materialism, consumerism, moral indifference are all part of the modern landscape. The responsibilities of family life confront us at every turn. With courage we must put our hand to the plow and not look back.

The Gospel today invites us again to ally ourselves with Christ and not with Satan. And once we grasp the good, let us be agents in bringing it to the world.

Points to Ponder

Civil authority and public morality
Our alliance with Christ
Seeking the common good

TUESDAY OF THE THIRD WEEK IN ORDINARY TIME

Year I

Hebrews 10:1–10
Psalm 40:2 and 4ab, 7–8a, 10, 11
Mark 3:31–35

To do the will of God summarizes the life of Jesus and his followers. Earlier in Mark 3, Jesus' family had shown their concern for him in claiming that his conduct did not appear normal. Today they stand on the edge of the crowd and ask for him. His response takes an unusual and unexpected direction. Told that his mother and brothers are asking for him, Jesus raises the discussion to a new level. Those who are the mother and brothers of Jesus are those who put God's will into practice.

This reply will eventually be understood in its full Christian sense. Once the Christian era is fully inaugurated with the Lord's death and resurrection and the Holy Spirit is conferred, we have access to a new life. That Spirit is shared with the risen Christ, and thus we are able to address the Father with the title "Abba" just as Christ himself does. But even apart from that fuller incorporation, discipleship with Jesus during his ministry constituted a new family, made in faith not blood. Thus we are members of Christ's family first, through discipleship and in addition, through the gift of the Spirit.

Hebrews today refers to Psalm 40 to highlight the superiority of Christ's offering over any other type of sacrifice. It is not sacrifices and offerings that God wants but rather a will that is in tune with his. That is exactly what Christ gave to the Father and in so doing established the new and better covenant. It is the offering of the "body of Jesus Christ once for all."

Sharing now in Christ's self-giving and in living in obedience to God, we become God's dwelling, a holy thing for a holy people.

Points to Ponder

The true family of Jesus
Daily obedience to God's will
The new and better covenant

Year II

2 Samuel 6:12b–15, 17–19
Psalm 24:7, 8, 9, 10
Mark 3:31–35

The day that David brought the ark of the covenant to its new home in Jerusalem is a moment of unmatched joy. He realizes that the true sovereign of this fledgling country is not himself but the Lord. David's intention to build a temple is thwarted by the Lord; that is to be the lot of his son Solomon. As mysterious as God's presence is, the ark still localizes the presence of Yahweh, and Jerusalem is its fitting resting place.

The Gospel underscores a new relationship to Christ that comes with discipleship. Adhering to him and his teaching, we become brothers, sisters, and mothers. What was the entire purpose of our being educated in the faith? Was it not to actualize God's will in our lives? Think of those years of instruction, the attendance at Catholic school or Confraternity of Christian Doctrine (CCD), the countless homilies heard over many years. All of it pointed to the daily task. The Christian life is not complicated, but neither is it simplistic. The opportunities to go astray are always present, but with it there is the master's voice: "Will you remain faithful?"

Pastoral ministry presents the various facets of life. There are people who have departed from the faith for years but then realize they have squandered a rich heritage. They realize how far they have wandered and want to return home. They do so, and life takes on a new meaning. Other people have never wandered. There might have been mistakes along the way, but they were never far from the beaten path. They have the joy of being the brothers, sisters, and mothers of Jesus. In the words of the psalmist today: "Be lifted up, O ancient doors! that the King of glory may come in."

Points to Ponder

> The ark of the covenant
> Living as members of Christ's family
> Remaining faithful

WEDNESDAY OF THE THIRD WEEK IN ORDINARY TIME

Year I

> Hebrews 10:11–18
> Psalm 110:1, 2, 3, 4
> Mark 4:1–20

The imagery in the parable of the sower and the seed might seem a little confusing. When Jesus is asked to explain the parable, we are first told that the seed is the word of God (v. 14), but then as the various categories are introduced, the seed represents the hearers, those sown on rocky ground (v. 16) and those sown among thorns (v. 18). Nonetheless, the teaching remains clear enough, with the categories as relevant today as in the time of Jesus.

The reading from Hebrews reminds us that Christianity is primarily a religion of the heart. Ours is a covenant that is deeply personal and calls for an internal response. The single offering of Christ is more than sufficient in which all sin is forgiven. Yet, as the parable states, the responses will vary. The seed sown on the footpath never takes root and soon loses its effectiveness. The rocky ground represents those who start well but whose faith is too superficial. Those sown among thorns show promise, but anxieties and worldly cares eventually choke growth and development. The good soil gives life to the seed and enables it to grow and produce a remarkable yield.

If we have felt our faith grow through the years, the seed is in healthy soil. For that we can only be grateful. But as we know well, there are those who never gave faith a chance. Some start off well but never reach a level of spiritual maturity. Today's readings call for a moment of thanks and a prayer for those whose faith is faltering. The weak, too, are loved by God and should not be forgotten.

Points to Ponder

> The seed on the footpath
> The seed on rocky round
> The seed choked by anxiety
> The seed on good ground

Year II

> 2 Samuel 7:4–17
> Psalm 89:4–5, 27–28, 29–30
> Mark 4:1–20

Chapter 7 of the Second Book of Samuel represents a watershed in Old Testament thought. It marks the beginning of the messianic hope in Israel. Nathan approaches David with a message from the Lord that will shape Israelite thought for centuries to come. David is to be the father of a lasting dynasty, kings who will preside over a nation that is blessed and peaceful.

The desire of David to build a house for the Lord in Jerusalem will not be realized. It will belong to his son, Solomon, to realize that dream. Even though subsequent heirs to David's throne may disappoint, punishment will follow but not rejection of the promise. The line of David will be perpetual.

Later prophets expounded on this Davidic theme. It explains why the evangelists were at pains to present Jesus as the son of David. The line of David continues in the person of Jesus.

Each year we celebrate the kingship of Jesus, even as we recognize that his kingdom is like no other. He rules by persuasion. To belong to him is entirely a matter of choice. To make his kingdom our own is to become that fertile soil of today's Gospel wherein the seed grows thirty, sixty, and a hundredfold. We are all part of God's special design, and we pray that we shall never disappoint.

The reign of God is sometimes referred to as "the sweet empire of God's love." It is a great blessing to be citizens of that empire.

Points to Ponder

> The kingdom of David
> The role of Solomon
> God's reign in our life

THURSDAY OF THE THIRD WEEK IN ORDINARY TIME

Year I

> Hebrews 10:19–25
> Psalm 24:1–2, 3–4ab, 5–6
> Mark 4:21–25

As the years roll by and life shortens, we may become a bit more apprehensive. But Hebrews today encourages us to be calm and confident. We have to realize that if Christ has gone this distance for us, he will not abandon us now. In going to death for us, he has carried the heaviest part of the load and will surely see us through to the end. He has gone to prepare a place for us and will not be content until we take our place at the heavenly table. Our present posture should be one of utter sincerity and absolute confidence.

The Gospel today urges us to be generous in sharing the message. Ours is not an esoteric religion, with the truth held only by the enlightened. Fully aware of the truths of our faith, let us share the hope that is in us. If we are generous, God will be generous with us. For God is never outdone in generosity. The candle of truth is not hidden under a basket but shines brightly on the lampstand. There are enough books written and films made that deride human values. But there are also commendable efforts in the media to elevate our tastes, to portray the good present in the world, and to draw our attention to the positive. Let us be promoters of the good and not solely critics of the bad.

Lord, teach me not only to avoid evil but also to applaud and imitate the good.

Points to Ponder

> Living in hope and confidence
> Applauding the good
> The lamp on the lampstand

Year II

> 2 Samuel 7:18–19, 24–29
> Psalm 132:1–2, 3–5, 11, 12, 13–14
> Mark 4:21–25

It is difficult not to become angry with David in reading the Books of Samuel. But there are also those moments that melt the heart, and all is forgiven. Today's passage is one of those moments. Following upon the promises made to David and his descendants, the king now turns to his God in grateful prayer.

In the first place, the king is thankful for the kindness Yahweh has showered upon him, the son of a rural sheep farmer. He has been singled out for kingship and protected by God through a number of harrowing experiences. But more than that, he has now learned that he is to sire a dynasty that will last forever. This carries David well beyond his fondest dreams.

"Who am I, O Lord GOD?" In posing the question at the start of his prayer, David realizes that he can make no claims on God. Everything has been gift, pure gift. Not only has he been personally favored, but the house of David as well. He can only pray for God's continued blessing on his house that future descendants will remain cognizant of such goodness.

None of us can make any claims on God, but, as the Gospel today reminds us, we can and should share what we have received. The ancients said, "Good is self-diffusive." Goodness wants to go out and touch others. Unfortunately we tend to become too self-absorbed. Let the good and positive features of our faith have greater play.

Let's not keep our candle under a bed or basket, but rather put it on a lampstand. There is no better way to express our gratitude.

Points to Ponder

> David's gratitude
> Jesus and the line of David
> The kingdom to last forever

FRIDAY OF THE THIRD WEEK IN ORDINARY TIME

Year I

> Hebrews 10:32–39
> Psalm 37:3–4, 5–6, 23–24, 39–40
> Mark 4:26–34

To live or to perish? To thrive or to wither on the vine? Hebrews today speaks of the deprivation and hardship endured by its readers. Suffering is the human lot but does not last indefinitely, only a "brief moment." Those with faith need only a little patience. The psalmist today reminds us, "The salvation of the righteous is from the Lord."

Today's Gospel parables are very life giving. The farmer sows the seed in the earth and then goes about his daily chores. But the seed experiences growth: the blade, the ear, and the wheat move in concert toward maturity, a process over which the farmer exercises no control. When the harvest times come, he appears with his sickle and reaps the harvest.

A parallel experience is then offered in the example of the small mustard seed. Small enough to be scarcely noticeable, it grows into a large and impressive plant. These are but natural manifestations of God's providence. The growth of the church will be similarly impressive.

Paul sums all of this up in a single statement regarding his ministry. "I planted, Apollos watered, but God gave the growth" (1 Cor 3:6). When it comes to work in God's vineyard or garden, we all make an investment. But the work of grace is in God's hands. And although there may be disappointment along the way, God will ultimately provide the final yield. Christ had many trials in addition to the cross. But his basic confidence in the outcome sustained him. That trust appears repeatedly in his teachings, his parables, and his miracles.

We all have our "What's the use?" days. But they too pass. Our objective stands clearly before us. Faith and love conquer all things.

Points to Ponder

Trials in the Christian life
God as the sustainer

Year II

2 Samuel 11:1–4a, 5–10a, 13–17
Psalm 51:3–4, 5–6a, 6bcd–7, 10–11
Mark 4:26–34

The David narrative today is more than a little disconcerting. His conduct is lustful, deceptive, and death-dealing. He could be grateful that he had to stand only before the court of God and not that of a human magistrate. The consequences would have been much more severe.

The story's deceit can be seen in three stages. David sees Bathsheba bathing on a nearby rooftop. Without knowing anything of her background, he lusts after her and arranges for her to be brought to his palace. When she becomes pregnant, he has her husband Uriah, a warrior in David's army, brought back from the front and given home leave. Uriah will then be the presumed father of the child and David, exonerated. When, upon his return, Uriah does not go to his home, David is infuriated. Upon his return to battle, the king arranges for him to be killed.

This is a David narrative that does not appear elsewhere in accounts of his life. The child of this illicit union does not live. And David expresses his profound sorrow and sense of repentance. His sorrow for his conduct is sincere and his sin forgiven.

The human failing aside, the forgiveness of God is paramount. And there are no limits drawn. People may be incarcerated for life because of their misconduct, but that does not mean that their sin is not forgiven. Peace with God can be made at will.

Today we can all say with the psalmist, "Have mercy on me, God, according to your steadfast love."

Points to Ponder

> The seriousness of David's sin
> David's sense of repentance
> Morality of the death penalty

SATURDAY OF THE THIRD WEEK IN ORDINARY TIME

Year I

> Hebrews 11:1–2, 8–19
> Luke 1:69–70, 71–72, 73–75
> Mark 4:35–41

Today Abraham's faith is applauded on a number of levels. He journeyed to an unknown land where he dwelt in tents with his son and grandson. His wife Sarah, well beyond childbearing age, believed in the power and will of God and bore Isaac. Even when asked to sacrifice this child of promise, Abraham was willing to obey, even though the request was later rescinded. The patriarchs died before seeing the results of God's promise, but they believed deeply in its realization.

The Gospel today presents the other side of the coin, with Mark's account of the storm on the lake. The fear of the disciples is so real in Mark that they do not use the deferential language found in the other accounts. "Teacher, do you not care that we are perishing?"

We often feel very much adrift as we ride out the tempests of life. Yet we must remain confident that Jesus travels with us through these difficult periods. In our times, parents are often dismayed as their children abandon their faith. Others are tested by marriages that are not, and perhaps cannot, be blessed. We must continue to pray with confidence. We never know when things might take a turn for the better. But we hope in the Lord, who is our encouragement.

The Old Testament likes to refer to Yahweh as "rock" and "deliverer." It is with that sort of confidence that we pray today.

Points to Ponder

Patriarchal faith
The fear of the apostle
Trust and confidence in prayer

Year II

2 Samuel 12:1–7a, 10–17
Psalm 51:12–13, 14–15, 16–17
Mark 4: 35–41

"You are the man!" The moment of truth. When seen against the background of David's liaison with Bathsheba, today's parable of Nathan is not hard to decode. With the entire court at his disposal, and its plethora of women, David took the wife of one of his soldiers for his adulterous philandering.

Yet the moment of truth is not without its salutary effect. David crumbles beneath the weight of his guilt. He is told that his own family is destined for great distress. The child to be born of Bathsheba will not live. Clothed in sackcloth, David lies on the ground praying for forgiveness. The psalmist captures his spirit: "Create in me a clean heart, O God" (Ps 51:10).

At times we are taken aback when full funeral rites are accorded someone who had long been separated from the church. But the fact is that none of us knows the dispositions of the human

heart when faced with mortality. We leave much in the hands of
God. None of us is really worthy. And how long does it take to be
truly sorry? In fact, in many instances, contrition is present long
before the end comes.

We pray daily for the grace to remain faithful. But we also
want to avoid being judgmental. With Paul, we can boast only of
our weakness. And that makes us ever grateful for the goodness
of God.

Points to Ponder

> Nathan's parable
> David's repentance
> God's mercy in our lives

MONDAY OF THE FOURTH WEEK IN ORDINARY TIME

Year I

> Hebrews 11:32–40
> Psalm 31:20, 21, 22, 23, 24
> Mark 5:1–20

As the Letter to the Hebrews draws to a close, the author lists
great acts of faith that appear in the Old Testament. A few
names are cited. Some of the heroic deeds mentioned can be identified, but, in the main, it is a general recollection of acts of
endurance through adversity, some of which occurred during the
Maccabean revolt in second-century Palestine.

These examples are stirring expressions of faith, yet with it
all, the author would have us keep one thing in mind. The many
Jews who endured these torments never lived to see the fulfillment of the plan. What they underwent, certainly exemplary and
praiseworthy, was still preparatory. Some were spared from death;
others were not. Everything was moving toward redemption in
Christ, and of that we are the beneficiaries. The plan of perfection
is to be found only in Jesus himself, the final Word of God. And

that includes all of us. Hence, we can read accounts of the past in a fuller light.

When we read the biblical history of salvation, we are not simply recalling a historical journey. We are watching a plan of God unfold—the patriarchs and prophets, judges, and kings, sainted figures and sinners, all were part of a plan that was ultimately to include us as well. It is a story long in the telling, sacred and secular. As Christians we believe that it all leads to Christ and is to be read with the eyes of faith.

In today's Gospel Christ casts out the unclean spirit and consigns it to a herd of pigs, who then hurls the swine off the cliff into the lake. It is a strange story, clearly Marcan in its directness and unelaborated form. And as so often happens, the people are left in a state of amazement.

Points to Ponder

Biblical examples of faith
Christ, the completion of the plan
Christ's power over evil forces

Year II

2 Samuel 15:13–14, 30; 16:5–13
Psalm 3:2–3, 4–5, 6–7
Mark 5:1–20

David's sense of guilt remains with him long after the Bathsheba incident. Different forms of adversity are beginning to appear in his life. The only major insurrection that occurs during his reign comes from his son, Absalom. Allegedly dissatisfied with his father's mode of governing, he organizes a rebellious campaign.

In today's reading, David takes his leave of Jerusalem, in the face of Absalom's threat, in a procession marked by pronounced grief. At one point, an unknown figure named Shimei makes an appearance and begins to curse the king, calling him a murderer and a scoundrel. He blames him for bloodshed in the time of Saul and shows that his sympathies lie with Absalom, David's son.

David staunchly prohibits any form of reprisal against Shimei. He sees the man's denunciation as God-sent and deserved. The king accepts the abuse and continues on his journey. His hope is that God will ultimately makes things right.

God's power is limited by the human will. We always retain the power to decide for better or worse. David does not act against Shimei because he sees this outrage against him as justified.

The man in today's Gospel, on the other hand, had benefited by Jesus' act of exorcism. But when told to go home and share his good fortune with his family, he follows his own whim and takes a tour through the region speaking of what Jesus had done for him. Self often takes precedence in our decisions.

We cannot be reluctant to see and recognize our wrongdoing, as David did. But at the same time, let us not refuse new directions if we feel that God is calling us.

Points to Ponder

> David's sense of wrongdoing
> David's refusal of reprisal
> Recognizing our wrong doing
> Adhering to God's will

TUESDAY OF THE FOURTH WEEK IN ORDINARY TIME

Year I

> Hebrews 12:1–4
> Psalm 22:26b–27, 28 and 30, 31–32
> Mark 5:21–43

If we don't want to get discouraged, then we have to keep our eyes on the goal, which is Jesus himself. During his earthly life, there were probably things he did not know, but he must have been certain of one thing: that his life would not be lived in vain. Jesus saw clearly what was ahead of him after all the pain and suffering was over. This is the message from Hebrews for us today.

We must continue the struggle, fully convinced that there are better days ahead.

The woman in today's Gospel is an example to all who suffer. After twelve years of terrible illness, with her patience and money exhausted, she wants only to touch Jesus' garment. She has an astounding faith. In our society, the number of citizens who do not have health insurance is in the millions. We think too little of their precarious situation. In the event of serious illness, many have nowhere to turn. In many countries of the world, health care is provided for every citizen. We spend billions for defense, but the number of our uninsured continues to grow!

At first, Jesus did not know who had touched him. Upon finding out, he commended the woman for her great faith. She was cured and finally saw the light at the end of the tunnel.

None of us longs to suffer. We accept it as part of our human condition, and we realize it is not terminal. We will not be taxed beyond our strength.

Courage, my soul, and ever onward.

Points to Ponder

Staying the course
Health care today
The woman's persistent faith

Year II

2 Samuel 18:9–10, 14b, 24–25a, 30—19:3
Psalm 86:1–2, 3–4, 5–6
Mark 5:21–43

With his great gifts of leadership and governance, David remains an outstanding biblical personality. But when it comes to the guidance of his own family, he falls far behind. Today in the first reading, David's son Absalom meets his end, and his father's grief is profound. But unfortunately this grief is too little too late.

Absalom has a blood sister who is sexually assaulted by their half–brother Amnon, David's eldest son by another woman. Absalom is enraged and vows vengeance against Amnon. In confronting this terrible conflict between his own sons, David chooses a nonconfrontational path. He does nothing to right the evil deed that Amnon has committed, since this guilty son is still privileged in his eyes. Absalom's anger turns against his father David. He goes into exile and remains distant from his father. Prevailed upon to return home, Absalom waits months for his father to receive him. Absalom then incites his father's opponents to revolt, the only insurrection that David has to deal with during his long reign. In today's reading, Absalom dies in battle, in a freakish accident. When his father receives the news, he is inconsolable. "O, Absalom, my son, my son," he cries. But the damage by then is irreparable.

In today's Gospel, Jairus approaches Jesus and pleads for his gravely ill daughter. Fully sympathetic, Jesus restores her health and returns her to her father. When faced with family ties in great strain, Jesus is never indifferent.

Strife among family members is still with us. Divorce, for instance, has become very common in our society. There is suffering on all sides, but the children suffer the most. They are caught between mother and father, both physically and psychologically. How often we see the child torn between parents or drawn to select one over the other. We realize ever more clearly the importance of the engagement period, the realization of what a lifelong commitment means, and the immense responsibilities taken on by those who enter into marriage.

Points to Ponder

> David as a father
> Grief at the loss of a child
> The children of divorced parents

WEDNESDAY OF THE FOURTH WEEK IN ORDINARY TIME

Year I

Hebrews 12:4–7, 11–15
Psalm 103:1–2, 13–14, 17–18a
Mark 6:1–6

One is always hesitant about paraphrasing the Bible, but today's Gospel suggests an old joke: "What is an expert? Someone who tells us what we know already, but who comes from out of town." Jesus was much too local to be taken seriously by his neighbors. The result was that he accomplished little among them.

The wise person is attentive to God's word under any and all circumstances. We may receive excellent insights from someone with whom we share life daily. But above all, let us not reject the message because we don't accept the messenger.

Hebrews reminds us today that sometimes we are disciplined by God. We are to be particularly concerned that others do not fall from the grace of God, especially if it might be occasioned by our own misdeeds. We must strive for peace with everyone. The customary greeting of Francis of Assisi was *pace e bene*, "Peace and all good." For him it was far more than a salutation, it was a reflection of an inner peace that came with a good conscience, of the joy that came with being a reconciler. To bring peace and reconciliation is the work of God. When a beautiful garden becomes defiled by weeds, it loses its attractiveness. We are called to be God's gardeners, tearing up the weeds that defile our relations with others and with God.

Each day we meet words and actions that have a prophetic ring. We do not want to ignore them. We have no trouble finding fault with others—would that we were as attentive to what we might *learn* from them! God's word comes to us in various forms. We reject that word to our own detriment.

Points to Ponder

The prophetic word in our lives
Speaking the truth in charity
Listening with openness

Year II

2 Samuel 24:2, 9–17
Psalm 32:1–2, 5, 6, 7
Mark 6:1–6

Today we see how the Lord gets angry with David for conducting a census of his people that includes counting the number of able-bodied men who can serve as soldiers. We may ask, "What's wrong with taking a census?" Nothing, in and of itself. God is opposed to this census because it reflects the belief that the strength of David's kingdom is due to its own size, not the result of God's favor. Human forces are not the reason for Israelite success. The Israelites triumph because God has strengthened his people. When they rely on their own strength, they meet defeat.

In today's Gospel we see how Jesus' contemporaries in his home region were unable to accept him. His family and his occupation were well known. Prophets are not found among hometown boys! But the truth is that many valuable insights into our character and conduct come from people who are close to us.

I have personal experience of this. On one occasion I received a valuable insight from some young seminarians who were part of my charge. They had to perform some ministry in a neighboring city. In granting them permission to travel, I sternly insisted that they be back in the seminary for evening prayer. On their way back home, running late, they saw an elderly man on the road who was struggling to change a tire. They passed him but got home on time. However, they felt that they had failed in a serious responsibility. They brought the case to my attention and in doing so taught me a very valuable lesson. Discipline is not the only value, nor, in this case, was it the principal one.

Points to Ponder

> Relying on God's help
> Prophets in our lives
> Being open to change

THURSDAY OF THE FOURTH WEEK IN ORDINARY TIME

Year I

> Hebrews 12:18–19, 21–24
> Psalm 48:2–3ab, 3cd–4, 9, 10–11
> Mark 6:7–13

While the value of voluntary poverty may be implied in today's Gospel, the main emphasis is on the need to "travel light." On their journey, the disciples are not to be encumbered or preoccupied. Their needs will be provided for; hospitality will not fail. The only accommodation allowed is that they are permitted to wear sandals.

There is a sense of urgency in their mission. The fathers of the church saw in their traveling in pairs an allusion to the importance of charity. Arriving at their destination, they were to stay with one family for the duration of their visit. Their message centered on the need for repentance in the light of the kingdom's arrival. Their work was a healing ministry. It was a moment of great anticipation.

Our liturgical prayers frequently reference the return of Christ, an event that, for most of us, seems quite remote. But there is a historical return as well as the one that will happen at the end of the ages. Sooner or later, we will personally meet our redeemer. We want to live our daily life in anticipation of the meeting. We have here no lasting home, but at times we act as if we did.

The account of the church's beginnings is infused with a great deal of excitement. We could use some of that excitement today. After all, the Gospel really is "good news", the assurance of a future life in God. If only we just respond!

Hebrews assures us today that as we draw near to the heavenly Mount Zion, the new Jerusalem, we should not be filled with the terror and trembling of Moses as he approached Mount Sinai. Full of hope, we must move forward with confidence.

Points to Ponder

> Gospel urgency
> Our approach to the new Jerusalem
> Christian confidence

Year II

> 1 Kings 2:1–4, 10–12
> 1 Chronicles 29:10, 11ab, 11d–12a, 12bcd
> Mark 6:7–13

Solomon had much to live for—perhaps too much. If only he had followed his father's final injunction. For all his proverbial wisdom, the fact is that he did not heed his father's counsel. It is true that Israel held together for as long as he lived. But preexistent seeds of separation were actualized at the time of his death, when the kingdom split politically into northern and southern parts. If he had kept the mandate of the Lord in avoiding religious syncretism and idolatry, things might have turned out differently. In many ways Solomon proved to be a disappointment.

On their first missionary journey, the disciples moved with agility and clear direction, as teachers and healers. If people rejected them, they were to leave the town and shake its dust from their feet. The message was clear, but people had the freedom to opt in or out. We are all asked to respond to God, but he will never tamper with our freedom. Love can not be forced; if it were, it would lose the name of love.

The disciples were told to travel light. In one way or another, every religious order in the history of the church has upheld this ideal. Members are taught to avoid the accumulation of goods. The reason is clear; they are an impediment to us on our journey. We eventually lose the agility and freedom to move as we should. But the counsel applies to all Christians. We are not to become entrenched in this world, which is passing away. We should regularly assess our needs and be attentive to the danger of going overboard.

Points to Ponder

The injunction to Solomon
Apostolic urgency
To travel light on the journey

FRIDAY OF THE FOURTH WEEK IN ORDINARY TIME

Year I

Hebrews 13:1–8
Psalm 27:1, 3, 5, 8b–9abc
Mark 6:14–29

Many people find it difficult to accept change in their religious life. We tend to insulate our faith from the swirling changes that meet us in our daily life. But certain things will never change, and Hebrews today list some of them. "Jesus Christ is the same yesterday and today and forever." Christ is the very core of our faith life— true God and true man. Born as a man and now exalted as Lord at God's right hand, he is the life giver risen from the dead. In the reading, Hebrews lists some of those essential features that must always characterize our life: love of neighbor, hospitality, concern for the disadvantaged, respect for marriage and the sacred.

These words of exhortation are as valid and timeless today as when they were first penned. Dedication to the sacredness of marriage cost John the Baptist his life, as is seen in today's Gospel. This principle has not changed, but our modern attitudes have. Behaviors that were at one time condemned are accepted today in the name of tolerance. There is where we fall short and may have to retrieve our principles.

And yet, at the same time, we have to remain open to change. For example, limbo was at one time a safe haven for infants who died without baptism. Today it is a theory that has been set aside in favor of our belief in an all-good God.

We pray for the strength to avoid an attitude toward our belief that is too dismissive or whimsical. At the same time, we pray for the ability to welcome authentic change as part of our belief in a faith that is fully alive.

Points to Ponder

> Jesus Christ, the immutable center of our faith
> Upholding principles of faith
> Adapting to change in our faith life

Year II

> Sirach 47:2–11
> Psalm 18:31, 47 and 50, 51
> Mark 6:14–29

Sirach sings David's praises, highlighting his virtues and remaining relatively silent about his failings, though he does say that God forgave David's sins. There is no doubt about David's military prowess, his praise of the Lord, his attention to the major feasts of his faith. These are aspects of his life that have immortalized him. There is a major difference between David and King Herod, a central figure in today's Gospel.

The story of Herod's stepdaughter and her famous dance (known in the theater as the "dance of the seven veils") has been a theme in drama and reached the operatic stage in Richard Strauss's opera *Salome*. Most of the characters in the now-famous story are unsavory, but the figure of Herod merits our attention. He has John the Baptist imprisoned for criticizing Herod's marriage to his brother's wife. One evening, in the midst of what must have been a drunken orgy, after his stepdaughter dances, he promises her whatever she might ask, even as much as half of his kingdom. After consulting her mother, she asks for the head of John the Baptist. The request is granted, much to Herod's chagrin.

John stood for principle, and it cost him his life. Today people are often more passionate about politics than they are about moral principle. This story is worthy of our reflection. Not that our lives equal it in drama. But because it highlights the importance of principle in conduct, something that cannot be put aside casually for personal reasons.

Points to Ponder

David's faith and accomplishment
David's recognition of moral failure
The figures of Herod, Herodias, and their daughter
John the Baptist and principle

SATURDAY OF THE FOURTH WEEK IN ORDINARY TIME

Year I

Hebrews 13:15–17, 20–21
Psalm 23:1–3a, 3b–4, 5, 6
Mark 6:30–34

Ordinarily we direct our prayers to Christ himself. Yet, in the liturgy, the official prayer of the church, our prayer is directed to God the Father through Christ. Today's reading from Hebrews speaks of God working in and through Jesus.

We are more inclined to pray to Christ because he shares our humanity. In him we believe we can find a ready ear that is attuned to our needs. This attitude is perfectly valid so long as we remember that God himself is the ultimate referent. The reign of Christ will ultimately come to an end when, as Corinthians states, all things have been made subject to him, when death and sin are no more. Then Christ will hand the kingdom back to the Father, Christ himself will step aside, and God himself will be all in all.

In today's Gospel, Jesus is once again overwhelmed by the crowd. His attempt to get away to a quiet place is thwarted. He cannot reach a place where the crowd does not find him. Yet, to quote Ezekiel, he sees the people as "sheep without a shepherd." And so, with a true spirit of availability, he begins to teach them.

There are those moments when we, too, feel overwhelmed. How can we deal with every request made of us? But then we respond as Christ did. He is always our exemplar and model.

Again Hebrews highlights God the Father as the one who acts on our behalf. He brought Jesus to the new and lasting covenant by the blood of redemption. We are in good hands: a loving Father, a Son who saves, a Spirit who makes us holy.

O God, accept our gratitude through Jesus Christ our Lord.

Points to Ponder

Praying through Christ
Jesus' desire for solitude
Availability
The new covenant and salvation

Year II

1 Kings 3:4–13
Psalm 119:9, 10, 11, 12, 13, 14
Mark 6:30–34

The wisdom of Solomon was a matter of the heart. We generally identify wisdom with the intellect. For the Hebrews, the heart was the seat of intelligence and wise judgment. In embarking on his kingship, Solomon prays for wisdom, as he realizes that decision making and judgment will form an integral part of his calling. He prays that as a judge he will not be swayed to follow any path except that of justice and fairness. Yahweh hears his request—one that did not center on perishable goods—and assures the king that it will be granted. It will be a wisdom that surpasses any that preceded or followed.

In modern society, there is a continual emphasis on good and qualified judges, magistrates who interpret the law and do not rewrite it. Unfortunately some of those who hold judicial office are unduly influenced by their own political philosophies. But this is true for all of us—we all have personal convictions that can influence our approach to thorny questions. The judge prays for an objectivity that will enable him to judge fairly, and so do we.

Wisdom was a gift that Solomon evidently enjoyed in good measure. Our own times have not lacked good and qualified judges. This does not, of course, mean that their decisions always meet with unanimous acceptance. They too are human and, with Solomon, must pray for enlightenment.

Points to Ponder

> The understanding heart
> The judge as interpreter of the law
> Fairness and honesty "from the bench"

MONDAY OF THE FIFTH WEEK IN ORDINARY TIME

Year I

> Genesis 1:1–19
> Psalm 104:1–2a, 5–6, 10 and 12, 24 and 35c
> Mark 6:53–56

Today we begin a series of readings from the Book of Genesis, starting with the first four days of creation. From the Catholic perspective, the creation accounts are not scientific explanations. This must be made clear. The purpose of these famous biblical passages is to present the idea, which is part of our faith, that the entirety of the cosmos is a place of order and ultimate purpose. Genesis does not tell us how the *physical* universe came about but conveys the idea that the universe is part of God's created order.

Today's reading shows how God fashions order from formlessness and chaos. We see this in the way he delimits the power of water (which the ancients saw as a force of destruction) by using a "dome" to separate the waters above (rainwater and storms) from the waters below (seas and lakes). This in turn provides suitable land for vegetation (third day). On the fourth day, the sun, moon, and heavenly bodies are created. The imagery of Genesis conveys an essential idea: order instead of disorder; purpose instead of purposelessness; goodness instead of emptiness and evil.

Many poets and musicians have drawn inspiration in meditating on creation. For most of us concern with nature seldom goes farther than the weather. Yet the scriptures repeatedly remind us that the heavens proclaim God's glory. Should it not elicit from us wonder, awe, and a deep respect for God's creative power? Should we not protect every aspect of that natural world that God, the ultimate architect, has brought into being?

Points to Ponder

Creation as God's handiwork
Spirituality and the environment
Genesis; a popular presentation of God at work

Year II

1 Kings 8:1–7, 9–13
Psalm 132:6–7, 8–10
Mark 6:53–56

Our readings today are full of movement. In the reading from Kings, there is a solemn procession bringing the ark of the covenant to its resting place in the Holy of Holies of the newly completed temple. Sacrifices are offered with the presence of the priests and elders. With the ark, the presence of the invisible God was "localized." It served as his throne or footstool and contained the tablets of the law that Moses had placed there. It remained in the most sacred part of the temple, where only the high priest entered once a year on the Day of Atonement (Yom Kippur) for ritual sacrifice. This description of the temple's dedication reflects the sacredness of the moment for the Hebrew people.

The Gospel reminds us that God is present in Jesus in a most unique way. In his ministry, he cannot escape the crowd. Wherever he goes, he is recognized, with people bringing their sick to him in ever greater numbers. In Jesus, God becomes accessible, something certainly worthy of our reflection.

Ours is not some distinct deity, infinitely separated from us. Our God shares our human experience in knowing what it means to be ill, to be alone, to be in need. And, in addition, there is our added access in the Eucharist, through that we can come to him to be nourished, strengthened, and consoled on our earthly journey.

The psalm today prays for our God to advance to his resting place. Yet in this new dispensation he has become the source of our rest. His great desire is to be of help. As Mark says today, all who touched him were healed.

Points to Ponder

The sacredness of the ark
The temple and the presence of the ark
Jesus as the presence of God
The Eucharist: our source of life

TUESDAY OF THE FIFTH WEEK IN ORDINARY TIME

Year I

Genesis 1:20—2:4a
Psalm 8:4–5, 6–7, 8–9
Mark 7:1–13

The crowning point in the creation narrative is the creation of man and woman. They are created in God's likeness, which is reflected in their dominion over the rest of the created order. They subdue the earth and have authority over all living things. There is no indication that the animals served as food for them; rather their diet is vegetarian. What is clearly seen is the stature of these humans towering over all other created things.

The rule of conduct for the human pair is derived primarily from their relationship to God. The Jewish norms that Jesus criticizes in today's Gospel reflect what can easily happen in religious experience. The observance of rules and regulations becomes the mark of true religion. Jesus indicates that the washing of hands is not necessarily indicative of a true religious spirit. Likewise, neglecting to financially support one's parents in order to satisfy the requirement to contribute money to the temple was misguided and disrespectful.

Certainly the human couple stands at the pinnacle of creation. Their dominion over the earth connotes a respect for the created order, not simply the observance of secondary legal precepts. We too can become legalistic in our religious practice. The great danger is that we lose sight of the forest for the trees.

Points to Ponder

Man and woman: the crown of creation
Sunday observance
Relations with God and neighbor as primary

Year II

1 Kings 8:22–23, 27–30
Psalm 84:3, 4, 5 and 10, 11
Mark 7:1–13

"How lovely is your dwelling place, O Lord of hosts!" Solomon stands in awesome wonder before God in today's first reading. How could it be that the God whom the heavens cannot contain should dwell in a house built by human hands. This suggests how closely God abides with us.

Hate crimes sometimes take the form of burning churches. This is seen as particularly sacrilegious, because in every church God comes close to his people. As Christians we believe that God dwells in Jesus in a totally unique way. God is also believed to be present in his word, and therefore we surround the scriptures with special reverence. Christ is also present in the form of bread and wine, not only symbolically but really. This is the great sacrament of God's love.

But it does not end there. Christ truly lives in the baptized believer. With Paul we can say, "And it is no longer I who live, but Christ who lives in me" (Gal 2:20). As Christians we respect each other as human beings but also as living temples of God, vessels of Christ.

These are primary considerations of our faith. Unfortunately, like the people in today's Gospel, we are preoccupied with secondary issues. Yet when all is said and done, this alone is necessary: to know God, and to know Jesus Christ, who was sent by God.

Points to Ponder

> Reverence for a church
> God's presence in his Word
> The Eucharist: Christ's presence
> Christ living in the Christian

WEDNESDAY OF THE FIFTH WEEK IN ORDINARY TIME

Year I

> Genesis 2:4b–9, 15–17
> Psalm 104:1–2a, 27–28, 29bc–30
> Mark 7:14–23

Today's Genesis reading comes from the second creation account, one that is more poetic and more lively than the first account found in chapter 1. Here we encounter the Garden of Eden—the garden of delights—where Adam has been placed by God. He is free to eat of any of the vegetation in the garden except the fruit of one tree, designated the tree of the "knowledge of good and evil." Up to this point, man's experience had been limited to "good." In eating of the forbidden fruit, he would turn his back on God and have his first experience of "evil."

It is interesting to note that the Genesis account is juxtaposed with the different perspective of today's Gospel, in which we are told that what despoils us is what comes from our heart, not from what goes into our mouth.

Do we realize the harm that we cause by letting our internal sentiments take possession of our lives? Some of these heart-centered evils are listed: adultery, greed, blasphemy, and arrogance.

Our experience attests to the truth of what is said. With the psalmist we say, "Create in me a clean heart, O God" (Ps 51:10).

Hardly a day passes that we are not tempted to undermine our relationship with God. A cruel comment about another person, a dalliance with pornography on the Internet, the unkind treatment of a person with whom we have had a dispute. These are all matters of the heart that draw us away from God. Let us be vigilant against them.

Points to Ponder

> The knowledge of good and evil
> Sentiments of the heart
> The source of wrongdoing
> Internal and external observance

Year II

> 1 Kings 10:1–10
> Psalm 37:5–6, 30–31, 39–40
> Mark 7:14–23

King Solomon's reputation for wisdom and insight has reached foreign courts—as far away as the queen of Sheba. The queen comes to see if his competence can be verified, bringing with her all manner of good things: gold, spices, and precious stones. The queen is not disappointed. Solomon addresses her questions resolutely, much to her satisfaction. Solomon's royal appointments, his table, his waiters, and his general opulence all make a deep impression on her.

On one occasion in the Gospels, Jesus mentions this visit of the queen of Sheba to Solomon and says about himself, "Something greater than Solomon is here" (Matt 12:42). Jesus is the Wisdom of God, and what he says must be taken with the utmost seriousness. In today's Gospel he speaks of the heart as the center of all evil.

Who of us cannot trace our own misdeeds to some movement from within? A friend of mine was once involved in a financial scam. He was neither the most nor the least guilty, but did have a part in some of the wrongdoing. I saw it as a misguided "once in a lifetime" mistake and wrote to the judge asking for leniency in view of his overall good conduct. The man, however, was sentenced to prison, with a sentence that the judge considered fair but not severe. The time was served and a good family life disrupted. There are times in life when we must pay the price for our wrongdoing. The greatest tragedy is not the mistake but not to have learned from the mistake. But it all begins in the heart with a "yes" or a "no." Indeed, it is the evil that comes from within that makes a person impure.

Points to Ponder

> The wisdom of Solomon
> Temptations from within
> Coping with temptation

THURSDAY OF THE FIFTH WEEK IN ORDINARY TIME

Year I

> Genesis 2:18–25
> Psalm 128:1–2, 3, 4–5
> Mark 7:24–30

The account of the creation of woman in the second chapter of Genesis is more colorful and dramatic than in the first chapter. First the animals are created and named by the man, demonstrating his dominion over the lower forms of creation. None of these creatures, however, is found to be a suitable partner for man. After putting the man into a deep sleep, God extracts one of his ribs and forms the woman. She is man's equal, bone of his bone, and flesh of his flesh. In perfect complementarity, the two become one.

The equality of the sexes is one of the hallmarks of our time. While it may not yet be totally uniform, great strides have been made. The role of wife and mother in the home is still of great importance, but the presence of the woman in the workplace is now quite commonplace. Women are prominently present in the professions today, including the military. In the ministries of the church, with the exception of priestly orders, women today play a vital role. This is a clear expression of what is so central in the Genesis account.

What is still worthy of note, however, and not to be bypassed, is the mother's role in the home. On the other hand, we have come a long way in recent times in acknowledging that the father also has an important role to play in the home. Parents are the first guides, the first teachers, and the first role models. Much of the strength or weakness of our society today can be attributed to the values lived in the home. Church and school can support the home but not substitute for it.

Jesus commends the Syro-Phonician woman for her faith in today's Gospel. Parents—fathers and mothers alike—have an obligation to set their children on the right path to faith. "It is the hand that rocks the cradle that rules the world."

Points to Ponder

> Man's dominion over creation
> Unity in marriage
> Sexuality and complementarity

Year II

> 1 Kings 11:4–13
> Psalm 106:3–4, 35–36, 37 and 40
> Mark 7:24–30

Two thoughts emerge from today's readings: "Politics over faith" and "faith over politics." The admiration we have had for Solomon up to this point is today badly shattered as we are brought face to face with his idolatry, his pandering to the religious interests of his pagan wives, and his construction of pagan worship sites. We are faced with an aching question: How could a man, divinely chosen and blessed with many gifts, fall to such a low level?

The disfavor of God is clearly registered in the text. Solomon's punishment will be political. The country that David had unified will be dismembered and form a northern and southern kingdom. The south will have only one tribe, Judah, with the other tribes making up the north. Solomon had made personal choices that overrode those of God. Now the price would have to be paid.

Faith brings the Syro-Phoenician woman to Jesus in the hopes of obtaining a cure for her daughter. The picture is an unusual one. The woman is a pagan. Not only is she a foreigner but a woman at that. Not concerned with social taboos, she addresses Jesus directly and is initially rebuffed. What may seem like untoward speech on Jesus' part is actually a form of verbal sparring to test the woman's tenacity. When Jesus expresses unwillingness to throw the food of "children" (the Jewish people) to "the dogs" (Gentile outsiders), the woman cleverly replies that even the dogs eat the scraps the children feed them. Her conviction wins out, and her daughter is healed. Faith has won over politics.

People sometimes are so fixed on their political outlook that they cannot see beyond it. Politics took Solomon away from his faith, while the faith of the Syro-Phoenician woman was emboldened by political obstacles. Both accounts today offer us food for thought.

Points to Ponder

> Compromising faith
> Foreign influences on Solomon
> The Gospel woman: Faith over all else

FRIDAY OF THE FIFTH WEEK IN ORDINARY TIME

Year I

> Genesis 3:1–8
> Psalm 32:1–2, 5, 6, 7
> Mark 7:31–37

The man whom Jesus cures in today's Gospel is both deaf and speech impaired. This is one of the accounts in which the action of Jesus takes an unusual twist. He puts his fingers into the man's ears and then, with spittle on his fingers, touches the man's tongue. He then commands that the impediments be overcome.

Without personal experience, it is difficult to determine the loss of which sense would present the greatest challenge. The loss of the sense of hearing, however, can have moral overtones in the Bible. This is not to imply that deafness results from sin or moral imperfection, but simply to say that in the Bible "hearing" can carry a metaphorical meaning. In our Genesis narrative, the woman has heard the command of Yahweh but she draws closer to sin through the enticement of the serpent. Certainly the command of God has been heard; however, the coaxing of the serpent proves more attractive. "Eat it and you will be like gods." That sounds worth a try! But what is the consequence? Subjected to shame and embarrassment, the man and woman try to hide themselves from view.

Who would deny that sin is an attractive choice? It may be deceptive, but it *is* attractive. In a moment of weakness, all of us are subject to its wiles. As St. Paul says, the saga of sin begins in Genesis, but there is no period in time when its effects were not felt. Any of us may fall prey at any time.

Yet, the remedy is there as well. The touch of Christ brings our attention to what he would ask. We pray ardently for the grace to listen and not be led astray:

Let our ears remain opened.

Lord, lead us not into temptation.

Points to Ponder

The touch of Christ
"To be like gods"
Moral deafness

Year II

1 Kings 11:29–32; 12:19
Psalm 81:10–11ab, 12–13, 14–15
Mark 7:31–37

The kingdom of David, at this early stage, is about to be divided in two. In a symbolic action, the prophet Ahijah tears his cloak into twelve pieces. Only one piece will go to Solomon's legitimate heir. The other eleven pieces, signifying the remaining eleven tribes of Israel, will form a new kingdom, greater in number and in size than Judah in the south. The sign was an omen of troubles to come. Rebellion was close at hand; the house of David would be assailed. The short-lived united kingdom was approaching its end.

The prophetic word had already come to Solomon. There had been sufficient warning. But it was also clear that to reject the teaching of Yahweh was to invite disaster.

Can we honestly say that we have never understood God's moral guidance? Hardly, though it may help to have a spiritual guide or director to assist us in discerning God's will. We should try to choose a person who is well equipped to understand us, to help us hold a mirror to ourselves, even if the counsel we receive is not what we expected.

The man in the Gospel today had trouble communicating. Jesus corrects the deficit. If we have trouble understanding, by turning to God or a spiritual director, the message will become clearer. It is always worth the effort.

Points to Ponder

> Listening to what God asks
> Hearing impairment
> The role of a spiritual director

SATURDAY OF THE FIFTH WEEK IN ORDINARY TIME

Year I

> Genesis 3:9–24
> Psalm 90:2, 3–4abc, 5–6, 12–13
> Mark 8:1–10

In the Garden of Eden we see the original case of "passing the buck." Adam blames the woman; the woman blames the serpent. But the transgression is real, and the resulting punishment reflects the ordinary (if uncomfortable) lot of the three culprits. The serpent's slithering form close to the earth suggests alienation. The woman's pain in childbearing and man's difficulty in making the earth productive suggest how sin disrupts our participation in creation. This is not to say that such hardships would not have otherwise been present, but it does highlight the negative effects of sin. What it does say is that if humans had remained faithful to God, the human lot would have been seen quite differently.

And where does the first couple find themselves in their exile? East of Eden. And speaking quite honestly, we might say that we share that destiny. Destined for a life of glory, we are still pilgrims. While we walk the path of eternal happiness, daily life reminds us that we are not there. Temptation, even failure, is our lot, but the forgiving Christ walks with us. That Messiah for whom the Old Testament yearned stands at the center of our life. East of Eden we may be, but our destiny is assured. We are all children of the Genesis "woman." Between her offspring and that of the serpent, there is lasting enmity. It is at the heel of the woman's descendants that the serpent strikes, while her descendants strikes at its head.

Death is now a cross to be borne. Hardship is now part of the human lot. We must read today's Gospel to complete the picture. We were not part of that wondrously fed multitude in the desert. But as the Marcan text itself makes clear, we are fed with the bread of life, which is the body of the Lord himself.

Points to Ponder

> The price of human rebellion
> Death as a penalty
> Eucharistic life

Year II

> 1 Kings 12:26–32; 13:33–34
> Psalm 106:6–7ab, 19–20, 21–22
> Mark 8:1–10

Jeroboam is the first king of the northern kingdom. Territorially, he is at a distinct advantage, with eleven of the tribes. But in not having Jerusalem and Judah, he lacks a center of Hebrew life, the temple and its cult. How can he hold the hearts of the people if they cannot journey to Jerusalem, their spiritual home? He would have to provide an appropriate alternative.

He proceeds to set up two new sanctuaries, each with its own calf of gold. The calves are images of Yahweh himself. "Here are your gods, O Israel, who brought you up out of the land of Egypt." It was an idolatrous act, forbidden by the Decalogue.

Jeroboam fed his people on deception. Jesus feeds people with the truth. In reading the Bible, we are impressed by the extent to which it is a human book, with more than its share of contrasts and contradictions. Jesus had no intention of sending four thousand people away hungry. With Jesus providing, they ate until they were filled.

But the evangelist makes it clear that we are no less privileged. Notice the action of Jesus. Taking the seven loaves, he gave thanks, broke the bread, and gave it to the people. Clearly the formula is eucharistic, and the sense is clear. We are no less blessed than that hungry crowd. Throughout life we are fed with the eucharistic bread. That is Mark's message for us in that wondrous feeding. In Eucharist we give thanks for that sacred banquet, our key to eternal life.

Points to Ponder

My own calf of gold
Contrast Jeroboam and Jesus
The Eucharist, our food for the journey

MONDAY OF THE SIXTH WEEK IN ORDINARY TIME

Year I

> Genesis 4:1–15, 25
> Psalm 50:1 and 8, 16bc–17, 20–21
> Mark 8:11–13

Most of the evildoers in the first eleven chapters of Genesis are, at best, literary ancestors of the various peoples with whom Israel had difficulties centuries later. For example, Cain is related to the Canaanites, whom the Israelites drove out of the land of promise.

Once sin is introduced with Adam and Eve, the "saga of sin" continues through chapter 11. Cain's sin is one of fratricide, killing his brother Abel in a frenzy of jealousy. Abel is described as a flock herder; Cain, a farmer.

The sad saga of evil, presented candidly in the Bible, takes various twists and turns. Yet Jesus states with utmost clarity that evil springs from the heart. In the case of Cain it was premeditated, and so it is in countless cases presented in the daily newspaper.

In today's Gospel, Jesus states that no sign will be given. Why? Because Jesus *himself* is the sign—in his life, his teaching, and his works. To know Jesus is to know that no further sign is needed. Cain's personality was devoid of God's presence. He lived on jealousy, anger, and disdain. Jesus clearly teaches that such a spirit has no place among his followers. This is the sign that Jesus gives. We need nothing more.

Points to Ponder

> The spirit of Cain
> Hatred and murder
> Jesus: the sign of love and forgiveness

Year II

> James 1:1–11
> Psalm 119:67, 68, 71, 72, 75, 76
> Mark 8:11–13

Early in his epistle, James introduces one of his central themes: it is the humble of this world who will ultimately be exalted, and it is the proud who, in their riches, will wither away. This is one of Christ's central teachings.

When the final reckoning is made, riches will dry up like flowers, and vegetation will perish under the blazing heat of the sun. It is unfortunate that so many of us are bewitched by temporalities. Yet there is great freedom in a life that is unfettered and not held hostage by material encumbrances. Of course, we all have responsibilities and people we must provide for. But our consumer culture continually tries to convince us that we need more, more, more. It is a danger that James does not hesitate to bring to light.

Jesus says in the Gospel that no further sign is necessary. He is the sign, the final word of God. We need only heed his voice.

Points to Ponder

> The danger of riches
> Humility as openness to God
> Jesus himself as the sign

TUESDAY OF THE SIXTH WEEK IN ORDINARY TIME

Year I

> Genesis 6:5–8; 7:1–5, 10
> Psalm 29:1a and 2, 3ac–4, 3b and 9c–10
> Mark 8:14–21

The saga of sin continues. By the time of Noah, sin is widespread. But God's disappointment and his promise of a flood is not without its ray of hope. Noah, his family, and an assortment of clean and unclean animals will enter the ark and be preserved from the devastating waters. An important Old Testament teaching holds that in the face of disaster a remnant will be spared. However severe the punishment, God's fidelity to this promise remains intact.

Yeast has both positive and negative qualities. Today Jesus advises his disciples to beware of the yeast of the Pharisees and Herod. Yeast may increase the volume of bread, but it may also be a corrupting element. It is in this latter sense that Jesus uses it today. The disciples incorrectly interpret Jesus' words as a reproach for their failure to bring sufficient bread. How could they have forgotten so quickly how Jesus had provided sufficient bread for the multitude in the wilderness?

It is often said that God's goodness appears more often than his punishment. The New Testament says much to support this idea. While sin is never approved, forgiveness is continually emphasized. Sin undoubtedly is part of our lives, but grace is even more abundant.

Points to Ponder

> God's intolerance of evil
> A remnant will be saved
> The forgiveness of Christ

Year II

> James 1:12–18
> Psalm 94:12–13a, 14–15, 18–19
> Mark 8:14–21

"Lead us not into temptation" is a petition in our daily prayer to God. Yet James says that God tempts no one. Our prayer simply means that we ask God to keep us free of situations in which temptations might arise. It does not imply that God does the tempting.

But trial has its positive value. To remain strong in grace in the midst of temptation is to receive ultimately the crown of life. What James wishes to emphasize is that God is the author of all that is good. That does not mean that our life is not beset by pain and trial, but we have been blessed as well. As James makes clear, all who have been baptized have been brought to birth "by the word of truth." We are the fruit of the new creation. Baptism is the key to life, the door to eternity.

In the midst of their distress, the disciples failed to recall the providence of God. Is not the same true of us on many occasions? We all too easily lose sight of God's providence. And we are assured that we will not be tested beyond our strength. The psalmist tells us today that the Lord will not forsake his people. Or to paraphrase Paul: If Christ has given his life for you, do you think he will abandon you now?

We are all tested, sometimes even to the point of discouragement. But we are never abandoned. Lord, give us the light to see and to know.

Points to Ponder

The spiritual side of the trials of life
Faith in our daily difficulties
God's providential care

WEDNESDAY OF THE SIXTH WEEK IN ORDINARY TIME

Year I

Genesis 8:6–13, 20–22
Psalm 116:12–13, 14–15, 18–19
Mark 8:22–26

In ancient mythologies, there are numerous flood stories. It is quite likely that one of these universal flood accounts was incorporated into the Genesis narrative as a striking example of sin's consequences. The main point is clear enough. Human evil was widespread, a fact that God could not simply overlook. In today's reading an uninterrupted rain of forty days covers the earth. At the end, the raven and the dove are sent forth to see if dry land had emerged. The raven returns, having found no place to perch. Then the dove first returns with a plucked olive leaf, indicating that the waters have begun to recede. On its second mission, the dove does not return at all, and Noah realizes that the punishment for sin has come to an end. He offers a sacrifice to God, who then declares he will never again submerge the world with a flood.

The two journeys of the dove from the ark parallel the blind man's journey to sight in today's Gospel. The dove first brings back a leaf, indicating that the flood waters are receding, although they are not completely gone. Later the dove does not return, indicating that the flood waters have receded enough that dry land has returned. The blind man, ministered to by Jesus, at first sees only indistinctly, so that people resemble trees. His sight is imperfect but is returning. Jesus again touches the man's eyes and he sees perfectly.

Our journeys to our goals come in stages. An unemployed person may find work that does not offer the desired salary. But it may well lead to something better. A slow cure for an illness is still a cure and offers the hope of ultimate healing. God loves a grateful heart—even gratitude for small blessings.

Points to Ponder

> Gratitude for small blessings
> Covenant sacrifice
> The seasons as a blessing from God

Year II

> James 1:19–27
> Psalm 15:2–3a, 3bc–4ab, 5
> Mark 8:22–26

Human anger can take a dreadful toll. James inveighs strongly against it in today's first reading. We are told to be good listeners and slow responders. Taking time to calmly deal with a conflict situation gives our anger a chance to subside and helps us more clearly discern the most appropriate way to respond.

The major guide in our human response should be the word of God. When faced with a critical or conflict situation, the best question to ask is, "How would Christ deal with this?" It is useless to hear the word of God but not act on it. Certain books of the Bible speak to us directly about appropriate behavior. We should return to these books regularly for insights on how to respond like Christians to difficult situations.

James also gives us a formula for the authentic worship of God: looking after the poor of this world, the "widows and orphans" who, in traditional societies, were at a severe disadvantage because they had been left with no male provider. All who have been left imperiled by misfortune have a strong claim on our concern. To serve the poor, we ourselves must remain unsullied by the enticements of this world. We must walk the path of the just and, in the words of the psalmist, speak truth from the heart.

Points to Ponder

> Reflection before acting
> The experience of anger
> The widows and orphans of today
> Authentic worship of God

THURSDAY OF THE SIXTH WEEK IN ORDINARY TIME

Year I

> Genesis 9:1–13
> Psalm 102:16–18, 19–21, 29 and 22–23
> Mark 8:27–33

The scriptures speak of God's relationship with his people as a *covenant*, a word that does not enjoy widespread use today. Its basic meaning is a "pact" or "agreement." The Genesis reading today is our first meeting with a covenant in the scriptures. God initiates this agreement with Noah, his family, and every living creature. In it, he promises never again to destroy the world with flood waters. In most covenants there is usually some concomitant obligation placed upon the contracting party, in this case Noah and all living things. Here this is not the case. God alone is held to the terms of the agreement. The rainbow stands in the sky as the bridge between heaven and earth, a permanent reminder of the covenant.

The sacredness of human life is underscored with the strongly worded prohibition against homicide. The dignity of the human person is related to his being created in God's image. Since life was seen as being in the blood, wanton bloodshed is forbidden. At this point, humans are no longer vegetarian but are permitted to eat animal flesh.

In today's Gospel, Peter recognizes Jesus as the Messiah and Jesus makes a prediction about his own future. Peter fails to connect messiahship with suffering and death. Yet this is the preordained path that will bring about another and final covenant. It is the covenant in the blood of Jesus that brings us from death to life. It is solemnly commemorated in every Mass we attend.

The covenant that began with Noah and will pass through Abraham and Moses reaches its crowning point in the death and resurrection of Jesus. As we say in unison at the Eucharist, "When we eat this bread and drink this cup, we proclaim your death Lord Jesus until you come in glory."

Points to Ponder

> God's concern for the universe
> The sacredness of human life
> The Jewish Messiah
> The "covenant": Noah and Jesus

Year II

> James 2:1–9
> Psalm 34:2–3, 4–5, 6–7
> Mark 8:27–33

Speculation about the identity of Jesus ranged from the prophet Elijah to John the Baptist or one of the prophets. Peter makes a quantum leap forward in seeing him as the Messiah, the royal descendant of David who would restore Israel to a faith-filled and just human community.

Peter is correct, but Jesus gives messiahship a new and different meaning. This is a Messiah who must suffer, be rejected, put to death, and eventually rise again. This is all too much for

Peter, and he attempts to turn Jesus' thinking away from such a destiny. In a strongly worded rebuke, Jesus refers to Peter as "Satan" for trying to obfuscate God's plan.

God does not judge things as humans do. In fact, the plan of salvation is in many ways quite alarming. So too, says James, is the way the kingdom of God is populated. Who can deny that we human beings revere rank and privilege? Yet, in God's sight, these merely human marks of social status have no priority. It is the little people of this world, the needy of every society, who show openness to God's love. Not entrapped by the transient values of this world, they are more open to God. There is a lesson here for a consumerist society. Our needs are not what modern-day profiteers would have us believe. The modern world continually tries to convince us that we need more material things, but the glory of eternity is the good we have done for others.

We can never forget the parable of Lazarus, who sat at the rich man's gate hoping for assistance. In the future life, the status of the rich man and Lazarus were radically changed. Wealth meant loss for the rich man, an eternity separated from God; and poverty led to true riches for Lazarus. We must not forget this lesson!

Points to Ponder

> Favoritism
> The desire for riches
> Concern for the poor
> The suffering Messiah

FRIDAY OF THE SIXTH WEEK IN ORDINARY TIME

Year I

> Genesis 11:1–9
> Psalm 33:10–11, 12–13, 14–15
> Mark 8:34—9:1

It can be frustrating to find yourself in a foreign country with no knowledge of the native language. The ability to communicate is essential to proper human relations. The last story in Genesis's "saga of sin" deals with the disadvantage of diverse languages. The people have decided on city life, with a lofty tower extending to the heavens (probably a reference to the "step temple" or ziggurat of the Babylonians). This symbol of human pride angers God. The price humans pay for their self-adulation is, perhaps paradoxically, their inability to communicate with each other.

There are interesting parallels here with today's Gospel. Ambition is of no use if it means the loss of one's soul. The heart of Jesus' teaching is a willingness to die to self, to shoulder one's cross, and to follow Christ. It is wrong to see this calling as a life of unhappiness. There is an unmatched joy that comes from adherence to Christ, from giving oneself for the benefit of others. Francis of Assisi lived a life of true sacrifice. He is not remembered today as a man of austerity but as one of intense joy. He brought that message of *pace e bene* ("peace and good") to every town he visited.

There is much more to life than amassing wealth and leaving a large estate. In a world that is "faithless and corrupt," let us pray for a clear spiritual vision, a life lived in the light of Christ. Where our treasure is, there will our hearts be also.

Points to Ponder

> Pride and its consequences
> The value of philanthropy
> Moderation in material goods

Year II

> James 2:14–24, 26
> Psalm 112:1–2, 3–4, 5–6
> Mark 8:34–9:1

Paul emphasizes that faith saves. James says that a faith that does not express itself in works is a very dead faith. How can one claim to be a believer and then bypass the person who is without food or clothing?

There is no contradiction between Paul and James. Paul insists that the gift of faith is never merited or achieved through human effort. James would not find fault with that. But, he would go on to say, once a person comes to faith, that faith comes to life through a virtuous life. Concern for others, cross bearing, and spiritual dedication find expression in good works. This means that faith is always pure gift, but it expresses itself in virtuous activity.

This is wholly consonant with today's Gospel. If a believer loses his spiritual vision and pursues only earthly benefits, that person is living a life of contradiction. That person's faith has been derailed.

A life lived in faith is not difficult to detect. The people who truly live in faith can be identified because they are the ones who give of themselves and their possessions without hesitation.

An old saying puts it well: "True faith means to live one's life in such a way that it would make no sense if God did not exist."

Points to Ponder

> Justification through faith
> The role of works with faith
> The faith that gives meaning to life

SATURDAY OF THE SIXTH WEEK IN ORDINARY TIME

Year I

> Hebrews 11:1–7
> Psalm 145:2–3, 4–5, 10–11
> Mark 9:2–13

A glimpse of glory summarizes the transfiguration scene. Jesus will not be present to his followers in a glorified state until his resurrection from the dead. As much as Peter desires to prolong this treasured moment, it was not meant to be. Jesus appears with Moses and Elijah representing the law and the prophets, respectively. Jesus represents the fulfillment of Old Testament hopes.

The voice of the Father gives fuller identification. This is God's Son, not by adoption but by nature. Drawing on the servant imagery in Isaiah, the Father sees his Son as the obedient servant, who through his death and resurrection will bring the Father's will to completion. The final injunction is strong in its brevity. We are to listen to him.

Hebrews tells us that faith is the confident assurance of what we hope for, the conviction regarding things unseen. All of which tells us that faith is not simply wishful thinking. The Old Testament figures of Abel and Enoch are cited as examples of that faith that was pleasing to God.

Think of the ways in which our faith comes to life. As we gather at the altar for the Eucharist, no one sees the body and blood of Christ, only the elements of bread and wine. There is the conviction of things not seen. When we accompany an infant to the baptismal font, it is not merely a question of ritual. It is a moment of Spirit infusion, of a new life in God.

If life without faith is futile and empty, a life with faith finds meaning in the most insignificant things. Our faith will carry us through many storms in life. Faith is never a burden, always a joy.

Points to Ponder

"Listen to him"; its meaning
Jesus: Son and servant
Jesus: the fulfillment of God's plan

Year II

James 3:1–10
Psalm 12:2–3, 4–5, 7–8
Mark 9:2–13

The Letter of James today speaks of the use of the tongue in two ways: as a way of promoting good and as a destructive force.

To control the tongue is to control the impulses of the whole body, to impose upon ourselves the kind of discipline that guides and directs our actions toward good results. Those who cannot control their tongues, who gossip, slander, and speak insensitively of others, probably have a difficult time controlling other vices in their lives. We should train ourselves to use our tongues to praise God and avoid conflict. Let us channel what we say to accomplish good and preserve peace.

In today's Gospel, Jesus underscores the amount of hostility he has experienced. It is worth our effort to reflect occasionally on the contempt that Jesus suffered. The rejection that we experience is minimal in comparison. It is good to remember that any attempt to devalue the work of Christ stands in opposition to that he has been sent to accomplish.

Points to Ponder

> The word of encouragement
> The crushing blows of the tongue
> Rejection in the suffering of Christ

MONDAY OF THE SEVENTH WEEK IN ORDINARY TIME

Year I

> Sirach 1:1–10
> Psalm 93:1ab, 1cd–2, 5
> Mark 9:14–29

Evil is violent; goodness is serene. Today's readings illustrate this point well. The evil spirit that has taken hold of the young boy throws him into convulsions and dreadful seizures. It has been suggested more than once that the boy's symptoms point to epilepsy as the illness. This may well have been the case, but the fact remains that the illness put the child in serious danger before he is cured at his father's request.

The reading from Sirach praises wisdom, God's first creation. The wisdom of God is personified in the Wisdom literature of the Old Testament. Wisdom appears clearly in the works of creation. It is "fine-tuned" in the countless sands of the seashore, the raindrops, and the endless number of days. It is present in the vastness of the heavens and the depths of the underworld. It is the Lord who stands behind wisdom and has lavished her so abundantly upon the earth.

And how does wisdom come to life in the hearts of humans? Through fear of the Lord, whose praises are sung so often in the Bible. This fear is not servile or full of dread. Rather it has the meaning of reverent recognition. Children "fear" their parents in the sense that they honor them. It is in this sense of honor and respect that humans have fear of the Lord. As free creatures, we have choices to make. We can go in the senseless direction of irreverence and chaos. Or we can take our place in a wise creation by a respectful adherence to God and his will.

The young boy in the Gospel was freed of the spirit of chaotic evil. Once cured, he lay as if dead. At the touch of Jesus he is brought to full consciousness. Jesus says that only prayer overcomes this type of demon. People ask today, half in jest, how they can get rid of their demons. Sirach gives the answer. Make better choices. Follow wisdom's lead. With prayerful attention, any demon can be expelled.

Points to Ponder

> Wisdom personified in God
> Human wisdom: Fear of the Lord
> Dealing with my personal demons

Year II

> James 3:13–18
> Psalm 19:8, 9, 10, 15
> Mark 9:14–29

Cunning may be clever and even humorous. It is also arrogant, self-seeking, and turns on others with little regard. How often do improper behavior, personal attacks, and character assassination spring from jealousy and envy? On the other hand, the wisdom that comes from God is innocent, peace loving, civil, sympathetic, and kind. It is worth noting that none of these virtues mentioned today by James seeks the upper hand. They are proper to a peace-loving personality that seeks the good of others rather than personal gain. It is for this wisdom that we earnestly pray.

The type of demon that Jesus casts out today called for a prayerful spirit. Unfortunately, one of the faults of our times is that we do not pray enough, or we find it inconvenient to pray. For example, many people admit that they make little or no effort to find a church for Sunday Mass when they're on vacation. Many priests argue that the time they spend looking after their daily responsibilities is their "prayer." But we all must make time to truly pray. Christ repeatedly returned to the necessity of prayer. To be casual about our spiritual life is to realize one day that we are running on empty.

A religious superior with whom I once lived was noted for his harsh responses. He seldom answered kindly and rather liked to "bark" orders. In going shopping one day, I asked if there was anything he needed from the store. He answered without losing a beat. "Yes, I want a better disposition."

To achieve the wisdom extolled by James we have to be patient with ourselves and, with God's grace, overcome one obstacle in our character at a time. The classic spiritual work *The Imitation of Christ* states that in addressing one fault at a time we will ultimately become perfect.

Our prayer is found in today's responsorial psalm. "Let the words of my mouth and the meditation of my heart be acceptable to you, O Lord, my rock and my redeemer."

Points to Ponder

The virtues of graceful acceptance
The evil of controlling others
Prayer, our daily companion

TUESDAY OF THE SEVENTH WEEK IN ORDINARY TIME

Year I

> Sirach 2:1–11
> Psalm 37:3–4, 18–19, 27–28, 39–40
> Mark 9:30–37

Have you ever felt as if one more day would be too much? Energy is gone, frustration is at maximum level, personal conflicts threaten to overwhelm. Sirach's message today is direct and simple: "Be steadfast." Stay with the Lord relentlessly. Trials do have their positive dimension if borne with patience and forbearance. As our faith grows stronger, so too does the assurance of God's assistance. In the lives of our favorite saints, hallowed figures from the past, we see that hardships were much a part of their lives. But God saw them through. Ours is a God of compassion and mercy, ever ready to forgive. One Italian word says it all: *coraggio.* Courage, courage, my friend!

The disciples in today's Gospel were engaged in a discussion as to which of them was the greatest. Jesus immediately alters their thinking. True faith is not about privilege, honor, or a place of superiority. These are all excluded. The great danger of ambition is that it can easily turn into control, self-centeredness, and manipulation. No Christian is called to lord it over anyone. The greatest service we can render is to help someone come to a point of self-actualization.

We must avoid taking the "high road" of self-exaltation, honor, and privilege. The only thing that matters is imitating Christ in his meekness and humbleness of heart.

Points to Ponder

> Dealing with weariness and frustration
> Trial as a form of testing
> Greatness in the kingdom of God
> Compassion for the weary

Year II

James 4:1–10
Psalm 55:7–8, 9–10a, 10b–11a, 23
Mark 9:30–37

We are not certain who the original recipients of James's letter were. But it was certainly a community beset with severe problems. Today the author speaks of conflicts and disputes. Misunderstandings are a part of life. And that is what they should remain: an understanding that has been "missed." But how often they are allowed to fester and extend into long periods of discord and dislike?

James draws an interesting parallel between those who love the world and those who love God. Those who love the world are characterized by a spirit of discord and antipathy. Those who love God operate on a different plane. God resists the proud and bestows his favors on the lowliest. In staying close to God, our hearts are purified and our hands cleansed.

Interestingly enough, James makes explicit what today's Gospel calls for. Discord and conflict often rise out of a spirit of "one-upmanship," putting people "in their place." But truly Christian speech never seeks to control or lord it over anyone. The one who is first, says Christ, is the servant of all and remains the least. Genuine Christians never try to place themselves over others. Even when they have to correct others, they do it with respect and concern.

This central teaching of the New Testament is unfortunately easily forgotten. Ambition takes people down ruthless trails both in society and, regrettably, within the church. Friendships are cultivated to pave the way for the future, to help "climb the ladder of success." But for the Christian, the only proper direction to move on the ladder is *down* to service and compassion, not "up" to self-glorification and worldly success. This is a descent that leads to eternal life.

Points to Ponder

Conflict resolution
Dealing with a jealous spirit
Becoming the "servant of all"

WEDNESDAY OF THE SEVENTH WEEK IN ORDINARY TIME

Year I

Sirach 4:11–19
Psalm 119:165, 168, 171, 172, 174, 175
Mark 9:38–40

There was a time when Catholic collaboration with other faith traditions in doing good was frowned upon and discouraged. Such cooperation could be construed, it was argued, as in some way giving approval to a religious body that was essentially flawed. Fortunately, that day has passed. Interfaith collaboration, especially in social outreach, is not only cost effective; it is a joining together of people in pursuit of a common cause.

Our Gospel today speaks about this issue. The disciple John is disturbed that an unknown man is casting out demons in Jesus' name. He is not even part of Jesus' company. Jesus excludes any action or reaction against the man. If he is acting in Jesus' name, he is at least on Jesus' side. Since he is not working against Jesus, he is at least an ally in doing good.

Do we have the same openness toward members of other congregations working for good causes? Since they are not working at cross-purposes from ourselves, their work should be seen as positive and worthy of support.

Sirach speaks of the importance of seeking and loving wisdom. But where are we to find this wisdom? God's will is found first in the scriptures. The Sermon on the Mount is a summary of Jesus' wisdom. If we reflect on it (Matt 5–7) and look at our lives in its light, we are undoubtedly in wisdom's company. It is a wisdom that unquestionably leads to eternal life.

Points to Ponder

Interfaith initiatives
Seeing the positive in other traditions
The wisdom of Christian morality

Year II

James 4:13–17
Psalm 49:2–3, 6–7, 8–10, 11
Mark 9:38–40

To visit Normandy on the French coast is to relive the Allied invasion of continental Europe in World War II. It is sad, indeed, to look out over those endless rows of crosses and stars of David and reflect on the thousands of young soldiers who died in the springtime of their lives, who never had children of their own or, if they did, who never saw them grow up, who never had the chance to assume the status of respected elderly people in their families or communities.

The lesson that James sets before us today is worth our reflection. We tend to live and move in certainties. We shall do this or that in our own time and in our own way. But how little attention we give to the all important proviso: If the Lord wills it. Only as we grow older do our absolutes change.

As our bones become more brittle and less agile; our physical condition, more fragile; our capacities, more limited, we do not so readily adopt the long-range plan. The desired vacation looks less likely. The project that sounds so engaging now seems less probable.

Like Jesus in today's Gospel, we may watch another accomplish the work we intended to do. It may make us a bit heavy-hearted. Yet when all is said and done, we are willing to pass the torch.

And so the oft-used expression has not lost its resonance: "If the Good Lord is willing."

Points to Ponder

Living in the "meantime"
The passing character of human life
Promising with a provisional clause

THURSDAY OF THE SEVENTH WEEK IN ORDINARY TIME

Year I

Sirach 5:1–8
Psalm 1:1–2, 3, 4 and 6
Mark 9:41–50

Companions of sin. There are strong warnings against courting evil in today's readings. Wealth brings power, and power makes us the master of our ship. But be warned. If there is a God in heaven, we are not omnipotent. How often have we seen powerful figures in corporate America fall from their pinnacles and be brought before the courts because of illegal gains? Sirach foresees all of this today when he calls for a heartfelt conversion. Remember that justice may seem delayed, but it will come. Live honestly, gently, and uprightly before the Lord.

The Gospel today wisely exhorts us to avoid whatever may do us damage. In the Act of Contrition, we resolve to "avoid the near occasions of sin." Good advice and that is precisely what Jesus is saying, in rather graphic language, when he speaks of removing hand, foot, or eye in today's Gospel. We all know that we are given opportunities that if pursued lead to moral shipwreck. It is sad when we return to them time after time, with the usual regrets. The solution is demanding but simple. Do not approach the danger. It may be the race track, the sleazy bar, the Internet porn site, or whatever. We have been called with the grace of God's love. As Jesus says, we have been salted, but if the salt goes flat, it is worth nothing.

Let us try today to be faithful to our moral compass. What may seem difficult is ultimately rewarding. We are also warned today against leading the innocent into sin; the abuse scandal within the church in modern times is an incredible moral tragedy.

Lord, forgive us our sins and lead us in the way of holiness.

Points to Ponder

Violations of people's trust
Personal occasions of sin
The tragedy of betraying the young

Year II

James 5:1–6
Psalm 49:14–15ab, 15cd–16, 17–18, 19–20
Mark 9:41–50

One of the keynote features of the church in the past century has been its emphasis on social justice. In a sense James today paves the way for this teaching in treating of the rich and poor, the employer and the wage earner.

All that the rich person has acquired will not only vanish in the final reckoning, it will bear witness against him. This is particularly true in the case of the person who has grown rich at the expense of the poor. History gives ample evidence of how often the rights of the worker have not only been disregarded but trampled upon. Such misuse of power will return to condemn the powerful in the final reckoning.

The Gospel reminds us today that even a glass of water given in Christ's name will not go unrewarded. How much more worthy of recognition are those who have worked to organize trade unions and collective bargaining. The Catholic Church was in the forefront of the trade union movement of the twentieth century, a moment of which we can all be proud.

In modern times we have undocumented workers from neighboring countries who work in our neighborhoods—in landscaping, at the car wash, at the diner. The government looks for ways to legitimize the presence of these workers, who seek to provide a livelihood for themselves and their families at home. Admittedly we cannot have an unrestricted open-door policy. But these people are now here and doing work that many native-born citizens would prefer not to do. Every worker must receive a just wage. James speaks to this issue today, a point that church teaching has repeated many times.

Points to Ponder

The right to a living wage
The unjust treatment of laborers
The Christian spirit in the workplace

FRIDAY OF THE SEVENTH WEEK IN ORDINARY TIME

Year I

Sirach 6:5–17
Psalm 119:12, 16, 18, 27, 34, 35
Mark 10:1–12

Sirach here speaks of the qualities of the true friend. The old adage holds that our lives are full of acquaintances, but few friends. Sirach holds that acquaintances abound, but only one in a thousand is a true friend. He offers ways of determining friendship. It must be tested, lasting, utterly sincere, not discarded at will. It must endure through reversal of fortune and remain steadfast during times of adversity.

Each of us knows when those qualities are present. We know who our friends are and are deeply grateful for them. A true friend is a treasure.

Our Gospel for today is Jesus' teaching on marriage and divorce. The fact is that the percentage of marriages today that end in divorce is alarmingly high. But this in no ways weakens the teaching of Jesus; rather it confirms it. The consequences of divorce are saddening. Its effects on children are particularly disturbing. One parent is awarded custody and the other visitation rights. The children find themselves caught in the middle of what is often a very divisive situation. It is not the way nature ordained things. Where there is antipathy or animosity between the parents, it all too often affects the child deeply.

But there is a further consideration: the effect of divorce on society as a whole. A strong family life is essential for community. Every child must mature with the loving presence of both mother and father. A child raised in conflict is often scarred for life.

Marriage begins with friendship. It must be rooted in deep personal ties that will sometimes be tested. This leads to engagement and a preparation for marriage.

All of which says that a couple considering marriage would do well to reflect on Sirach's teaching today.

Points to Ponder

Value of a lasting friendship
The pain of friendship betrayed
The permanence and indissolubility of marriage
The negative effects of divorce

Year II

James 5:9–12
Psalm 103:1–2, 3–4, 8–9, 11–12
Mark 10:1–12

On the question of oath taking, James is as straightforward as Jesus in the Sermon on the Mount. The Christian community must be marked by honesty and candor. Duplicity is neither expected nor accommodated. Taking oaths should be unnecessary—an honest "Yes" or "No" will suffice.

On the other hand, one doesn't have to live very long within church structures without being subjected to oaths. A certain wise priest was involved in academia and church government for many years, where oaths of fidelity were regularly taken. The only conclusion he could reach was that some people in the church did not wholly accept the scripture's teaching on taking oaths. They were being "double safe."

When trials come our way, James advises us not to give in to bad temperament or a critical spirit. Our state of mind can easily lead us into negative criticism and fault finding. We are asked to put our shoulder to the plough and imitate the prophets, many of whom were called to endure much in the course of their ministry. We will not be tested beyond our strength. The psalmist today reminds us that our God is kind and merciful.

Our first reading today is not directly related to the marriage and divorce theme of the Gospel. But it plays its part. If our character is patient and persevering, then these difficult moments that arise in marriage can be dealt with. Marriage crises do not arise overnight. They are often related to smaller issues that were never properly addressed.

Points to Ponder

My word or my oath
A critical spirit versus a spirit of trust
Addressing issues in marriage

SATURDAY OF THE SEVENTH WEEK IN ORDINARY TIME

Year I

Sirach 17:1–15
Psalm 103:13–14, 15–16, 17–18
Mark 10:13–16

Sirach today gives us a litany of the glories of humanity. Created in God's image, the human person is given strength and unmatched power on earth, the human senses and an understanding heart, wisdom, knowledge, and moral discernment. All of these qualities are highlighted, and yet there is not a word about personal immortality. Why? Because our spiritual forbears had not yet come to fully comprehend this idea.

As Christians we are inclined to see life after death as the greatest gift. At the same time, it is worth the effort to consider the ways in which humanity has been blessed on *this* side of the grave. Consider the achievements of the human intellect. Our broader understanding of the universe, especially outer space, is greater than ever before. The triumph of modern medicine over many diseases, even if not complete, has made incredible strides. And from antiquity to modern times, the human spirit has been elevated by the arts, by great works of literature, by musical geniuses such as Mozart.

But Jesus in today's reading from the Gospel of Mark carries us further. He receives children and sees them as the prototype of openness and total dependence. We too must have this attitude with respect to God. The realization that all good flows from God is the key to eternal life.

Today then we are thankful for earth and heaven, for what is now and what is to come. It has taken us centuries to come this far, and there is even more ahead.

We are grateful, Lord, for all that we are. Let my prayer come like incense before you.

Points to Ponder

> Homily help
> The dignity of the human person
> The right to life
> The added blessings of eternity

Year II

> James 5:13–20
> Psalm 141:1–2, 3 and 8
> Mark 10:13–16

The anointing of the sick about which James speaks today is a forerunner of our sacrament of the sick. At one time the latter was referred to as "the last rites" and was conferred only when death was imminent. Today it is conferred with any serious or prolonged illness, and often during a Mass offered for the sick of the community.

James returns again to the importance of prayer, not only in times of illness, but especially in moments of hardship. It is difficult to pray when there is no human solution. But the Lord's ways are not our ways. James has especially encouraging words for those whom Paul refers to as ambassadors who bring about reconciliation. There is nothing more rewarding in ministry than helping to restore a person to the faith. James extols this service by saying it will not only save the sinner but benefit us as well. It brings with it a boundless joy and a deep sense of gratitude to the reconciler and the reconciled.

Heaven does not require academic credentials. But it does require a childlike spirit. That is the sense of the Gospel today. It is a kingdom of open hands and open hearts. Children have no doubts about their human needs and the role that their parents play in filling them. Hence, our eyes are on the Lord, our constant refuge in the journey of life.

Points to Ponder

> The anointing of the sick
> The forgiveness of sins
> A reconciling heart
> The joy of conversion

MONDAY OF THE EIGHTH WEEK IN ORDINARY TIME

Year I

> Sirach 17:20–24
> Psalm 32:1–2, 5, 6, 7
> Mark 10:17–27

Our understanding of the afterlife differs considerably from that of Sirach. Death for us is not so definitive that praise can no longer be given to God. The belief in life after death was only clarified with the passage of time. But the principal teaching of today's passage is in no way obscured. The mercy of God is always available for people who turn to him.

Some people are so weighed down by their mistakes in life that they often wonder if life is worth living. What is often most needed at such a time is the presence of an understanding friend, a friend who can bring assurance that the Lord's mercy is always limitless to those who seek to return to him.

Today's Gospel represents one of the few instances when the invitation of Jesus was refused. The young man was evidently good and God-fearing. Riches were his major obstacle. His wealth stood between him and the following of Christ. This leads to Jesus' statement that wealth stands strongly in the way of entering the kingdom of God. But it is an obstacle that God can overcome.

Discouragement and riches emerge strongly in today's readings. We pray that the discouraged may realize that, as Paul makes clear in Romans 8, no power, not even death, can separate us from the love of God in Christ Jesus.

Riches, too, will pass. We ultimately stand before God with the wealth of our lives, our response to God's love.

Points to Ponder

Our life today as the key to eternity
The overarching forgiveness of God
The proper use of wealth
The primacy of Christ in our life

Year II

1 Peter 1:3–9
Psalm 111:1–2, 5–6, 9 and 10c
Mark 10:17–27

The First Letter of Peter begins on a very positive note. Yes, trials there are in life, but through them, faith can become stronger. The bottom line is this: we have received a new birth in baptism, and it is a birth with hope, that hope that springs eternal in the human heart. It is a birth to a full and eternal life in God. This is our destiny, an inheritance that is kept in heaven for us.

We struggle with many things in life, even in ministry within the church. As long as we have human dealings, there are going to be hardships. But as we work patiently on the "nuts and bolts" that make things work, let us never lose sight of the goal, our ultimate objective. We never want to turn away from that "imperishable inheritance."

We are saddened by the decision of the gentleman in today's Gospel. We wonder how he could turn away from an invitation from Christ himself. It is a reminder that our vision can always be obscured, that we can refuse to divest ourselves from many material things that clutter our lives, that our freedom can be impaired. An honest inventory of our attitudes and desires can do us much good. Ask yourself: What do I really need to provide for myself and my family? Of course, material goods are not evil in and of themselves, but an excess of them can end up burdening us.

Where our treasure is there is also our heart. Francis of Assisi achieved freedom when, standing before the Bishop of Assisi, he gave back to his father even the clothes on his back. God has indeed given his people the inheritance of the nations. We have an incomparable birthright.

Points to Ponder

Baptism and hope
Faith tested by trial
Material wealth and God's kingdom
Dangers of accumulation

TUESDAY OF THE EIGHTH WEEK IN ORDINARY TIME

Year I

Sirach 35:1–12
Psalm 50:5–6, 7–8, 14 and 23
Mark 10:28–31

God is never outdone in generosity. This comes through clearly in today's readings, where Sirach speaks of worthy sacrifices offered to God. Even before offering a sacrifice, one must lead an upright, law-abiding life. The observance of the law and works of charity should underlie every cultic or sacrificial offering. Every offering is an expression of gratitude, an attitude in which the Lord delights.

Peter shows a measure of self-interest in reminding Jesus that the disciples have left everything to follow him. Jesus acknowledges their good will and assures them of blessings both here and hereafter.

This is the experience of most people who have dedicated themselves to the reign of God. Of course, there may be a certain pain in abandoning much that we hold dear in order to follow God's will more perfectly. But, by the same token, those who dedicate themselves to the church have a home, new family ties—in short, a wealth of benefits. A life led on the Gospel path is not a life of "gloom and doom."

The generosity of God is constantly before our eyes. This commentary has repeatedly held up gratitude as the keynote virtue of the Christian life. If we keep this before our eyes, our lives will have to be positive.

The psalmist says today, "Those who bring thanksgiving as their sacrifice honor me." Let us praise him for he is good and his mercy, everlasting.

Points to Ponder

> Cult with a pure heart
> God's goodness and service of the kingdom
> Gratitude to God

Year II

> 1 Peter 1:10–16
> Psalm 98:1, 2–3ab, 3cd–4
> Mark 10:28–31

"You shall be holy, for I am holy." This closing injunction from Peter today appears frequently in the Bible. But what does it mean to be holy? Too often we identify holiness with those sainted figures in our churches, statues with hands folded and eyes directed heavenward.

The basic idea behind the Hebrew word for *holiness* is "otherness," to be distinguished, to be different from. Have you ever been so deeply impressed with someone or something that it immediately raised your thoughts and emotions to a higher level? Perhaps it was a great work of art, like Bernini's sculpture, *St. Teresa in Ecstasy*—or a great piece of music, like Mozart's *Requiem*. Or maybe it was a person whose attitude toward life and other people transported us beyond ourselves.

God himself is totally other. He is not visible in himself but is known from what he does. We, too, are known by what we do. To live upright lives, to look after the homeless, to see that all families are properly fed, that children do not "fall between the cracks" of society's abundance, to take the road less travelled in order to serve God—to do these things expresses our sacred "otherness." They are all aspects of holiness.

Jesus implies in today's Gospel that to live for others is to live in holiness. It can all be summarized in one expression: To be holy is to live our lives in such a way that they would make no sense if God did not exist.

Points to Ponder

> Experiences of holiness
> The secular and a holy life
> The otherness of God
> Our call to otherness

WEDNESDAY OF THE EIGHTH WEEK IN ORDINARY TIME

Year I

> Sirach 36:1, 4–5a, 10–17
> Psalm 79:8, 9, 11 and 13
> Mark 10:32–45

"Use them to show your glory to us."

No one prays for misfortune. Sirach wants the nations to see the glory and power of the one and only God. This is the God who knows the past and the future and preserves all of creation in its glory. It is the splendor of God that we all want to retain.

But Jesus says repeatedly that it will not be that way. In the Gospel today, there is a note of anxiety as he and his apostles make their way to Jerusalem. Jesus again shares with the Twelve the events that will soon transpire. He will be betrayed, condemned, mocked, spat upon, flogged, and killed, only to rise again.

Much to our surprise, especially at this moment, the brothers James and John approach Jesus and ask for places of singular prominence at the time of glory. The request is, at best, very inappropriate. Jesus once again states that he has not come to bestow honors. Such will be decided at another time by another authority.

The other ten then show their indignation with the two sons of Zebedee. Jesus takes it as a teaching moment. In the pagan world, people seek honors and privilege and want to exercise authority over others. But this attitude has no part in the plan of the Son of Man. The only criterion is service. This is to be a kingdom of hands outstretched, not of royal enthronement.

This is a hard lesson to learn, and we have not always learned it well. But one thing is unquestionably true. The church's Hall of Fame through the centuries is peopled with noble souls who have given their lives for others and have asked nothing in return. They learned well the lesson of today's Gospel.

Points to Ponder

> Honor seeking in the kingdom
> Humility, a keynote feature of the kingdom
> Christian service

Year II

> 1 Peter 1:18–25
> Psalm 147:12–13, 14–15, 19–20
> Mark 10:32–45

It is worth taking a little time today to examine the rich imagery used by Peter to describe what God has done for us in Christ. First of all, we have been bought at a dear price, redeemed from a life of utter futility. No sum of silver or gold has been paid for us, but we are redeemed by the blood of a most precious lamb. This is the lamb chosen by God from all eternity but only revealed in these final days. This is the lamb raised from the dead and given glory.

In accepting this teaching ("obedience to the truth"), we have been born into a community of love. We are born not of a human seed, one that is limited in time and duration, but by the indestructible seed that is the word of God. This is a word that will not pass away, unlike the glories of humanity, which will vanish like the vegetation of the field. This word that has been preached to us is a saving word that will not pass away.

All of this makes the self-aggrandizing aspirations of the apostles in today's Gospel even more foolish. What do temporal places of honor mean in comparison with the incomparable eternal honor that has already been conferred? The word of God teaches humility and gratitude, not prestige and status. In running the good race, what is the sense of getting off the track and running in reverse?

What is sorely needed in our time is good catechesis. Even many well-educated professionals still have only an elementary or high school understanding of their faith. Our scriptures are so rich. How anxious we should be to share them!

Points to Ponder

> Bought at a great price
> The word of God: indestructible seed
> The dignity of the Christian life

THURSDAY OF THE EIGHTH WEEK IN ORDINARY TIME

Year I

> Sirach 42:15–25
> Psalm 33:2–3, 4–5, 6–7, 8–9
> Mark 10:46–52

The glory of God appears in his creation. And he has given humans the ability to recognize and appreciate that glory. It is through his creation that human beings can come to a better understanding of God. There is a remarkable commonality and diversity in the world that surrounds us. It is about this that Sirach speaks to us today.

Blind Bartimaeus calls out to Jesus with a note of recognition. Twice he appeals to him as the Son of David. The people try to silence him but to no avail. The strength of his faith leads to his salvation.

We are reminded today that faith and sight go hand in hand. Bartimaeus teaches us a lesson in perseverance. Our cry for mercy repeatedly goes out to God. Let us never despair. If we cry to him for mercy, his compassion will not fail.

Points to Ponder

> God in nature
> Helping the blind to see
> The gift of perseverance

Year II

> 1 Peter 2:2–5, 9–12
> Psalm 100:2, 3, 4, 5
> Mark 10:46–52

Most people identify the priest as the "God person" in the neighborhood; he represents the interests of humans before God and offers counsel about God to humans. We may be a little surprised to realize that the First Letter of Peter refers to the Christian community as a "holy priesthood." This means that all of us make up a priesthood, sacred to God. It means that all of us stand before God as intercessors on behalf of other people, just as we bring the teaching of God to our brothers and sisters. We proclaim by the glorious works of the One who has called us out of darkness into light. Like the blind Bartimaeus, we are called to follow the Lord on his way. The evil desires to which we are all prey should be channeled into conduits of good that we may inspire rather than degrade our neighbor. Our lives should give glory to God.

In terms of the liturgy, we are co-offerers of the Mass, together with the ordained priest, in bringing our lives and our lot before God. We should reflect more often on our priestly calling. In fact we belong to two worlds: one from earth and one from above; and we have responsibilities in both.

Points to Ponder

The priesthood of the faithful
Our response to a request for prayers
Living in a God like way
Dealing with carnal desire

FRIDAY OF THE EIGHTH WEEK IN ORDINARY TIME

Year I

Sirach 44:1, 9–13
Psalm 149:1b–2, 3–4, 5–6a and 9b
Mark 11:11–26

Mark's story of the barren fig tree serves as a parenthesis surrounding the account of Jesus expelling the merchants from the temple. This is a key to its meaning. Jesus first curses the tree for lack of fruit (even though it is not fig season) and then subsequently, after the temple incident, passes the tree and sees that it has withered to its roots. This is an indication that in Mark the fig tree story has become a symbolic action and is tied in with the temple account. Just as Jesus disrupts the temple to protest the elevation of elaborate religious ritual over spiritual substance, so too he curses the fig tree because despite its abundant foliage it has no edible fruit. The temple, intended as a house of prayer, will soon be replaced by Jesus himself, who as the heart and center of faith becomes the temple of the new era (John 2:19–21).

Martin Luther insisted that the power of sin could never be stronger than the power of faith in the saving work of Jesus. Sirach today praises the faith of the holy people of Hebrew history. A life of faith is a life of prayer. Jesus reminds us that we must pray with a clear conscience, forgiving grievances just as we ask for forgiveness.

It is easy to become deeply involved in "church matters." This is fine in itself but can easily become a delusion. The heart of everything connected with church is Jesus Christ and him alone. This is what gives meaning to everything we do. It is not difficult to lose sight of essentials in a pursuit of secondary considerations. The fig tree had beautiful leaves but nothing of substance. The temple had maximum activity but was lacking in faith.

Points to Ponder

The meaning of Jesus' action in the temple
The barren fig tree as a symbol
Faith in Jesus, the center of life

Year II

1 Peter 4:7–13
Psalm 96:10, 11–12, 13
Mark 11:11–26

One thing emerges clearly in today's Gospel. Jesus was displeased with the manner in which temple ritual was being observed. It was a question of too much "fluff" and not enough substance. The cornerstone of all worship offered to God is faith, and it can easily happen that in caring about secondary features of cult we can lose sight of what is truly essential.

The letter of Peter today highlights some of the primary manifestations of faith. Within the community, faith must mean above all "love for one another." Love is shown in various ways. Hospitality without complaint and placing our gifts and talents at the service of one another, speaking in God's name and acting with God's strength. When called to endure suffering we are to unite our hardship with the suffering of Christ. In short, in all that we do, God is glorified.

What we are speaking of here is a manner of living. It does not mean that we consciously spiritualize everything we do in the course of a day. But it does mean that we so thoroughly incorporate the Gospel values into our daily actions that we strive to do what is right as a matter of course.

The tree in today's Gospel was filled with foliage but nothing more—it had the appearance of life but was not nourishing. As regular churchgoers, we sometimes settle for the externals, the beautiful "foliage" of religious observation that is barren of true spiritual fruit. That is why it is so important to keep our spiritual life before our eyes. Today's readings touch on the heart of our faith. They raise questions that we should certainly heed.

Points to Ponder

> Concern with externals
> Faith and charity in our lives
> Acting with faith reflexively

SATURDAY OF THE EIGHTH WEEK IN ORDINARY TIME

Year I

> Sirach 51:12cd–20
> Psalm 19:8, 9, 10, 11
> Mark 11:27–33

Today Jesus presents a question to his critics: "Did the baptism of John come from heaven, or was it of human origin?" This puts them in a dilemma. If they answer, "From heaven," they know that Jesus will ask next, "Then, why did you not believe in it?" But if they say, "Of human origin," they know that the people listening in will be angry, since they all believed that John was a true prophet. Therefore, Jesus' critics simply plead ignorance.

Today's Gospel can be seen as a simple plea for honesty and candor. Jesus left no doubt about the authority with which he acted. He was God's emissary and clearly stated it. Sly cleverness is no substitute for clarity. In the Christian life, our answer is to be "Yes" or "No," no oaths required. Hypocrisy expresses itself in duplicity and a lack of honesty.

Sirach today speaks of the young person's search for wisdom, who is presented as the attractive woman. Wisdom, of course is the way to God, the expression of his will. The young man pursues her, burning with desire. He is preoccupied with her; she is never far from his mind. He quietly opens her gate and then loses himself in her secrets. The language borders on the erotic. Once found and engaged, wisdom imparts understanding and is never forsaken.

Points to Ponder

Honesty and candor
The dangers of religious hypocrisy
Our search for wisdom

Year II

Jude 17:20b–25
Psalm 63:2, 3–4, 5–6
Mark 11:27–33

The letter of Jude is easy to overlook. It is only one chapter in length and deals with a number of issues that were present in the community to which he wrote. There were evidently teachers who were departing from the accepted Christian teaching, and this was creating tensions within the community.

He reminds his listeners that the apostles themselves had predicted that there would be scoffers and those who ridicule the faith. But as for you, he says, stand firm. Be prayerful and persevere in the faith. Correct confusion; rescue those led astray.

With a total reliance on Christ, we will be protected from a fall.

Even today we can be misled. We must be wary of latching onto every new opinion that makes the rounds. On the other hand, we cannot be closed-minded. New insights into theological positions may convince us to change our perspective. That is an encouraging sign of growth. There is nothing that so ends discussion as the belief that everything important has already been decided.

The people who confronted Jesus in today's Gospel had their minds made up before the discussion began. We realize that we are not all-knowing, nor do we claim to be. As Christians, we do however believe that Jesus taught with an authority received from God. New questions arise at every turn in our lives and in the histories of our communities, our cultures, our nations. But the Jesus of the Gospels is the same "yesterday and today and forever."

Jesus' enemies tried to trip him up at every turn. But he stood his ground with resoluteness. His manner of speaking left no doubt about the source of the authority with which he preached. If we respond to challenges to our faith with joy and courage, we stand in the truth, a truth that leads to eternal life.

Points to Ponder

Today's problem: heresy or indifference
Fidelity; adherence to the gospel
The certainty of faith

Lent

Lent is our major season of penitential conversion. Recalling Christ's forty-day fast in the desert, we dedicate ourselves to a more profound and more intimate union with Christ our Savior. It is a season marked by prayer, charity, abstinence, and fasting. It is for many people a spiritual "wake-up call."

This is a time when people will enter the church or be reconciled with the church at Easter. We think especially of those people in our community who are engaged in the Rite of Christian Initiation of Adults (RCIA), and with them we are united in prayer and companionship as they make their spiritual journey.

ASH WEDNESDAY

Joel 2:12–18
Psalm 51:3–4, 5–6ab, 12–13, 14 and 17
2 Corinthians 5:20—6:2
Matthew 6:1–6, 16–18

The theme of Lent is aptly expressed in today's reading from Corinthians. Paul speaks of himself as an ambassador for Christ. An ambassador is a country's representative before a foreign state. He conveys the message that he receives from his superior that he is not free to change, modify, or adapt. Christ's message is divine in its origin and is simple and direct: "Be reconciled to God."

Theologians have long speculated as to whether or not Christ would have come if man had not sinned. It is a debate that has long endured and will not be resolved here. The fact is that sin is a reality and is the cause of our spiritual alienation from God. The coming of Christ reversed the tide of woe. In Christ we have been brought home.

We are first reconciled in baptism. But like anything else in life, our spiritual life needs "fine-tuning." Lent is the time for us to give expression to our gratitude by deepening the spirit of reconciliation.

Our readings today strongly emphasize this being done without ostentation. Joel tells us to rend our hearts and not our clothing. Reconciliation is a matter between God and you. It needs no publicity or display. Our praying may be done effectively in the silence of our home. Nor is our fasting a matter for the public forum. A fellow student from my seminary days fasted so vigorously that he was very unpleasant most of the time. I often wondered what was gained by it all.

Lent, while penitential, is also a time of joy. It is a special time of the year to say "Thank you" to the God who first loved us.

Points to Ponder

Lent, a time of fuller reconciliation
Almsgiving
Fasting
Remembering the oppressed

THURSDAY AFTER ASH WEDNESDAY

Deuteronomy 30:15–20
Psalm 1:1–2, 3, 4 and 6
Luke 9:22–25

"Choose life." Those words from today's Deuteronomy reading have become a mantra for those promoting the life issues in modern times. It resonates with those who uphold the dignity of human life from the womb to the final illness. Its original meaning is connected with the divine promise of tranquility and blessings in the land of promise that Yahweh is entrusting to his people. Observance of God's law leads to the blessing of all temporalities needed for life. A life of sin, on the other hand, was the choice of death, which would only bring tragedy and havoc to a dissident population.

Christianity promises life as well, but life with a fuller understanding and with different choices. Suffering in the Old Testament, especially the suffering of the innocent, was an enigma. The innocent Job was at a loss to explain the suffering he had to endure. For the Christian, suffering is woven into the texture of life itself. Cross bearing is the way God brings us to eternal life, as is clearly stated in today's Gospel. That cross that comes to us in different forms must be embraced, and Jesus' road to Calvary followed as we move ahead. This may mean illness, difficulties in the workplace, unexpected unemployment, or disappointment in family situations. We may know that these are not troubles of our own making. But when borne with patience and resignation—and a smile—they terminate with a life in God.

As Lent begins, it is time to reassess our lives, recognizing those obstacles that are part of our journey. We want to unite our crosses with that of Christ and move forward, with grace and dignity, toward that goal, which means more than gaining the whole world.

Points to Ponder

> The good life for the Hebrews
> The role of suffering in our life
> Material wealth as a goal in life
> Christian asceticism: bearing the cross

FRIDAY AFTER ASH WEDNESDAY

> Isaiah 58:1–9a
> Psalm 51:3–4, 5–6ab, 18–19
> Matthew 9:14–15

There is room for fasting in our lives now that the bridegroom has gone to the Father. Sackcloth and ashes? Fine as far as they go, but Isaiah points out that they are not the heart of the matter. We can go through as many penitential practices as we wish, but as long as people are suffering around us, such practices mean very little.

We may think that the age of collective charity and justice is past. But personal experience tells us otherwise. There are Catholic hospitals that have never in their history turned a patient away for lack of money or insurance.

When a piece of national legislation threatened to make assistance to illegal immigrants a felony, the cardinal of America's most populous diocese said that, if such legislation passed, he would direct his priests to disobey it.

There are moments in our lives that call for true Christian courage. There are times when it is necessary "to obey God rather than men." The task cannot simply be left to others. We are called to bring personal support to the disenfranchised. One cannot read the daily papers without being struck by some human need in some part of the world. There are religious organizations equipped to respond quickly to worldwide catastrophe. They offer us the opportunity to respond.

"Share your bread with the hungry, and bring the homeless poor into your house." This is the call of the prophet. If we do, "your vindicator shall go before you, and the glory of the LORD shall be your rear guard."

Yes, fasting is appropriate, as the bridegroom has left. But, in another sense, he is still with us, urging us on to comfort our brothers and sisters, the needy of the world.

Points to Ponder

> A Lenten priority: responding to need
> Caring for the sick poor
> Gospel over law

SATURDAY AFTER ASH WEDNESDAY

> Isaiah 58:9b–14
> Psalm 86:1–2, 3–4, 5–6
> Luke 5:27–32

Repairer of the breach. Restorer of ruined homesteads. Those designations would have been apt and welcome in 2005 when a mammoth hurricane destroyed a large part of the city of New Orleans. Many people did their part in the midst of such a calamity, but when all was said and done, there was still much reconstruction to do.

But there are other breaches to repair, ways in which we can respond honorably to disaster, especially moral failure. And Isaiah today outlines some of them. In the matter of living God's law there is a strong incentive: happiness in doing what God wills. This happens when the Sabbath is not a burden, but a delight. It is commended to honor the Lord's day by not following our own will nor speaking of others with malice. If we do so, all will be well. The avoidance of false testimony and improper speech, coupled with a sense of outreach and care for the sick—such are signs of a correct conscience, worthy of a holy people.

When Levi gave a reception for Jesus, he was not discriminating of the people who attended. He was, after all, a tax collector and would certainly have had friends among such people, who were agents of a foreign, pagan power. Tax collectors were not table companions for believing Jews.

But once again Jesus breaks the barrier. It is precisely for the unwanted that he has come. They are the sick in need of help, much the same as the sick in the emergency rooms of our hospitals. Jesus sees his role largely in terms of care for the morally ill. They, not the well, need the physician.

Today's readings are a call to an upright life. Of course, we all fall short. But we still return to the task. In doing our best, we add to the collective good. We help repair the breach. And if we feel a bit wounded at time, the physician is there to see us through.

Points to Ponder

Choosing God over ourselves
Christ's embrace of the unwelcome

MONDAY OF THE FIRST WEEK IN LENT

Leviticus 19:1–2, 11–18
Psalm 19:8, 9, 10, 15
Matthew 25:31–46

We have no trouble understanding the validity of the norms set forth today in Leviticus. The sinfulness of stealing, swearing falsely, defrauding, or being dishonest is something of which we are well aware. They are basic norms of morality, important for any Hebrew to observe in his daily community dealings. Their applicability to our own lives is equally clear.

However, the move to the Gospel teaching represents a quantum leap. This is not a question of harm done to anyone but is rather a question of doing good. This is the heart of the Christian ethic, as captured so well in the Sermon on the Mount. Is any person in need (whether a member of the Christian community or not) to be ignored? It is not a question of avoiding injury but rather of being present to anyone in need. This may mean food, clothing, or comfort. The word *compassion* means "to suffer with." And it is on that subject that the final judgment dwells.

The word today could not be clearer. Our personal lives, as well as the life of society itself, are kept at a high level if these norms of charity are observed. It is not that we neglect other teachings, it is just that we want to give Matthew 25 a high priority. The emphasis of Lent is on the importance of the "now." Now is the acceptable time, now is the day of salvation.

Charity delayed is charity denied.

"Lord help us to judge rightly." Much of our moral life is centered on the Ten Commandments. We review them before reconciliation and our act of contrition. But today's Gospel has pointed out our authentic calling. Behold these Christians, how they love on another. Give us the light to see.

Points to Ponder

> Gospel and law
> Primacy of the law of love
> The human needs I see each day

TUESDAY OF THE FIRST WEEK IN LENT

> Isaiah 55:10–11
> Psalm 34:4–5, 6–7, 16–17, 18–19
> Matthew 6:7–15

We don't have to invent a "prayer wheel." It seems that every time a group prays together, prayers are always being added. Jesus today warns us against multiplying prayers and gives us an example of prayer in as direct and simple a fashion as one could imagine. His prayer is brief but very comprehensive.

Isaiah tells us today that the word of God does not fail. Nothing that God wills or executes is done in vain. It accomplishes its purpose just as surely as does the rain or snow. The prayer of Jesus is equally efficacious.

The Lord's Prayer has two major divisions. The first part deals with God and his concerns. We pray that his person be honored and revered ("Hallowed be thy name"), that the full establishment of his kingdom, rooted in uprightness and justice be brought to fruition ("Thy kingdom come"). The second part of the prayer deals with our needs. It is remarkably encompassing. We pray that our daily needs be met ("Give us our daily bread") that we overcome our faults and stand in grace ("Forgive us our sins"). In addition we pray to be delivered from the final test between good and the powers of evil and find ourselves always on the side of God.

There is a Matthean caveat after the prayer, underscoring the importance of forgiveness. This oft-repeated warning never fails to touch our conscience. We can hardly ask God to forgive us if we fail to forgive others.

There are various moments in every day when we can pray the Lord's Prayer. As the only prayer that Christ has taught us, it always has priority and is so all-embracing that any need can fit.

The Lord has eyes for the just, and ears for their cries.

Points to Ponder

> Daily prayer
> Praying that God's will be recognized
> Praying that our needs be met
> Forgiving others before asking for forgiveness

WEDNESDAY OF THE FIRST WEEK IN LENT

> Jonah 3:1–10
> Psalm 51:3–4, 12–13, 18–19
> Luke 11:29–32

Jonah, the reluctant prophet, carried a call to conversion to an obstinate and unbelieving people. At his call to reform, the

Ninevites accepted his word and changed their lives. When Jesus' contemporaries asked for a sign, he replied that the only sign to be given is that of Jonah. Just as Jonah preached to hard-hearted unbelievers, so to does Jesus. And what will be the effect of Jesus' call to conversion of life? The tone of the Lucan passage read today indicates that Jesus did not see the fruit of his preaching as did Jonah. Indeed, foreigners who turned to God in the Old Testament (the queen of the South and the Ninevite population) stand on higher ground than Jesus' contemporaries and can well stand in judgment on them.

The story of Jonah, contained in a short, four-chapter book, was written centuries after the city of Nineveh and its Assyrian population had ceased to exist. The story is an extended parable and should be read in that light. It underscores strongly Yahweh's concern for all people and points forward to that age when all barriers between Jew and Gentile will fall.

We live in an age of ethnic and religious rivalry and intolerance. It is well to remember that there are narrow-minded and bigoted people in every faith. But they are not normative, nor are they representative of the faith as a whole. The readings this morning remind us of the universal character of our faith. Ours is a church that is termed *catholic*. Any shade of disdain or disrespect toward people of other beliefs has no place. We cannot forget the fact there was a strain of Catholic anti-Semitism in heavily Catholic populations that lasted for centuries.

The Second Vatican Council has ushered us into an era of respect and dialogue.

If Jesus is the sign of Jonah, let us find ourselves with the Ninevites of old in hearing our call to love and understanding, as we stand on the side of acceptance.

Points to Ponder

Understanding the sign of Jonah
Openness to God's word
A gospel of acceptance and love

THURSDAY OF THE FIRST WEEK IN LENT

Esther C:12, 14–16, 23–25
Psalm 138:1–2ab, 2cde–3, 7c–8
Matthew 7:7–12

A photograph once circulated in which a father was playfully tossing his young son into the air. The father's arms were open to receive the descending child, and a broad smile wreathed the face of the son. It was a picture of total confidence and trust. Today's scriptures highlight the prayer of petition. In the reading about Queen Esther, a Hebrew in a Persian court, the stage is set for the extinction of the Jewish people. She turns to God in an ardent prayer for help. As the story unfolds, her prayer is heard. This liberation of the people from the threat of death is celebrated annually in the Jewish feast of Purim.

Of the four forms of prayer—adoration, contrition, thanksgiving, and petition—it was once said that petition is the least noble since it centers so much on the petitioner. This is hard to accept in view of the great praise given this form of praise by Christ himself. In the New Testament, it is repeatedly given high commendation. The reason for this is that it is an expression of a key Christian virtue, the spirit of dependence on God, and our bringing our requests before God is wholly consonant with that spirit.

Christ says today that God's attitude toward us is that of a loving father. If a son asks for bread he will not be given a stone, or for a fish and he will not be given a serpent. We are encouraged to bring our needs before the Lord; we will not be given a deaf ear.

It often happens in life that when faced with a critical situation, God becomes an afterthought. We turn initially in different directions for help. But we must be honest. If God is first in our life, then he doesn't stand at the end of the line. In the course of human events, we first ask, then we seek, and finally knock to receive a response. This implies a certain perseverance. It all begins with conviction, the conviction that we are loved. If so, then we will certainly not be forgotten.

Points to Ponder

The prayer of petition
Children of a loving God
Perseverance in prayer
In difficult moments: putting God first

FRIDAY OF THE FIRST WEEK IN LENT

Ezekiel 18:21–28
Psalm 130:1–2, 3–4, 5–7a, 7bc–8
Matthew 5:20–26

When a major racial uprising occurred some years back in Los Angeles, a truck driver found himself in the wrong part of town, was dragged from his truck, and nearly died at the hands of his assailants. Later when the trial took place, the man's testimony left a lasting impression. He insisted that he had forgiven his assailants and wished them well. When asked why he had such a tranquil position, he claimed that this is what his faith asked of him and he could do no less.

Ezekiel today presents an interesting picture of conversion: one can be converted to good or to evil. The prophet makes a strong appeal to leave evil behind and embrace the good.

And what does our Gospel say apropos of this topic? It centers wholly on forgiveness, even things that we might consider of secondary importance. But the Gospel does not consider forgiveness secondary. Any spirit of anger, which means holding on to an injury, is excluded. When anger is allowed to fester, the situation worsens, often with forms of invective foreign to the Christian spirit. We are told not to come before the Lord in worship until peace is made. Christians should avoid public litigation and make every effort to settle out of court.

Some people say, "I will forgive, but I won't forget." But this is incomplete forgiveness. In the course of daily life, differences and disagreements are inevitable. But a spirit of animosity gains us nothing and is a constant reproach to our conscience. Often in public prayer we ask God to forgive us as we forgive others. We pray that this be a blessing and not a reproach.

Points to Ponder

The courage to forgive
Forgiveness, a sign of moral strength
Forgiving and forgetting
"Forgive us as we forgive"

SATURDAY OF THE FIRST WEEK IN LENT

Deuteronomy 26:16–19
Psalm 119:1–2, 4–5, 7–8
Matthew 5: 43–48

The love of neighbor is clearly stated in Leviticus 19:18, but the hatred of enemies is not found in any Old Testament text. Jesus is evidently attacking a common mindset that sharply contrasted relations with one's countrymen and those outside.

Racial profiling has become part of our modern vocabulary. It signifies suspicion regarding people of a particular ethnic or racial background solely on the basis of their appearance. It has come into play in more cases than we would like. And can easily affect our own outlook as well. There was a time when African Americans were the people of lesser status in America. That has not completely disappeared. But it has been preempted by negatives feelings toward Middle Eastern people, people of the Muslim faith. The roots of this are found in the acts of terrorism that have been perpetrated on the West in modern times by people from the Arab world.

Our Gospel today addresses this problem very directly. The law of the former covenant commanded love of one's fellow citizens. The mandate of Christ looks to love for everyone. We may say that we have no enemies. But when we begin to look down on the people of a particular ethnic strain because of terrorist activity of a very limited number, then our love of all is being limited. The majority of people want to live in peace and harmony. Our attitudes to each other should be characterized by fairness and equality.

For those who harbor enmity against us for whatever reason, we should pray regularly for a change of heart. It is also quite easy for us to develop a hostile mindset. From such an attitude we pray to be delivered, always confident that God's grace will not be lacking.

Points to Ponder

> Racial profiling
> Causes of racial hatred
> Forgiveness after a grievous offense

MONDAY OF THE SECOND WEEK IN LENT

> Daniel 9:4b–10
> Psalm 79:8, 9, 11 and 13
> Luke 6:36–38

Despite Israel's sinfulness and waywardness, Daniel prays today for God's forgiveness. He cannot make any claims on the basis of the conduct of his countrymen but relies wholly on God's compassion. Compassion is a very distinct form of charity. The English word is derived from two Latin words meaning "to suffer with."

When mistakes are made in life that deeply affect a person, it is not reproof that is sought. It is an understanding heart. When we say that a person is nonjudgmental, it does not mean that the person is indifferent to wrongdoing. It simply means that judgment is left to the Lord and the person is willing to stand with the wrongdoer through trying and difficult times.

When St. Francis expresses concern that thieves seeking food have been turned away by his friars, it is not because he approves of the thieves' criminal behavior. But he is concerned about their hunger, and he sends one of the friars to find them and provide them with food.

When someone dear to us decides to pursue a course of action that we know is wrong, we are not asked to alter our convictions. But by the same token that person should not be separated from our love. The Gospel today enjoins us to avoid judgment and condemnation and be willing to extend pardon just as we ask God to pardon us. If we measure our forgiveness in large portions, pardon will be extended to us by a generous God in equally large measure.

Be prepared. Charity will probably carry us in directions never imagined. Harshness brings no comfort. Condemnation is best left to the courts. The understanding person says simply, "I stand with you and am willing to suffer." If we do not forget others, we will not be forgotten ourselves.

Points to Ponder

> Examples of compassion
> Being nonjudgmental
> The heavy burden if guilt

TUESDAY OF THE SECOND WEEK IN LENT

> Isaiah 1:10, 16–20
> Psalm 50:8–9, 16bc–17, 21 and 23
> Matthew 23:1–12

The Gospel today emphasizes the importance of service and humility, which must characterize the Christian community. Honors and titles—rabbi, father, and teacher—that were proper to other states of life were to be avoided when they conferred an authority that belonged only to God. This prohibition does not extend to such titles in society at large, but only to leaders in the community. The male head in the family remains "father" and the presider in the classroom is still "teacher." But such titles must not become designations of high office or exalted status within the ecclesial community. The reason for this is that in the realm of faith, the one teacher and father is God himself or the Messiah whom he has sent.

So what title is appropriate within the Christian community when speaking of our co–religionists? There is a title that appears repeatedly in the New Testament: "brother and sister." It is a title that relates us to Christ as brother and to God as father. It is a designation that binds us together as members of one family. It is a term dear to the New Testament and bears no connotation of a superior position.

During my assignment in Rome in the 1970s, I once traveled with the minister general of the Capuchin Franciscans to the town of Aquila, some few hours from Rome. He spoke of his determination to see that all Capuchins be designated brothers or friars, not fathers, in keeping with the mind of St. Francis himself. And he had had a considerable measure of success. I congratulated him on his initiative. Arriving at our destination, we approached the friary driveway. Facing us was a large sign that read "Capuchin Fathers"! "Well, Paschal," I said, "you win some and you lose some!"

Points to Ponder

> Titles and honors in the church today
> The role of the Christian leader
> The humble are exalted

WEDNESDAY OF THE SECOND WEEK IN LENT

> Jeremiah 18:18–20
> Psalm 31:5–6, 14, 15–16
> Matthew 20:17–28

Two questions arise from a consideration of today's scriptures. We know that there is much good in this world of ours. But why is it that it is so abused? And the second question: Why is the good so misused?

In considering Jeremiah and Jesus, we are dealing with the presence of God in the world, and yet a battery of opponents come up against both of them. Jeremiah's opponents take steps to silence him and his prophetic voice. The prophet prays for deliverance. Jesus once again tells his disciples that there is much for him to endure before the end. He speaks of rejection, condemnation, and death. While we might admit that the message of Jesus could create controversy, it is much more difficult to understand the death he envisions, death at the hands of his enemies.

And why is the good misused? The two sons of Zebedee have their sights centered on position and status. In today's account of the request for honors, there is a slight difference from its parallel account in Mark; there the disciples themselves, not their mother, make the request. With his usual deference to the apostles, Matthew makes the request through the mother. When Jesus assures the two that they will have to drink of the cup of suffering, he indicates that places of honor are not his to give. When the other disciples initiate a conversation of dismay at the two, Christ raises the discussion to a new level.

The reign of God has nothing to do with presiding over others or receiving human recognition. There is no room there for domination or manipulation or self-seeking. It is simply a question of standing shoulder to shoulder with others in their need, of being agents of comfort, solace, and direct assistance. Had Jesus not told them that his mission was one of service, even to death? Our life is not different. It may include many hardships and inconveniences. It is a life of self-giving, not of honors. We may even have to suffer rejection. But in dedication and perseverance, our goal shall be reached.

Points to Ponder

The mistreatment of the good
The dangers of ambition
Service in the kingdom of God
Disinterested self-giving

THURSDAY OF THE SECOND WEEK IN LENT

Jeremiah 17:5–10
Psalm 1:1–2, 3, 4 and 6
Luke 16:19–31

If we take today's two readings as a unit, then Lazarus, the beggar, is represented by the flourishing tree planted near the water. The wealthy man is the barren bush, withered and dry, on the desert floor.

The point of the parable is clear enough. A person's material and physical circumstances in life do not tell the whole story. A person may be poor but rich in spiritual values. Or a person may be very wealthy but at the same time self-absorbed, with little or no interest in the well-being of others. Afterlife belief changes the complexion of human destiny. Upon his death, Lazarus is taken to the place of bliss, spoken of as "with Abraham." The lot of the rich man, on the other hand, is one of separation and unhappiness.

From his place of grief, the rich man asks Abraham for relief for himself and a warning for his living brothers. But the warning is already present. The norms of human conduct have already been set forth by Moses and the prophets. To follow the counsel of the scriptures is to be assured of salvation.

We believe deeply that God is not only just but kind and merciful. His will is clearly set forth in his word. But like the rich man, especially in our day and age, we can become immersed in values that carry us far from God. There is always the "something better" drawing our attention: the larger and better home, the newer model car, the extended vacation. But there are people, never far from us, who lack the necessities of life: clothes that are old and tattered, a daily diet that seldom varies, the lack of means to give the children a summer break away from home.

The fact is that no joy matches bringing happiness to others. Now is the acceptable time, or as the ancients said, *Carpe diem!* "Seize the day!"

Points to Ponder

Using wealth for the kingdom of God
Being lost in our own concerns
The joy of sharing

FRIDAY OF THE SECOND WEEK IN LENT

Genesis 37:3–4, 12–13a, 17b–28a
Psalm 105:16–17, 18–19, 20–21
Matthew 21:33–43, 45–46

Violence is not a suitable answer to provocation. In the Genesis narrative, the brothers of Joseph are jealous of the favor that their father shows Joseph. They therefore plan to kill him. Feeling a certain measure of remorse, they devise another plan as a compromise settlement. They will sell their brother to a passing caravan of Ishmaelites. The act was a despicable act of treachery against a member of their own family.

The parable in today's Gospel is an allegory. The owner of the vineyard is God himself; the tenant farmers are the Jewish people. When, at harvest time, the owner sends his messenger to obtain a share of the harvest, the delegation is subjected to a violent attack. A second group is sent with the same results. These represent the prophets and teachers of the Old Testament that had been sent to the Jewish people. When there is question of sending the owner's son, the allegory takes on a strong New Testament hue. The reference is to Christ himself, God's Son, who is rejected and killed at the hands of his oppressors. The kingdom of God, with Christ as its cornerstone, will now pass to a foreign people.

Our world is so marked by violence that we have become inured to it. People are raped and killed by unknown assailants. Robberies all too often end in bloodshed. Sometimes a simple provocation can lead to violence and death. We cannot escape the fact that the New Testament contains a strong pacifist ethic. It should be a rule of our life that we will never lift a hand against another person. We oppose the death penalty for various reasons—one is the infliction on the guilty person of the same evil that we decry in his conduct.

Christians are essentially agents of peace and harmony. Let us point out mistakes or failings when this is justified, but never inflict harm on anyone. That is the only response possible from those to whom the owner has now consigned the vineyard.

Points to Ponder

> Jealousy and anger
> The evil of violence

SATURDAY OF THE SECOND WEEK IN LENT

> Micah 7:14–15, 18–20
> Psalm 103:1–2, 3–4, 9–10, 11–12
> Luke 15:1–3, 11–32

This well-known Gospel story is named after the wayward son, not because of his sterling qualities, but because of the forgiveness showered upon him by a gracious and loving father. The story illustrates the teaching of Micah in today's first reading. Ours is a God who does not persist in anger but delights in clemency, the one who is compassionate and treads guilt underfoot.

The younger son not only makes a mistake but persists in wrongdoing. He squanders his inheritance, is left without income, and finally engages in an unsavory occupation for a Jewish man: feeding pigs. Without any real sense of sorrow, he realizes that even the employees on his father's estate are better off than he. Deciding to return home, he prepares a short speech admitting his guilt and sets forth. Upon his approach, the father, throwing convention to the wind and with a complete loss of composure, runs to greet his son, does not allow the short speech to be given in its entirety, and restores his son to his former status. Finally, he prepares a major homecoming feast. He asks no question but gives unqualified acceptance.

The reaction of the other son is, in a sense, quite understandable. He has always rendered valuable service to his father, has never wavered from his sense of duty, and has never been feted like his "ne'er do well" brother. In speaking with his father, he does not refer to the returning son as "my brother," only "this son of yours." But his father subtly corrects him: "This brother of yours was dead." By the same token, his compassion and love for his younger son is profound.

People often return to sins of the past and wonder about forgiveness. The fact is that God has long since put guilt away; there is no doubt about forgiveness; now there is only cause for rejoicing. God's forgiveness is well described by the psalmist today: "As the heavens are high above the earth…, as far as the east is from the west."

Points to Ponder

> The selfishness of the younger son
> The indignation of the older son
> The total forgiveness of the father
> My son was lost and is found

MONDAY OF THE THIRD WEEK IN LENT

2 Kings 5:1–15ab
Psalm 42:2, 3; 43:3, 4
Luke 4:24–30

It all seemed just too ordinary. Naaman, an army commander in a neighboring country, is a respected military leader but suffers from some form of leprosy. One of his servant girls suggests that he visit the prophet Elisha in Israel. Naaman decides to act on the proposal, but, following the proper protocol, he first presents himself to the king of Israel, with the proper letters from his own king.

The king of Israel is distraught with the request that is made. He has no interest in finding a prophet healer. Elisha the prophet hears about the case and asks the king to send Naaman to him. Elisha then directs Naaman to go to the Jordan and wash himself seven times. But the Jordan waters are insignificant in comparison with the rivers of Syria, Naaman's home country. He is not going to follow the directive until his servants urge him to give it a try. He does so, is immediately healed, and returns home a convinced believer in the God of Israel.

Faced with the continued obstinacy of his opponents, Jesus drawn on the Naaman story to highlight the openness of foreigners to God's action while Israelites were frequently left behind because of intransigence and hardness of heart. Naaman was dubious but remained open to what was asked of him.

Perhaps many of us are slow to see the hand of God in the ordinary events of life. A person who had lived a life far from God is at some point drawn to God by conversion of heart. Or a quiet unassuming pastor becomes God's instrument in bringing a hardened sinner back to Christ.

It may be that at times we stand too close to an event to see God's hand. We would do well to be spiritually attentive. Miracles may not appear with undue frequency—but they do appear.

Points to Ponder

> The presence of God in daily events
> Conversion: a moment of God's grace
> Being alive to the sacred in life

TUESDAY OF THE THIRD WEEK IN LENT

Daniel 3:25, 34–43
Psalm 25:4–5ab, 6 and 7bc, 8–9
Matthew 18: 21–35

The plea made by Azariah in the Book of Daniel, written in the second century before Christ, is full of pathos. The Jewish people have once again been subjected to ruthless invaders. Sacrifice is gone, leaving room only for an internal sacrifice of spirit. Sinfulness is recognized and forgiveness sought. Only one element is missing, one found repeatedly in New Testament requests for forgiveness.

This added dimension is underscored in today's Gospel parable. Forgiveness cannot be asked from God if we do not forgive others. And how often? "Seventy times seven," which says forgiveness everywhere and always. Any minister of the gospel has met cases repeatedly. A very good person is approaching the end of life but needs to be reconciled with someone before the end. It may be a close family member or a childhood friend. But the sentiment is wholly in keeping with the Gospel teaching. It is expressed each time we recite the Lord's Prayer as we ask for forgiveness in the measure to which we extend it. One hardly wants to think of the indictment involved in reciting this prayer while harboring hostility toward others.

The fact is that we are all capable of hurting in word or deed. We can also find ourselves on the receiving end through the actions of others. When we are guilty, let us be quick to heal the breach. In so doing we are assured of God's forgiveness in whatever circumstances.

If Christ in his final sufferings can offer his prayer from the cross, "Father forgive them," it is hard to imagine what excuse we might offer. The king in the parable forgives an indebted servant, canceling the debt entirely. But the same servant mistreats a fellow debtor, with no sense of compassion. Shylock still wants his "pound of flesh." Yet as Portia says in the same Shakespearean drama: "The quality of mercy is not strained." May those sentiments be our own.

Points to Ponder

> To be forgiven and forgiving
> Settling discord before prayer
> Bearing grudges

WEDNESDAY OF THE THIRD WEEK IN LENT

> Deuteronomy 4:1, 5–9
> Psalm 147:12–13, 15–16, 19–20
> Matthew 5:17–19

There are few verses in the New Testament more widely debated than those from the Matthean Gospel read today. The claim for the lasting value of the Torah seems to be the antithesis of Paul's teaching on freedom from the law. Moreover, there is no historical evidence that the church ever retained every precept of Torah. The fact is that most of its legislation did not continue.

It is helpful to begin with the facts. Paul insisted that the precepts of the Jewish law must not obtain among Gentile Christians. His position prevailed. If we are correct in the assumption that Matthew's Gospel was written for a largely Jewish Christian community, then law observance may well have obtained for some period of time. This would have been seen as consonant with Jesus' basic respect for the law during his lifetime.

The examples used in Matthew 5 of fulfilling the law and not destroying it do not in any way violate Paul's thought. The Decalogue contained basic moral norms that Jesus did not ignore but raised to a new level. Where the law forbade killing, the teaching of Christ excludes even personal hostility. The law is fulfilled in going beyond it. Both Matthew and Paul champion a new ethic that in its premises respects and upholds the basic principles of Torah.

The reading from Deuteronomy today provides insight on why Torah was held in such esteem. It brought God close to his people. His will for them was expressed with clarity. It did not require mental gyrations to divine God's intentions.

As we make the journey of life, we are comforted by the fact that God's will for us, especially as expressed in Jesus, is a guiding light, a beacon on what are at times stormy seas. At times we find it difficult to live as a Christian. We make mistakes. But the will of God remains a great grace for which we can only be grateful as we make the journey.

Points to Ponder

> Moving beyond the Decalogue
> Understanding Matthew and Paul
> The God who is near to us

THURSDAY OF THE THIRD WEEK IN LENT

Jeremiah 7:23–28
Psalm 95:1–2, 6–7, 8–9
Luke 11:14–23

There can be no real conversion without breaking from evil. God and evil are antithetical. Jesus points out the absurdity of his being an agent of Satan in casting out devils. Such would mean that Satan is working against himself. But if Christ is acting as an agent of God, then the reign of God has come.

The plight of Jeremiah lay in the insensitivity on the part of the people who refused to heed God's warning. It was not uncommon for the prophets to be disregarded until it was too late. It is sad enough to be distant from God, but to give his warnings a deaf ear is even worse.

Our experience today tells us that many people are at ease with the prevailing spirit of evil. Wrongdoing is diminished, and all manner of compromise is introduced. There was a time when sin was called by name; today it is often justified in terms of "changing times." Pornography today is a multimillion-dollar business. A movie that is suitable for all ages is difficult to find. Cohabitation before marriage is rapidly moving from the exception to the rule.

We all have to remember that we have been richly blessed in our Christian faith. We have been truly favored. What wisdom is there in discarding a precious gift?

Jesus was criticized for casting out devils. Today it seems that we are comfortable in compromising our convictions. There is a helpful caveat in today's Gospel. In safeguarding our faith, let us always be wary of the one stronger than we who may overpower us. With conviction and the will to distinguish between right and wrong, that will not happen.

"O that today you would listen to his voice! Do not harden your hearts."

Points to Ponder

Jesus identified as an agent of Satan
Remaining strong in faith
Our compromising times
With him or against him?

FRIDAY OF THE THIRD WEEK IN LENT

Hosea 14:2–10
Psalm 81:6c–8a, 8bc–9, 10–11ab, 14 and 17
Mark 12:28–34

The Great Commandment has been saved for this third week of Lent. If one can speak of the genius of Christianity, it certainly finds expression in the first and greatest commandment. It is a summary of the entire Christian ethic.

This precept combines two concepts from the Old Testament. The first is the great *Shema* from the Book of Deuteronomy, an unequivocal statement of monotheistic faith. Yahweh is God and he alone; the response required is total and uncompromising. As the only God, he is to be loved with the totality of one's forces (heart, soul, and mind). This recognition of God's absolute sovereignty is coupled with a thought from Leviticus. It expresses the horizontal dimension of our moral life. Our neighbor is to be loved as we love ourselves, and neighbor here is to be taken in a broad sense. Unlike its earlier meaning, it is not limited to other Israelites. It calls for openness to any human being. To answer the question of the Good Samaritan parable—"Who is my neighbor?"—the answer is anyone who has need of me.

The recognition of God and neighbor leaves no middle ground. It is a summary of the entire New Testament ethic, especially the Sermon on the Mount. We are called to recognize from the heart the sovereignty and goodness of God and to respond to the needs of others as they occur.

Hosea's insistent call to conversion is at the heart of his message. Sadly Israel had abandoned her first love and gone after empty idols. In this moving book, the prophet calls, with insistence for a "return."

The lesson of forgiveness is a good benchmark here. As John asks, How can I say that I love God whom I do not see and do not love my neighbor whom I see? In short, the Christian is the one who loves prayer but also has a spirit of availability toward brother and sister. Be sure that in making an examination of conscience, the Great Commandment is a worthy tool. In a real sense, that says it all.

Points to Ponder

Does God have full sway in my life?
The relationship between love of God and neighbor
Recognizing one's neighbor in today's world

SATURDAY OF THE THIRD WEEK IN LENT

Hosea 6:1–6
Psalm 51:3–4, 18–19, 20–21ab
Luke 18:9–14

Ritual has meaning when it is the expression of an inner spirit. Otherwise practice becomes an empty shell. The scriptures today illustrate this principle with considerable clarity. Hosea speaks to Ephraim and Judah, the northern and southern kingdom of the Hebrew people. They have long since shown their lack of an authentic commitment to the Lord; their expressions of faith are transient and vanishing. Their piety is like a morning cloud, like the dew that quickly passes away. Yet the ritual continues, but to no avail. "For I desire steadfast love and not sacrifice, the knowledge of God rather than burnt offerings."

The Gospel today goes on to make an added point in saying that one cannot judge by externals. The Pharisee was a member of a respected and bonafide Jewish body; the tax collector was the employee of a foreign power, an occupying force. The Pharisee practiced worthy expressions of faith—fasting and tithing—but it had led to self-adulation and very clear shades of superiority. The tax collector, with head bowed, could make no religious claims, but his heart was right. In a spirit of sincerity, he simply asks God's mercy. It is he who went home justified, totally dependent on the goodness of God.

Since comparisons are odious, we do well to avoid them. If we strive to be faithful, it ill behooves us to compare ourselves with others, who, at least by external standards, show little or no effort. Paul tells us that if anyone would boast, he should boast in the Lord. We are what we are by the grace of God to whom we remain deeply grateful. A man cannot get to daily Mass but never fails to stop in church for a short time as an expression of his faith. Religious is ultimately a matter of the heart, a theme to which Christ returns time after time.

My sacrifice, O God, is a contrite spirit, a heart contrite and humble you will not spurn.

Points to Ponder

> Religious practice versus a religious spirit
> A piety that vanishes as quickly as the dew
> Humility, a recognition of God's goodness

MONDAY OF THE FOURTH WEEK IN LENT

Isaiah 65:17–21
Psalm 30:2 and 4, 5–6, 11–12a and 13b
John 4:43–54

With a very earthbound vision of end-time blessedness, Isaiah today sees a long life as a sign of divine favor. In Jesus' time it was life itself that was cherished. In today's Gospel it is the restoration to health of the royal official's son. It becomes one of the "signs" in John's "book of signs."

Before Jesus gives the parable of the Good Samaritan in Luke's Gospel, the question is posed to him, "Who is my neighbor?" The parable gives the answer. The Samaritan passes near the man who had been badly beaten and abused and immediately offers assistance. The question is answered. My neighbor is anyone in need. In today's Gospel, Jesus proves himself to be a neighbor to a royal official. The story has a familiar ring; it may well be another version of Matthew's centurion's son (Matt 8:5–13) or Luke's servant (Luke 7:1–10). As a royal official, the man is either not a Jew or a Jewish appointee of Roman authority. He is clearly not a believer but becomes one at the story's conclusion.

If we are selective in our charity, we may be on the track of loving others because they love us. But being willing to extend ourselves to anyone who needs us brings the Christian ideal to life. At one point, Francis of Assisi was incensed when three robber-beggars were hungry and were turned away by the friars because of their poor reputation. He gave the order for them to be found and fed.

Years ago a priest pastor in New York's lower Manhattan was well known for giving something to everyone who knocked on the door. A friend once chided him, saying that he had been taken advantage of more times than he probably realized. His reply was simple: "God is never going to ask me about that. But he will bring up the one person who was in need and was turned away."

Points to Ponder

> My response to the person in need
> The joy of doing good
> The agent of love: an instrument of peace

TUESDAY OF THE FOURTH WEEK IN LENT

> Ezekiel 47:1–9, 12
> Psalm 46:2–3, 5–6, 8–9
> John 5:1–16

Water is an element that prolongs life and takes on rich symbolism in the Bible. In Ezekiel today it has an end-time significance. It represents that new life in God that flows from the temple itself and actually envelops people.

On the other hand, the restorative power of water meant little to the man lying by the pool in Jerusalem, hopeful that when the curative waters stirred, someone would assist him in immersing himself. That day never came.

Christ, in his compassion, substitutes himself for the healing water. He cures the man and tells him to pick up his mat and leave. The man is immediately subject to criticism for carrying his mat on the Sabbath. Jesus' final words are significant. The man is told to avoid sin so that he might not again find himself in a debilitating state.

In the curse of life there is no free ride, no cheap grace. How often in the Gospels Jesus links a cure with the injunction to avoid sin. Even after they had experienced God's favor, the Hebrew people repeatedly reverted to sinful ways. Their gratitude was short-lived. We too often speak of our gratitude to God for a specific favor and then frequently revert to business as usual.

Very impressive in the lives of the saints is their spirit of lasting gratitude. They want to share their sense of wholeness. St. Thérèse of Lisieux prayed that she might spend her heaven in doing good upon earth.

Christ is our cleansing water, our enabler. If we have come this far as children of God, it is because of him. If we are to go farther, it will be due to him.

The Lord of hosts is with us, our strength is the God of Jacob. In our moments of weakness, help us to do your will.

Points to Ponder

Water as the symbol of life
The frustration of the sick man
Christ's admonition: Sin no more

WEDNESDAY OF THE FOURTH WEEK IN LENT

Isaiah 49:8–15
Psalm 145:8–9, 13cd–14, 17–18
John 5:17–30

In the face of a dismal outlook, Isaiah today encourages a downtrodden people. The day of help and salvation is at hand. Zion may well have thought that she was abandoned. But that was no more likely than that a mother would forget her child. The Johannine Jesus today clearly indicates that the time of salvation has arrived.

Christ's opponents are determined to kill him, not only for violating the Sabbath but for making himself equal to God. Jesus responds to the charge on various levels, clearly affirming his equality with God. Let us take a look at these claims.

There is no Sabbath observance for the Father, who is always at work, as is the Son. There is, moreover, a mutual ongoing communication between Father and Son. The Son does only what he had learned from the Father. The Father is a life giver, as is the Son. The Spirit life, so dominant in John, is the first gift of the risen Christ to his apostles; it is this life that Jesus shares with the Father.

One of God's principal functions in the Old Testament is that of judge. This too he has consigned to the Son. Whoever honors the Son honors the Father as well and is destined for eternal life. The one who refuses is destined for death with a negative judgment. But as Christ states elsewhere, a negative judgment is self-inflicted. Condemnation comes from the "naysayer" himself and is simply affirmed by the judge.

Finally the Son has made his own the will of the Father. Nothing will happen to Christ by human devices; everything is in accord with what the Father has directed.

The equality of Father and Son is clearly affirmed. Jesus' right to heal on the Sabbath is upheld. To know Jesus is to know God; he is "the way, the truth and the life." In our Christian dispensation, there is no other way to reach the Father except through him.

Points to Ponder

Jesus' right to work and to heal
To know Jesus is to know God
Jesus, the life giver
Jesus, our judge

THURSDAY OF THE FOURTH WEEK IN LENT

Exodus 32:7–14
Psalm 106:19–20, 21–22, 23
John 5:31–47

To the unbelievers, Jesus today submits a number of reasons why he should be accepted: the witness of John the Baptist, the works of Jesus, the scriptures themselves, and Moses. John, widely recognized as a prophet, clearly attested that Jesus was the "true light." Jesus also performed any number of works that highlighted the presence of God in his life. His miracles were clearly "end-time" signs and worthy of belief.

In addition, the scriptures with their strong messianic thrust pointed to his day and spoke of it in a variety of ways. Finally, Moses in his own times led God's people toward a final destination and in so doing gave witness to Christ. If Moses is not to be believed, then faith has lost its meaning.

In our times we would probably add the witness of history. For more than two thousand years, the positive contribution of Christianity has resulted in remarkable good in the world. This too authenticates the mission of Christ.

When the Israelites fashioned a molten calf in the desert, they consciously rebelled against the God of the exodus, the God of their deliverance. God was set to exterminate them until Moses succeeded in dissuading him.

Today when people make wrong choices and embark on paths of moral ruin, we often wonder why punishment is delayed. The reason is that God's patience far outdistances our own.

The evil in the world bears witness to its rebellion. We are always grateful for that extra chance.

O Lord, remember us for the love you bear your people. Do help us, Lord, to remain faithful.

Points to Ponder

Seeing Christ in the Old Testament
The scriptures and the "end-time"
John the Baptist: the forerunner of Jesus

FRIDAY OF THE FOURTH WEEK IN LENT

Wisdom 2:1a, 12–22
Psalm 34:17–18, 19–20, 21 and 23
John 7:1–2, 10, 25–30

Evil finds good intolerable. It will do whatever it can to eradicate it. This is what comes to the fore in today's reading from Wisdom. Evildoers plot against the just person. Why? Because he is a reproach to them. He follows the path of righteousness, claiming God as his father. Therefore, he is to be tortured and handed over to death. If he is all that he claims to be, God will deliver him. Once again it is question of rejecting the message by killing the messenger.

Jesus fares no better at the hands of his accusers. His opponents claim that his origins are a matter of common knowledge. But when the messiah comes, his origins will be unknown. Jesus came from Nazareth, a small northern town and a biblical nonentity. In short, Christ had no noteworthy credentials and thus was worthy of rejections.

But they have failed utterly in determining Christ's real origins. The true believer knows that Jesus' origins are with the Father who sent him into the world. In knowing neither the Father nor the Son, Jesus' enemies are far from the truth. This is the great irony of John's Gospel. Many of those who had seen and experienced Christ remained far from him. They never took the leap of faith.

It is one thing to fail to respond to God's call; it is quite another to try to rewrite the script. It is better to say simply and directly, "Lord, I am a sinner." In an effort to make wrong seem right, we only do damage to ourselves. We are only one step from forgiveness. It is far better to admit our sin than to try to make black be white.

Lord, be merciful to me a sinner.

Points to Ponder

Faith in the origins of Jesus
The antithesis between good and evil
Admitting, and not excusing, guilt

SATURDAY OF THE FOURTH WEEK IN LENT

Jeremiah 11:18–20
Psalm 7:2–3, 9bc–10, 11–12
John 7:40–53

Jeremiah came to realize that the plot being hatched by his opponents was directed against him. Once again we are reminded of how much the biblical defenders of the truth had to suffer. Here the prophet realizes that only God can deliver him from their hands.

The Gospel today finds Jesus' opponents turning in any direction to help their cause. Since Jesus was from Galilee in the north and not from Bethlehem in the south, he cannot be the messiah; the messiah was to come from Bethlehem, the city of David. Their position indicates how a little scripture can be a dangerous thing. The messiah was to be a descendant of David, whose home city Bethlehem is often portrayed as a place of divine privilege. The New Testament does indicate that the birth of Jesus took place in Bethlehem, but, even if it had not, his Davidic origins would have remained intact. Geography was not the central issue. Jesus spent most of his life in Galilee but that did not contradict his Judahite origins.

There is considerable discussion in our time about scientific positions that are seen to be at odds with the Bible. Evolution versus creationism. Was it seven days or seven million years? Regrettably, it is a question of apples and oranges. The biblical authors had no idea of the age of the universe, nor was there any reason why they should. In the Bible, God is presented as working like a human artisan in a popular description of the world's origins. The scientific questions are best left to science, and religious questions to the Bible. Both have a very different scope. The ancient maxim said it well. "The Bible tells us how to go to heaven, not how the heavens go."

Points to Ponder

> The meaning of the Davidic messiah
> The dangers of biblical fundamentalism
> Religion and science

MONDAY OF THE FIFTH WEEK IN LENT

> Daniel 13:1–9, 15–17, 19–30, 33–62
> Psalm 23:1–3a, 3b–4, 5, 6
> John 8:1–11

The stories of both Susanna and the adulterous woman, powerful expressions of justice and divine mercy, have had a troubled textual history. The Susanna story from the Book of Daniel is evidently an appendix to the original Hebrew and has come to us only in its Greek translation. The adulterous woman narrative is not found in any of the earliest Greek New Testament manuscripts. There is further question as to its original provenance, since its language and style are not typically Johannine but seem to be more Lucan.

That having been said, the narratives and their teaching remain perennially strong. The false accusations made against Susanna are overturned by the prophetic insight of the young Daniel. Her accusers are found guilty of slander, and she is completely exonerated.

The story of the sinful woman of the Gospel leaves no doubt about her guilt or the malice of her accusers. The question posed to Jesus was more entrapment than a hoped-for sentence of death, since evidence indicates that the Jews in Roman times had no authority to render a death sentence. Jesus prescinds from the question of guilt or innocence. Was there a guiltless person in his audience who was in a position to move against the woman? One by one they take their leave. Left alone with the woman, Jesus sends her away in peace and exhorts her to sin no more.

Forgiveness lies at the very center of Christ's mission. For this he came into the world, to lift the sentence that lay upon us. It is this sense of forgiveness that permeates the whole of his mission, and he clearly indicates that his followers are to be like-minded. Forgive not seven times but seventy times seven.

As Holy Week approaches, we are again reminded of the price of our exoneration. Regardless of the sin, forgiveness is ours for the asking. We are now called to extend that same spirit to others.

Points to Ponder

The death penalty and Catholic teaching
Forgiveness for the asking
Forgiveness of others when not asked
Personal reconciliation with God
The sacrament of reconciliation

TUESDAY OF THE FIFTH WEEK IN LENT

Numbers 21:4–9
Psalm 102:2–3, 16–18, 19–21
John 8:21–30

The term *lift* is used in our times in a variety of figurative ways. It may mean to give someone a ride, or it may indicate some object or event that gives someone a more positive outlook. In John's Gospel, it means a move toward a new level of existence.

The biblical background to this is found in the narrative from Numbers, read in today's Mass. Struck by a plague of deadly serpents in the desert, the Hebrews were saved by looking upon a bronze serpent that Moses had set upon a pole. This sign of God's providence is seen in the Johannine Gospel as a forerunner of Christ's being "lifted up" on the cross, the divine emissary of definitive salvation. Those, in turn, who look upon Christ as their savior and life giver are themselves "lifted up" in the Holy Spirit, the key to eternal life.

When Christ tells the Jews in today's Gospel that where he is going they cannot come, he is referring to his return to the

Father, a venue to which only the believer will be admitted. He identifies himself once again as "I AM," the personal name that God revealed to Moses at the burning bush.

In our faith we believe that we have been "lifted up" and are convinced that Jesus is truly the "I AM." We cherish and are grateful for that life in the Spirit that gives meaning to our life in its entirety.

We must strive and not grow weary. The liturgy repeatedly, especially in these final days of Lent, brings our destiny to the fore. We are not only moving toward God, but in him we live and move and have our being. Things will never be the same again. We have been given a "lift" and can respond only with grateful hearts.

Points to Ponder

> Jesus "lifted up"
> The Christian "lifted up"
> The Spirit life
> Salvation as a gift

WEDNESDAY OF THE FIFTH WEEK IN LENT

> Daniel 3:14–20, 91–92, 95
> (Ps) Dan 3:52, 53, 54, 55, 56
> John 8:31–42

Candor and honesty. These virtues are striking in today's readings. The three young men in the blazing furnace refuse to compromise the truth of their convictions by surrendering to idolatry. They are vindicated and liberated because of their adherence to principle.

Jesus insists in the Gospel that sin reduces us to slavery. His Jewish opponents recognize no form of slavery; as the descendants of Abraham, they are the heirs of freedom. But in opposing Jesus, who speaks the truth of the Father, they are sinners, and sinners are enslaved to the "father of lies" (John 8:44). His opponents bend the truth at every opportunity, and in so doing they are slaves of evil and far from the freedom of God's children.

In today's world, enslavement to sin takes various forms. One example is child pornography, which has reached alarming proportions. Young children are drawn to immorality through cunning and depravity. It is an enterprise that produces millions of dollars each year. Its evil is multifaceted, but it is rooted in deception and depravity.

Today we also hear much about "spin." It is a reporting technique that alters the truth to make the report more palatable. It is now a commonplace in the reporting of news. This, too, is a distortion of the truth. It may not be done to dishonor the person of Christ, but anytime that we doctor the truth, we move farther away from the candor of the Gospels.

Sometimes the truth hurts. But we cannot betray it. Let us pray for the grace to respond honestly to every inquiry, to relay the facts of any given situation, and not garnish the truth for personal or other motives.

Let us keep the word with a generous heart and yield a harvest through perseverance.

Points to Ponder

Deception for immoral ends
Garnishing the truth

THURSDAY OF THE FIFTH WEEK IN LENT

Genesis 17:3–9
Psalm 105:4–5, 6–7, 8–9
John 8:51–59

Two important biblical texts are in play in today's readings. The first deals with the covenant God made with Abraham (Gen 17), the second, the identity of God (Exod 3). There is no more sainted ancestor in Jewish tradition than Abraham, with whom the covenant of perpetuity was made. God pledges himself to remain with his people and promises the land of Israel to them as a lasting reminder of his fidelity.

In today's Gospel the question arises as to the relationship between Jesus and Abraham. Is Jesus greater than the patriarch? As daring as the implication is, Jesus answers it unequivocally in the affirmative. Abraham rejoiced to see the day of the Messiah. Then drawing on the way God identified himself to Moses in Exodus 3 (I AM WHO I AM), Christ not only show his anteriority to Abraham but also indicates his equality with the Father. Before Abraham came to be, Christ was. He is the great I AM.

Jesus is not only the Word of God. He is God's last Word. There is nothing better or subsequent to this. In Jesus a new and lasting covenant has been forged in his own blood. This is the new covenant promised by Jeremiah, a covenant written not in stone but in the human heart, a deeply personal relationship between the believer and God.

If Lent has any lesson it is this: Realize who you are and how much you mean to God. Not only is Christ superior to Abraham, he is the son of God who has died for love of us. We are confident about the future because we have reason to be. We trust in God's word that endures forever.

Points to Ponder

The covenant with Abraham
Jesus the I AM
The new covenant of the heart

FRIDAY OF THE FIFTH WEEK IN LENT

Jeremiah 20:10–13
Psalm 18:2–3a, 3bc–4, 5–6, 7
John 10:31–42

In the midst of hatred and the threat of terror, Jeremiah prays for deliverance and the defeat of his adversaries. God alone is his vindicator. The Johannine Jesus continues to present him-self—with theological persuasion—to his opponents, but their animosity is unabated.

The title "Son of God" is prominent in today's controversy. The term was originally used in the Old Testament of an exalted person, notably the king. It signified the unique status a person held before God. As Jesus uses the expression, however, it says much more. Between his Father and himself there exists a oneness that can be claimed by no other human being. As Jesus states, it means that "the Father is in me and I am in the Father."

Yet the expression takes on an even fuller meaning when applied to the Christian life. In baptism, the Christian is incorporated into Christ, in his dying and rising. Christ now shares his own Spirit life with the believer. We are now members of a new household, privileged to call God our Abba and Christ, our brother. This is not merely spiritual "wishful thinking." It is the reality in which we live.

At one point in his life when Jesus is told that his family wishes to see him, he moves the discussion to another level: Who are my mother and brothers? Those who do the will of God.

Lent is much concerned with our calling. It is a time to dedicate ourselves to God anew and to realize who we are. Members of the household of God. It is well to remember that the unkind word offends our brother or sister. Uncharitable speech takes its toll on the body of Christ. Improper language is unworthy of a son or daughter of God.

Points to Ponder

> Faith in Jesus as Son of God
> The Christian in the family of God
> Responsibilities of the Spirit life

SATURDAY OF THE FIFTH WEEK IN LENT

> Ezekiel 37:21–28
> Jeremiah 31:10, 11–12abcd, 13
> John 11:45–56

The storm clouds gather....The Gospel narrative today picks up immediately after the restoration of Lazarus to life. The spectators to that event are now split. Some place their faith in Jesus;

others report him to the Jewish authorities. At this point, the machinery is in place to arrest and condemn him.

Faced with the quandary of further acceptance of Jesus and its political consequences, the authorities are at a loss as to what to do. It is the high priest Caiaphas, who will play a part in the forthcoming passion narrative, who makes the deciding proposal. It is better to have one man die than to have the nation destroyed. (The decision is seen as prophetic for John. In fact, the death of Jesus will bring salvation, not destruction, to the people.)

The Passover approaches. Confident that Jesus will appear in Jerusalem, the people watch for him. The Jewish authorities, meanwhile, have given orders that any appearance of Christ is to be reported. The stage is set for the denouement as the events of the last week of Jesus' life begin to unfold.

The reading from Ezekiel, speaking of the restoration of Israel, is placid and serene. Exile will come to an end. There will no longer be a divided kingdom. Idolatry will be no more. The royal descendant of David will preside over a country marked by an authentic religious spirit. There will be a new covenant of peace. This idyllic picture is about to be fulfilled in the paschal mystery of Christ's death and resurrection. It marks a triumph bought at a very dear price. The memories of that final week will be set before us in the next few days.

Yes, it was better that one man die than for the country to be lost. But it was God's Son who endured everything, even a sense of abandonment by the Father. Recalling the event of his death is to lead us to a renewed spirit of love and commitment. This is the door to a life in God, which surpasses anything imagined heretofore.

Points to Ponder

The prophecy of Caiaphas
Ezekiel's vision of restoration
A populace divided over Christ
Belief and betrayal

Holy Week
and Easter

MONDAY OF HOLY WEEK

Isaiah 42:1–7
Psalm 27:1, 2, 3, 13–14
John 12:1–11

The readings of Holy Week converge around the suffering and death of Christ. The Isaian reading today is the first of four songs of the unidentified servant of the Lord, with the other three songs appearing in the course of the week. In the first song, the servant is introduced as a prophetic figure whose work will effect God's will, not only in Israel but among the nations as well.

The character of the servant is described; he is mild mannered and not given to clamor or violence. The damaged stalk of a plant he will not break and the smoldering wick he will not extinguish. His work will be done in a peaceful fashion.

The Johannine story of Mary of Bethany anointing the feet of Jesus is a variant of an event recounted in the other Gospels as well. Unlike in the other accounts, here the woman is clearly identified. The anointing done with a precious ointment evokes Judas's criticism. He sees it as a waste of money that might well have been used for the poor. Jesus sees through the ruse and commends the woman. Jesus sees it as an act of love done in anticipation of his death, which is now imminent.

From the servant we learn the lesson of determination with a gentle expression. Conviction is often identified with an aggressive thrust; here it is evident that a gentler spirit can be equally effective.

Mary's expression of love was not hindered by the fear of criticism. Extravagance in the cause of good can be praiseworthy. The enemies of Jesus are already planning to eliminate him. Yet his goodness is praiseworthy, especially, in this case, his restoring Lazarus to life. We should not be afraid to applaud the good, even if it be costly. Where Mary did not hesitate to act, we often walk in the opposite direction.

Points to Ponder

The servant's peaceful witness
Mary's expression of gratitude
The damage of harmful criticism

TUESDAY OF HOLY WEEK

Isaiah 49:1–6
Psalm 71:1–2, 3–4a, 5ab–6ab, 15 and 17
John 13:21–33, 36–38

In the second song of the servant, his mission is well under-
way. Like Jeremiah, he was called from his mother's womb. He
had been directed to call Jacob and Israel to conversion, as well as
to be "a light for the nations." Yet his mission has not been an
unqualified success. So unresponsive have his hearers been that he
has felt frustration and a sense of failure. Yet he remains confident
that the Lord will see him through.

The Johannine Gospel moves us steadily toward the denouement of Jesus' ministry. He is to be betrayed and handed over to
his enemies by one of his own, one who reclines at the table with
him. It is a clear reference to Judas's treachery. Jesus urges him to
carry out his nefarious plot quickly and without delay. Judas leaves
the upper room. The scene is punctuated by a simple statement:
"It was night." The darkness theme, a major motif in this fourth
Gospel, comes to the fore. Judas goes off into the darkness of
betrayal and sin. The time has now come for the Son of Man to
be glorified, a reference to the paschal mystery of Jesus' death and
resurrection.

Peter's protestation of loyalty is all too shallow. His fidelity
will vanish all too quickly. That very night he will deny his Master
three times.

There is great human pathos in this narrative. There is the
closeness and affection of the unnamed disciple "whom Jesus
loved." Jesus the Servant wrestles with the sadness of betrayal and
denial. Have we not in life met some form of such disappointment? The absence of a friend in a time of need? The sorrow of

desertion by someone we had trusted? The need for a defender in a moment of mistrust?

What we see before us today is the psychological dimension of Christ's ordeal. It is one thing to suffer physically; it is another to feel forsaken.

O my God, rescue me from the hand of the wicked.

Points to Ponder

> The servant's disappointment
> Betrayal in the life of Jesus
> The denial of Peter
> Human disappointment; a test of faith

WEDNESDAY OF HOLY WEEK

Isaiah 50:4–9a
Psalm 69:8–10, 21–22, 31 and 33–34
Matthew 26:14–25

Often termed "Spy Wednesday" because of the biblical account of Judas's betrayal, the Gospel narrative is accompanied by the third song of the servant. As he continues his mission, the servant meets with greater trials, this time, in terms of physical abuse. While never backing away from his call, the servant recounts beatings, buffeting, and spitting. All of this notwithstanding, he continues resolutely on his path, always confident of Yahweh's continued assistance.

In the Matthean Gospel narrative, Judas bargains with the Jewish leaders and receives the notorious thirty pieces of silver, the price given to the rejected shepherd in Zechariah. The treachery of Judas is compounded by the fact that he later sits with Jesus at the final supper. An avowed enemy did not share food with his opponent, since the sacred character of meal sharing and its intended good will would be reduced to mockery. In making his disclaimer of guilt, Judas incriminates himself.

The readings today issue a clarion call for honesty, candor, and transparency. This is the authentic Christian response, even in matters of lesser moment. We are subject to the temptation to bend the truth at times in our own favor. The result is that our responses do not always reflect the facts. Sometimes the truth is painful, but we are asked to bear it with courage.

It is the work of the judiciary to ferret out the truth—not always an easy task. As Christians we are called to settle out of court. To seek the truth is to seek the good, and it is the truth that sets us free. Any shade of hypocrisy is to be avoided. Christ is the luminous example of eternal truth, and it is he we wish to emulate.

Points to Ponder

Suffering for a good cause
The betrayal of friendship
The sin of hypocrisy
Thirty pieces of silver: the price of the Good Shepherd

HOLY THURSDAY

Exodus 12:1–8, 11–14
Psalm 116:12–13, 15–16bc, 17–18
1 Corinthians 11:23–26
John 13:1–15

The church sets before us today three central aspects of our faith: the Eucharist, the priesthood, and the commandment of mutual love.

In three of our Gospels, Jesus institutes the Eucharist at a Passover supper. This major Jewish feast celebrates the deliverance of the Hebrew people from the slavery of Egypt and their subsequent bonding with God in covenant. Christians, with Paul, declare that Christ is our Passover, delivering us from the bondage of sin and establishing a new covenant in his blood. He is our paschal lamb.

At the final supper, Jesus assures his followers of his continued eucharistic presence. The apostles are told to do what he did in his remembrance. On this day we celebrate the Catholic priesthood. As we see clearly in difficult circumstances today, without the priest there is no Eucharist. In memorializing this saving act of Christ, the priest participates in the one eternal priesthood of Christ, our high priest. In fact, no individual in the New Testament is designated a priest of the new era except Christ himself. Today we may well remember all the priests who have served us through the years. Some were profoundly configured to the person of Christ; others perhaps less so. But through it all, we have been well served. Today we pray in a special way that others will respond to this call of service, at a time of great need.

Our Gospel for Holy Thursday recalls Christ's washing of the apostles' feet. It was a profound act of humility. There is no mention of the Eucharist at the Last Supper in John's Gospel, although the Gospel as a whole contains strong eucharistic teaching. But it is the self-abasement of Christ that gives meaning of the entirety of his mission.

Francis of Assisi stood in awe before three great mysteries: the incarnation, the cross, and the Eucharist. Each of them manifests the great humility of God. Holy Thursday calls us to remember and to emulate. Our love goes to God in Eucharist and to our neighbor in generous service.

Points to Ponder

> Redemption as a new Passover
> Eucharist: the saving blood of the Lamb
> Self-giving to others in the Christian life

GOOD FRIDAY

> Isaiah 52:13—53:12
> Psalm 31:2, 6, 12–13, 15–16, 17, 25
> Hebrews 4:14–16; 5:7–9
> John 18:1—19:42

On this Friday, which history has long called Good, we directly recall the great cost of our redemption. The three scriptural readings today center on the sufferings of Jesus.

The first of our readings is the fourth and last song of the servant. Introduced in the first song, frustrated in the second, reviled in the third, he is brought to his death in the fourth. One of the results of his ordeal has been the alienation of his acquaintances. Harshly treated, he remains silent before his persecutors. But his death takes on a very distinctive meaning, bringing us to one of the major insights of the songs. His suffering is vicarious. His ordeal has been endured on behalf of a sinful people. This is a new and important insight into the "why" of suffering. Suffering may be endured on behalf of others. Although the servant remains unnamed, the church has long seen him as an image of Christ. As the epistle to the Hebrews sees Jesus today, "He learned obedience through what he suffered; and…became the source of eternal salvation for all who obey him."

Our passion narrative today is from the Gospel of John. It is strikingly different from the Synoptic accounts. While never minimizing Christ's ordeal nor diminishing his sufferings, the Gospel portrays a Christ who stands above and, in a certain way, directs the course of events. His death is a free-will offering in obedience to the Father, a faith-filled event, not one of human manipulation or control. Jesus becomes a key player, engages Pilate in conversation, and goes to the cross thirsting for souls and consigns the disciple whom he loves to Mary, the symbol of church. He dies with resignation with the task accomplished ("It is finished") and hands over the Spirit to his followers.

We have inherited a rich patrimony. The worst is now behind us. As Paul says, if Christ has gone this far for us, how can we doubt that we will make the last mile?

Points to Ponder

> Vicarious atonement
> The Johannine Jesus in the passion narrative
> The Spirit and church from the cross

HOLY SATURDAY

Reflection

"There is a great silence on earth today, a great silence and stillness." So begins a Christian classic, the homily on Holy Saturday found in the Liturgy of the Hours. Holy Saturday is a day of quiet, a day of mourning for the Christ who will rise from the dead only on the morrow. Liturgically, today everything moves toward this evening's Easter vigil and the first Mass of the resurrection. There is no other liturgy celebrated today.

But this is not a vacuum, a day of spiritual emptiness. It is quiet time, something that we all need, a time of reflection in our very busy lives. In the aforementioned ancient homily, the unknown author speaks of Christ today going to awaken our first parents who live in darkness and the shadow of death. He goes to release them from their captivity and share with them the new life in God, the first fruit of redemption.

Today we stand in waiting for that Easter triumph that is about to break forth. We relive the painful experience of the cross in a spirit of quiet reflection. We need Holy Saturday and should not see it solely as a preparation day. Christ today touches those who have gone before us. The bridal chamber is adorned, the banquet is ready, the eternal dwelling place is prepared.

Lord, instill within us a deep love for all that you have done for us.

EASTER MONDAY

Acts of the Apostles 2:14, 22–32
Psalm 16:1–2a and 5, 7–8, 9–10, 11
Matthew 28:8–15

If Christ is not risen, then vain is your faith; you are still in your sins. The centrality of the resurrection in the catechesis of the church touches on the whole mystery of salvation. This was not solely for apologetic purposes. Certainly, if crucifixion has been the end, sin would have triumphed. But the resurrection has an importance beyond that. It is the risen Christ who confers the

Holy Spirit. Without the Spirit, we would be in no position to be a true believer and to overcome personal sin. As Paul teaches, no one can profess Jesus as Lord except in the Holy Spirit.

In his Pentecost proclamation, Peter sees David the Psalmist as an early proclaimer of the messiah's resurrection. When the psalmist spoke of freedom from corruption and the path of life, he was not speaking of himself. David died and his tomb was still frequented. So he spoke not of himself but of the Messiah, the risen Christ.

To offset any idea of resurrection, the religious leaders in today's Gospel advise the Roman guards to claim that the disciples had stolen the body of Jesus while the guards slept. (A sound sleep it would have had to be, since the large stone had to be rolled back and the body absconded!) But such a story circulated among the Jews even to the end of the first century when the Matthean Gospel was written.

Easter is so pivotal that every mystery of our faith is viewed through that prism. Because of Easter, baptism is an immersion into the risen Christ; the Eucharist is a sharing in his true body and blood; Christian division is a rending of the one body of Christ. We are Easter people; Christ has triumphed; *Allelujah* is our cry!

Points to Ponder

> The psalms adapted for Christian use
> Early denial of the resurrection
> Resurrection and the forgiveness of sins

EASTER TUESDAY

> Acts of the Apostles 2:36–41
> Psalm 33:4–5, 18–19, 20 and 22
> John 20:11–18

The Johannine account of Mary Magdalene's initial encounter with the risen Christ provides considerable food for thought. Her fidelity to the Lord through his passion and death is legendary. Now standing by the empty tomb, she is addressed by the two angels within. Asked why she is weeping, she replies that she does not know what has become of Jesus' body.

It is at this point that Christ addresses her directly. Not recognizing him and believing that he is the gardener, she again expresses her grief at the loss of Christ's body. Recognition comes with a single word: "Mary." She immediately addresses him as "Rabboni" or Teacher.

In the Gospel of John, the resurrection, ascension, and Pentecost are united. Christ tells Mary not to detain him, since he is ascending to his Father and will return on that same Sunday evening to confer the Spirit on the apostles. His journey is not interrupted.

Mary then becomes the first witness to the resurrection. This woman from Jesus' earthly company carries this central mystery to the apostles. In our times, when Mary is seen as an important woman of the Gospels, we see her today as the first ambassador of the risen Christ.

There are two points that come quickly to mind. One is the expanding role of women in the church. This is an encouraging development. This is true not only of teaching, catechetics, and human outreach but in worship as well. We can only be grateful and supportive of the contribution women do and can make to church life.

The second point is the force of the name. Our name is singularly our own. We are recognized by it, and we claim it unfailingly. To remember a person's name does him or her honor. That name is to be reverenced and honored. Its proper use is an unmatched sign of respect.

Points to Ponder

Mary's grief
Name recognition
The ascent of Jesus
Women in the church

EASTER WEDNESDAY

Acts of the Apostles 3:1–10
Psalm 105:1–2, 3–4, 6–7, 8–9
Luke 24:13–35

Christ lives and continues his saving work. Peter and John restored a crippled man to health in the name of the Lord Jesus. In addition, the risen Christ continues his saving work in each one of us as the Lucan story of the men on the road to Emmaus makes clear.

The two men are moving away from Jerusalem. Strange indeed, considering that in Luke's Gospel the movement is always toward Jerusalem. They are puzzled and uncertain, with no idea as to the identity of the stranger who joins them. Disillusioned by the outcome of Jesus' life, they are left only with the account of the empty tomb.

It is here that the teaching of Jesus begins. Drawing on the scriptures, he presents those passages that point to the suffering and death of the messiah. With the approach of evening, the Lucan theme of hospitality emerges as the two men urge the stranger to join them in the inn. As they are at supper, the eucharistic motif emerges anew. Jesus takes bread, breaks it, and distributes it. At this point, the men recognize the Lord. There is no further need for a visionary presence. He is present in the "breaking of the bread."

What can we carry away with us from this reading? Christ is truly present in each Mass that we offer. Initially, in the scriptures that we draw upon each day, and in which we hope, our hearts too burn within us. Then we move to the altar and the "breaking of the bread." Christ is truly present as our food for the journey.

This narrative is rich in its teaching and reminds us that Easter is not simply a matter of historical recall. Christ is truly present in word and sacrament. It should be noted that at the account's end, the two disciples return to Jerusalem.

Points to Ponder

> Sin, our move away from Jerusalem
> The scriptures and the Eucharist
> The breaking of the bread
> Christ's presence in our life

EASTER THURSDAY

Acts of the Apostles 3:11–26
Psalm 8:2ab and 5, 6–7, 8–9
Luke 24:35–48

The curiosity seekers who rush to see the cured lame man are addressed by Peter in a speech of reproach as well as forgiveness. The Jews in the audience had turned Jesus over to the authorities and were thus accomplices in his execution. But forgiveness can still be theirs. They must first recognize Christ as the healer of the crippled man and repent of their sins. Peter recognizes that they had acted out of ignorance, but with repentance forgiveness can still be theirs.

In his first appearance to the apostles in Luke's Gospel, Jesus highlights more than personal immortality. His visible form is not a vision or a phantasm; rather it involved his whole physical makeup. Jesus' resurrection would not necessarily have had to include his body, but the Gospels are at pain to show that it did. The disciples are invited to touch his hands and feet. Jesus asks for something to eat and then consumes it in their presence. Although totally transformed in indescribable ways, this is the same Jesus who had spent his earthly ministry in their company.

The risen Christ is a Spirit-filled presence, a Spirit that Christ communicates to his followers. There is no sin that cannot be remitted. What is necessary is to recognize that Jesus of Nazareth is truly Lord and Messiah and then to accept the forgiveness of sins.

It is impossible for us to understand fully what a true resurrection entails. For Christ it meant a totally different form of existence. But it did include the body that had been given to him.

There were Christian heresies that disdained the physical and saw the human body as ignoble. But authentic faith teaches that we share a common nature with our Messiah and Lord. Totally human, we desire to make holy that which comes from God.

Points to Ponder

> Forgiveness for the death of Jesus
> The corporeality of Jesus
> Sanctity of the whole person

EASTER FRIDAY

> Acts of the Apostles 4:1–12
> Psalm 118:1–2 and 4, 22–24, 25–27a
> John 21:1–14

A fine surgeon who was also a devout Christian once commented, "If the patient makes a speedy recovery after surgery, God gets the credit. But if things go badly, I get the blame." Yet, it is commendable that the Christian conscience sees the hand of God in many events of daily life. It brings us closer to God and God closer to us.

Many of the resurrection narratives find the disciples deferring to the risen Lord. In today's reading from Acts of the Apostles, after the crippled man is cured and the crowds begin to gather, Peter speaks boldly and resolutely before the religious authorities, in claiming that the man was restored to health in the name of Jesus Christ the Nazarene. The cornerstone of the new reign of God is Jesus himself; the stone that his own people had rejected is now the cornerstone. His words are both a reproach to his hearers and a clear affirmation of the resurrection.

In the Johannine Jesus' apparition at the Sea of Tiberias, the disciples have returned to their initial occupation. They set off with Peter in a boat to make a catch. Their nocturnal effort is futile, however. Only at daybreak, at Jesus' direction, do they make a remarkable catch. The impetuous Peter jumps into the water. As they enjoy their breakfast, it is clearly Christ himself who is the host and the one around whom the entire narrative converges.

We do not want to reach a point in life where everything that happens is attributable to God. But we have all experienced those moments when our prayers are clearly heard and something deeply desired is realized. In acknowledging this, we utter a prayer of thanksgiving, a theme deeply woven into the prayer of the scriptures. It says nothing more than that we as people of faith believe that God is very close at hand.

The first of the disciples to recognize Christ on the shore was the unnamed "disciple whom Jesus loved." Recognition came as the result of fidelity. From the supper to the passion to the cross, this was the faithful disciple. Running with Peter to the tomb, he is the first one to understand its emptiness. Now seeing the figure on the shore, he says simply, "It is the Lord!" Faith must be steadfast. Faith gives understanding. This is the lesson of the beloved disciple.

Points to Ponder

> The healing power of Christ
> God's presence trough the charity of others
> The prayer of thanksgiving
> Recognizing the Lord

EASTER SATURDAY

> Acts of the Apostles 4:13–21
> Psalm 118:1 and 14–15ab, 16–18, 19–21
> Mark 16:9–15

Today's Gospel is taken from the longer ending of Mark's Gospel. The earlier abrupt ending was later emended with this summary of Jesus' appearances after the resurrection, taken from different Gospels.

In the Acts of the Apostles conclusion to the account of the cure of the crippled man, the Jewish authorities forbid the apostles any further mention of Jesus or his teaching. However, in having been commissioned by the risen Christ, their mandate is from God himself. In accepting the decree of the Jewish authorities, they would be clearly disobeying God. Hence, for them there is no choice in the matter. They must continue to preach what they have heard and seen.

Conflicts between conscience and civil government are not uncommon today, the abortion debate being a case in point. Religious belief holds that life is given by God himself and is sacred at every stage of development. Therefore, abortion rights advocates find no ally in the Christian conscience. In another case, there are some twelve million illegal immigrants in this country at the present time, with many of them here for many years. Mass deportation is no solution, but tighter border control is. What flies in the face of basic Christian values is to make material assistance to a needy immigrant a felony. One cannot ask for a green card in the face of genuine need. Here God must be obeyed, not man.

Conflicts between conscience and human authorities are not infrequent. But the basic principle remains the same. It is to God that we owe our first allegiance.

Points to Ponder

Conflicts between conscience and human authority
Charity: Christianity's first law
Suffering for principle

MONDAY OF THE SECOND WEEK OF EASTER

Acts of the Apostles 4:23–31
Psalm 2:1–3, 4–7a, 7b–9
John 3:1–8

Easter faith with conviction! No sooner have Peter and John advised their people that the priests and authorities had ordered them not to speak of Jesus than a prayer of rightful indignation goes up from the crowd. There was no way they could be silent about their newfound faith. They ask the Lord's support as they continue to speak the word.

The position of these first Christians cannot be explained apart from faith. That which had transpired in their lives was occasioned by the new birth from above, about which Jesus speaks to Nicodemus in today's Gospel. As happens so often in John, the talk of a new conception and birth is misunderstood by the Jewish leader. How can a grown person be born again? Yet, there is another, a heavenly birth that occurs when two forces converge. The first of these is the Holy Spirit, which is as mysterious as the wind itself. The origins of the wind are unknown, and it remains invisible. It is experienced in the effects that it produces. The second force is the material element of water. When the two converge in the sacred rite of baptism, a new birth takes place. By this sacrament one is empowered from on high; it explains the profound change in the apostles and the first believers. Prior to Christ's death, the apostles were largely undistinguished and even weak in their convictions. Following Easter, they are emboldened and fearless in their commitment to the truth.

It is often said that two topics should be avoided in conversation. They are religion and politics. If a discussion of religion means an inconsiderate brow beating, its avoidance is understandable. If, however, it means an openness about our beliefs and a willingness to speak honestly, then we have no choice. We have a heavenly birthright, about which we can never be ashamed.

Points to Ponder

> Spirit like the wind
> Conviction and discipleship
> Speaking the truth in love

TUESDAY OF THE SECOND WEEK OF EASTER

> Acts of the Apostles 4:32–37
> Psalm 93:1ab, 1cd–2, 5
> John 3:7b–15

The key to Christian belief is to see the death of Jesus as the saving action of God. In the Book of Numbers, Moses raises a bronze serpent to save the Israelites who gazed upon it and were saved from a plague inflicted death. In John's Gospel, the serpent is seen as a type of Christ. Years ago a person once commenting on modern church furnishings was taken aback to see an altar crucifix with Christ depicted in a serpentine style. Yet the image was totally biblical. Belief in the person of Christ crucified is rewarded with eternal life, which in the here and now means life in the Spirit.

In the teaching of Jesus, love of God and love of neighbor are inseparable. Today's reading from Acts of the Apostles finds the earliest Christians earnestly providing for each others needs. Property, housing, and material needs were available through mutual sharing.

We can see evidence of this spirit to the present day. When a family grieves, friends or acquaintances appear with prepared meals. There are those people in life for whom the words *enough* or *too much* are never used. Their reserves of giving are never exhausted. In countless ways they put that spirit of Acts into practice. But the fact is that we live in a very selfish world. Think of the impatience and anger at work behind the wheel of a car, the absence of a word of thanks when a door is held for someone, physical abuse inflicted upon a child. We deeply appreciate the giving and generous person. It is the spirit of Acts at work.

Points to Ponder

> The lifting up of Jesus
> Sharing in the early church
> The spirit of Acts today

WEDNESDAY OF THE SECOND WEEK OF EASTER

> Acts of the Apostles 5:17–26
> Psalm 34:2–3, 4–5, 6–7, 8–9
> John 3:16–21

Among the factors that many of the New Testament person-alities had in common, one often unmentioned is the fact that many of them had to do "jail time." From John the Baptist to Jesus to Peter and Paul, encounters with religious and civil authorities often led to imprisonment. In today's reading from Acts of the Apostles, the apostles as a group are apprehended but then set free by divine intervention; they return to their preach-ing mission, much to the amazement of their stunned jailers.

We are reminded in today's Gospel that no human judgment can compare with that which comes from the rejection of God's Son. The term *world* is used in two different senses in John's Gospel. Used negatively, it is the arena where evil is at play and therefore worthy of disdain. In the positive sense, it is the focus of God's love, the locus of redemption, the springboard to eternal life.

Where condemnation enters the picture, it is self-inflicted. It is a question of refusing God's Son and choosing darkness over the light. Works that are evil survive only in the realm of darkness, while those who have the truth love the light and have nothing to fear.

As the baptized we have been snatched from the grasp of evil. We are people of light, truth adherents. Therefore, we are called to walk in the daylight, to do the work of God, with no fear of the dark. The only imprisonment that we have to fear is that of the soul. The "jail time" served in the New Testament was pro-ductive of good. But if the spirit is imprisoned we sit in darkness and death.

Taste and see how good the Lord is; happy the person who takes refuge in him.

Points to Ponder

Imprisonment for a worthy cause
Spiritual imprisonment
God's love for the world
Self-condemnation

THURSDAY OF THE SECOND WEEK OF EASTER

Acts of the Apostles 5:27–33
Psalm 34:2 and 9, 17–18, 19–20
John 3: 31–36

When the question of illegal immigration became a major issue some time ago, there was a proposed law before Congress to make it a felony for anyone to give public assistance to an undocumented person. The archbishop of a large American diocese said that if such were to become law, neither he nor his clergy or social outreach personnel should consider themselves bound by a law that blatantly flew in the face of the supreme law of Christianity, the law of love.

These are precisely the sentiments expressed by the apostles in today's reading from Acts of the Apostles. Their first allegiance was to God whom they must obey rather than to human authority. As Jesus states in today's Gospel, "The one who comes from heaven is above all." In the parable of the Good Samaritan, the priest and the Levite pass by the dying man on the road to Jericho. They probably did so out of religious concerns. Thinking that he might be dead, they knew that they would not be able to perform their cultic duties if they came into contact with a corpse. This was to give a secondary law a priority it did not deserve.

We are sometimes faced with conflicts of this type. But with any set of laws there are certain priorities. Basic religious principles also have rights, primarily the right to be recognized, especially in matters of fundamental importance. We must always stand firm when something as basic as our relationship with God is called into question.

Points to Ponder

Obeying God rather than humans
Religion and the civil rights issue
Christian pacifism
Illegal immigration

FRIDAY OF THE SECOND WEEK OF EASTER

Acts of the Apostles 5:34–42
Psalm 27:1, 4, 13–14
John 6:1–15

There is a wisdom motif in today's two readings. Before the court, Gamaliel argues from precedent in the matter of Jesus. Religious claimants had appeared in the past, but upon their death, their cause evaporated and their followers disbanded. The court would now show itself wise in abstaining from any action against the apostles. If their cause was from God, it would succeed; if not, it would disappear.

In John's recounting of the story of the loaves, there is a distinct eucharistic imprint. We are surprised by the fact that John's Last Supper narrative makes no mention of the institution of the Eucharist, since the Gospel as a whole is strongly sacramental. In today's narrative, Jesus took notice of the crowd with no food, he "took" the bread, gave "thanks," and "distributed" the loaves to those reclining on the plain. The language clearly reflects the Last Supper account of the Synoptic Gospels. What we have here is a distinctly eucharistic catechesis.

The Johannine wisdom in many parts of the Gospel stresses the continued presence of Christ in his church. If the people were blessed who followed Jesus personally during his life, so too are we. If we wish, we can receive daily that bread of life that sustains us on our journey. Christianity is an historical religion not only because it finds its origins in the person of the historical Jesus Christ but also because it relives the Christ event in every moment of history. Our belief tells us that Christ lives in the Spirit-filled Christian and in each one of the sacraments, especially the Eucharist. This sacrament is both sign and reality: the sign of Christ's self-giving and the reality of his true body and blood.

The psalmist today prays to dwell always in the house of the Lord. With the assurance of faith, this is precisely what we do in the Eucharist.

Points to Ponder

The wisdom of Gamaliel
The Eucharist in the story of the loaves
Christ, our food for the journey

SATURDAY OF THE SECOND WEEK OF EASTER

Acts of the Apostles 6:1–7
Psalm 33:1–2, 4–5, 18–19
John 6:16–21

When the goodness of God is truly appreciated, it leads to service and ministry.

Although they are not called "deacons," this passage from Acts of the Apostles is often seen as the institution of the order of deacons. In the past the diaconate was a stepping stone to priesthood, with its singular ecclesial value frequently overlooked. Since Vatican II, men are ordained deacons as a permanent ministry, appreciated in and for themselves as a distinct part of the church's hierarchy. There is evidence in the New Testament that in its earliest stages the order included women as well.

When the first wave of deacons appeared after Vatican II emerged, the results were uneven. Today the quality of deacon candidates has improved dramatically, and in many parishes they play an indispensable role in the daily life of the church.

In today's reading from Acts of the Apostles the deacons are installed to provide for the material needs of the poorer members of the community. Many deacons continue to fill that role in our times. What is important to note here is that the social ministry was an integral part of the church's life from the start. There is no place where the church is present and people in need do not exist. One of the earliest synods of bishops after Vatican II spoke of social justice as an integral part of evangelization. In other words, the church cannot ignore human need and be true to itself.

When the disciples in today's Gospel recognize Jesus walking on the water, after they had rowed several miles on a turbulent sea, Jesus did not enter the boat. But the disciples quickly found themselves at their desired destination. So, too, in the church, it is through the collaboration of various ministries that a difficult task becomes easier. Ministry in the church is multifaceted in its Spirit-filled direction.

For our deacons and all those who serve the needs of our people in the church we can only be grateful.

Points to Ponder

The ministry of deacons
The various ministries in the church
Social justice, integral to church life

MONDAY OF THE THIRD WEEK OF EASTER

Acts of the Apostles 6:8–15
Psalm 119:23–24, 26–27, 29–30
John 6: 22–29

The readings today deal with people's motives for acting. Stephen's enemies, determined to rid themselves of his presence, invented charges against him. This was the only way they could defeat his cause, because he was a Christian in whom the presence of "grace and power" proved a formidable mix. He is accused of blasphemy against Moses and God. Yet, in the midst of the charges, Stephen's face was like "the face of an angel."

The so-called spin on the truth has become so much a part of contemporary discourse that we often fail to take notice. But, for whatever reason, a distortion of the truth is a falsehood and unworthy of Christian argumentation. Jesus promised that the truth would make us free. Thus we want to stand unwaveringly committed to the truth. Even if events do not turn out exactly as we had hoped, it is a question of character to remain faithful to the facts. Stephen's enemies brought him to death but did not deprive him of his place with the Christ whom he has served so well.

John's Gospel today recounts the crowd's following after Jesus, going as far as Capernaum to reach him. But Jesus questions the reason for this pursuit. They had eaten of the bread that he provided and now saw him as one who would miraculously provide for their physical needs. He reminds them that is not perishable food that they should seek but rather the food of eternal life, God's Word.

Their future is assured only if they have faith in the One whom God has sent.

In church life we have many secondary benefits about which we have no quarrel. But the ultimate criterion is the only one that counts: faith in the person of Jesus as our personal Lord and Savior. It is that belief that retains primacy of place.

Points to Ponder

> Distorting the truth
> Shading the truth
> Speaking the truth in love
> Christ as the bread of life

TUESDAY OF THE THIRD WEEK OF EASTER

> Acts of the Apostles 7:51–8:1a
> Psalm 31:3cd–4, 6 and 7b and 8a, 17 and 21ab
> John 6:30–35

At God's direction, Moses was the intermediary for the Israelites' deliverance from hunger in the desert. As providential as this bread from heaven was, it pales in comparison with the true heavenly bread, which is Christ himself in his life and in his teaching.

The death of Stephen bears a striking resemblance to that of Jesus. Jesus speaks of the Son of Man as an eschatological figure, the one "coming on the clouds of heaven" (Matt 24:30), just as Stephen sees him standing at God's right hand. As Jesus commended his spirit to the Lord, so too does Stephen. Both Jesus and Stephen die with a prayer of forgiveness on their lips. Clearly the martyr had made the teaching of Christ his own; even in his death he is the faithful witness.

Is it not true that our own moral failures in life reflect the absence of Christ's spirit? And when we know that we have acted correctly, do we not feel that such is the way that Christ would have acted? After his conversion, Paul became such a model of Christ that it is hard for us to believe that he concurred publicly in the killing of the first martyr.

The meaning of faith is to mirror Christ in our daily lives. This is what is meant by "having the mind of Christ." St. Thérèse of Lisieux lived her short life behind a cloistered wall. But her "little way" of holiness was to be an echo of Christ himself in the way she lived her daily life. This meant humility, forgiveness, and above all, charity. Hers was a love of neighbor that went beyond the grave as she prayed that she might spend her heaven in doing good upon earth. This was her "little way," to walk the walk of Christian holiness.

Points to Ponder

> Jesus the true bread from heaven
> Stephen echoes the sentiments of Christ
> Paul an accomplice in Stephen's death

WEDNESDAY OF THE THIRD WEEK OF EASTER

> Acts of the Apostles 8:1b–8
> Psalm 66:1–3a, 4–5, 6–7a
> John 6:35–40

During the conflict between Hindus and Muslims in India in the twentieth century, Mahatma Gandhi was once visited by a troubled Hindu who had just killed a Muslim man, the only parent of a young boy. His remorse was so great that he sought Gandhi's counsel. The latter advised the man to take the boy and provide a home for him. Furthermore, he should raise him as a Muslim.

Many wars have been fought over religious convictions, but such wars are contrary to genuine religious spirit. In today's reading from Acts of the Apostles, Philip brings the gospel to Samaria, to a people despised by the Jews and yet viewed in a very positive way by Christ himself. These apostolic efforts were crowned with success, with the church experiencing continued growth in Samaria.

In John's Gospel today, we have the beginning of Christ's bread of life discourse. Three themes are highlighted. First, to come to Christ is to find an inexhaustible source of food and nourishment. Second, it is the will of Christ that none of those committed to him by the Father be lost. Finally, Christ is the pledge of eternal life. In this passage, Christ is not speaking explicitly of the Eucharist. The bread of life is Jesus himself; in his life and his teaching he is the true bread of life.

There are people today who identify themselves as Christians because they have been baptized. But that says far too little. There is the need for an ongoing catechesis following baptism, coupled with a true sense of commitment. The bread of life must take deep root within us.

In most major endeavors today, education must be ongoing. With our faith it can be no different. If it can be said that to know is to love, then to know more should mean to love more. Christ wants to lose none of us. But are we willing to lose him? The quality of our love gives the answer.

Points to Ponder

> Evangelization: sharing the faith
> Hostility toward other faiths
> Jesus' desire that none be lost

THURSDAY OF THE THIRD WEEK OF EASTER

Acts of the Apostles 8:26–40
Psalm 66:8–9, 16–17, 20
John 6:44–51

The Ethiopian, a royal official, wrestles with the celebrated text from Isaiah, much as have scripture scholars of the past and present. The passage is from the last of the four servant songs, in which the servant is clearly individualized but not identified. What is clear is that he suffers in the cause of good. Regardless of who it was the original author intended, there is no doubting the fact, as is evident from today's reading that early Christians saw the text realized in a remarkable way in Jesus of Nazareth.

The Ethiopian evidently found Philip's explanation of the text convincing. Upon reaching a location where water was present, the servant asks for baptism, following which Philip's duties are ended and he is seen no more. In the church in our time, catechesis precedes baptism. In the earliest days of the church, the opposite was the case. After professing faith in Christ's salvific death and resurrection, the candidate was baptized, with the fuller teaching on Christ coming only later.

This narrative is illustrative of the message of today's Gospel. It is the Father who draws the believer as the first instructor in the faith. And it is this faith, centered in the person of God's Son Jesus, that brings eternal life. Christ is the true bread from heaven, which, unlike the manna in the desert, is imperishable.

Why is it that we have such confidence in our belief?

It is because we have it on the word of God himself, a fact that is hard to explain to an unbeliever. Belief is not of our own doing; it is God who draws us to himself. A celebrated author once said that she abandoned her faith because she could not accept the teaching on the Eucharist. To see it as a sign was fine but not as the reality of Christ's body and blood. We admit the mystery, but with the apostles we have nowhere to go, for Christ has the words of eternal life.

Faith is not easily upheld; sometimes it is very costly. Martyrs have gone to their deaths in its defense. But most of all it bears us up as we travel the bumpy road of life.

Points to Ponder

The central truths of our faith
Identifying Jesus as the Servant of the Lord
Faith and eternal life
The true bread from heaven

FRIDAY OF THE THIRD WEEK OF EASTER

Acts of the Apostles 9:1–20
Psalm 117:1bc, 2
John 6:52–59

Today's readings contain the account of Paul's conversion and the eucharistic discourse at the end of John 6. The conversion of Paul was sudden and unexpected. It is retold three times in the Acts of the Apostles. The point of our reflection today centers on the way that Christ identifies himself to the man who was "breathing threats and murder against the disciples of the Lord." Christ says that he is the one Paul is persecuting. This is the doctrine of the body of Christ that Paul will develop at considerable length in his writings. The relationship between Christ and the believer is so intimate that the two can be used interchangeably. Here in its initial appearance it is an allusion in Paul's conversion encounter.

The end of John's bread of life discourse takes a different turn. Heretofore, the bread referred to the person of Christ in himself and in his teaching. At this point, Jesus speaks of eating his flesh and drinking his blood as a source of mutual indwelling. It is this reference to the Eucharist that precipitates a split among his followers. Some will leave and no longer walk in his company.

The two mysteries of the body of Christ and the Eucharist complement one another. What the Eucharist accomplishes is an intensification of our life in Christ: "Those who eat my flesh and drink my blood abide in me and I in them."

We cannot remain indifferent to the great gift of the Eucharist, a mystery about which Paul also writes at some length. The conversion of Paul highlights the incredible transformation that occurred in his life. Initially blinded by this heavenly intervention, he regains his sight only at his later meeting with Ananias.

Where blind spots may exist in our own life, we pray today for the grace of sight.

Points to Ponder

> The body of Christ
> The Eucharist in our life
> The real presence of Christ in the Eucharist
> God in bread and wine: the great humility of God

SATURDAY OF THE THIRD WEEK OF EASTER

Acts of the Apostles 9: 31–42
Psalm 116:12–13, 14–15, 16–17
John 6:60–69

Faith is the "conviction of things not seen." These words from Hebrews 11 point to things not seen—that is, things that are not the object of direct and immediate knowledge. Faith is the only evidence of such things. Thus Jesus is credible on the attestation of God himself.

At the end of Jesus' eucharistic discourse in John, some of his disciples were so nonplussed that they could not accept his word. To eat the body of Christ could only be seen as cannibalism and, therefore, beyond human acceptance. Hence, there were some among his followers who walked with him no longer. When Jesus asks the Twelve what they choose to do, they can only breathe a sigh of relief at the response of Peter: "Lord, to whom can we go? You have the words of eternal life."

We should not be surprised if at times we are troubled by doubts. We walk by faith and not by sight. We continue on solely because it is Christ who gives meaning to our lives. His is a teaching that is consistent and coherent, but not always easy to accept and to obey. We stay on course because he is the way, the truth, and the life. Even in our moments of doubt, we realize that his is a message of eternal life. To walk in another direction is inconceivable. We accept the Eucharist as a mystery of faith. Based on God's own word, we have total assurance, to pray:

Lord, "I believe; help my unbelief" (Mark 9:24).

Points to Ponder

Faith as evidence of the unseen
The Eucharist and the real presence
Understanding moments of doubt

MONDAY OF THE FOURTH WEEK OF EASTER

Acts of the Apostles 11:1–18
Psalm 42:2–3; 43:3, 4
John 10:1–10

In the tenth chapter of John's Gospel, read in part on Good Shepherd Sunday, two distinct images appear. One depicts Christ as the Good Shepherd; the second speaks of him as the sheep gate. It is the latter that appears in today's Gospel. To enter the sheepfold through Christ is the sole recognized way of access; to enter through others ways is the route of deceivers and robbers. The authentic leaders of the faithful remain faithful to the voice of Christ.

The image certainly underscores the importance of orthodoxy and authenticity of teaching. But it also points to a willingness to accept change.

The first major issue that early Christianity had to face was the decision to accept Gentile converts, a question that arises in today's reading from Acts of the Apostles. One of the major obstacles to religious homogeneity centered on the question of the Jewish food laws. A considerable part of the Jewish legal code distinguished between clean and unclean foods. Therefore table fellowship with unbelievers was excluded. In today's reading, at the direction of the Lord himself, all foods were declared clean. The full acceptance of the Gentiles is authenticated with the giving of the Holy Spirit, in a scene often referred to as the Gentile Pentecost.

It was moments such as this that made Christianity a universal religion. Otherwise it would have withered on the vine or remained a sect, albeit a fringe one, of Judaism.

Both in early Christianity as well as in later centuries, there were moments of great change. Change is an integral part of growth and development. It should not cause us dismay. As long as we enter through the sheep gate, we need have no fear.

Points to Ponder

Christ: Shepherd and sheep gate.
Jew and Gentile, co-equal in the church
Adjusting to change

TUESDAY OF THE FOURTH WEEK OF EASTER

Acts of the Apostles 11:19–26
Psalm 87:1b–3, 4–5, 6–7
John 10:22–30

With the growing number of Gentile converts entering the church, the break with traditional Judaism became more pronounced. Gradually the center of the church's life shifted from Jerusalem to Antioch. It was there that the so-called followers of the Way first became known as Christians.

This is a title that all of us carry with pride, but it is worth our effort to explore briefly its connotation. It was only when Christianity became fragmented that we adopted denominational names. *Catholic* may be fine, but it says far less than *Christian*. In our baptism we are united with Christ; our religious education centers on his teaching. Every milestone in our life—graduation, marriage, ordination—is laden with Christian meaning. It is in Christ that our final destiny is assured.

The opponents of Jesus in today's Gospel want him to state clearly whether or not he is the Messiah. There were reasons why Jesus did not so proclaim himself, one of which was the heavy political baggage that the term had acquired. Once again Jesus appeals to his works, which give clear indication of his position. But only faith will bring about acceptance. His disciples adhere to him as the Good Shepherd, with a faith that gives full assurance.

The title "Christian" is the noblest that we shall ever bear. It is not of our making or choice. It is part of the gift that God gives us. One of my relatives named a son "Christian" but always insisted that his name not be abbreviated to Chris or any other shortened form. Christian is a man today and still carries the name with pride. The same should be said of all of us.

Points to Ponder

Antioch, an early Christian center
The title "Christian"
The separation from Judaism
Hearing the voice of the shepherd

WEDNESDAY OF THE FOURTH WEEK OF EASTER

Acts of the Apostles 12:24–13:5a
Psalm 67:2–3, 5, 6 and 8
John 12:44–50

Transmitting the message. In today's Gospel, Jesus affirms that to accept him is to accept the Father who sent him. In seeing Christ as the visible expression of God himself, faith in Christ embraces the message that God has sent into the world. Jesus comes as savior, not as one who condemns. Condemnation is self-inflicted when God's word is rejected.

The message is then communicated within the Christian community through a legitimate mandate. When, in Acts of the

Apostles, Barnabas and Saul become bearers of the message, the sending community in Antioch imposes hands on them and sends them off. In the Christian tradition, the imposition of hands in the ordination rite authenticates the ordinands as legitimate carriers of the message. As Saul and Barnabas set off on their mission, they are one in spirit and teaching with the Antioch community.

We too are part of that Christian tradition, recipients of a patrimony two thousand years old. We want to recall gratefully those who have gifted us with the faith: parents, teachers, members of the clergy. The transmission of the faith has endured difficult moments. The way was not always smooth and welcoming.

Now, by the same token, the task is laid on our shoulders. We are to convey the message to others—first of all, as parents. The home is the first and primary school of Christian values. We may, in addition, be catechists or teachers in religious education. It is a serious and indispensable task. If our children are to become faith-filled adults, the great part of that responsibility rests with us. How often today we meet young adults with little or no appreciation of their faith. It is an inestimable loss.

Jesus was the first bearer of the message; the apostles were the second. We now play our own part in that great tradition.

Points to Ponder

> Jesus, the image of the Father
> The imposition of hands
> Our duty to transmit the faith

THURSDAY OF THE FOURTH WEEK OF EASTER

> Acts of the Apostles 13:13–25
> Psalm 89:2–3, 21–22, 25 and 27
> John 13:16–20

Rising to speak in the synagogue of Antioch in Pisidia, Paul summarizes the favor God has shown the Israelites through the ages. The culmination, of course, is God's gift of Jesus, who comes as his people's Savior. In John's Last Supper narrative, Jesus performs the great act of humility in washing his disciples' feet. They are told that, in turn, they should do the same for one another. Jesus goes on to say that anyone in the future who receives one of his disciples receives him, as well as the One who sent him. Drawn by the Holy Spirit, the one who receives a disciple in humble charity is then enveloped in the Trinity itself.

Yet a somber note is struck in this idyllic, grace-filled picture. There is one seated at the table who is about to become the betrayer. Jesus alludes to him in a free adaptation of Psalm 41:10: "The one who ate my bread has lifted his heel against me." Meal sharing was a sacred act, a convivial expression of desired well-being and blessing. For an enemy or a deceiver to share a meal was a grievous act of dishonesty. The allusion, of course, is to Judas, who is about to turn Jesus over to the authorities.

Is this not a situation that comes to us in life in ways seldom foreseen? To be betrayed or discarded by a friend is a cruel blow. It is felt deeply when inflicted by one whom we esteemed and cherished. And how should we deal with this? If we are the recipient of an offense, we gain nothing by allowing the wound to fester. If, on the other hand, we cause an injury, we want to ask forgiveness, in the words of scripture, before offering our gift at the altar. Forgiveness is fundamental to New Testament teaching.

But the words "I forgive" or "You are forgiven" do not fall easily from our lips, because it is very difficult to utter them insincerely.

Points to Ponder

> The humility of Christ in the foot washing
> The reception of a disciple of Christ
> The evil of character assassination
> The act of forgiveness

FRIDAY OF THE FOURTH WEEK OF EASTER

Acts of the Apostles 13:26–33
Psalm 2:6–7, 8–9, 10–11ab
John 14:1–6

In today's reading from Acts of the Apostles, Jesus becomes Son of God with his resurrection. But was he the Son of God before that? The answer is "yes" if we are speaking solely in terms of his being. But the true Christ as a life-giving son, constituted in power, comes only with his resurrection, as Paul himself teaches (Rom 1:1–4). And regardless of how he may have been seen previously, he is now confirmed as Son of God, as the agent of effective sanctification.

In one of John's most celebrated passages, Jesus today speaks of the dwelling places that have been prepared for us in the life to come.

Jesus himself is the access to our heavenly dwelling. In a full acceptance of Christ—his person and his teaching—we have accepted the way. No one can approach the Father except through him. In the truth as well, he stands as the living expression of God's fidelity to his promises. In the life, we share the Holy Spirit that unites him and the Father.

Tolle et legge! "Take up and read!" St. Jerome said that to be ignorant of the scriptures is to be ignorant of Christ. There are many spiritual treatises that shed light on our calling. Roman documents serve as guideposts on our way. But none of these is a substitute for the scriptures.

To take one Gospel and read prayerfully one chapter each day would take us less than a month. To respond to the Gospels in faith leads ultimately to that heavenly dwelling that has been prepared for us.

Points to Ponder

Jesus as son of God
The heavenly home prepared for us

Jesus, way, truth, and life
Loving the scriptures

SATURDAY OF THE FOURTH WEEK OF EASTER

Acts of the Apostles 13:44–52
Psalm 98:1, 2–3ab, 3cd–4
John 14:7–14

Many people in the course of their lives echo the request of Philip: Show us the Father. Since God in himself is invisible and unseen, it is not unusual to hear the query, "What is God like?" The truth of the matter is that for the Christian the question has already been answered. God is like Jesus. To know the person and teaching of Jesus is to know God.

There are countless illustrations in the scriptures where this becomes evident. What, for example, is the lesson to be drawn from the parable of the prodigal son (Luke 15)? God's forgiveness is boundless. Whom does God resemble? The forgiving father. Or if we want to know where God's concern lies in a particular way, we read the account of the final judgment (Matt 25). There we can see God's love for the poor and underprivileged. Or for the suffering, as in the story of the Good Samaritan.

As we look at today's reading from Acts of the Apostles, we see Paul and Barnabas rejected by their own people. Disappointment and persecution have become part of their ministry. But in looking upon Christ, they see the suffering that was part of his life. Yet God stood by the side of Christ, saw him through his mission, and ultimately brought him to victory. All of this is showing us the Father.

When Christians act in a Christlike manner, they too bring us the Father in different ways. The friend by our side in time of distress. The person who stays by our bedside in time of illness. The one who forgives and does not condemn when we make a serious mistake.

In the scriptures as well as in our personal experience, there are countless ways in which we are being shown the Father.

Points to Ponder

The Father in Jesus
Examples of Jesus' revelation of the Father
God's presence in our daily life

MONDAY OF THE FIFTH WEEK OF EASTER

Acts of the Apostles 14:5–18
Psalm 115:1–2, 3–4, 15–16
John 14:21–26

"Not to us, O LORD...but to your name give the glory." These words from Psalm 115, found in today's responsorial, express well the sentiments of Paul during his ministry. It is seen in the attempt of the citizens of Lystra to deify him and Barnabas after the cure of the lame man. The apostles emphasize that it was the true God who had effected the cure, albeit through human instruments.

Paul instinctively drew back from any form of hero worship. The community at Corinth was drawn into camps that championed Peter, Apollos, or Paul. Paul states clearly that he wants no part of it. He asks, "Was Paul crucified for you? Or were you baptized in the name of Paul?" (1 Cor 1:13).

Young people today look for role models, a pursuit that can have its positive features. The problem lies in the fact that so often in those heroes human weaknesses soon emerge. In church life, the same situation may obtain. A pastor who serves his people diligently and tirelessly is recognized as such. But it can happen that our vision is too centered on human qualities, while the purpose of all ministry is to keep us centered on the Lord. Our sense of admiration may never deflect from that singular vision.

It all too often happens that we may have a pastor for a number of years who is gifted with leadership and a caring spirit, only to be followed by a pastor who lacks those qualities. When all is said and done, it is the Lord whom we serve, and that remains true when times are good or bad.

Jesus in today's Gospel sums it up well. "Those who love me will be loved by my Father, and I will love them and reveal myself to them." That is the leader around whom we all place our fidelity.

Let us praise the name of Jesus Christ, now and forever!

Points to Ponder

Christ as the center of our lives
The place of human role models
A faith that goes beyond the human

TUESDAY OF THE FIFTH WEEK OF EASTER

Acts of the Apostles 14:19–28
Psalm 145:10–11, 12–13ab, 21
John 14:27–31a

Hope and peace emerge as significant themes in today's readings. Paul and Barnabas come to the end of their initial journey. There had been moments of joy, but adversity also had dogged them along the way. Today Paul is stoned by the Jews and left for dead. But restored to health, he is able to complete his journey.

It is in the midst of suffering that hope proves its mettle. It does not stand simply as a conviction that the ultimate goal will be reached. It means that in the midst of trial and severe human misgiving, there is the conviction that the future remains intact. We cannot separate hardship from the meaning of hope.

Hope has major importance in the church today. The storm clouds of dissension, polarization, and misconduct weigh heavy. In addition, we look at those parts of the world, traditionally strong in the faith, where in our time belief is severely threatened and the future uncertain. It is hope that convinces us that the final word will be God's.

Peace has been cynically described as a "period of preparation between two wars." In the biblical sense, however, peace is the restoration of primitive accord. Peace was lost when humanity rebelled against God. Pain and suffering became our common lot, as well as moral disorientation. There was a rupture in the relationship of God and the world. As Christ comes to his disciples in the upper room, he announces the reestablishment of peace between heaven and earth. In our new covenant in the Holy Spirit, our restoration is attained, not only with God but with our fellow human beings and the created world, which is also redeemed. He has made us one through the blood of the cross.

"War, war—never again" is not simply an ardent wish. It is a Christian mandate. Peace is held in contempt in a world of strife and conflict. The Gospel states today that the evil prince of this world may make temporary gains, but only the Father who lives in Jesus, our hope and our peace, will triumph.

Points to Ponder

> Hope rooted in the promise of Christ
> Hope the virtue of difficult times
> Peace, a story of reintegration
> Blessed are the peacemakers

WEDNESDAY OF THE FIFTH WEEK OF EASTER

> Acts of the Apostles 15:1–6
> Psalm 122:1–2, 3–4ab, 4cd–5
> John 15:1–8

Paul respected Jewish tradition as part of his own heritage. Nonetheless, his Christian belief saw no place for circumcision as necessary for salvation. Such a position would fly in the face of the all-sufficient saving work of Christ. When Jewish Christians came to Antioch from Judea, urging circumcision, Paul saw at once the moral conflict that their demand made. It was then decided to bring the matter to the attention of the Jerusalem authorities in order to seek a definitive solution.

Paul's perspective is characterized by collegiality. Where opinions conflict, the effort must be expended to arrive at a consensual solution. Paul has no intention of being a "lone ranger" in the matter. He wants to hear the voice of the church and so makes his way to Jerusalem as the emissary of a developing church.

There is only one avenue of salvation: adherence to Christ. Just as the branch only lives when united with the vine, so too the Christian must be one with Christ. There is no independent way of bearing fruit. Christ stands as our life and our greatest benefactor.

The door to life is opened in baptism, not circumcision. In being called to do good, it is Christ who enables us. In walking away from sin and remaining on the path of virtue, it is because we are one with the vine. There are many devotions in the church; in their variety they satisfy many spiritual needs. But they are to be seen as ways to express gratitude for the gift that is ours, not as stepping stones to holiness.

The psalmist says it well today. We make our way to Jerusalem so we can give thanks to the Lord.

Points to Ponder

> Christ alone as the center of faith
> Living as a branch on the vine
> Salvation, the gift of a gracious God
> Governing through consensus

THURSDAY OF THE FIFTH WEEK OF EASTER

> Acts of the Apostles 15:7–21
> Psalm 96:1–2a, 2b–3, 10
> John 15:9–11

It would be difficult to overestimate the importance of what is recorded in Acts of the Apostles 15 and is read today. The burning question centered on the extent to which a Christian's new-found freedom would require submission to the Jewish law in accepting circumcision. The issue was discussed at what has been called "the Council of Jerusalem."

James was the head of the Jerusalem community where the adherents to Jewish tradition resided. Peter, Paul, and Barnabas were spokesmen for the position excluding circumcision as part of Christian practice. Peter makes an impassioned plea, arguing from his own experience. He had witnessed the Holy Spirit given to Gentiles without any restrictions. Barnabas and Paul follow up with the same argument. After what was probably a heated debate, a decision is reached and is enunciated by James. Gentile Christians were not held to the Jewish law, except in four areas that he presents.

This decision had profound effects. Up to this point, there was still a strong belief that the Jewish population would accept Christ and be baptized. However, that conclusion now became more remote. The legal tie with Judaism was now practically severed, as the church became increasingly Gentile in its makeup. However, it is worthy to note that the decision of the Council of Jerusalem pertained to Gentile Christians only; nothing was said about Jewish Christians in their approach to the law. It was only a question of time, however, until the Jerusalem decision came to characterize the whole church.

John's Gospel again today highlights the heart of the Christian call. Love unites Father and Son, and the Son and his followers. Love remains the first and greatest commandment. Such love produces a joy that is indeed complete.

Points to Ponder

> Freedom from the Jewish law
> The overriding law of love
> The early church and consensus

FRIDAY OF THE FIFTH WEEK OF EASTER

> Acts of the Apostles 15:22–31
> Psalm 57:8–9, 10 and 12
> John 15:12–17

When a church is named, it is often after a sainted person whose life places in relief one or more aspects of Christ's teaching.

Or it may be named for Christ himself under one of his many titles. Therefore, it is more than a little surprising that we do not meet a church named for "Jesus, our friend." In today's Gospel, Jesus clearly designates himself as our friend, the clear proof of which was his willingness to lay down his life for us.

One of the main thrusts of the Johannine teaching is to underscore Jesus' initiatives in our regard. We are chosen; we are friends. Our relationship now is one of friendship, not slavery; it is through his presence that we now bear fruit. And it was for our sake that he laid down his life.

Perhaps the absence of the title of Jesus as friend is due to the fact that friendship in modern parlance has lost much of its force. We use it today even of people who may be no more than acquaintances, whereas true friendship must be tested and proven. Christ is the greatest example of such true friendship.

When the Jerusalem assembly had completed its work, a delegation was commissioned to bring its decision to the broader church. Judas and Silas accompany Paul and Barnabas to bring the decision to Antioch.

The decision regarding freedom from the law was to have widespread consequences. It meant that Gentile Christians did not have to pass through the portals of Judaism in coming to Christ.

The way to Christ is a one-way route. It is not complicated even though it sets a high standard. It is a loving response to the One who calls us friends and walks with us on our journey.

Points to Ponder

> Jesus as friend
> What greater love than this?
> The chosen friend

SATURDAY OF THE FIFTH WEEK OF EASTER

Acts of the Apostles 16:1–10
Psalm 100:1b–2, 3, 5
John 15:18–21

After his conversion, Francis of Assisi entered upon the path of holiness with renewed strength. There was no indication initially that he planned to do this in the company of others. At a certain point, other men expressed their desire to share his vision. But this was God's doing, not his. In his Testament, Francis says, "The Lord gave me brothers."

Such a statement could be written off as medieval piety. Or it could arise from a deep spiritual conviction. In today's reading from Acts of the Apostles, Paul's zeal for evangelization led him to places he had not previously visited. The Spirit of Jesus led him and even determined his route.

Timothy was part of Paul's missionary group. Paul, no champion of mandatory circumcision, had Timothy circumcised; he was the son of a Jewish mother and a Greek father. Although a man of strong conviction, Paul was not inflexible, but he was capable of necessary accommodation in the interest of a greater good.

Today's Gospel reminds us that we have been chosen out of this world and it now has no claims on us. If the disciples belonged to this world, they would be embraced by it. But if their vision and aspirations belong to a higher realm, their stay here will be marked by discomfort. In many ways, our life here is countercultural. At the same time we recognize the God-given good that is present in the world. But we and the world will always have our differences. Without enmity or hatred, we still walk a different path. The road may not always be clear, but, with the Lord's help, it is his will that will take the lead.

Points to Ponder

The Lord, our shepherd and guide
Making necessary accommodations
The rejection of conflicting values

MONDAY OF THE SIXTH WEEK OF EASTER

Acts of the Apostles 16:11–15
Psalm 149:1b–2, 3–4, 5–6a and 9b
John 15:26–16:4a

As we move liturgically from the Easter season toward Pentecost, our scriptures begin to speak of the Holy Spirit, today defined as the Spirit of Truth, elsewhere as the Paraclete. The function of the Spirit today is to bear witness to Jesus, a witness that is to be coordinated with that of the disciples themselves.

The Spirit is presented as occurring during a time of trial or persecution. The days will come (and by the time John is written, have already arrived), when the disciples find themselves alienated from their Jewish co-religionists and subjected to persecution and even death. They are told that through it all their faith will remain intact. Their enemies will even see the maltreatment of the disciples as a service to God. But they are to remain strong. Their hearts will be fortified by the spirit of truth. They cannot forget that their opponents accepted neither Christ nor his Father. They can expect no better treatment.

The rhythm of life has its positives and negatives. While the Gospel today speaks of persecution, the story in Acts of the Apostles is one of peace and serenity. Here begin the "we" passages in Acts, where the author Luke seems to include himself. One sometimes sees Lydia depicted in religious art as a woman dressed in purple, engaging Paul in conversation. She stands among the women of Philippi who listened to Paul's preaching. The heart of this God-fearing woman was opened, and she and her household received baptism. She then provided lodging for the itinerant Paul.

Our own experience gives us the evidence of faith-filled lives. Some people, even when they wander, manifest a deep appreciation of the faith that is theirs. Other people, under different circumstances, make a mockery of religious belief and are detractors from the truth. Sometimes we are consoled by our faith; at other times, we suffer for it. But it is the Spirit who gives us the strength to live in accord with what we believe.

Points to Ponder

Dealing with religious animosity
Indifference toward the faith
The love of faith
The courage of conviction

TUESDAY OF THE SIXTH WEEK OF EASTER

Acts of the Apostles 16:22–34
Psalm 138:1–2ab, 2cde–3, 7c–8
John 16:5–11

Our Gospel today makes it clear that only with the departure of Jesus will the Paraclete come to guide and direct the nascent community. Here, in fact, it is Christ himself who will send the Spirit. With his coming, the Spirit will perform three important functions in the public forum. The world had taken a position on Jesus and will be proved wrong in the time to come.

The three areas of the world's error are sin, justice, and condemnation. The sin consisted in their not believing in Jesus and thus rejecting God's plan. The world had also judged wrongly in thinking that by condemning Jesus to death his cause had been vanquished. Finally the world was wrong about condemnation. The true condemnation was not sentencing Jesus but in banishing Satan, the prince of this world. In three distinct ways, the correctness of Jesus' cause is made evident and the world is proven wrong.

Today's reading from Acts of the Apostles is an illustration of Christ's truth. In the liberation of Paul and Silas from their prison cells, due to the shattering effects of an earthquake, the conscience of their jailer is awakened. The frightening episode is crowned with the joy of the jailer's conversion. The world once again is convicted of sin, judgment, and condemnation.

The season of Pentecost, soon to begin, reminds us of the victory that Christ has attained for us. The sin of disbelief is overcome; the wrong judgment about Jesus vanishes in the light of his victory, and the power of evil, while still seeking its own, has been subdued. How true the words of the psalmist today: "Your stead-fast love O LORD endures forever."

Points to Ponder

> Sin in the failure to accept Jesus
> God's justice in Jesus' victory
> The condemnation of evil
> The victory of the Paraclete

WEDNESDAY OF THE SIXTH WEEK OF EASTER

Acts of the Apostles 17:15, 22–18:1
Psalm 148:1–2, 11–12, 13, 14
John 16:12–15

If we surmise correctly, Paul put a good deal of thought into his first presentation of the faith in the Areopagus at Athens. It differs considerably from the customary Pauline apologetic, and we can only regret that it did not meet with a great measure of success, as the author of Acts of the Apostles admits. While visiting the shrines to the various Greek deities, Paul comes upon one dedicated to a God Unknown. He seizes the moment and makes an impassioned plea for the God of Israel and the Christ. He assures his hearers that this is the true God, the one in whom "we live and move and have our being."

The turning point in Paul's apologetic presentation occurs when he mentions Christ's resurrection from the dead. This was an idea that was repulsive to a sophisticated Greek audience. He is met by sneers and an unwillingness to hear more at that time. Only a few converts were made.

Worthy of note is the fact that Paul's presentation centered almost wholly on the God of the Old Testament. There is only a single reference to Christ, not as Son of God or Messiah but simply as the man raised from the dead and appointed judge of the world. Paul's words were carefully selected to appeal to the

Hellenists, with none of the usual apologetic surrounding Christ's life and mission.

The Gospel today reminds us that the Spirit was to bring enlightenment after Christ's departure. There are many ways in which the Spirit has enlightened the church since the dawn of Christianity. The mystery of the incarnation and redemption has unfolded for us through the teaching of countless fathers and doctors of the church. The theological enterprise has been the source of untold good.

Paul selected the way in which he felt the faith could best be presented. It was not a great success. We have the opportunity to draw on the wisdom of the ages. Sometimes our efforts are blessed with remarkable success; other times not. Some occasions call for new approaches; others, for those which are more traditional. In any case it is always the one risen Christ who remains at the center of our efforts.

Points to Ponder

> Christ as the wisdom of God
> We are God's offspring
> The resurrection of Christ: a core belief
> Dealing with success and failure

THURSDAY OF THE SIXTH WEEK OF EASTER

> Acts of the Apostles 18:1–8
> Psalm 98:1, 2–3ab, 3cd–4
> John 16:16–20

The words of Jesus today foretell a period of grief for the disciples to be followed by one of joy. Commentators discuss at length the meaning of these two periods of time. The time of grief refers to the time of Christ's passion and death when he was removed from their presence. The world rejoiced in being rid of Christ's presence, but for the disciples it was a time of sadness.

But when do the disciples see him again? This would seem to go beyond the few post-Easter appearances and point rather to the giving of the Spirit after the resurrection. This was the clearest evidence that his triumph over sin and death was complete. The former sense of loss gave way to an overriding joy of new life.

This mixture of sadness and joy characterized Paul's stay in Corinth. In preaching first to the Jews, as was his custom, Paul experienced hostility and opposition. He asserts his willingness to turn to the Gentiles. Working out of the house of one Titus Justus, Paul gains access to willing listeners. The Corinthian community, which will play such a dominant role in Paul's ministry, begins to grow and flourish.

Our faith tells us that we live in the era wherein Christ is alive and experienced. Our sorrow has indeed been turned into joy. Through the sacraments, God's word, and the Christian community, we live in the end-time. Faith will one day give place to vision, but in the meantime we are not left orphans. We now live in the risen Lord. This reality should carry us through our days of sorrow and frustration. Our grief has truly been turned into joy.

Points to Ponder

> The joy of the Spirit
> To see Christ again
> Sorrow and joy in the life of Paul

FRIDAY OF THE SIXTH WEEK OF EASTER

Acts of the Apostles 18:9–18
Psalm 47:2–3, 4–5, 6–7
John 16:20–23

The church in Corinth was one in which Paul took no small amount of pride, and this, even when taking into consideration the problems present there, is amply seen in the two letters he wrote to this community. In today's reading, Paul is again beset by his Jewish listeners who bring him before the civil authority, Gallio, who refuses to hear the case being brought against the apostle, seeing it as a purely religious matter.

What is impressive is the equilibrium that Paul maintains in the face of repeated opposition. It is the calm of a man of faith who knows well where the truth lies.

In his Last Supper discourse, Jesus today tells the disciples that their future too will be marked by grief and mourning. But it will not last. Their ultimate joy is compared to that of a woman whose pain in giving birth is converted into happiness at the birth of the child. Certainly the time of Jesus' suffering and death was a period of disappointment and grief. But his emergence from the tomb marks the dawn of a new era, an era of grace and the Holy Spirit, in which "no one will take your joy from you." This is the era in which we now live.

The longer we live, the more aware we are that pain and suffering are a prominent part of many people's lives. We marvel at the fact that just when things seem to be on an even keel, sadness strikes in some unforeseen way. It is at moments like that that we must be convinced that our Spirit life enables us to cope. In faith we shall persevere and our joy will not be taken from us. As the psalmist says today:

"Sing praises to God, sing praise;
sing praises to our king, sing praises."

Points to Ponder

Paul's perseverance
Dealing with present sorrow
Our joy: life in the Spirit

SATURDAY OF THE SIXTH WEEK OF EASTER

Acts of the Apostles 18:23–28
Psalm 47:2–3, 8–9, 10
John 16:23b–28

Can you imagine being a Christian without being baptized? Well, it happened in the case of Apollos, and other disciples in the early church as well (Acts 19:1–7). This incomplete incorporation may be an oblique indication of the respect accorded the life and ministry of John the Baptist, a fact also noted by the Jewish historian Josephus. In the case of Apollos and the other disciples mentioned in Acts of the Apostles, the absence of baptism is quickly remedied and full incorporation granted.

In our day baptism is held to be important, but its true meaning is often laid aside. It very often has social significance and little more. Yet this sacrament's importance is strongly underscored in the scriptures. Its reception calls for commitment on the part of the baptized or, in the case of an infant, the parents. Baptism is the key to eternity and the door to the church's spiritual riches. We wonder how it could have been by passed, as in the case of Apollos. At the same time, we should be equally distraught by its casual acceptance today.

Our prayers at Mass are directed to God the Father through or in the name of Jesus, his Son. And this is the way we are told to offer prayer in today's Gospel. Jesus insists on his intermediary role. To offer prayer in Jesus' name is to accord him his rightful place in the order of faith. No one else is ever given such an exalted position. But with the recognition of Jesus as Lord, and, as in John's Gospel, to be called God, he is placed on equal footing in nature with the Father himself. The person praying already loves the Son and for that fact is already loved by the Father.

As both a grace and commitment, baptism links us with Christ. We can now address the Father as "Abba," as Jesus did, and pray in the name of Jesus, our brother.

Points to Ponder

The importance of baptism
The esteem for John's baptism
Praying to God in Jesus' name

MONDAY OF THE SEVENTH WEEK OF EASTER

Acts of the Apostles 19:1–8
Psalm 68:2–3ab, 4–5acd, 6–7ab
John 16:29–33

Today's reading from Acts of the Apostles offers us another example of delayed catechesis. It is hard to believe that the company of twelve at Ephesus became Christian believers without knowing either of the Holy Spirit or the necessity of Christian baptism. The baptism of John, certainly widely respected, was evidently seen by some as sufficient. After learning of this erroneous idea, Paul sees to their baptism in the name of the Lord Jesus and the Holy Spirit becomes part of their lives.

There may be more to this issue than meets the eye. It may well have been that there were disciples who saw John's mission as "parallel" to Jesus' mission, with a certain level of equality between the two. This may go some way in explaining something else. The Gospels are at pains to honor John but also to emphasize his inferior status to that of Jesus. Behind all of this may well have been champions of John who were overstating his case.

In the Gospel today, Jesus tells his disciples that they will too be scattered and be left to endure his passion alone. But suffering will be their lot as well. Yet confidence and trust remain the order of the day. The world is set against Jesus and his followers. But fear not! He has overcome the world.

An incomplete understanding of the truth of our faith is a serious concern today. Many of those people today whose faith is firm and education complete learned their religion at an early age. Today the majority of our children are not in Catholic schools. Their religious instruction is limited to one hour a week, in after-school hours. It is often geared solely to their reception of the sacraments. It is seldom a high priority. Parents and Catholic educators have to see this as a major responsibility.

The education and formation of the young is a matter of major importance. It is essential to the transmission of the faith and must be a high priority for parents and for all those who seek to positively shape the minds and souls of children.

Points to Ponder

Belief in Jesus without a Spirit baptism
Our problems today in religious education
Belief in Jesus' triumph over the world

TUESDAY OF THE SEVENTH WEEK OF EASTER

Acts of the Apostles 20:17–27
Psalm 68:10–11, 20–21
John 17:1–11a

What is necessary to obtain eternal life? The question is answered in today's Gospel reading from John. The first requisite is to know the true God. This can only be done in accepting the God revealed through Jesus and to accept him in faith. The second requisite is to accept Christ as God's son, as the one who has come into the world, not simply as a spiritual presence but as one who has come in the flesh.

The glory of God plays a central role in Jesus' life and work. In accomplishing the task the Father has given him, Jesus gives glory to the Father. The Father, in turn, acknowledges the Son and with his death and resurrection restores the glory that he had before the creation of the world. The Father, then, is the primary agent of glory. In their accepting Christ and his teaching, God's glory is now present in the disciples as well. In this acceptance of the work of Jesus, the cycle of glory is complete. Jesus is glorified by both the Father and the believer. The Father is glorified by the Son and the believers. Christ is further glorified in the believing disciples, whose lives give evident testimony to God's presence in the world.

In today's reading from Acts of the Apostles, we have the beginning of Paul's celebrated farewell to the elders of Miletus. He reminds his hearers of the work that has been done. He preached Christ humbly but courageously to both Jew and Gentile. His message was a call to repentance and faith in Jesus as Lord. Now he is about to return to Jerusalem certain only that hardship and trials are before him. He has no sense of shame; he has preached consistently and honestly the full message of Jesus, issuing a call to repentance.

We may never be ashamed of Christ, much less dilute his message to make it more acceptable. Paul did not preach some esoteric mystery cult, but always the full message of Christ. His hearers will never see him again. He takes his leave with the conviction that God's design has been proclaimed fully and faithfully.

Points to Ponder

> Speaking the full truth of Jesus
> The glory of God in Father, Son, and believer
> The Holy Spirit as the source of glory

WEDNESDAY OF THE SEVENTH WEEK OF EASTER

Acts of the Apostles 20:28–38
Psalm 68:29–30, 33–35a, 35bc–36ab
John 17:11b–19

The responsibilities of those entrusted with pastoral care are front and center in today's readings. It is worth the effort to review them briefly.

The exhortation of Paul to the elders of Ephesus emphasizes vigilance. Any notion of indifference with reference to the needs of the flock is excluded. The leaders must be constantly alert. Such was a main characteristic of Jesus himself in the Johannine Gospel. One of the reasons for vigilance is to maintain the unity of the community. An essential feature of the Godhead is the unity of persons; it is also to be characteristic of the church itself.

Another quality of leadership is generosity, a giving of self without reserve. Paul indicates that he always shunned being a burden to others. He worked and provided for his own needs and those of his companions. Providing for others held primacy of place, as he quotes from an otherwise unknown saying of Jesus: "It is more blessed to give than to receive."

True spiritual guidance must be rooted in a plea for heavenly assistance. Protection from evil is not solely a human endeavor; it requires assistance from God. The Christian leader must be a person of prayer.

Christianity is not an esoteric faith. It is to be brought to the world. Jesus in today's Gospel sees mission as another aspect of responsibility. Just as Jesus was sent into the world, so too are his followers. While never surrendering to worldly values, the message of Christ is destined for the marketplace. In a special way, our daily lives are to reflect our heavenly values.

We have all known Christian leaders who were men and women of vigilance, generous service, prayerful and dedicated to unity. In the last quality we often lose sight of the scandal of a divided Christianity. We may accommodate ourselves to Christian sectarianism, but we remain certain that such is not the mind of Christ. Ecumenism must remain one of our primary concerns.

As we give ourselves generously to the Christian task, let us not forget to pray for those called to leadership in the faith.

Points to Ponder

> Maintaining vigilance in our faith life
> Giving of ourselves generously
> The work for Christian unity
> Our personal sense of mission

THURSDAY OF THE SEVENTH WEEK OF EASTER

Acts of the Apostles 22:30; 23:6–11
Psalm 16:1–2a and 5, 7–8, 9–10, 11
John 17:20–26

The Catholic Church became an active participant in the ecumenical movement only after Vatican II. In an earlier era, it was felt that the church could not be involved in a search for unity, because it already possessed that unity. The only solution for the problem of disunity was for other Christians to convert to Catholicism. Today there has been a dramatic shift in the position. All Christians feel the pain of disunity, which has held sway for centuries. Every Christian body has in some way contributed to division and separation. It will require a united effort for our differences to be resolved.

Today's Gospel centers on Christ's strong appeal for unity. Just as the Father and Son are united in an inseparable unity, Jesus prays that the same may be true of his followers. In fact, unity is a sign to the world of the Spirit's presence in the Christian community, an apologetic sign of God's presence in the world.

Love is the integrating force. It was love that prompted God's intervention in the world in the mission of Jesus. A bond of love came into being in the Christian community in appreciation of what God had done in Jesus. Unity is an important sign to the world of what God has accomplished, an apologetic sign of God's work in the lives of his disciples.

It is the integrating force of love that unites Christians as well. It is to remain as a permanent sign to the world of Christ's continued presence, as well as a sign of the Father's love for his Son and his disciples.

Christian unity remains an unfinished task. Steps in recent years toward healing division and overcoming separation have been welcomed in many quarters. The work for unity exists on two levels. One is theological or doctrinal. Theologians of various denominations meet periodically to seek ways to reach agreement on thorny doctrinal issues. The second level is the grass-roots response wherein people of different denominations undertake common initiatives, join in common prayer, and bury outdated stereotypes that only engender division. The latter is an ecumenism in which we can all participate.

Points to Ponder

> Ecumenism in our daily life
> Joint moments of prayer
> The pain of a divided Christianity

FRIDAY OF THE SEVENTH WEEK OF EASTER

> Acts of the Apostles 25:13b–21
> Psalm 103:1–2, 11–12, 19–20ab
> John 21:15–19

The lives of both Paul and Peter now move toward their respective conclusions. Paul, as a Roman citizen, wants his case to be heard by Roman authorities and not by the Jews, who wanted to confront him on religious grounds. Peter, after his threefold profession of love, is told that his death will take place at the hands of oppressors. Then he is simply told by Jesus, "Follow me." In death as in life, the lot of the disciple is configured to that of the Master.

The manner in which Peter is singled out for special responsibility in the church is different in John. In Matthew, authority is conferred through the image of the keys and the power to bind and loose. Here the risen Lord addresses Peter to ascertain whether the apostle who three times denied him is now prepared to assume pastoral responsibility. He is first questioned as to whether or not his love surpasses that of the other disciples. Peter responds with an unqualified affirmation.

True love, as true sorrow for sin, finds expression in service to others. The desire to make amends moves away from the selfishness of the offense to the generosity of genuine concern. Have we not seen a parallel instance in which the sinful woman of the

Gospel expresses her repentance in anointing the feet of Jesus? Peter, as a leader among the Twelve, distinguishes himself in his willingness to spend himself in the pastoral care of the flock. "Feed my sheep."

Our gratitude for God's boundless forgiveness expresses itself in our desire to serve. The scriptural mandate to love will never fail to be present in the church. Let the world say about us what nonbelievers said about our ancestors in faith (according to Tertullian): "Behold these Christians, how they love one another!"

Points to Ponder

> Paul's appeal for Roman justice
> Peter's failure converted into love
> Love in community: the unmistakable sign of God's
> presence

SATURDAY OF THE SEVENTH WEEK OF EASTER

> Acts of the Apostles 28:16–20, 30–31
> Psalm 11:4, 5 and 7
> John 21:20–25

In the readings today we come to the end of the earliest Christian era. Paul, now under house arrest at Rome, is still sharing the good news of Jesus with members of the Jewish community. The disciple whom Jesus loved in the fourth Gospel is here identified as the author of the Gospel itself. Confusion had arisen as to the length of his life with some believing that he would not die before the return of Christ. But, as the narrative is at pains to explain, Jesus had not said that such would be the case. This apologetic note would seem to point to the fact that the beloved disciple had already died.

With the end of the apostolic age, we realize that the essentials of this definitive entrance of God in history are now in place. And those essentials remain with us today. Their very antiquity is a source of inspiration. In establishing the canon of inspired books, the church has brought us into contact with the authentic beginnings of the Christian faith.

St. Jerome said, "To be ignorant of the Scriptures is to be ignorant of Christ." One of the main objectives of the liturgy, as well as of this book, is to encourage us to take up the Scriptures. It is an enterprise that will not disappoint; we are drawn into inexhaustible spiritual riches. The author of the fourth Gospel reminds us today that he has been selective in his composition. Many things about the life of Jesus are left unrecorded. But that which is written is to intensify faith in the person of Jesus, who came into the world to bring us new life.

The scriptures that we hear each day are meant to underscore in one way or another this basic fact.

Points to Ponder

Paul reaches Rome
The fourth Gospel and the beloved disciple
The Bible and our spiritual life

Ordinary Time
Weeks 9 to 34

MONDAY OF THE NINTH WEEK IN ORDINARY TIME

Year I

Tobit 1:3; 2:1a–8
Psalm 112:1b–2, 3b–4, 5–6
Mark 12:1–12

The parable of the vineyard finds its origins in Isaiah (5:1–7). There the vineyard is the house of Israel that the Lord (the master of the vineyard) had been at pains to prepare for a plentiful harvest of grapes.

But such was not to be, since the vineyard produces only wild grapes. The owner then strips down the vineyard and leaves it desolate. The house of Israel suffers for its disappointing yield.

In the Gospel parable the owner of the vineyard has entrusted it to tenant farmers. At harvest time he sent his servants for his share of the yield, and all are badly mistreated. Finally he sends his son, who is killed by the tenant farmers. The owner is left with no choice except to destroy the tenants. The allegorical features are clear enough. God's son has been rejected by his people and has died at their hands. The final denouement will come with the destruction of temple and country.

In our times we see violence as something abhorrent. Yet it retains its force in the telling of a story. When one considers Jesus' message as one of peace and respect, his treatment at the hands of the people whom he desired to save is tragic in every way.

The story of Tobit is another biblical example of an historical background in the service of faith. The story is set in the period of the Assyrian Empire in the eighth century but is actually written centuries later. It is an engaging story of profound respect for religious tradition. In learning of a violent death, Tobit orders his son Tobias to bring the man to his house and sees that he is buried later that day.

Unfortunately in a culture of hatred and war, the value of human life is often diminished. Violence and murder have become all too common in today's society. If every human life is sacred, its destruction is always a matter of grief. Every death brings grief to those who are left behind. Someone will mourn even the most despised. As we look upon the cross, we see the greatest act of love rejected. Of that we must be always mindful, as we strive to make God's love our own.

Points to Ponder

> Respect for the good name of the deceased
> Violence committed in God's name
> The value of a human life

Year II

> 2 Peter 1:2–7
> Psalm 91:1–2, 14–15b, 15c–16
> Mark 12:1–12

The Letter of Peter reminds us that divine power has made the life of authentic virtue a true possibility. With faith at its base, many virtues emerge in our lives. Knowledge, self-control, perseverance, concern for others are all effective because of God's power, with love as the crowning virtue.

The great tragedy of the vineyard parable is not only the rejection of Christ but the rejection of all that his gift of the Spirit life makes possible. The human being is intended to be the glory of God, fully alive. That means living the qualities that love of God will infuse in us. That is the meaning of the great Easter gift. To turn our backs on Christ is to walk away from all those qualities that make of life such a precious gift. As the reading from Peter today states, God has bestowed on us everything necessary for a life of genuine piety.

In turning our backs on the Son of the vineyard's Owner, we suffer an immense loss. Let us pray that we persevere in faith with courage and love.

Points to Ponder

Grace in a variety of virtues
Appreciating the goodness of God
The primacy of love

TUESDAY OF THE NINTH WEEK IN ORDINARY TIME

Year I

Tobit 2:9–14
Psalm 112:1–2, 7–8, 9
Mark 12:13–17

For the Jews to pay taxes to a foreign occupier could easily be seen as religious compromise. Since the Roman emperor was considered divine, the problem was compounded. Jesus' opponents in today's Gospel present him with a dilemma. To deny the tax to Caesar would be seen as an act of civil disobedience. To concede the paying of the tax could be seen as a serious concession to an illegitimate religious authority. Jesus responds clearly and without equivocation.

The coin bears the image of Caesar and therefore rightly belongs to him. It has nothing to do with the reign of God, Jesus' sole concern. Therefore, what belongs to Caesar should go to him. If the government provides us with certain temporalities, then the government should be compensated. In other words, "If you want roads and use them, then pay for them." But this has nothing to do with the reign of God. Material temporalities in life are necessary and are often provided by the state. Due compensation is logical.

There is no question here of God's authority being exercised in two realms, church and state. Jesus' answer is not an admission of two realms or a divided realm. As good citizens, we pay our taxes (sometimes reluctantly!) in recognition of our indebtedness to the state. But the state can never be a competitor for our spiritual allegiance. There is only one kingdom of God, and both civil government and individual are beholden to it.

Tobit's misfortune lay in his loss of sight and the false judgment of his wife. The goat was given to Anna out of a sense of gratitude. Tobit's insinuation that it may well have been stolen is entirely without merit. His wife wonders about his virtue and sense of good judgment. Do we not often jump to conclusions that are unfounded and sometimes quite hurtful? We pray for a sense of fair-mindedness and understanding in our daily dealings.

Points to Ponder

Tax paying and civic duty
The single reign of God
Justice and propriety in daily dealing

Year II

2 Peter 3:12–15a, 17–18
Psalm 90:2, 3–4, 10, 14 and 16
Mark 12:13–17

Peter's letter today exhorts us to grow in the "knowledge of our Lord and Savior Jesus Christ." But the knowledge spoken is not mainly that of the mind, it is an experiential knowledge that is spoken of, as is so often the case when it appears in the Bible. When Mary is told by the angel that she is to become a mother, she is perplexed because she does not know man. It is the knowledge of experience that is meant.

Each of us may pose the questions: How well do I know Jesus Christ? Do I understand grace as a personal extension of Christ in my life? When I hear the scriptures, does my heart grow warm within me, as in the case of the disciples on the road to Emmaus? Is the Eucharist a personal experience of Christ in my life?

Knowledge here is not a question of verbalizing; there is not much to say. An elderly woman who spent long periods of time each day in church, was absorbed in prayer. When asked what she said, she answered, "I don't say anything. I look upon him and he upon me. It is quite enough." It is the language of love.

In today's Gospel, Jesus' questioners are utterly amazed. But they remain closed to his invitation. Many people stand in amazement of Christ, admire him at a distance, but refuse the invitation to discipleship. "Give to God what is God's": our lives, our gifts, our needs, our misgivings. The knowledge of God leads to a surrender as well as to untold blessings.

Points to Ponder

> To know is to cherish
> The simplicity of prayer
> Giving to God what is his

WEDNESDAY OF THE NINTH WEEK IN ORDINARY TIME

Year I

> Tobit 3:1–11a, 16–17a
> Psalm 25:2–3, 4–5ab, 6 and 7bc, 8–9
> Mark 12:18–27

Life after death is a truth we can more easily affirm than describe. We speak of it in the language of the present, the only vehicle at our disposal. The marriage question, raised in today's Gospel, is a classic example.

According to Jewish law, if a man died without offspring, his brother was obliged to take his widow and raise children to his brother's name. This would have been the case with Sarah in today's reading from Tobit. Sarah becomes the reproach of her own maidservants. So distraught is she after the death of seven husbands that she asks God to take her life.

A question surrounding what is called the "levirate law" is presented to Jesus in today's Gospel. If a woman has been married to seven husbands, whose wife would she be at the time of the resurrection? It is interesting to note that the question is posed by Sadducees who do not believe in the resurrection. The question is purely hypothetical but reflects the type of casuistry employed by Israel's teachers. Jesus transposes the discussion to an entirely different key: In heaven marriage will no longer exist, and childbearing will cease as well. The afterlife is a completely new way of being.

We are all given to a certain amount of speculation about the afterlife, much of it based on our present experience. But the fact is that life beyond the grave is part of the mystery of God. It is part of God's plan, and we are destined to be part of it. But determining its particulars must be left for that final day.

Points to Ponder

The purpose of the levirate law
The essence of life in the hereafter
The danger of excessive speculation

Year II

2 Timothy 1:1–3, 6–12
Psalm 123:1b–2ab, 2cdef
Mark 12:18–27

The two letters to Timothy and the one to Titus, referred to as the "Pastoral Letters," are markedly different in content and style from Paul's other writings. If authored by Paul, they come from a period late in his ministry. If authored by another, they probably date from the early second century. They are of particular importance in pointing up the development of ministry within the early church.

If the Gospel today warns against too literal a transposition of this world's reality to that of the future, the epistle underscores some of the basic values relative to our future existence.

The Spirit that has been given to us enables us to bear hardships with strength. The difficulties of the present are as nothing compared to the glory that is being revealed in us. With no merit of our own, it is by God's favor that we are being saved. Death has lost its power; the path of life and immortality lie before us. This has been accomplished through Jesus Christ our Savior.

This great message of light and hope has been entrusted to the ministers of the church, of whom Paul is one. Paul preaches that message unashamedly, fully aware that the One in whom he believes will see him through to the end.

The casuistry of the Sadducees would have little meaning for Paul. They are raising questions of little consequence. Are we not also guilty of posing questions of little value? The unassailable fact is that we have an eternal destiny with a loving God. That belief is most important.

Points to Ponder

> The Spirit and suffering
> Talking about eternal life
> Ministers of a message of hope

THURSDAY OF THE NINTH WEEK IN ORDINARY TIME

Year I

> Tobit 6:10–11; 7:1bcde, 9–17; 8:4–9a
> Psalm 128:1–2, 3, 4–5
> Mark 12:28–34

Our readings today point up the meaning of a God-centered life. Tobias is given the hand of his relative, Sarah, in marriage. This after the tragic loss of the seven men to whom she had previously been married. But rather than shrink from the possible consequences of his marriage, Tobias resolves to place his case before the Lord with confidence.

On their wedding night, Tobias and Sarah leave their bed to pray earnestly before the Lord. Theirs is a hymn of praise to God for his goodness in creation and in providing for the married life. Tobias prays that his marriage to Sarah may last many years and be blessed abundantly. It is a selfless prayer, simple and unadorned, but reflective of a deep faith and confidence.

The scribe who approaches Jesus in the Gospel asks about the primary commandment. Jesus' answer is a summary of the entire life of faith. In drawing on the great *Shema* from Deuteronomy, Jesus places love of God as the first and primary commandment. To it he joins a relatively obscure verse from Leviticus that calls for a love of neighbor at least equal to the concern for self. The scribe applauds the teaching and sees it as superior to any form of sacrifice. Jesus recognizes the man's sincerity and his proximity to the reign of God.

A moment's reflection shows us that there is no norm of Christian conduct that does not fall within the ambit of this first and greatest commandment. The grateful love of God underlies any good that we do, and our love of neighbor finds a place for others, regardless of status or background. This commandment is indeed the sum and substance of the Christian life.

Points to Ponder

The dignity and sanctity of marriage
Placing God first in our life
Who is my neighbor?

Year II

2 Timothy 2:8–15
Psalm 25:4–5ab, 8–9, 10 and 14
Mark 12:28–34

The word of God is not chained, although its proponents often are. Paul today speaks of his suffering for the gospel and sees it as a definite gain. To be baptized is to die with Christ only to be brought to new life in the Spirit. To persevere with him is to reign with him eternally. To deny Christ brings about a voluntary alienation, but, even though we should be unfaithful, he remains ever faithful.

The epistle urges us to put worthless discussion behind us and to keep our spiritual priorities before our eyes. Our preaching is to be the unvarnished truth; it is after all the gospel of salvation.

It is the gospel of Jesus Christ, a descendant of David, who was raised from the dead. It is the same Jesus Christ who with his resurrection from the dead was constituted Son of God in power. It is he who gave his life for our salvation and who, as today's

Gospel indicates, asks for an unqualified and total love of God and to love our neighbor as ourselves.

In a world so marked by selfishness and lack of concern for the interest of God and others, we are called to a completely different set of values. This is the gospel that has been preached to us and in which we stand. It is the path to life, truly the "good news" of God.

Points to Ponder

> The heart of the gospel message
> The cost of discipleship
> Gospel values and worldly values

FRIDAY OF THE NINTH WEEK IN ORDINARY TIME

Year I

> Tobit 11:5–15
> Psalm 146:1b–2, 6c–7, 8–9a, 9bc–10
> Mark 12:35–37

Jewish belief held that the messiah would be a descendant of King David. In this regard Jesus today raises a pointed question. In Psalm 110, historically attributed to David, the king refers to the messiah as his Lord. How then can he be David's son? The answer lies in the fact that, on one hand, the messiah is a son of David; on the other hand, he is also superior to David. It is because Christ is both God and man that the psalm can refer to him.

Attempts to deny either the humanity or divinity of Christ date back to the early centuries of the church. Yet both features are essential to any true understanding of Christ, and for this reason the church has always emphasized both the human and the divine natures of Christ.

Tobit's prayer was heard and his sight regained through the ministration of his son Tobias. "Lord, please help me see" is the repeated plea of the blind in the gospels. In the spiritual sight that only faith provides, we are able to uphold Christ as both God and man. The New Testament is at pains to see Christ as the Lord. It also strongly emphasizes his role as a man. Exaggerations on either side fail to see him as the one who would redeem humanity, who while being God shared our common human nature. Without humanity there is no suffering; without divinity there is no heavenly intercessor.

In faith we are fully aware of our human weakness, but that same faith opens our hearts to the access beyond which Christ has gained for us.

Points to Ponder

The messiah as David's son
The messiah as David's Lord
Christ, the God-man

Year II

2 Timothy 3:10–17
Psalm 119:157, 160, 161, 165, 166, 168
Mark 12:35–37

The praise of the scriptures in today's reading from Timothy underscores its centrality in the Christian life. It is honored and respected as inspired by God. How inspiration takes place is widely discussed by scholars; opinions on the subject are numerous. But the fact remains that from earliest times certain compositions have been confirmed by the church as inspired, while numerous competitors have not. They include books that have been received from the Hebrew tradition as well as those written in the light of New Testament revelation.

These books are normative for the Christian life. We are not free to pick and choose, although we certainly have our favorites. We are told that the scriptures are useful for correction and refutation. Since they constitute the inspired norm of our faith life, deviations can lead to wrong judgment and error. But most important, the Bible is important for teaching, to make us equipped for teaching in holiness and for every good work.

Today's Gospel is a classic example of biblical teaching. The first and greatest commandment is the love of God and neighbor. With this as our guiding norm, we quickly realize that there is no commandment or precept that falls outside its domain. To be schooled in the scriptures is to be totally at one with God's will.

In the past fifty years there has been a remarkable growth in our understanding of the Bible. Scripture formation is now part of the life of many parishes. We learn from the Bible's towering figures and from the mistakes of some of its heroes. Above all, Christ stands as its center and heart. The scriptures are multifaceted, a rich source of inspiration.

Points to Ponder

> Daily scripture reading
> The Bible: inspired and inspiring
> Teaching from the scriptures

SATURDAY OF THE NINTH WEEK IN ORDINARY TIME

Year I

> Tobit 12:1, 5–15, 20
> Tobit 13:2, 6efgh, 7, 8
> Mark 12:38–44

Raphael, the companion of Tobias on his journey, is today revealed as an angel of God. His advice to Tobit and Tobias is to live a life of praise of God and generous almsgiving for the needy. The good things that have some to Tobit's family are wholly due to God's goodness, for which praise and honor are due. Almsgiving means awareness of those who are less fortunate in life; to have their cause at heart is a sign of faith.

Jesus in today's Gospel sees true generosity exhibited in the concern of the poor widow. Most of the contributors to the temple treasury were people of means who gave of their wealth. There was little or no sacrifice involved. But the widow gave of the very small amount that she had. As Jesus states, that means so much more than what is given from abundance. For this she is warmly extolled.

Of course, no gift made in God's name is to be despised. But the depth of generosity varies. Sometimes it seems that the easiest way to deal with a problem is to write a check. It can alleviate pain and cost the donor little. But when true sacrifice is involved, there is much more to be said. It is not the amount that is given that weighs in but the sentiments of the donor.

In villages of northern India, the rural poor often contribute to the church in kind. The collection basket often contains eggs and a quantity of rice. This is as much as the people can give. Yet what is little in the eyes of the world counts for much before God. Of greater value than the gift is the heart of the giver.

Points to Ponder

> The value of almsgiving
> The danger of ostentation
> Jesus' praise of the poor widow

Year II

> 2 Timothy 4:1–8
> Psalm 71:8–9, 14–15ab, 16–17, 22
> Mark 12:38–44

The Letter to Timothy concludes with a strong exhortation to persevere. As the author has previously stated, the gospel of God is not chained. It will not be thwarted, but it requires evangelizers to make its message known. This will not be an easy task. In the midst of countless difficulties, its bearers will be tempted to withdraw and to lose patience. It is a saving message, but it is not always welcome. Teachers will appear with a message enticing enough to lead astray even the believers. Fables rather than the truth will prove attractive.

For his part, the apostle is self-confident. He has cherished the faith, fought the good fight, and finished the race. There remains now only the fulfillment of the promise; the merited crown awaits him.

It is a great grace to finish life with the assurance that the interests of the faith have been served. One leaves behind no financial inheritance of great worth, no perishable crown. But God's cause has been at the center of one's life. One stands confident before the Jesus Christ who comes in judgment. As the Gospel tells us today, even the widow's small contribution made an important difference. We have received the faith as a gift, have passed it on, and tried to live the ideals that it proposes. We confidently hope to hear the words, "Well done, good and faithful servant."

Points to Ponder

> The gospel for life
> Perseverance and fidelity
> The final reward

MONDAY OF THE TENTH WEEK IN ORDINARY TIME

Year I

> 2 Corinthians 1:1–7
> Psalm 34:2–3, 4–5, 6–7, 8–9
> Matthew 5:1–12

The prelude to Paul's Second Letter to the Corinthians is a practical presentation of the Matthean second Beatitude: "Blessed are they who mourn, for they will be comforted."

Depression is a word that I never fully understood until I was well into my ministry. It is not simply experiencing a "low" or "feeling bad." It is a psychological state of mind that calls for the help of a professional person. At one time I sat for lengthy periods with a man who twelve years prior had urged his pregnant fiancée to terminate an unwanted pregnancy. His failure had been dealt with sacramentally and spiritually years before. But he never succeeded in overcoming his deep sense of guilt. His failure kept returning and, try as he would, he remained unconvinced that God had forgiven him.

Paul speaks today of the encouragement in his life and ministry that comes from God the Father. It is that spirit of endurance that flows from faith that enables Paul to bring encouragement to those who suffer. Just as his difficulties are endured for others, so too the encouragement that he receives redounds to the good of others. He is quite confident for the Corinthians. If they share in his sufferings, they share in his encouragement as well.

Encouragement goes beyond words. There are times when there is nothing to say. What is needed is simply a calming presence. To sit quietly at the bedside of a very sick person. To hold a hand, to say a prayer, to kiss a furrowed brow. These are ways in which encouraging comes to life.

Points to Ponder

Enduring hardship
Compassion in ministry
Blessed are they who mourn

Year II

1 Kings 17:1–6
Psalm 121:1bc–2, 3–4, 5–6, 7–8
Matthew 5:1–12

The Matthean Beatitudes read today declare blessed those who work for the reign of God and those who endure for it. The mourners, the meek, and the persecuted are called to suffer with patience and to persevere for the love of the Lord. The poor in spirit (those who remain always open to God), those who pursue the cause of righteousness (those who hunger and thirst), the merciful and the peacemakers actively pursue the cause of God's kingdom.

There are many people who question their lot in life. It is not easy to explain why good people suffer, and for some, suffering continues for years. But has it not always been so. Christ did nothing to incur the hatred and hostility of his opponents. But in enduring such a lot, he opened the door of hope in his example of goodness. We are at times at a loss to explain why people turn against us, or why one family is called to drudgery and hardship. Some people never escape the edge of poverty. And yet they never give up, and in countless instances give an example of unfailing dedication.

And we also know people who are tireless in the pursuit of good. They work for peace and harmony within family and community. And the "poor in spirit" live a life of spiritual transparency. They have no hidden agenda; honesty lies at the root of their lives. They live without recrimination, only with an outstretched hand that says, "There is someone here for you."

These are not the qualities of which an aggressive society stands in awe, which tells people that there is room for them in what can seem a very cold and indifferent society. Heaven is comprised of people who endure to the end. The Beatitudes express what that means in practice.

Points to Ponder

> Being poor in spirit
> Enduring rejection
> Peace making and seeking justice

TUESDAY OF THE TENTH WEEK IN ORDINARY TIME

Year I

> 2 Corinthians 1:18–22
> Psalm 119:129, 130, 131, 132, 133, 135
> Matthew 5:13–16

An unforeseen change of plans prevented Paul from reaching Corinth at the expected time. This led to the comment on the part of some that he vacillated and was not resolute in his intentions.

In today's reading he takes issue with the negative charges. He is not a "Yes" and "No" leader. In his commitment, he is not one day "Yes" and another day "No." Taking Christ as the model of an affirmative response, he affirms that in everything God asked of him, Jesus gave an unqualified "Yes." He insists that the same is true of Silvanus, Timothy, and himself. In his ministry and vocation, he is one resounding "Yes" to God. Any change of plans is due to unforeseen circumstances, and he claims strongly that he is not an indecisive person.

Ostentation in religious practice smacks of hypocrisy. Yet in the Sermon on the Mount we are called to be salt and light. Salt served two purposes in antiquity. First, it was a preservative, in the absence of refrigeration, and second, it gave savor to food. We are called to be salt in a similar, if analogous, way. We remain true to the revealed truth of God's message in Jesus and protect its authentic value. In so doing we give a special flavor to life. In seeing human existence in its comprehensive sense, we are a savory condiment in the human endeavor.

Matthew takes the light image, found elsewhere in the Synoptics, and gives it a distinctly personal meaning. We are not to be ostentatious or self-proclaimers but rather people in whom the truth of the gospel shines forth. In living the values in which we have invested our lives, we give direction and meaning to others.

Points to Ponder

> Affirming our commitment to God
> He salt of the Christian life
> The light of lived Christian values

Year II

> 1 Kings 17:7–16
> Psalm 4:2–3, 4–5, 7b–8
> Matthew 5:13–16

When Elijah insisted on a part of the small quantity of food that the widow of Zarephath possessed, he is not unmindful of her own need. He assures her that in providing for him in his want, she will be amply provided for. She goes to fetch for him the water and cake requested, in the midst of a crippling drought that had left the land hard and dry. Initially she had denied his request. But when he assures her that the God of Israel will reward her generosity with an unfailing supply of oil and flour, she quickly complies.

There are moments in life when we are called to step out in faith. It may be when the salt has become flat and the light dim. But in giving our "Yes" to God, his generosity will not be diminished. Christianity is not an esoteric faith, a set of beliefs destined only for the enlightened. It is to radiate throughout the world, and we are called to be its emissaries. At times it seems easier to hold on to our faith tenaciously and ignore our role in the world. But if the salt goes flat, it has no value. And if the light is encumbered and not placed on a lamp stand to be seen, it will never attract the human spirit.

The widow gained biblical prominence because she gave of the little that she had. We become salt and light when we let God's goodness show forth in our lives. It is always better to light one candle than to curse the darkness!

Points to Ponder

Sharing our little with confidence in God
Letting conviction show forth in what we do
Images of salt and light

WEDNESDAY OF THE TENTH WEEK IN ORDINARY TIME

Year I

2 Corinthians 3:4–11
Psalm 99:5, 6, 7, 8, 9
Matthew 5:17–19

It would seem that the Christian community for which Matthew writes is pro-law and religiously conservative. It is certainly true that Jesus held the main lines of the Jewish law in respect, but to argue that he would uphold the law in all its features even to the end of the age exceeds the evidence. That he was God's agent of fulfillment is certainly the case. But he was to be the author of a different type of observance, which went beyond simply observing the letter of the law.

Paul, as we know, takes a very different tack. For him the law had seen its day and was passing away. Its glory was a fading one. Giving his own interpretation of the brilliant face of Moses when he communed with God, Paul believed that Moses' face was covered to conceal a glory that was passing away. For this reason he calls the ministry of Moses a ministry of death. The new ministry of the Spirit, however, is a glorious one that will not pass away. Paul does not see the ministry of the law as having permanent value. It is destined to pass away.

It is clear that the new covenant of Jesus, the covenant of the heart not written in stone, far surpasses that which preceded it. It is the covenant of which Jeremiah spoke, a covenant that comes from within. A covenant not written in stone but on the flesh of the heart.

We belong to the Judeo–Christian tradition. Christianity can never be understood if it is detached from its Jewish roots. On the other hand we are not simply a law-observing people. We are made holy not by anything we do but because we have been graced and favored. Christian fulfillment lies in the spirit not the letter. It is the response of a grateful heart.

Points to Ponder

> The role of the law in Christian life
> Matthew and the law's lasting value
> The new covenant of the heart

Year II

> 1 Kings 18:20–39
> Psalm 16:1b–2ab, 4, 5ab and 8, 11
> Matthew 5:17–19

When Elijah challenged the prophets of Baal, he was convinced that there was no god to champion their cause. Nevertheless he taunts them, suggesting that the god Baal may be occupied or away on a journey and therefore incapable of responding. But when the God of Israel is invoked, his presence is felt at once as the burnt offering was consumed.

The story has folkloric qualities but also a contemporary application. People today have their own gods: financial success, theft, corruption. Even our most famous contemporary celebrities turn out to have feet of clay. They are properly called "idols"!

Yet the person of God lives by the faith and conviction that God will ultimately see him through. The gods of our own making are unreliable. We have a centuries-old tradition, one that Christ brought to fulfillment. If we place our confidence in Christ, we will not be disappointed. Other gods may disappoint us. But our faith tells us that there is only one God who counts. He is a God of mystery, of course, a God who is totally other, but a God who has spoken to us in Jesus and will not disappoint.

Points to Ponder

> The gods of our own making
> The presence of the one God in our life
> Standing firm in faith

THURSDAY OF THE TENTH WEEK IN ORDINARY TIME

Year I

> 2 Corinthians 3:15—4:1, 3–6
> Psalm 85:9ab and 10, 11–12, 13–14
> Matthew 5:20–26

Paul continues today with the "veil" imagery. Moses veiled his face so that the Israelites might not see the fading glory of the former covenant. Today, he speaks of another veil, the one that hides the glory of Christ. The unbelievers are thus incapable of seeing the light that shines in the darkness, the light that reveals the glory of God in the face of Jesus Christ.

In failing to see the light, people remain unconvinced of Christ's teaching. The Gospel today deals with the question of anger. Previously it had been taught, "You shall not kill," but the Sermon on the Mount goes to the root of violent action, which is anger. There are escalating forms of anger, hateful terms of reference, all of which merit punishment.

Anger is simply counterproductive. Its fruit is pain and hurt for ourselves and for others. To harbor hostility toward another makes us unworthy to come before the Lord in worship or cult. In knowing the person of Jesus, we move away from sin and strive to remain in the spirit of forgiveness, the spirit of him who taught this message even from the cross.

Points to Ponder

> The lifted veil and the person of Jesus
> Anger and forgiveness
> Settling disagreements "out of court"

Year II

> 1 Kings 18:41–46
> Psalm 65:10, 11, 12–13
> Matthew 5:20–26

Seven is a perfect number in biblical terms. Elijah's servant finds relief from the drought only after scanning the sky seven times. It was a case of pure perseverance.

When it comes to the ethic of the Sermon on the Mount, today's Gospel gives a clear example of the distance between the demands of the Decalogue and those of Christian discipleship. Unjust killing was seen as seriously sinful in the Hebrew dispensation, much as it is today in Christian thinking. But the Christian teaching is very incisive. It depends on one of the root causes of homicide: a hostile spirit.

One of the dangers of anger is its tendency to escalate. It harms the person harboring it as well as the person at whom it is directed. Name calling goes from the less grievous to the more injurious. Furthermore, as the Letter of John states, how can we say we love God whom we do not see if we don't love the brother whom we see? Thus, to bear a spirit of animosity toward another is to render fruitless any offering we might make before the Lord.

Charity is the queen of all virtues, but its ramifications are very practical and close to home. Certainly homicide is excluded from the Christian vision, but one cannot escape the fact that, if anger were dealt with more directly, crimes of murder would decrease. But even when anger does not turn violent, it is destructive of our honesty and equanimity.

Points to Ponder

> The spirit of perseverance
> Loving the neighbor whom we see
> Anger as a destructive agent

FRIDAY OF THE TENTH WEEK IN ORDINARY TIME

Year I

> 2 Corinthians 4:7–15
> Psalm 116:10–11, 15–16, 17–18
> Matthew 5:27–32

We are weak but God is strong. The more that fragility shows forth in our human makeup, the more the power of God appears in our all-too-human flesh. In our weak humanity, we are afflicted in every way. All of this is part of the dying of Jesus, now lived out by extension in the life of the Christian. But Jesus died in order to bring forth life, and it is in our human weakness that this new life appears. Although we are repeatedly beaten down, the life of Jesus, that of the Holy Spirit, becomes ever more evident.

The Gospel today sets forth Jesus' teaching on adultery and divorce in a very strong statement of opposition. And once again, it goes deeper than the evil act. The seeds of adultery lie in the heart, and therefore we are enjoined to uproot every semblance of lust. And lust, to be sure, means more than impure thoughts, something to which are all prone. Lust is an internal struggle marked by attempts to actualize the evil desire. And it is this that Jesus' teaching excludes.

We all face the struggle of the Christian life, but we are also assured that in Christ victory will come. Just as the righteousness of God triumphed in Christ, so, too, it will in us if we remain faithful.

Points to Ponder

> The death of Christ in each of us
> The life of Christ in each of us
> Our weak human nature

Year II

> 1 Kings 19:9a, 11–16
> Psalm 27:7–8a, 8b–9abc, 13–14
> Matthew 5:27–32

At the time of Catherine Drexel's canonization as a saint of the church, one of the sisters who had lived with her for many years was asked what it was like to live with a saint. The sister responded unhesitatingly, "I never thought of her as a saint, just a very fine woman."

In today's reading from Kings, Elijah returns to Mount Horeb, the same location where God had spoken with Moses in the great theophany of covenant making. The prophet was advised to exit from the cave to witness the Lord's passing by. There was first a heavy wind in which the Lord was not present. This was followed by an earthquake and then a fire, but the Lord was not present in either. Finally there was a still whispering sound in which the Lord's voice was heard. God frequently manifests himself in the least pretentious manner. It may be an unexpected act of kindness, a moment of good news, or the tragedy of an unexpected loss. These are our "sounds of silence" in which the presence of God is so clearly felt. They are moments we want to cherish, small revelations of the divine, and often contain insights for our own spiritual life.

In events of great importance, it is often difficult to hear the voice of God. At times it seems as if God is absent. But in the sounds of silence," we are often led to prayer and reflection. They are quiet ways in which God is at work, and we should not underestimate their importance.

Points to Ponder

Listening to God in the sounds of silence
Following God's lead
Hearing God's whisper

SATURDAY OF THE TENTH WEEK IN ORDINARY TIME

Year I

2 Corinthians 5:14–21
Psalm 103:1–2, 3–4, 9–10, 11–12
Matthew 5:33–37

The principal work of Christ as God's emissary to the world was reconciliation. This is clear in Paul's Letter to the Corinthians, in which he speaks of our being ministers of reconciliation. In Christ we have all died. In dying to the old unregenerated self, we have now put on a new life, by which we live no longer for ourselves but for God.

We now have the responsibility of proclaiming this to the world. God reconciles the world to himself in Christ because this is his principal work. He who knew no sin was made sin for us, meaning that all the effects of sinful conduct have been heaped upon him, while he himself was innocent. By his vicarious atonement, the burden of sin has been lifted from our shoulders. In the midst of all manner of suffering and affliction, he remained the faithful ambassador.

Living in a new era with a new life, there is no need for some of the practices of the past. Oath taking was one of those practices. False oaths were clearly discredited. Now all oaths are excluded. When asked to testify, our answer itself is our testimony to the truth. Truth flows from the new life in Christ that we possess, not from any oath or formulaic affirmation of the truth.

Points to Ponder

> Christ as the reconciler
> Our sharing in Christ's reconciling work
> Honesty in testifying

Year II

> 1 Kings 19:19–21
> Psalm 16:1b–2a and 5, 7–8, 9–10
> Matthew 5:33–37

Oaths call upon God to witness the truth of what is asserted. They played a part in Old Testament life, just as they have been part of church practice for centuries. Whatever else an oath may do, it infringes on God's sovereignty in drawing him to matters of lesser concern. The Sermon on the Mount is clear in its condemnation of oaths.

Why then do we continue to take oaths? Some would argue that the Matthean prohibition of oaths is part of an ideal toward which we may strive but continually fall short. But such an argument also is weak, since it has long been held that the provisions of the Sermon on the Mount are not simply ideals but norms to be lived in everyday life. Perhaps the best answer is simply to recognize that it is an area in which we fall short. We fail to speak the unvarnished truth with honesty.

In our reading from Kings, Elisha is so determined to share the lot of Elijah that he destroys his instruments of agriculture and destroys the animals that provided for his livelihood. This was as total a commitment to the future as could possibly be made. Here there is no putting his hand to the plow and looking back. Elisha prays for a double share in Elijah's spirit. It is that type of determination that was so much a part of the prophetic tradition as well as true Christian discipleship.

Points to Ponder

> The truth of the simple and direct answer
> The witness of total commitment
> Elisha's prophetic call

MONDAY OF THE ELEVENTH WEEK IN ORDINARY TIME

Year I

> 2 Corinthians 6:1–10
> Psalm 98:1, 2b, 3ab, 3cd–4
> Matthew 5:38–42

In what might seem to be a series of defeats, Paul sees victory and new life. Paul exhorts the Corinthians not to assume that God's grace had failed. When he speaks of his ministry, his conscience is clear. He has had more than his share of setbacks—from constraint to outright imprisonment—but his response has always been patience, kindness, unfeigned love, and uprightness. Despite being attacked as a deceiver by those who are against him, Paul knows that he has been truthful and has lived life in God. Though he may appear sorrowful, he rejoices; though he may seem poor, he is enriched; though he has nothing, he possesses everything. These are some of the apparent contradictions of the Christian life.

The law of retribution, cited in the Gospel, was known to both the Israelites and the neighboring cultures. Known as the *lex taleonis*, it sounds worse than it actually was: it put limitations on retaliation for injury. Retribution was not to be excessive. If someone knocked out your tooth, you were not justified in killing them, but only knocking out *their* tooth! True, this was violent, but it was nevertheless an ancient attempt to control a person's response to evil or criminal acts.

But in the Christian life, there is an entirely different standard. The only acceptable response is love and forgiveness. When struck, turn the other cheek. When asked for a tunic, give your cloak as well. When asked to walk for a mile, go two.

We live in a violent and vengeful world. But Christians must walk a different path, one that may seem foolhardy at times but is actually replete with its own riches.

Points to Ponder

Sorrowful yet always rejoicing
Living in the day of salvation
Turning the other cheek

Year II

1 Kings 21:1–16
Psalm 5:2–3ab, 4b–6a, 6b–7
Matthew 5:38–42

Nothing but malice can explain the vicious tactic of Jezebel to obtain Naboth's vineyard. It is hard to explain Ahab's extreme anger over his failure to purchase Naboth's ancestral property, but there is no doubt about Ahab's single-mindedness. With his consent, his scheming wife Jezebel arranges for Naboth's death, with the sole intent of expanding the royal holdings.

Perhaps the only difference between Jezebel's cunning and cases of modern dishonesty is the open shamelessness of her actions. She does everything she can to possess Naboth's land. She succeeds in her ploy. Ahab gets the vineyard, and Naboth is killed.

How different is the teaching of today's Gospel. Every Christian response is marked by charity and forgiveness. In this case, the rights of Naboth would have been recognized, and the king would have looked elsewhere for ways to increase his holdings.

Greed characterizes many human transactions today. People will set upon a course of action and leave no stone unturned in obtaining their objective. Yet nothing is more important in life than personal integrity. All material things, regardless of their worth, are fleeting. What profit have we if we gain the whole world and lose our own soul?

Points to Ponder

Greed and its destructive character
The unjust taking of human life
The value of personal integrity

TUESDAY OF THE ELEVENTH WEEK IN ORDINARY TIME

Year I

2 Corinthians 8:1–9
Psalm 146:2, 5–6ab, 6c–7, 8–9a
Matthew 5:43–48

Among the ancient Hebrews it was legitimate to hate certain enemies, but this hatred never appears as a commandment of the Torah. There is no explicit precept that states, "Hate your enemies." Love of neighbor, on the other hand, is mandated, though it refers to love for fellow Israelites. It is not universal in its extension. Christ's offers us a new mandate: we are enjoined to love our enemies and pray for our persecutors. God himself is seen as the model of nondiscrimination. The sun rises upon the good and the bad; the rain falls in the same manner. To be selective about those we love makes us no different than anybody in secular society. Christians will be able to effectively promote a more just and forgiving society only when the law of love has primacy in their lives.

This principle of universal caring is concretized in Paul's appeal to the Corinthians on behalf of the poorer churches. He cites the example of the church in Macedonia which, though poor, wanted to be part of the charitable efforts on behalf of the churches in need.

The collection basket is not the sole measure of good will, but it is a barometer. Christ became poor for us that we might become rich through his poverty. We become rich with the grace of Christ when we are generous to those who are poor.

Points to Ponder

> Ways in which we show our dislike
> God's universal love
> The Christian response to natural disaster

Year II

> 1 Kings 21:17–29
> Psalm 51:3–4, 5–6ab, 11 and 16
> Matthew 5:43–48

The crime of Ahab and Jezebel against Naboth in order to lay hold of his property was so serious that it called for major retribution. The Lord promises Elijah that punishment will not be slow in coming. It is delayed in Ahab's case only because he manifested sincere contrition and performed salutary works of penance.

Even we could see why Naboth's kin might harbor hatred for Ahab and his family. Yet, even here, the teaching of the Gospel is that love must prevail. Does this mean that justice is not to be served? The commandment does not say so. The scale of justice is set to counter evil actions with just punishments, but there must always be room for forgiveness.

In our times, crimes of treachery have been perpetrated against entire communities of people. The term *genocide* has become commonplace because of the unspeakable horrors of the twentieth century. Some acts of inhumanity are so evil as to defy the imagination. Yet when evildoers seek forgiveness, even for the most despicable crimes, forgiveness must be extended. To extend forgiveness in certain cases is not only difficult, but one might say even humanly impossible. But the law of love is not conditional. It is where "the tire hits the road" in the Christian life. We were never told it would be easy.

Hatred is only destructive. Peace is the way to God.

Points to Ponder

The consequences of Ahab's greed
The taking of innocent human life
Forgiving one's enemies

WEDNESDAY OF THE ELEVENTH WEEK IN ORDINARY TIME

Year I

2 Corinthians 9:6–11
Psalm 112:1bc–2, 3–4, 9
Matthew 6:1–6, 16–18

The clear message of today's scripture is to avoid ostentation—or prideful showiness—in any form. Whether it is donations, praying, or fasting, what you do should be solely between you and God. There is a great temptation to let others know of our spiritual practices. Of course, there are times when we legitimately speak of our spiritual lives without the intention of drawing attention to ourselves. But if we use religion in any way to advance our personal agenda, the value of our spiritual actions is diminished.

There is nothing in and of itself wrong with publicly performing a action of faith or prayer. Public charitable contributions can be very good, and communal (or public) prayer certainly has its place in our lives. It is when these things are done expressly *to attract attention* that they are misdirected.

Paul today applauds generosity and concern for others. "God loves a cheerful giver." God has provided for our needs, and in being generous with them, they are not diminished. If we are the providers of seed for the field and bread for the table, we are assured a good harvest, "the harvest of your righteousness."

The poor widow who provided food for Elijah in his hunger was rewarded. Her personal store of food, despite drought and famine, was never exhausted. If we give of what we have with love and kindness, whether we are rich or poor, we will never be the losers.

Points to Ponder

Attracting attention in doing good
Doing good for its own sake
The spirit of generosity

Year II

2 Kings 2:1, 6–14
Psalm 31:20, 21, 24
Matthew 6:1–6, 16–18

We still live in anticipation of the final times. Even the arrival of Christ pointed to his return at the end of time. The departure of Elijah in the whirlwind was not definitive. He had not died; therefore, it was believed that he would return in the final days. In the Lucan Lord's Prayer, Christ prays for the full inauguration of the kingdom. But Elijah had not departed without showing special favor to Elisha. When the latter strikes the water with Elijah's cloak, the waters are parted. Elisha has captured the spirit of Elijah.

No greater affirmation of Elijah surpasses the gift of the twofold spirit to his disciple. Today so many people are captured by sinful example. But between the two prophets there was only the exchange of the good. Many young people are immersed in the example of evil. How inspiring it is to see them captured by the good. Some young people today give of their vacation time to assist people in the underdeveloped and developing world in agricultural projects or housing developments to assist the needy.

Jesus today warns against forms of ostentation. When charity is done, let it be done quietly, without fanfare. Likewise, praying and fasting be done without attracting attention. It is our heavenly Father who sees all and rewards all. That is quite sufficient. Humans can too easily become self-centered. And it may not be in serious ways. But it is to the Lord that all good is to be attributed. God brooks no competitors.

Points to Ponder

Wise imitation
Improper self-seeking

THURSDAY OF THE ELEVENTH WEEK IN ORDINARY TIME

Year I

> 2 Corinthians 11:1–11
> Psalm 111:1b–2, 3–4, 7–8
> Matthew 6:7–15

To the Corinthians, Paul insists that he preaches the gospel free of charge. He either supported himself or was helped by other churches. He preached the authentic gospel and asked only that his hearers remain faithful to the word he preached and not be seduced by those who teach to the contrary.

The Matthean Jesus today teaches us how to pray. It is not a question of how many words we use, but rather the sincerity of the heart. Jesus teaches us only one prayer to pray daily, and it is composed of two sets of three petitions each. The first three petitions deal with the concerns of God: the holiness of his name, the ushering in of his kingdom, and the realization of his will. The second three petitions deal with our needs: the provisions of daily life, forgiveness, and delivery from temptation and all that is evil.

There is only one invocation about which Jesus adds further comment, the oft-repeated lesson of forgiveness. We can only ask God to forgive our misdeeds if we do the same in our dealings with others. If we bear continued hostility toward others, our prayers for forgiveness ring hollow indeed. If we ourselves are forgiving, God is never far from the yearnings of our own heart.

Points to Ponder

> Paul's willingness to serve
> Praying that God's interests be served
> The lesson of forgiveness

Year II

> Sirach 48:1–14
> Psalm 97:1–2, 3–4, 5–6, 7
> Matthew 6:7–15

Sirach sings the praises of the elders, especially the prophets Elijah and Elisha. By the power of God, Elijah controlled the elements. He confronted kings and nobles and was fearless in the service of God. Carried aloft in a whirlwind, he was destined to return prior to the "day of the Lord" in order to soften hardened hearts. Elisha was blessed with a double spirit of his predecessor. He moved with power and was intimidated by no one.

The New Testament sees John the Baptist as the returning Elijah, and at least one evangelist saw Jesus himself as an Elijah figure. These two figures are the earliest prophets in the Old Testament, though they are not considered "literary prophets" because they left nothing in writing. They lived at a critical time in Israel's history, during the early years of the monarchy when religious infidelity was on the rise.

When we pray the Our Father's first petition, the prophets come to mind. Elijah and Elisha stood firmly for God's interests: the recognition of his sovereignty, the coming of his kingdom, and the fulfillment of his will. Much discussion in modern times deals with similar issues. What does the will of God mean in contemporary life? Does the separation of church and state mean some sort of intolerance toward faith? It is one thing to uphold "nonestablishment" of religion and quite another to say that there is no place for religion in public discourse.

Points to Ponder

> The dauntless faith of the early prophets
> John the Baptist and the return of Elijah
> The role of faith in public life

FRIDAY OF THE ELEVENTH WEEK IN ORDINARY TIME

Year I

> 2 Corinthians 11:18, 21–30
> Psalm 34:2–3, 4–5, 6–7
> Matthew 6:19–23

Strength and weakness. To boast or not to boast. Paul today views features of his life about which he might justifiably boast. With his former co–religionist, he is able to stand on equal ground. A Hebrew and a descendant of Abraham, he is moreover a member of Christ. But he does not boast of these things; rather he speaks of the trials he has endured: beatings, shipwreck, dangers from Jew and Gentile, sleepless nights, hunger and thirst. It is through these moments, when he was most weak, that the power of God is made manifest in Paul. This is his boast.

The Gospel continues along the same line. It is not treasures or human accomplishments that count but rather the spiritual treasures that are stored in heaven. These are the goods that will endure because there is no earthly force that will destroy them. And of this bounty it can be said, "Where your treasure is, there your heart will be also."

Many people we know in life never gain prominence, never are seen in a newspaper headline. Yet their willingness to do good is boundless. They see a need and respond spontaneously. They wear themselves out for the gospel and ask for nothing in return. Their passing away may be largely unheralded, but they have lived lives of limitless good. The grace of God in them has not been fruitless, and now a treasure in heaven awaits them.

Points to Ponder

Glorying in our weakness
Our spiritual treasure
What makes true greatness?

Year II

2 Kings 11:1–4, 9–18, 20
Psalm 132:11, 12, 13–14, 17–18
Matthew 6:19–23

Athaliah is an unsavory character. It was through violence that her hold on the people was broken. Joash, the legitimate heir to the throne, is saved from her clutches through the action of one of the king's daughters. It is the priest Jehoiada who paves the way for the young prince to take the throne. Finally Athaliah is put to death, the king's position is reaffirmed, and the temple of the false god Baal is destroyed. The royal line is preserved, evil is overthrown.

The proponents of both good and evil are part of the biblical narrative. The lamp of the body is the eye, says the gospel. If there be light in the eye and the organ sound, the whole body will be filled with light. But if the eye is bad and not receptive to light, darkness is the inevitable result. How often today is the guiding light we seek in our religious, cultural, and political leadership shrouded in darkness!

So much of the evil today is caused by misplaced values. If we were to build our treasure with God, it would remain free of any destructive force; it would never lose its value. For in God's kingdom, evil has no place.

Points to Ponder

> The machinations of the powerful
> The abuse of authority
> Retaining light in the eye

SATURDAY OF THE ELEVENTH WEEK IN ORDINARY TIME

Year I

> 2 Corinthians 12:1–10
> Psalm 34:8–9, 10–11, 12–13
> Matthew 6:24–34

A priest once asked a Hindu driver who worked for his mission in India and bathed daily in the Ganges what he would like to be when reincarnated.

Without hesitation, the Hindu answered, "A bird. They don't work hard yet they live very well." The priest smiled as he thought of today's Gospel.

Providence is the belief that God cares about us and urges us not to be anxious or concerned. The Gospel today introduces various comparisons. If God provides for the birds of the sky and the lilies of the field, are we not of greater importance than they? Therefore excessive worry about food, drink, and clothing is not consonant with a life of true faith.

Paul today describes his earlier mystical experiences. Caught in rapture and lifted to the third heaven, it was an experience about which he can boast. But he declines to boast and speaks only of his weakness, even of a severe temptation that had managed to keep him humble. Exactly what his "thorn in the flesh" was we are not told, but it was enough to keep him mindful of his need to depend on the power of God.

All of this is but to say, "Whatever I am is due to the goodness of God." The realization of that truth will keep us holy and humble.

Points to Ponder

The experience of God's providence
Strength in weakness
Paul's "thorn in the flesh"

Year II

2 Chronicles 24:17–25
Psalm 89:4–5, 29–30, 31–32, 33–34
Matthew 6:24–34

Despite the messages of its prophets, Israel all too readily falls into the sinful practices of the past. When the priest Jehoiada dies, the princes of Judah converge on King Joash and quickly revert to pagan worship of idols and sacred poles. They are unwilling to listen to prophetic voices, and even Jehoiada's son Zechariah is eventually put to death. Punishment comes from Aramean forces, which, with a few men, were able to defeat Judah because of its infidelity.

The call to conversion is made repeatedly in the pages of the Old Testament. The people are never left without God's mouthpiece, but sadly it makes little difference. Death and destruction are the results of religious waywardness.

In the Gospel today we are reminded that God is our provider. Yet we are continually faced with the Horatio Alger philosophy of our time. We want to go it alone and make a success of our lives. Yet on the world stage we all come and go. None of us is really the master of our fate. We need to be attentive to God's voice and realize that if we heed his voice our lives will always have purpose.

Points to Ponder

>   Listening to the voice of God
>   Seeing God as the director of our lives
>   The providence of God

MONDAY OF THE TWELFTH WEEK IN ORDINARY TIME

Year I

>   Genesis 12:1–9
>   Psalm 33:12–13, 18–19, 20 and 22
>   Matthew 7:1–5

In this chapter of Genesis, the "epic of sin" that has dominated the first eleven chapters has come to an end. At this point a new era of faith appears with the call of the earliest patriarch Abram (whose name only later is changed to Abraham). His origins lay in Ur of the Chaldees, deep in present-day Iraq; from there he had migrated north to Haran where he had settled with his family. Called by God to move west and settle in Canaan, subsequently named Israel, he is initially blessed in a very singular way. From him is to come forth a great nation, and so great will his name become, that future generations will use it as a blessing. "May you be blessed as was Abraham."

Abram makes the journey to Canaan where he passes through regions destined to play a major part in the history of the

Hebrews: Shechem, Bethel, the Negeb. In this, as in his future life, Abram is the obedient servant of the Lord, whom at one time he had never known.

It is this willingness to respond to God's will that will play such a prominent part in the history of the people of God. Revelation will grow in its grasp of God, but the human response remains the same: "Speak, Lord, your servant is listening," so clearly evident from Abram to the prophets, from David to Josiah, to Mary at Nazareth and to Jesus himself. It lies at the heart of the Judeo-Christian tradition. "Thy will be done."

Points to Ponder

> Abram's obedient response
> Obedience and the Christian message
> Modern examples of Christian obedience

Year II

> 2 Kings 17:5–8, 13–15a, 18
> Psalm 60:3, 4–5, 12–13
> Matthew 7:1–5

Judgment is mine, says the Lord. The Assyrian invasion of Israel was as severe as it was destructive. The deportation of captives to Assyria was widespread, with Israel suffering the consequences for many years after. In today's reading from Kings, it is asserted that the reason for such destruction was Israel's moral waywardness. Idolatry had become the order of the day; the covenant and its statutes were disregarded. The prophets went unheeded. The invasion was an act of God's judgment.

The Gospel, however, presents judgment in a different light. It is really quite a compliment when we refer to someone as being "nonjudgmental." We may see things in another's conduct that make us put them on trial in our minds. But that is not our responsibility, and in any case we usually don't know all the facts.

Moreover, Jesus reminds us that our own faults are often more glaring than those of the person we judge. It is clear that we should avoid judging or making comments about others. If we are generous in our dealings with others, God will be generous with us. It is a question of "measure for measure." Harshness never makes friends; generous feelings almost always do. If we take the wooden log out of our own eye, we will see others in a different light.

Points to Ponder

> The lesson of the Assyrian invasion
> Our proclivity to judge others
> The virtue of being nonjudgmental

TUESDAY OF THE TWELFTH WEEK IN ORDINARY TIME

Year I

> Genesis 13:2, 5–18
> Psalm 15:2–3a, 3bc–4ab, 5
> Matthew 7:6, 12–14

Abram's nobility of spirit emerges in his decision to give the first choice in the selection of land to his nephew Lot. As the senior member, the first choice would ordinarily be his. Lot selects the verdant Jordan plain, occupying the cities that border the locale. Yet divine favor is still showered upon Abram, who is promised by God a vast extent of land that will fall to him and his posterity.

In today's Gospel it is a question of holy things for holy people. The dogs and swine who are to be denied the mysteries of the kingdom may have originally meant the Gentiles, in keeping with Matthew's emphasis on an exclusively Jewish mission for Jesus during his lifetime. Its use here probably refers to those who dishonor or reject the ministry of the apostles.

In our dealings with others, we must abide by the Golden Rule: Treat others as you would have them treat you. Our treatment of others should match exactly what we expect of them. "Equal justice, equal treatment."

The Gospel passage closes with a striking antithesis. In entering through the narrow gate, one accepts the teachings and directives of Jesus, which leads to eternal life. To follow false teachers or champion "another gospel" is to set out on a broader road with a broader gate, which may seem more accommodating but which ultimately leads to perdition.

Points to Ponder

> Abram's spirit of generosity
> Carelessness with the things of God
> Believing in the authentic gospel

Year II

> 2 Kings 19:9b–11, 14–21, 31–35a, 36
> Psalm 48:2–3ab, 3cd–4, 10–11
> Matthew 7:6, 12–14

Today's reading from Kings is illustrative of the gospel's teaching. It is important to enter by the narrow gate, since the wide gate is the one that leads to devastation and destruction. The Assyrian king, Sennacherib, was set on the destruction of Jerusalem and its environs, but, by the power of God, 185,000 troops of Assyria were destroyed and Assyria was forced to retreat.

The great irony of religious history is that things do not always work as expected. The size of the invading force did not outweigh the designs of God. And all too often it was human designs our forces opposed to Christianity that failed while Christianity survived. In our own times, we have seen religious men and women who refuse to bear arms or prepare for war for reasons of conscience.

Pope Paul VI pleaded in the United Nations, "War, war— never again." One hopes that we have set upon a new course where mutual antagonism will be offset by diplomacy and negotiation. Many of the most diffident nations would choose to find peaceful solutions to solve conflicts.

Rather than engage in warfare, Francis of Assisi went to the Muslim world to engage the sultan in dialogue. We live by the Beatitude: "Blessed are the peacemakers...."

Points to Ponder

Military solutions: right or wrong?
Entering by the narrow gate
The possibility of a just war

WEDNESDAY OF THE TWELFTH WEEK IN ORDINARY TIME

Year I

Genesis 15:1–12, 17–18
Psalm 105:1–2, 3–4, 6–7, 8–9
Matthew 7:15–20

In addition to the major covenant between God and Israel (Exod 19–24), there are other subordinate covenants centering on the God-Israel relationship. In today's Genesis reading, the covenant with Abram is highlighted. God's promise is that a great progeny will spring from Abram. There is nothing expressly asked of the patriarch except the implicit pledge of unwavering fidelity.

The covenant ritual seems strange to us. A number of animals are split in half. A smoking fire pot and a blazing torch passes between the parts of the dead animals. Originally the contracting parties would walk between the parts, showing their willingness to suffer the same lot as the animals should they not be faithful to the covenant terms. Here Yahweh in the form of pot and flame is the sole negotiator, with Abram close at hand in a trancelike state. Yahweh promises the patriarch the land of Canaan with borders that will extend from Egypt to the Euphrates.

The Gospel today speaks of false prophets preaching an inauthentic gospel, of which the early church had its share. To be honest, faithful, and forthright is to bear good fruit. To do otherwise is to cut oneself off from the tree.

We must also note that the idea of God's covenant with Abraham is not just a powerful religious concept; it continues to have political ramifications in our modern world. There are no easy answers to resolve the difficulties between the Israelis and the Palestinians in present-day Israel, with passionate feelings on both sides. The solution lies in a peaceful two-state solution. It is a solution for which we should ardently pray.

Points to Ponder

The significance of the covenant with Abram
The dangers from false prophets
The situation in Palestine today

Year II

2 Kings 22:8–13; 23:1–3
Psalm 119:33, 34, 35, 36, 37, 40
Matthew 7:15–20

The celebrated book of the law found in the temple during a period of restoration is identified by many scholars as an early copy of the Book of Deuteronomy. Its discovery brings King Josiah to a solemn renewal of the covenant, a public reading of the book's contents, and most important, to a far-reaching religious reform in the country. There were a number of attempted reforms in the country's history, many of them limited in their effects. The reform of Josiah is often singled out as one of the major reforms. In recounting the kings of Israel, the Book of Kings sees most of them as religious failures, but Josiah, a devout Yahwist, is praised as an ardent reformer.

For the most part, the Israelite monarchy was a disappointment. The kings of Israel and Judah were not unlike the false prophets of today's Gospel. If they were not themselves idolatrous, they did little to stem the tide of infidelity. They exemplified the dangers of the monarchy expressed in the words of Yahweh at the institution's beginnings.

Are there not shades of all of this in many of the problems that face us today? We are asked to be "broad–minded" in many of the controversies that swirl about us, but are we faithful to God? We must always remember our baptismal commitment to the one Lord and Savior of us all. In the spirit of Josiah, we must take up the word of God and reaffirm its importance, and remain always fruitful branches on the tree.

Points to Ponder

> The book of the law in the temple
> Religious infidelity
> Fruitful branches on the tree

THURSDAY OF THE TWELFTH WEEK IN ORDINARY TIME

Year I

> Genesis 16:1–12, 15–16
> Psalm 106:1b–2, 3–4a, 4b–5
> Matthew 7:21–29

Abram's decision to have intercourse with Sarai's maid, Hagar, resulted in the birth of a son who was anything but a blessing. Ishmael was the eponymous ancestor of the Israelites' neighbors and enemies, the Ishmaelites. He was something of a wild man, notorious for his hostile and boorish conduct. The true son of promise, Isaac, was to be born later of the legitimate union between Abram and Sarai.

The antithetical parable in today's Gospel speaks its own truth. Jesus stresses that the person true to the word of God is like a house built on rock. The natural elements may rage against it, but it will remain firm and not be endangered by natural forces.

Those who hear the word but fail to internalize it are like the fool who builds his house on sand. With the coming of the rain and winds, the house soon collapses. It cannot perdure.

It is one thing to be identified as Christian and quite another to embrace the faith with conviction and tenacity. There is no one in the church who is not at times beset by doubt and uncertainty. Questions arise about the validity of what we believe. But in faith we hold firm and ride out the storm. Abram was too eager to have relations with a slave girl. He paid a dear price by begetting an unruly and uncontrollable son. Let us pray that we do not surrender to convenience when our basic values are at stake.

Points to Ponder

The curse of Ishmael
A strong faith
The house built on sand

Year II

2 Kings 24: 8–17
Psalm 79:1b–2, 3–5, 8, 9
Matthew 7:21–29

In today's reading from Kings, one of the saddest chapters in the history of God's people is recounted. The previous invasion of the Assyrians had taught Israel a sad lesson, but with the coming of the Babylonians a century or so later, every shade of past glory vanished. The Babylonian king, Nebuchadnezzar, attacked and destroyed Jerusalem, deported its citizens, including the king, his mother, and the royal entourage. The temple and palace treasuries were pillaged and thousands of Jews deported. Imperial power may explain some of this; religious infidelity, much more.

The lesson of today's Gospel is well illustrated in the sixth-century fall of Jerusalem. It is not sufficient to invoke the Lord's name with the idea of manipulating his will. Nor is it sufficient to go through the motions of religious cult. It is only the house built on solid rock that survives. This had been the message of the prophets for centuries, but the warning had not been heeded.

Nothing in life that is valuable lasts without attention. No lasting goal is attained without effort. The Israelites learned the hard way that there is no sure and easy way to survive. There is a lesson here for all of us. We ignore it to our own grief.

Points to Ponder

The biblical reason for Jerusalem's fall
Those who say "Lord, Lord"
The house built on rock

FRIDAY OF THE TWELFTH WEEK IN ORDINARY TIME

Year I

> Genesis 17:1, 9–10, 15–22
> Psalm 128:1–2, 3, 4–5
> Matthew 8:1–4

In today's readings it is the will of the Lord that is highlighted. The Lord tells Abram that he and Sarai will soon have a son, Isaac, even though their advanced age would seem to make that impossible. The child will be a living sign of the covenant between God and his father. The visible sign of the covenant will be the circumcision of every male child.

Acting outside of the legal boundaries, the leper in today's Gospel approaches Jesus directly and asks for a cure. "Lord, if you choose, you can make me clean." Jesus responds in the affirmative. "I do choose. Be made clean."

To express our desires before the Lord conditionally is a sign of a mature faith. Is what I am asking truly in accord with God's will? We have only partial vision; God sees the picture in its entirety. There was once a case of a child inflicted with a debilitating mental illness. Her family ardently prayed for a cure, which did not happen. But the family developed a new sense of compassion for those with mental illness and their families. This led them to sponsor treatment centers where such patients and their loved ones could have care and support.

There are times when our prayers are redirected. Indeed, God does write straight with crooked lines!

Points to Ponder

> A covenant's visible sign
> The courage of the leper
> A conditional request of God

Year II

> 2 Kings 25:1–12
> Psalm 137:1–2, 3, 4–5, 6
> Matthew 8:1–4

Only the poor were left behind in a torched and ravaged Jerusalem. The Babylonians had leveled the city, and the temple was destroyed. The Judean king's son was murdered and the king himself was hauled off to Babylon, a captive.

Who were the poor of God who become such a privileged people in the scriptures? Originally it was a social category: the poor people of the land, with precious little of this world's goods. Materially they may have suffered, but they were in the best position to be responsive to God. God alone was their true provider, and the recognition of this was at the heart of biblical spirituality.

As time went on, it was the spiritual qualities of the true *anawim* or "poor of God" that were emphasized. The anawim lived with a true sense of dependence on God, one that went beyond social status and looked to basic dispositions of the heart. It could apply to anyone in society, although there was always the recognition that the socially deprived were in an ideal position to have the spirit of the anawim.

It is this spirit that characterizes the leper in today's Gospel. He knows what Christ is capable of but prefaces his request with trust in the willingness of the Lord. "Blessed are the poor in spirit, for theirs is the kingdom of heaven."

Points to Ponder

> The spiritual qualities of the poor
> Poverty as openness to God
> Poverty in religious life

SATURDAY OF THE TWELFTH WEEK IN ORDINARY TIME

Year I

> Genesis 18:1–15
> Luke 1:46–47, 48–49, 50 and 53, 54–55
> Matthew 8:5–17

The power of God is highlighted in today's readings. The three men who visit Abram mediate the one God, the principal actor. Abram and his wife were well beyond the age of beginning a family. When Sarai overhears the guests speaking of her forthcoming birth, she laughs. The story itself reflects norms of ancient hospitality. After the guests are treated to a fine meal, one of them indicates that upon his return within a year, Sarai will have a child.

In the Gospel story of the Roman centurion, the soldier requests Christ to cure his servant, even though he knows that, by their law, Jews were not free to enter the homes of Gentiles. Jesus replies that he is willing to come and cure the servant. Jesus marvels at the man's belief and commitment to his servant, signs of true good will. The servant is healed without Jesus' physical presence.

While in Capernaum, Jesus also heals Peter's mother-in-law, who then gets out of bed and starts to serve her guests. This is the model for all Christians: having been saved by Christ, we must now serve others.

After the healing of the servant, Jesus reflects on the future makeup of the kingdom. Some will enter to take their place with the great patriarchs, while others will continue to resist. Those who were excluded from society because of their love of Christ will enter the heavenly kingdom.

It is the power of God that colors both readings, a God for whom nothing is impossible. It is a valuable lesson to retain, especially when we think our human resources have been exhausted.

Points to Ponder

> The birth of Isaac and the seemingly impossible
> The respect of the centurion
> The kingdom of God and the Gentiles

Year II

> Lamentations 2:2, 10–14, 18–19
> Psalm 74:1b–2, 3–5, 6–7, 20–21
> Matthew 8:5–17

In our reading from Lamentations today, the sad lot of Jerusalem and the towns of Judah is graphically depicted. All forms of protection have been torn down. The old and the young are equally distraught. The glory of Zion exists no more. The people have listened to false prophets, who spoke only specious lies and failed to confront the people with their guilt. Daughter Zion is encouraged to repent and bewail her guilt with loud lamentations.

One is reminded of the Franciscan penitent, St. Margaret of Cortona, who, in her hilltop town of central Italy, would cry out for her sins throughout the night—often to the dismay of the villagers!

All of this makes the compassion and goodness of Jesus even more touching. In this early cycle of miracles in Matthew, Christ stands ever ready to extend himself and the goodness of his Father to all those who were sick or beset by demons. As tired as he was by day's end, he was still pressed to respond to those who needed him, as the living expression of the goodness of God. In the spirit of Isaiah, he took away our infirmities and bore our diseases.

Points to Ponder

> The destruction of Jerusalem and Judah's guilt
> Sorrow for sin
> The forgiveness of God

MONDAY OF THE THIRTEENTH WEEK IN ORDINARY TIME

Year I

> Genesis 18:16–33
> Psalm 103:1b–2, 3–4, 8–9, 10–11
> Matthew 8:18–22

So grave is the scandalous conduct connected with Sodom that the Lord moves toward its destruction. But first Abraham bargains with God, much like a customer in an eastern bazaar. If fifty innocent people could be found in Sodom, would the Lord spare the city? Yes, says God. Encouraged by his success, Abraham first drops the number by fives. Forty-five? Forty? God continues to affirm his intention to save the city. Emboldened, Abraham then drops the number by tens. Thirty, twenty, ten? The Lord is willing to withhold judgment, if even ten innocent people are found. In this account, God demonstrates his flexibility.

The Gospel narrative, on the other hand, operates on a principle of single-mindedness. The intention to follow Jesus must take precedence over all other considerations. On a very practical level, Jesus is not going to object to a disciple's burying his father. But what he will not accept is half-measures. One does not become a disciple by merely testing the waters. It must be a whole-hearted, single-minded commitment.

When it comes to treating others, compassion is paramount. When it comes to adherence to Christ, it's all or nothing.

Points to Ponder

> Sin as God's nemesis
> Compassion for the innocent
> Faith as a total commitment

Year II

> Amos 2:6–10, 13–16
> Psalm 50:16bc–17, 18–19, 20–21, 22–23
> Matthew 8:18–22

The preexilic prophet Amos is often termed the prophet of social justice. He certainly addresses many of the serious injustices of his time. Today's reading is a case in point. The poor are being impounded and sold for a pittance. Prostitution, primarily of a cultic nature, lures fathers and sons into sin. Amos cites both social injustice and idolatry as terrible evils.

The Israelites fail to remember what God has done on their behalf. They escape from Egypt, survive the desert experience, and finally take possession of the land, all thanks to God. Now they have disregarded the covenant and engaged in wanton disobedience. For their failures they will soon pay a dear price. The Assyrian hordes will descend upon them. There will be no escape; the strongest warriors will flee in disarray.

Our Gospel today again reminds us of the importance of dedication and complete allegiance to Christ. Half-measures count for nothing. As Christians we have been bought at a great price; in gratitude, every day we should commit ourselves anew to the service of the Lord, with a loving desire to give ourselves to the concerns of our God.

Points to Ponder

> Faith and social justice
> Sin as a rejection of God
> Christian commitment

TUESDAY OF THE THIRTEENTH WEEK IN ORDINARY TIME

Year I

> Genesis 19:15–29
> Psalm 26:2–3, 9–10, 11–12
> Matthew 8:23–27

The minimum number of innocent people in Sodom was evidently not to be found; hence God's punishment is visited upon both cities. Abraham's nephew Lot and his family are spared, however. As they flee, they are urged to move on, even in their weariness. When they ask to be allowed to find refuge in the plain city of Zoar, the request is granted. Told not to look back on the cities of the plain, Lot's wife disobeys and becomes a "pillar of salt." The rugged terrain of the Dead Sea area may have suggested the punishment. But the moral point is clear enough. Once deliverance is at hand, there can be no looking back.

In the Gospel, a sudden change of weather incites fear in the hearts of the disciple, even though Christ is present with them. In Mark's Gospel, they cry out to the sleeping Jesus, essentially reproaching him for his lack of concern. In Matthew, they offer a prayer for deliverance. The answer is swift in coming as calm is restored. The point is clear. On the stormy sea of life, trouble often leads to discouragement. But we are not to fear. Christ is with us in the storm. With faith and assurance, Lot was saved as were the disciples. Even when he seems to be absent, God is closer than we realize.

After suffering years of spiritual aridity, Teresa of Avila asked the Lord where he was in her suffering. His answer was, "Right in the middle of your heart."

Points to Ponder

> The sin of "looking back"
> Confidence in trial
> The Lord as our deliverer

Year II

> Amos 3:1–8; 4:11–12
> Psalm 5:4b–6a, 6b–7, 8
> Matthew 8:23–27

With our salutary emphasis today on God's goodness, we sometimes lose sight of his justice. The prophets, however, will not let us forget it. In a whole series of parallel images, Amos reminds Israel that its rejection of God will not be overlooked, for as Paul tells us, God will not be mocked.

Amos offers a series of analogies about how events don't simply happen without reason or cause. Two people don't travel in each other's company unless they have agreed to do so. Lions only roar when they have their prey. Birds can only be snared when there is a lure in the trap. When a trumpet sounds in a city, the people will be afraid. And if something bad happens to a city, isn't this also part of God's plan?

When God scourged Sodom and Gomorrah, a clear message was given, but God's own people did not return to him. So now, says Amos, they must bear their guilt. "Prepare to meet your God."

It is quite true that sorrow for sin can overcome every sinful obstacle. The concern of the apostles on the stormy sea brought quick deliverance. We should always be confident. But it is good to remember that God, too, suffers rejection. He is a Lord whom none of us should take for granted.

Points to Ponder

> The justice of God
> Spiritual indifference
> Sorrow begets forgiveness

WEDNESDAY OF THE THIRTEENTH WEEK IN ORDINARY TIME

Year I

> Genesis 21:5, 8–20a
> Psalm 34:7–8, 10–11, 12–13
> Matthew 8:28–34

The ambivalent feelings of the Hebrews toward the Ishmaelites, at a later date, is reflected in today's reading. As the son of Abraham and Sarah's maidservant Hagar, the young boy Ishmael has a certain status. On the other hand, as the eponymous ancestor of an historically hostile people, the negative side could not be overlooked. Sarah insists that Hagar and her son bring an end to their association with her son Isaac. Afraid that Ishmael might find favor with her husband, Sarah tells him to send mother and son away. Although dismayed by her request, Abraham at God's direction carries out Sarah's request. It is stated clearly that Ishmael is not the child of promise but in subsequent history will be a considerable force.

The presence of Jesus' power over evil is evident in the story of the Gadarene demoniacs. The desire of the demons to enter the swine was in accordance with Jewish attitudes about both pigs and demons. The demons enter the swine and precipitate their headlong charge into the sea. The herdsmen are justifiably upset, as well as the local citizens. They ask that Jesus not further damage their livelihood and leave the region.

Evil will be dealt with effectively by God in whatever form it comes, however uncomfortable it might be for us to observe it. This is a sobering thought for us today.

Points to Ponder

> Isaac: the exclusive heir of the promise
> The lot of Ishmael
> Jesus as the opponent of evil

Year II

> Amos 5:14–15, 21–24
> Psalm 50:7, 8–9, 10–11, 12–13, 16bc–17
> Matthew 8:28–34

Jesus' expulsion of the demons from the possessed Gadarenes takes an unusual twist. The unclean pigs become the recipients of the demons and then charge into the sea. Evil deserves no better treatment.

Amos exhorts his people to seek good and avoid evil in order to assure a blessed future. Only when justice is at the gate will God look favorably and have pity on them.

It is useless to spend time on observances. Feasts and offerings have no value if life is not correct before God. Music and song will not succeed in tempering God's wrath. These are things that will have value when justice pours forth like water and goodness like a constant stream.

Liturgical planning is an important part in parish life today, and with good reason. We do not want the sacred to be treated irreverently. But liturgy must always be one part of a lived and conscious expression of our Christian faith. To emphasize only the beauty of our rituals and hymns, while neglecting to witness God in our everyday behavior, is to lose sight of the forest for the trees.

Points to Ponder

> Desisting from evil
> Liturgy and faith
> Music: something beautiful for God

THURSDAY OF THE THIRTEENTH WEEK IN ORDINARY TIME

Year I

> Genesis 22:1b–19
> Psalm 115:1–2, 3–4, 5–6, 8–9
> Matthew 9:1–8

Isaac was not only the son of Abraham's advanced years; he was also the son of the promise. God's intention of making Abraham's descendants as numerous as the sands of the seashore was to be realized through Isaac. But in today's reading, Abraham is put to the supreme test. Is he willing to sacrifice this special son to God in a spirit of faith? As the story unfolds, with its strong sense of drama, the patriarch complies unquestioningly. His hand is stayed only at the final moment. God commends his obedience, again promises abundant blessings and a numerous progeny.

The relationship between sin and suffering is highlighted in the story of the paralytic in today's Gospel. He is brought to Jesus for a cure. There is no mention of sinfulness. But the gospel tradition links healing and forgiveness. Which is easier to do, asks Jesus, to cure sickness, or to forgive sin, which requires no visible proof? But on the level of faith, the remission of sin is a prerogative of God alone and not a human accomplishment. Jesus has forgiven the man's sins, but in order to verify the truth of what he does, he also cures the man's illness.

Jesus has a twofold mission: healing and forgiveness. We have frequently been beneficiaries of the forgiveness of sins. But do we take God's forgiveness too much for granted?

Points to Ponder

The greatness of Abraham and Jesus: total obedience
The carriers of the paralytic: companions in suffering
Sin forgiveness and the power of God

Year II

Amos 7:10–17
Psalm 19:8, 9, 10, 11
Matthew 9:1–8

In preexilic Israel, there were groups of prophets who carried their messages throughout the country. Their conduct was frequently ecstatic, oftentimes self–induced. Amos, however, works alone; although a southerner, he preaches at a northern sanctuary.

Amaziah, the priest of the Bethel sanctuary, is clearly annoyed by Amos's presence and orders the prophet to leave the Bethel sanctuary. Amos argues that this seems to be a case of mistaken identity. He is not part of any prophetic group but rather a sheep herder and a vine dresser by profession. Even though commanded not to speak, he utters his message of destruction. He does so because he is not his own man.

The word of truth is not always welcome and is often flat-out rejected. In today's Gospel Jesus vindicates his power to forgive sins in his dealing with the paralytic. Even in the face of hostile opposition, he continues to speak the word of truth.

The word of God cannot be silenced. We cannot fail to speak it because of human respect. Amos suffered for his mission but he could only remain steadfast. Jesus never shrank from the truth; for this he had come into the world. At times we remain silent when our convictions are attacked. But we too must remain firm.

Points to Ponder

Bands of prophets and the classical prophets
The duty of the prophet
Jesus' mission: forgiveness of sin
Faith and courage

FRIDAY OF THE THIRTEENTH WEEK IN ORDINARY TIME

Year I

Genesis 23:1–4, 19; 24:1–8, 62–67
Psalm 106:1b–2, 3–4a, 4b–5
Matthew 9:9–13

Exclusion or inclusion? Abraham is very much a man of his own culture. After Sarah's burial, he must now provide a wife for Isaac. He makes his servant swear that she will not be chosen from among the Canaanite population but from among his own people. Purity of the genealogical line was essential for the descendants of the patriarchs. The servant gives his assurance. But there is another issue. Isaac must not be taken back to Abraham's country. He must remain in Canaan, since this was the land that God had promised to his people. The servant's mission was blessed with success. Rebekah makes the return trip with him to become Isaac's wife.

Abraham insisted on exclusivity. Jesus is exactly the opposite. The latter would find place for everyone who would come to him. The Jewish prohibition against contact with public sinners finds no place in Jesus' vision. In fact, it is the sinner who needs him most. He takes no issue with sinners sitting and eating with him. When his conduct is questioned by the Pharisees, he answers them directly. It is for the sake of the sinner that he has come into the world. The healthy do not need a doctor; the sick do.

The teaching is a very important one. Ours is not a church of the perfect or the sinless but rather the weak and the needy. We should be grateful that anyone can find a home with us. If the church were only for the sinless, none of us would be here.

Points to Ponder

> Abraham's condition for a wife for Isaac
> The embrace of the sinner
> A holy church for the less than holy

Year II

> Amos 8:4–6, 9–12
> Psalm 119:2, 10, 20, 30, 40, 131
> Matthew 9:9–13

The prophet of social justice again inveighs against the unfair advantage taken against society's neediest. Business transactions were prohibited during sacred times (the new moon, the Sabbath), yet merchants in their greed were anxious for such special times to end so that they could once more pursue their financial interests. They were accustomed to buying and selling the disenfranchised and "fixing the scales" in business transactions.

But on the future day of the Lord, happiness will come to an end. Sackcloth and mourning will be signs of the times. The greatest tragedy will be the loss of God's word. It will no longer be announced as the people wander in a moral wasteland. God's message will be nowhere to be found.

The tax collectors, a despised segment of society, who appear in such a poor light in the Gospels were guilty of some of the same misdeeds that Amos mentions. First of all, they were collaborators with Rome, a foreign pagan power. In addition, they were often accused of dishonest conduct and taking undue advantage of the less fortunate. Yet, all of this not withstanding, Jesus repeatedly invites them to conversion. Today he does so in the Gospel as Matthew sits at the customs post.

Then and now Christ extends the invitation. "Follow me." This is not embarking on some slippery slope to disaster. Rather it makes us true citizens of the reign of God. It is well worth the effort. The only acceptable response is "Yes."

Points to Ponder

Dishonesty in public life
Taking advantage of the poorest
Our "Yes" to God in discipleship

SATURDAY OF THE THIRTEENTH WEEK IN ORDINARY TIME

Year I

Genesis 27:1–5, 15–29
Psalm 135:1b–2, 3–4, 5–6
Matthew 9:14–17

There is no doubt that the ruse devised by Rebekah to see that Jacob receives the all-important paternal blessing was deceptive. It was unthinkable that it be given to Esau, the son of a slave girl. For the Hebrews the superiority of Jacob over Esau was an established fact, and the way of obtaining the blessing would have been seen as clever and enterprising. Although he raises some questions himself, the failing Isaac is duped into thinking that the blessing goes to Esau, but he is mistaken. The blessing once given could not be revoked. Jacob is told that he will be the first among his brothers and eventually a focal point for many nations.

In the Gospel today John's disciples ask Jesus why he does not fast when the disciples of John and the Pharisees do. Jesus answers in terms of the eschatological wedding feast of God and his people. During this celebration in the days of Christ's ministry, fasting is inappropriate. Moreover, a new era calls for new measures; there is no sense in putting new wine into old wineskins.

In what would seem to be a later addition of the early church, it is stated that with the bridegroom's departure, forms of fasting will again be observed.

It should be noted that there is a distinctly new asceticism present in Jesus' teaching, one that goes beyond fasting. This is summarized for us in the Sermon on the Mount. To live that teaching is the highest form of asceticism and takes precedence over any form of penitential practice.

Points to Ponder

> Jacob's blessing: deception or destiny
> Fasting in the Christian life
> The principal ethic of Christianity

Year II

> Amos 9:11–15
> Psalm 85:9ab and 10, 11–12, 13–14
> Matthew 9:14–17

For the prophets, even those with the most dire prophecies, there is always a bright horizon. Amos is no exception. He speaks today of the reconstruction of the fallen "booth" of David, the restoration of the Davidic monarchy, a kingship of honor and justice, as was true in the days of old. It will be a kingdom whose authority will spread beyond its borders.

When that day comes, the harvest of field and vineyard will be astonishing in its abundance. No sooner will a crop be reaped than the plow will prepare another planting. The formerly devastated population will again dwell in peace and security. With an abundance of the good things of the earth, the people will never again go needy nor will they again be uprooted from their land.

Jesus today speaks of the end-time with a different image, that of the wedding feast. It is a period of joy and happiness when the dark and somber have no place. The fact is that in faith we believe that we are living in that final period. God has spoken to us in his Son; it doesn't get any better than that. When we stop and think of the Holy Spirit, the scriptures, and the sacraments, the privilege to participate at the altar in the solemn memorial of his death-resurrection, we realize how blessed we are. Christianity is a religion of gratitude. Of that we should never lose sight.

Points to Ponder

Biblical images of the end-time
Our life in this final period
The wedding imagery

MONDAY OF THE FOURTEENTH WEEK IN ORDINARY TIME

Year I

Genesis 28:10–22a
Psalm 91:1–2, 3–4, 14–15ab
Matthew 9:18–26

Bethel was one of Israel's most sacred worship sites. Today's reading is an account of the site's discovery by Jacob. The place was formerly known as Luz, but, now in light of Jacob's vision there, it becomes Bethel, the house of God. It was a place of strong divine–human exchange, illustrated by the heavenly messengers ascending and descending. There Jacob is assured a future kingdom and a far-reaching domain.

Both individuals in today's Gospel are aware that Jesus is in some way the walking presence of God among them. The daughter of the official has died and he asks that she be restored to life. The anonymous woman has suffered with a hemorrhage for years without an effective cure. Because of their great faith, both of them receive the desired healing.

In John's Gospel, Jesus tells his disciples that they will see the angels of God ascending and descending on the Son of Man. It is not without reason that people pray for particular benefits. And when people claim that a blessing has been received, why do we not rejoice with them rather than be incredulous? We do believe in the power and greatness of God—but perhaps our faith can run a little thin in practice.

Points to Ponder

> The church as God's dwelling
> Human fate: shades of darkness
> Turning to Christ in faith

Year II

> Hosea 2:16, 17c–18, 21–22
> Psalm 145:2–3, 4–5, 6–7, 8–9
> Matthew 9:18–26

There is probably no passage from the Old Testament that has a clearer New Testament ring than today's reading from Hosea. God's intention is to engage his people in a conversation so full of love and endearment that betrayal will never again be thought of.

When the Hebrews first emerged from Egyptian bondage, they were one with the God who had championed their cause. Their installation in the land of promise, however, had brought its own set of woes. Idolatry, cultic prostitution, and the worship of Baal was the slippery slope down which they had slid. They were in short an immense disappointment. But God would allure them again to a figurative desert and reconstitute them in those strong biblical qualities of right, justice, love, and mercy.

Humans look at appearances; God looks at the heart. Isn't this the lesson of today's Gospel? Regardless of the background or status of the supplicant, Jesus has a willing ear and a sympathetic heart. But the discourse does not end there. We are those who today walk in his shoes. How can we turn our back on the needy, the grieving parent of a lost child, or the elderly woman suffering years of pain? To walk the walk is more costly than to talk the talk.

Points to Ponder

> The desert experience in our spiritual life
> Conversion always a possibility
> Sensitivity to pain

TUESDAY OF THE FOURTEENTH WEEK IN ORDINARY TIME

Year I

Genesis 32:23–33
Psalm 17:1b, 2–3, 6–7ab, 8b and 15
Matthew 9:32–38

We will probably be forever at a loss to determine what happened to Jacob at the Jabbok on that mysterious night, and yet there is no doubt that it represented a bitter struggle between God and the patriarch, and through it all Jacob prevailed. Was it a question of Jacob's doubts about his mission? Or was it simply a test of faith? Although the stranger refuses to give his name, Jacob names the place "Peniel" because there he had dealt with God face to face.

Some people struggle with their faith for years on end. They may feel trapped by beliefs inherited from their forebears, or they may struggle with limitations placed on their conduct by the church. Or perhaps they have suffered rebuff or hostility from a member of the clergy. The causes may be many, and the solutions are not always easy. But faith for such people is not simple acquiescence. Out of hard questioning, faith can be strengthened. And that is a real plus.

In today's Gospel, Jesus casts out demons. The demons were the antithesis to everything godly. Jesus' mission in the world was to overcome evil and offer the pathway to eternity. We too may have our struggles with God, but we must have courage. Faith is not easily acquired nor easily surrendered. Questioning often leads to clarity and a fuller access to God.

Points to Ponder

Struggles with faith
Courage in the struggle
Dealing with the forces of evil

Year II

> Hosea 8:4–7, 11–13
> Psalm 115:3–4, 5–6, 7ab–8, 9–10
> Matthew 9:32–38

Nothing had greater importance in Israelite life than the authentic worship of Yahweh, and yet the Israelites were continually falling short in this area. Not only did Israel establish its own monarchy, but Samaria became a center of illicit worship. Two calves of gold, set up in the early years of the northern monarchy, were created to offset Jerusalem as the center of worship.

The altars that had been erected in the northern kingdom became places of sin. Hosea shows deep concern for the waywardness of his people and assures them that punishment for sin will not be delayed. Jesus' frontal attack on evil appears today in his exorcisms and healings. The contrast is striking. The Israelites stand in opposition to the God who had saved them. Jesus, the agent of forgiveness, brings healing and God's gentleness to troubled souls. This is at the very heart of Christian ministry—concern for the suffering, outreach to the needy.

Christ prays today for laborers for the harvest. The opportunities are countless, but it takes willing collaborators to bring Christ to others. Each of us has a distinct Christian calling to bring Christ to the world. The need has never been greater than it is today. Ask yourself, In what way can I contribute to the work of the harvest?

Points to Ponder

> Human disregard for God's love
> Jesus' way of confronting evil
> My contribution to the harvest

WEDNESDAY OF THE FOURTEENTH WEEK IN ORDINARY TIME

Year I

Genesis 41:55–57; 42:5–7a, 17–24a
Psalm 33:2–3, 10–11, 18–19
Matthew 10:1–7

Twelve is an interesting biblical number. It immediately suggests the twelve sons of Jacob, the fathers of Israel's twelve tribes. Their conduct was not always beyond reproach, as in today's reminder that they had sold their brother Joseph into slavery and now lived as if the event had long been forgotten. In today's reading, they come before their exalted brother in Egypt in search of food at a time of serious famine. They do not recognize Joseph. He, on the other hand, while stern with them during the encounter, is moved to tears. He asks that they bring their youngest brother, also dearly beloved of Jacob, to Egypt, and all will be well.

The thought of separating their youngest brother from their father evokes the memory of the cruel separation of Joseph from his father years before.

Christ chose twelve apostles, symbols once again of the twelve tribes of Israel and the sons of Jacob. Today they are commissioned to announce the reign of God to the children of Israel. During the earthly ministry of Jesus in Matthew's Gospel, the kingdom is proclaimed only to the Jewish people, the universal mission coming only after the resurrection.

Life is a series of successes and failures, of joys and disappointments. The brothers of Joseph begin to feel the remorse for their brother's loss that they should have felt years earlier. The twelve apostles, so buoyed up by their faith, set forth to proclaim the inauguration of God's reign. Sadness and joy, failure and success—these are the lot of Jesus and of every disciple.

Points to Ponder

God's providence in Joseph's life
The twelve apostles and the reign of God
Sorrow and joy in the Christian life

Year II

Hosea 10:1–3, 7–8, 12
Psalm 105:2–3, 4–5, 6–7
Matthew 10:1–7

In many books of the Old Testament, we read accounts of repeated failure. Perhaps no one describes God's favor and human negligence as graphically as Hosea. In today's reading Israel is described as a luxurious vine with abundant fruit. The children of the covenant, favored with God's law, had a future that was assured. But what resulted? Altars to pagan gods; productivity turned into wasted ingratitude. Their sacrifices, tainted with idolatry, were worth nothing. Their only future would be a return to bondage.

And yet hope for that dawn of a better was never lost. It came, although it turned out differently than expected. It involved a kingdom with a different kind of king. It came at a moment of strong eschatological hope, but it did not follow the path of ordinary expectations. It was a kingdom of gentleness and humility. Its king came humble and riding on a donkey. This new kingdom introduced a time of forgiveness and hope, an opportunity to let the past be forgotten. Announced to Israel by unlettered Galilean laborers, it would soon spread to the world. The kingdom of God is at hand. It is now present in *our* hearts and on *our* lips. We now live in the era of the great pardon.

Points to Ponder

Formalistic religion
The unexpected character of Christianity
Grateful for forgiveness

THURSDAY OF THE FOURTEENTH WEEK IN ORDINARY TIME

Year I

Genesis 44:18–21, 23b–29; 45:1–5
Psalm 105:16–17, 18–19, 20–21
Matthew 10:7–15

The moment of Joseph's self-disclosure to his brothers is one of the Bible's most poignant scenes. It would have been cruel and disrespectful for Jacob's youngest son to be taken from his father and brought to Egypt. It would have broken the patriarch's heart and indicated that the brothers had not learned the lesson of what they had done to Joseph years before.

All of this proves to be too much for the kind–hearted Joseph. He dismisses the others present and speaks only to his brothers, revealing that he is the one they had rejected years before, that he is Joseph, their brother. He tells them not to feel deep remorse because God has turned misfortune into good. Through his present office, Joseph is now able to save many lives.

Early in his pontificate, Pope John XXIII received in audience a group of rabbis. His simple greeting touched them all: "I am Joseph, your brother." This friendly posture of the pope opened a new era not only of Jewish-Christian relations but one of positive developments with those of other faiths, a harbinger of things to come in the ecumenical life of the church.

Jesus today sends his emissaries on that initial mission of peace and love. Or in the words of Francis of Assisi: *Pace e bene!* "Peace and good." This is not a cry of condemnation or reproach, only a message of saving peace. The truth is that more good is accomplished through kindness and understanding than through harshness.

It is a lesson worth heeding.

Points to Ponder

The lesson of Joseph's reaction
The "peace" that Christ brings
Kindness, not harshness

Year II

> Hosea 11:1–4, 8e–9
> Psalm 80:2ac and 3b, 15–16
> Matthew 10:7–15

In speaking of God's love for Israel, Hosea passes from the image of husband and wife to that of a parent and child. It was God who taught the child how to walk, held him in his arms, and hugged him. He brought his child out of Egyptian bondage.

And yet with all the care showered upon the child, he only wanders farther from his parent, ultimately burning incense to pagan gods. And still God's constant love emerges, the unwillingness to abandon his child. Israel will not be destroyed. This song is a great testimony to God's fidelity.

The good news of Jesus was to be carried with haste by those who received it. The apostles are not to be impeded—by money, clothing, or personal belongings. The message they bear is one of peace and joy. To reject it is to reject the kingdom; to accept it is to find the key to life.

Lord, give us hope in discouragement. Be always the light of our lives. We have failed many times, but we are grateful that you have never given up on us.

Points to Ponder

> God's fidelity
> The imperative of preaching the good news
> Hope in discouragement

FRIDAY OF THE FOURTEENTH WEEK IN ORDINARY TIME

Year I

> Genesis 46:1–7, 28–30
> Psalm 37:3–4, 18–19, 27–28, 39–40
> Matthew 10:16–23

One of life's greatest tragedies is a parent's loss of a child. It seems so unnatural. Parents follow the unborn child through gestation, with the accompanying joy at the birth. They follow with love the processes of growth and development. It is a crushing blow when the child is there no more.

The Joseph story is full of family pathos. The aging Israel (Jacob) today is about to be reunited with his son Joseph, after many years of belief that the son was dead. The story has been brought to a happy ending. Joseph's brothers have shown remorse; food has been provided for the family in Egypt. Jacob can only exclaim that now his life may be brought to an end, bringing him peace and tranquility.

Jesus assures his disciples today that life will take unusual turns for them, as well. They will have to defend their beliefs before civil magistrates. Families will be sharply divided over the acceptance and rejection of their message. But as they carry out their mandate, they are assured that their commitment will be vindicated.

Turmoil is always difficult. Family discord is particularly painful. Conflict resolution has more than psychological value. It fulfills a gospel mandate to be at peace with our family members. Joseph waited years for reconciliation. We may not have that much time.

Points to Ponder

Joseph's forgiving spirit
Addressing family conflict
Overcoming religious differences

Year II

Hosea 14:2–10
Psalm 51:3–4, 8–9, 12–13, 14 and 17
Matthew 10:16–23

Despite his severe warnings, Hosea remains always a prophet of hope. The first step to total reengagement is conversion. Idols must be abandoned, reliance on foreign powers must be shunned. In the face of noble sentiments, God's love will be deeply felt.

With God himself providing rain, Israel shall blossom like the lily; she shall strike root like the olive tree. Never again shall she be desolate. If she walks in the way of justice, her future is assured.

The trials that beset the first Christians, so well illustrated in today's Gospel, underscore the crosses that accompany the life of faith.

To read the Acts of the Apostles is to see how accurate were the prophecies of Jesus. Imprisonment became a fact of life. It is interesting to note the large number of New Testament personalities who spent time in prison.

This was a great hardship for the apostolic church, but it always led to a brighter day.

The only question remaining is, Shall we persevere to the end? With conviction and God's help, we will. The world is the Lord's and everything in it. The Son of Man will one day return and will graciously embrace those who remain faithful.

Points to Ponder

>Agricultural imagery in the Bible
>Carrying the cross and the life of faith
>Perseverance in suffering

SATURDAY OF THE FOURTEENTH WEEK IN ORDINARY TIME

Year I

>Genesis 49:29–32; 50:15–26a
>Psalm 105:1–2, 3–4, 6–7
>Matthew 10:24–33

Despite his brothers' fears, Joseph was much too magnanimous to consider making them pay for their earlier act of betrayal in attempting to rid themselves of him. As they make their plea before him, Joseph forgives them and promises to provide for them in the future. Always faithful to his origins, he asks that his remains be brought back to Canaan for burial.

God's providence is a key feature of the Joseph story. The Gospel today speaks in the same terms. Just as Jesus indicates to his followers that persecution will be their lot, he also assures them that God will provide for them. The body may be tormented but the spirit will survive. God will never forget those who profess the name of Christ.

The primary lesson of the Joseph story is forgiveness, a lesson that all of us can take to heart. How often we treat others with austerity and coldness. There is the added lesson of maintaining that broader vision. Disappointment in life does not spell the end. The One who is faithful remains ever so. With courage and determination we continue the journey.

Points to Ponder

Fraternal forgiveness
The cost of discipleship
Joseph's magnaminous spirit

Year II

Isaiah 6:1–8
Psalm 93:1ab, 1cd–2, 5
Matthew 10:24–33

In today's Gospel Christ exhorts us to speak boldly of our beliefs and not to conceal them. Experience shows us that it is not always easy to stand firmly for our beliefs. Be not afraid! If the birds of the air and the beasts of the field fall under God's providential care, how much more those of us who are part of his company?

The account of Isaiah's call to mission is awesome. It takes place within the temple precincts. Yahweh appears in majestic splendor as attendant seraphim acclaim the holiness (otherness) of God. The unworthy Isaiah fears that he is about to die. But once his lips are purified, he is clearly destined for a preaching mission.

When the Lord asks of the heavenly court, "Who will go for us?," the prophet answers enthusiastically, "Here I am....Send me."

In the face of spiritual challenges, how reluctant we often are. We fade away rather than express our willingness. A longtime friend once made a vow never to pass by a person in distress on the highway. It is a vow he has faithfully fulfilled. A troubled "Yes" is better than a reluctant "No."

Points to Ponder

> Our baptismal calling
> A willing giver
> Standing for conviction

MONDAY OF THE FIFTEENTH WEEK IN ORDINARY TIME

Year I

> Exodus 1:8–14, 22
> Psalm 124:1b–3, 4–6, 7–8
> Matthew 10:34—11:1

To the throne of Egypt came new king who knew nothing of Joseph. Times change. Favor today may mean disfavor tomorrow. As the Book of Exodus opens, the golden era of Joseph has passed, and the Hebrews, having grown in numbers, are now subjected to cruel servitude by a later pharaoh. To prevent their increase in number, the pharaoh ordered the death of all male babies.

The Gospel today indicates that the reception of Christ was mixed. Certainly, Christ did not come with the message of a sword. Peace was always his central theme. But the acceptance of his message often resulted in deep divisions within a family. Members turned on one another in a way that was destructive of the peace desired by Christ.

Christ goes on to speak of the allegiance that is expected of those who follow him. To place others before him is to subordinate the primary calling. By the same token, kindness toward one of Christ's disciples is kindness to him.

Because of our human condition, we are all at times tempted to put Christ in second place. But when we stop and consider our Christian calling, we know that nothing can take precedence over that. In him is our life and destiny, our Savior and inspiration. Deep in our conscience we know that he must have priority of place.

Points to Ponder

> Christ as the bearer of the sword
> Charity in the name of Christ
> Living at peace with one another

Year II

> Isaiah 1:10–17
> Psalm 50:8–9, 16bc–17, 21 and 23
> Matthew 10:34—11:1

For some people, religion is largely identified with ritual, the proper way to worship. Every aspect of worship must be executed with correctness. It is true that a proper way of worship is as important as many other aspects of life, but it is by no means the heart of our belief.

The prophets repeatedly inveigh against ritualism, as Isaiah does today. Yahweh makes it eminently clear that his concern is not with animal offerings, calendar observance, or the worth of offerings. Of these things he stands in no need.

In all this concern with ritual observance, the important things are forgotten. Orphans and widows are the special responsibility of the community, since they have been left with no male provider. They are neglected by the community. And yet this is at the heart of a true worship of God. Today's Gospel stresses the importance of even a cold glass of water extended to a disciple. Such counts for more than any carefully planned sacrifice.

It happens in life that we meet people who are continually giving of themselves in the service of others. And yet they never darken a church door. One has the distinct feeling that they are not far from the kingdom of God.

Points to Ponder

Legitimate concern for ritual
Religious priorities
Concern for the unfortunate

TUESDAY OF THE FIFTEENTH WEEK IN ORDINARY TIME

Year I

Exodus 2:1–15a
Psalm 69:3, 14, 30–31, 33–34
Matthew 11:20–24

Exodus gives a popular explanation for the name of Moses by relating it to the account of the child's discovery by Pharaoh's daughter and his being taken out of the water. Not strict etymology but not bad catechesis!

It is interesting to note how often water in the scriptures becomes a symbol of baptism. It is true of the Noah story, the Red Sea crossing, and the Israelites crossing the Jordan. It is always a question of a deliverance through water. The Moses story lends itself to such symbolism.

Moses is first and foremost a Hebrew. When he comes upon a fight between an Egyptian and a Hebrew, he unhesitatingly kills the Egyptian. When he later learns the homicide has become known, he flees to Midian.

Jesus today speaks of the imminence of judgment. Clear signs of the final age in the person of Jesus had been given, but still there was hardness of heart. Who can honestly say that the opportunity to turn from a life of sin to God is not given? But how often do we pass up the chances he offers us! Let us always respond to the voice of the Lord.

Points to Ponder

Moses: delivery from the water
Turning to God
The joy of the life of grace

Year II

Isaiah 7:1–9
Psalm 48:2–3a, 3b–4, 5–6, 7–8
Matthew 11:20–24

"Do not fear" are the words of Isaiah to Ahaz, king of Judah, who stood in fear of a stronger northern coalition. Within a determined period of time the threat from the north will pass, but Judah is forewarned. If they do not remain strong in faith, they too will suffer the consequences.

The scriptures today address at least two different types of response. The cities of Jesus' time were simply lacking in faith, despite the wonders they had seen. Before Jesus they remained unmoved. Judah held to a belief but it proved weak and untested. It lacked the firmness Isaiah saw as necessary.

Our faith is real but it often remains untested. We seldom suffer the ultimate cost of discipleship. Archbishop Romero of El Salvador, at great personal cost, preached the gospel fearlessly and paid for it with his life. We have countless examples in the history of the church.

We are grateful for our faith. At the same time we never want to see faith imposed on anyone. We pray that we always remain strong.

Points to Ponder

Hardness of heart
An untested faith
Courage in faith

WEDNESDAY OF THE FIFTEENTH WEEK IN ORDINARY TIME

Year I

Exodus 3:1–6, 9–12
Psalm 103:1b–2, 3–4, 6–7
Matthew 11:25–27

The patriarchal figures, despite their unique call, had frequent and prolonged relations with neighboring cultures. Moses married a Midianite after fleeing Egypt and in today's reading is depicted as feeding her father-in-law's flock not far from Mount Horeb.

Seeing a bush that burned but was not consumed, Moses goes over to take a closer look. A voice tells him that he stands on sacred soil and that he must remove his shoes. The God of his fathers has heard the cry of his people in slavery and desires to deliver them. The only identity that he gives at this point is that of the accompanying deity. The liberating God.

God revealed himself in various cultures and a various moments of time. The gospel reminds us that we have relived all of that and more. Jesus today gives thanks that this revelation was not made to those who are exalted and of superior intelligence. It is the little people of his own time who are most receptive. We have come to know the fullness of God's revelation in his Son. The gift is inestimable: our gratitude must be profound.

Points to Ponder

Standing in sacred space
God's identity: Savior
Appreciating revelation

Year II

Isaiah 10:5–7, 13b–16
Psalm 94:5–6, 7–8, 9–10, 14–15
Matthew 11:25–27

A gift that is much discussed today but often lacking is discernment. In looking for answers to serious questions, we often settle for surface answers. We are not interested in getting to the root of the question. In looking at war in the Middle East, we often find superficial answers for why the West is so disliked.

Isaiah dealt only with the fundamental questions. Assyria certainly was a power to be reckoned with, and its anger was directed against Israel and Judah. Yet Yahweh does not hesitate to call it his rod of anger.

Israel is paying the price for its sins. In the face of great tragedy, we are often reluctant to acknowledge our own possible fault. Yet the scriptures are clear. A wanton disregard for God's law will lead to unfortunate consequences.

When we read today's Gospel, we are led to ask, Are we too self-inflated to see where we fail? Are we more concerned about victory than we are about life? How important is it for Americans to be the only world superpower?

There is such a thing as social sin. As Christians we ignore it at our own peril. It is the childlike who hear and receive God's saving word.

Points to Ponder

Discerning our national sins
Seeking justice in an unjust world
Living a childlike spirit

THURSDAY OF THE FIFTEENTH WEEK IN ORDINARY TIME

Year I

Exodus 3:13–20
Psalm 105:1 and 5, 8–9, 24–25, 26–27
Matthew 11:28–30

God's name and accessibility. Pressing God for his name, Moses is given what he asks, but the answer is not so simple. "I

AM WHO I AM." Certainly the name *Yahweh* is related to the verb "to be" and, in the simplest terms, he is identified with the God who truly "is" as opposed to the gods of the heathens who "are not." He goes on to identify himself with the God of the patriarchs: Abraham, Isaac, and Jacob. Whatever the etymology of the name, it became sacred in Israel, was at first pronounced only under sacred circumstances, and then, in the course of time, was not pronounced at all.

Many of us grew up with a marked respect for God's name, but much of that respect has vanished with the passing of years. Gratuitous and even vulgar invocations of God's name have become commonplace in our culture, so much so that we hardly notice them. We cannot change the way other people speak, but as Christians, we ourselves should not invoke sacred names in a negative fashion. The name of Jesus Christ is particularly sacred in view of all that God has accomplished for us through his son.

While there is a certain awesome quality to the revelation of God's name, it is a note of intimacy that appears in Jesus' words today. Where there is grief or discouragement, it is to him that we should turn for solace. While our responsibilities may at times lead to discouragement, the path of the Christian life is ultimately one of vision and great joy.

The truth is that the one God whom we adore has drawn close to us in Jesus Christ, who calls us to find hope and consolation in his life and message.

Points to Ponder

> Reverence for God's name
> Our closeness to Christ
> Bringing our worries to Christ

Year II

> Isaiah 26:7–9, 12, 16–19
> Psalm 102:13–14ab and 15, 16–18, 19–21
> Matthew 11:28–30

Isaiah recalls vividly that the country's pain has ended in joy. But the crushing hand of God's anger had been felt in punishment. As pain precedes childbirth only to break forth in joy, such is the similar lot of God's people. While final salvation still remains on the horizon, his glory is already being enkindled. At some point even the dead will rise.

We all suffer pain in one way or another—war, unemployment, illness. But the Christian life is never overwhelmed. Jesus reminds us today to bring our sorrows to him. He is not an overbearing dictator but a servant-prince who is meek and humble of heart. If we stand firm, we will be refreshed. That is the assurance of today's Gospel.

Some people are forever downcast. A professor I had years ago never smiled. He carried the weight of the world and his students got the brunt of it. One student remarked, "Well, he's strict, but he's fair." Another responded, "I don't know about his fairness, but I've never had any trouble finding his strictness."

Rejoice in the Lord, for the world is his.

Points to Ponder

> Christian hope
> Confiding in the Lord
> Jesus, the meek and humble Master

FRIDAY OF THE FIFTEENTH WEEK IN ORDINARY TIME

Year I

> Exodus 11:10—12:14
> Psalm 116:12–13, 15 and 16bc, 17–18
> Matthew 12:1–8

Passover is a feast of great significance for Jews and Christians. Its beginnings are recounted for us today in the reading from Exodus. It was a spring feast, marked by rites wherein a young lamb was slain and cooked and consumed in its entirety. The lamb's blood was then sprinkled on the doorposts of the homes. The avenging angel would recognize the homes of the Israelites and spare their children from death. This was the great act of God's love and power in bringing his children to freedom.

Jesus' Passover awareness appears in a number of ways. He is depicted as the new Lamb of God who delivers all people from the slavery of sin. In all of the Gospels, the passion and death of Christ take place at Passover. In three of the Gospels, the Eucharist is instituted during the Passover supper. All of this clearly views the saving work of Christ against the background of its Old Testament type.

The Gospel issue of picking and eating grain on the Sabbath had its own importance, but it pales in insignificance to the larger picture of Christ's saving action. When all is said and done, it is not what a person eats that makes him unclean. Purity springs from the workings of the heart.

Points to Ponder

> The Christian Passover
> The generosity of God's love
> Food laws and holiness

Year II

> Isaiah 38:1–6, 21–22, 7–8
> Isaiah 38:10, 11, 12abcd, 16
> Matthew 12:1–8

Law is necessary for life in any well-ordered society. But laws are not all of equal value; at times they can even be bypassed for good reason. They may be divine or human, social or ritual, some having greater value then others. In today's Gospel, Jesus' opponents object that his disciples are violating the Sabbath by plucking and eating grain on the Sabbath.

Jesus objects. The law of necessity has greater value than a law of abstinence. There are other exceptions to the abstinence law that are found even in the scriptures. Moreover, the overriding issue is rooted in the person of Jesus. The Son of Man as God's personal emissary has authority over the Sabbath laws.

It is well to keep the lesson in mind. We at times feel a certain conflict in the law. But the overriding law is that of love. If the urgent needs of my neighbor require that I miss Sunday Mass, there is certainly no sin involved.

This may seem quite clear, but many Catholics fail to see the difference. How often people confess that they missed Mass because they were ill. This is not and cannot be a sin.

Hezekiah, repenting of his sins, is told that in three days he shall go up to the temple. But he wants even further assurance. We trust in the word of our God. "Say but the word and my soul shall be healed." That word has been said; we must have confidence in it.

Points to Ponder

Distinguishing types of law
The supreme law of love
Christ as lord of the Sabbath

SATURDAY OF THE FIFTEENTH WEEK IN ORDINARY TIME

Year I

Exodus 12:37–42
Psalm 136:1 and 10–12, 13–15, 23–24
Matthew 12:14–21

It is certain that the number of people participating in the exodus is highly inflated, as happens frequently in biblical narratives.

Six hundred thousand people would have been impossible to organize and lead through the Sinai desert. However, it is still not difficult to understand Pharaoh's reaction to their departure, whatever the actual number. Egypt was losing its workforce with the acquiescence of its leader. The importance of the Hebrews after 430 years of slavery cannot be contested. Their departure had to be stopped!

Jesus, on other hand, is not concerned with numbers. In today's Gospel, he is the silent healer, a true likeness of Isaiah's servant of the Lord. Quietly and without fanfare he goes about his mission of bringing a saving Word to the people. To the sick he brings healing. His works will speak for themselves, but he wants to avoid any unwanted publicity.

At times, it is impossible to avoid recognition. But it must be received gratefully and humbly. To seek honors and to have ourselves exalted is at odds with Jesus' teaching. We should be pleased when well-deserved recognition is accorded someone. But there is nothing good about striving for success no matter what the cost. Pride comes before a fall. If we are content with our lot in life and glad to do good whenever we can, we can be assured that the just Judge will see our lives in a positive light.

Points to Ponder

>Egyptian fears in the face of the exodus
>Doing good without personal interest
>The dangers of self-seeking

Year II

>Micah 2:1–5
>Psalm 10:1–2, 3–4, 7–8, 14
>Matthew 12:14–21

An old saying goes, "Those who plot evil shall live to reap it." Unjust scheming for personal gain is not a modern phenomenon but is at least as old as the biblical prophets. Micah in today's reading sees greedy people who plot to dispossess the poor and underprivileged. It is a blatant disavowal of the Hebrew ethic and its concern for the needy.

But Micah sees sorrowful days of foreign invasion on the horizon, and it will be a day of woe for the greedy and misguided. Wealthy landowners will see their own property portioned out by the invaders, and they will find themselves among the dispossessed.

What a contrast we have in today's picture of Jesus, who goes about healing and comforting and asks only that he be able to act with quiet and discretion.

In our time crimes of every sort fill our daily papers. Even some public officials are guilty of working against the common good. Regrettably, not even the church is exempt. Religious leaders have freely helped themselves to parish funds until they are apprehended by the law. Rare indeed, but still a great misfortune.

We should pray each day for the grace of honesty and candor and live a life of concern for others that is at the heart of the New Testament message.

Points to Ponder

> Dishonesty in public office
> Sacred office and profane conduct
> Christ as a social figure

MONDAY OF THE SIXTEENTH WEEK IN ORDINARY TIME

Year I

> Exodus 14:5–18
> Exodus 15:1bc–2, 3–4, 5–6
> Matthew 12:38–42

Jonah is a type of Jesus in the three Synoptic Gospels by reason of the fact that he preached repentance to a reluctant people. Jesus did the same but with less success. Jonah met an overwhelmingly positive response; Jesus met closed-mindedness and opposition. Matthew sees a second likeness to Jonah. As Jonah was three days in the belly of the fish, so Jesus was three days in the tomb.

Prophetic voices are so frequently met by reluctant believers. In our reading today from Exodus, shortly after they leave Egypt the Israelites are lamenting their lot in the desert. How often in life it happens that we are shown the better way, the way of virtue.

When we respond positively, our lives can take on a completely different tone. To settle for momentary gratification or passing satisfaction is unworthy of the call we have received.

Christ, our savior, stands at the door of our heart and knocks. His message is one of goodness and peace. Are we listening as did the Ninevites of the Jonah story? Or do we hear and then turn away as did so many contemporaries of Jesus?

Points to Ponder

Living a life of compromise
Choosing God over self
Harden not your hearts

Year II

Micah 6:1–4, 6–8
Psalm 50:5–6, 8–9, 16bc–17, 21 and 23
Matthew 12:38–42

In the course of a strong prophecy upbraiding Israel, Micah gives a brief summary of a true life of faith: "To do justice, to love kindness, and to walk humbly with your God." A brief reflection on each of these qualities is helpful.

When we "do justice," we weigh the word of God to determine what it is that God asks of us. This applies to our everyday lives and our general pattern of conduct as well as to critical situations that may arise.

The just thing will not always be the easier thing; in fact it is often difficult. But the person of faith seeks always to do what is just.

When we love kindness, we are clearly on God's side. Why should we settle for the tawdry and unseemly when we see God's kindness so apparent in the world that surrounds us? When we see an elderly person in need, we can ignore that person or help him in a spirit of "loving kindness."

A day does not pass that we are not met with the opportunity of practicing loving kindness.

To walk humbly with our God is to recognize ourselves as being God's creation and belonging to him. Self-exaltation is pride and must be avoided. To lord it over others is to lose sight of our servant status and our true dependence on God. We are weak; we are human; we falter and fail. To acknowledge that and see God as our protector is to live in humility.

Points to Ponder

Examples of doing justice
Availability: loving kindness
Humility: taking the lower place

TUESDAY OF THE SIXTEENTH WEEK IN ORDINARY TIME

Year I

Exodus 14:21—15:1
Exodus 15:8–9, 10 and 12, 17
Matthew 12:46–50

Even if the Israelites crossing through the Red Sea did not occur with the epic-like proportions that Exodus presents, it made an overwhelming impression on the Hebrews and remained so throughout their history. The pursuing Egyptians are dealt with severely by the Lord, and the fleeing Hebrews walk safely across the dry sea floor. This was undoubtedly the great saving act of their history, and it was recounted annually within every family as an unfailing reminder of God's power.

This is also part of our Christian history, since through our water baptism we too are made part of the people of God. But our Gospel account today transposes all of this to a distinctly higher key. As disciples of Christ, we are infused with the life-giving Spirit that makes us part of his family. We are now brothers, sisters, and mothers. Can there be a closeness greater than that?

Through our baptism we too have passed through the waters and have been saved by the blood of the lamb. Christ, our starting point and our final point, our Alpha and Omega, is both our Savior and our brother. There are many factors that call us to faithfulness, but family loyalty is high on the list!

Points to Ponder

Dramatic buildup in the crossing of the sea
The people of God
The family of God

Year II

Micah 7:14–15, 18–20
Psalm 85:2–4, 5–6, 7–8
Matthew 12:46–50

Today's Gospel once again introduces the question of Jesus' attitude toward human relationships. When it came to his own family, Jesus showed the respect and love that would be expected of a son. But it is not his father and mother whom he holds up for special recognition. When he is told that his family is present looking for him, he quickly addresses the question of his real family ties. His disciples, the ones who do the will of his heavenly father, are his true relatives. At another point in Luke's Gospel, when a woman in the crowd raises her voice in praise of Jesus' mother, Jesus again gives precedence to those who make God's word their own.

All of this ties in closely with Jesus' sense of his own mission as the unique emissary of his father with a very distinctive message. The acceptance of that message results in a very special relationship with Christ, one in which we become his family members.

This idea also appears in the Lucan story of Jesus being lost for three days in the temple as a boy. Jesus is separated from his mother and father so that he might identify with his true mission, bringing others to the family of God.

Are we as willing to give the concerns of God the priority that Christ gave them? Nothing can ever be of greater importance than God's will in our life.

Points to Ponder

> The true family of Christ
> The bonds of Christian community
> Micah: God's delight in clemency

WEDNESDAY OF THE SIXTEENTH WEEK IN ORDINARY TIME

Year I

> Exodus 16:1–5, 9–15
> Psalm 78:18–19, 23–24, 25–26, 27–28
> Matthew 13:1–9

Despite the Hebrews' murmuring and discontent, Yahweh continues to shower blessings on them. They are given bread from heaven (manna) and quail meat for their daily sustenance. So many times in Exodus we read of happenings that have clear New Testament echoes.

Jesus provides us with bread from heaven in his teaching and in a special way in the gift of his body and blood under the form of bread. "The bread that I will give for the life of the world is my flesh" (John 6:51). Imagine, if you can, what it would mean for us to traverse the desert of life without the Eucharist!

We all pray that we may be the good seed of today's Gospel, the seed that produces abundant fruit. This will happen if we remain rooted in our faith and always grateful for the bread from heaven, the greatest sign of God's providential love.

Points to Ponder

> Yahweh's providence in the desert
> Jesus as the bread of life
> The Eucharist and our spiritual life

Year II

> Jeremiah 1:1, 4–10
> Psalm 71:1–2, 3–4a, 5–6ab, 15 and 17
> Matthew 13:1–9

Today's first reading is the account of the call of Jeremiah, the reluctant prophet. Told that he was predestined for his mission from before his birth, he pleads to be excused because of his youth. But the Lord assures him that he will not walk alone. In placing his words in Jeremiah's mouth, Yahweh sets before the prophet his twofold task: to destroy and to build up. In short, Jeremiah will be a prophet of woe and a prophet of hope.

The role of the prophet is like that of Jesus himself. There were various reactions to the teaching of Jesus, as today's Gospel illustrates. Some individuals never accepted; some responded favorably initially but did not persevere; some succumbed to other attractions that proved more appealing. Some, however, remained faithful and became sturdy believers.

Is it any different today? Some prophetic voices have been silenced through violence; others, ignored. Yet in most cases, there have been those who were open to God's teaching. Let us pray for the grace to be attentive and alert to the Lord's call, for it will come.

Points to Ponder

> Prophetic voices in modern time
> The pain of the prophet
> The willingness to be taught

THURSDAY OF THE SIXTEENTH WEEK IN ORDINARY TIME

Year I

> Exodus 19:1–2, 9–11, 16–20b
> Daniel 3:52, 53, 54, 55, 56
> Matthew 13:10–17

The covenant at Mount Sinai between God and his people is recounted for us in Exodus 19–24. Today's reading from chapter 19 is God's act of self-presentation and his offer to enter into a covenant relationship. It is the majesty and the otherness of God that comes into play. It is a frightening scene of thunder, lightning, and dense clouds. The people give their consent and are given ritual prescriptions to prepare themselves for the Lord's return. The Old Testament Yahweh is a God of loving concern and faithfulness, but he is also a God of singular power and might.

The parables of Jesus were a practical means of illustrating the truth through popular images. They were primarily a way of communication, though they were not always direct. Because of this it was also possible to miss the point. This is precisely what happens to some of Jesus' listeners in today's Gospel. There are some people who hear but never understand because of their hardness of heart.

It is common today to speak of God in endearing terms, the God who is close and understands. But this is still the Lord of awe and majesty, the God who can be understood as well as misunderstood. His ways are not our ways. As we approach him each day, let us never lose sight of God as mystery. Our insights into God are inexhaustible.

Points to Ponder

> The meaning of theophany
> The parable as a way of communication
> Understanding God as mystery

Year II

> Jeremiah 2:1–3, 7–8, 12–13
> Psalm 36:6–7ab, 8–9, 10–11
> Matthew 13:10–17

A person is naturally grieved when a beloved decides to terminate a relationship, but the pain is even greater when that partner leaves for another person. Such was the case with the fickle Israel. Jeremiah today speaks of their earlier relationship in idyllic terms; she was like a bride, following him in the desert, the first fruits of the harvest, led by him into the garden land. But what has transpired? The priests do not seek him, the shepherds have rebelled, the prophets prophesy by Baal. Promise has turned to tragedy.

Jesus' hearers, children of Israel, make no attempt to understand his message. His parables, which are intended to illustrate the truth, become obstacles to understanding. It is one thing never to have known the true God, but it is sadder indeed to have known him and rejected him.

The prayer for final perseverance is a worthy one indeed. Our hearts can become cold; we may become beguiled by other attractions or even tempted to despair. But alertness is always a good medicine. *Sursum corda* says the Latin. "Lift up your hearts!" We may waver, but he is forever faithful.

Points to Ponder

> Cherishing the faith
> Abandoning the truth
> Praying for perseverance

FRIDAY OF THE SIXTEENTH WEEK IN ORDINARY TIME

Year I

> Exodus 20:1–17
> Psalm 19:8, 9, 10, 11
> Matthew 13:18–23

It is sometimes said in our days that the Ten Commandments have lost their relevance. What can the commandments possibly say to modern society? But is the problem with the Decalogue or with *us*? Let us look at the first three commandments and ask some hard questions.

Few people totally abandon their belief in God and turn to the worship of pagan idols. But who can deny that there is erosion in our belief and therefore an implicit idolatry? There is the man in the television commercial with car keys in hand who says, "I want to live well, with the car I want, the house of my choice, plenty of vacation time. That's all I need to be happy." There is no room for God in such an attitude.

And reverence for God's name? Today many of the rules of propriety and civility have vanished. Not only are the names of God and Christ bandied about, but much of our speech seriously violates the norms of human decency.

As for Sunday worship, it remains steady in the United States, but in other traditionally Christian countries it has sunk to historic lows. If we are not careful, the decline in religious observance will happen here as well.

We need a new *world evangelization*, a revitalization of the faith. We have been gifted in Christ the Lord. Gifts require thanks, and that means recognition of who God is and what God has done. We must be continually aware of those false attractions that can choke our faith.

The recognition of God, reverence for God, and the worship of God—three ideas as old as the Decalogue and still meaningful today.

Points to Ponder

> Today's spiritual lethargy
> Reverence for God's name
> The Mass as Christ's great gift

Year II

> Jeremiah 3:14–17
> Jeremiah 31:10, 11–12abcd, 13
> Matthew 13:18–23

The ark of the covenant, the sacred footstool or throne of the Lord, was lost at the time of the Babylonian destruction of Jerusalem and was never recovered. Jeremiah tells his people that it is not an irreparable loss, because someday a new era will dawn. At that time Jerusalem will be the center of all religious attention.

There all nations of the earth will converge in recognizing the universal lordship of Yahweh.

The New Testament reminds us that we are citizens of the new Jerusalem. The church has become a center of religious life for people of all ethnic and national backgrounds. This is the church founded on the apostles and their predecessors the twelve tribes of Israel, with Christ himself as the cornerstone. In fact, in the study of our religion, no city emerges with an importance equal to Jerusalem.

As citizens of the New Jerusalem, let us cherish our faith.

Points to Ponder

> The early significance of the ark
> The supplanting of sacred symbols in a new era
> Understanding our spiritual origins

SATURDAY OF THE SIXTEENTH WEEK IN ORDINARY TIME

Year I

> Exodus 24:3–8
> Psalm 50:1b–2, 5–6, 14–15
> Matthew 13:24–30

The covenant between Yahweh and Israel on Mount Sinai was essentially bilateral. It required the agreement of both parties. In today's reading from Exodus 24, the covenant is solemnized. In response to Yahweh's question as to their willingness to observe the covenant terms, the people respond in the affirmative. The bond is then actualized in blood. For the Hebrews, life was in the blood, which made of it a sacred element. An altar had been erected that symbolized God himself. A portion of the animal blood is sprinkled on the altar and a portion on the people, thus bonding the two together in a permanent and sacred relationship. The words of Moses are climactic—"See the blood of the covenant"—and will be heard again at the Last Supper. Christ has made of us a holy people, a priestly people in his own sacrificial blood. We are continually reminded that we stem from a rich tradition. It is only from an understanding of our Hebrews roots that we begin to understand our relationship to God.

The wheat and the weeds, the good and the bad. We live in a distinctly imperfect church. It is unrealistic to believe that the church is made up of only the perfect. It is encouraging to know that we are surrounded by the weak and the strong. It means that the goal is open to all of us, and progress is never out of sight. The offer is always present.

Points to Ponder

> Blood significance in the Bible
> The covenant and mutual consent
> The coexistence of the wheat and weeds

Year II

> Jeremiah 7:1–11
> Psalm 84:3, 4, 5–6a and 8a, 11
> Matthew 13:24–30

Some people love to wear a gold crucifix. Others carry a medal on their person at all times. These can be healthy signs of a strong spiritual attachment. Or they may be merely security totems, assuring us that we have divine protection. Today's message of Jeremiah is much to the point. He tells his contemporaries that it is hopeless to assume God's protection simply because they continue to have his temple in their midst. As long as their conduct violates the terms of the covenant, they are beyond God's protection. Guilty of idolatry, adultery, robbery, and murder, they are hardly the reflection of God's otherness in the world. Their possession of the temple is purely symbolic and gives no assurance of God's protection.

But the situation is not dire. As long as we live in a church made up of wheat and weeds, of the good and the not so good, conversion is possible. That is the consoling side of today's Gospel. There are people whom we love deeply but whom we meet in church only very infrequently. Sometimes it is members of our own family whose faith is very weak. We can never rule out a day of conversion. What is remarkable is the number of people who have unexpectedly come to God in real conversions that stay for life.

We pray that God strengthen our faith, a faith that rests in Christ our Savior who desires nothing more than our love for him and the Father.

It is the same Christ who assures us that he has prepared a place for us in his heavenly kingdom.

Points to Ponder

> The significance of wearing crosses and religious medals
> Religious identity and false security
> The fidelity of God and conversion

MONDAY OF THE SEVENTEENTH WEEK IN ORDINARY TIME

Year I

> Exodus 32:15–24, 30–34
> Psalm 106:19–20, 21–22, 23
> Matthew 13:31–35

The seriousness of the calf of gold incident lies in the fact that such idolatry came on the heels of a solemn covenant with God. Moses' anger leads him to destroy the calf, smash the tablets of the law that Yahweh had given him, and upbraid the Hebrews for their faithlessness. Aaron offers a lame excuse for such a serious violation and downgrades his own culpability as much as possible.

But it is the magnanimous spirit of Moses that stands out. In asking God's forgiveness, he is willing to surrender his own role in the event that the Lord cannot bring himself to absolve his people. Moses is told that punishment will be meted out to the guilty only at a future date. Moses is reconfirmed in his leadership role.

For an innocent person to substitute himself to another requires a great deal of spiritual fortitude. It recognizes the seriousness of sin and shows a deep sense of generosity. It is not unusual to hear a parent offer him- or herself in the place of a very sick child. For an innocent person to substitute for the guilty calls for even greater virtue.

St. Paul reminds us that this is exactly what Christ did for us. In the face of our serious guilt, he offered himself as the innocent victim. His vicarious atonement deals sin the death blow. The innocent Lamb has offered himself for the world's sins.

Points to Ponder

> Homely helps
> Israel's sin of idolatry
> Moses offers his own rejection
> Forgiveness in Christ Jesus

Year II

> Jeremiah 13:1–11
> Deuteronomy 32:18–19, 20, 21
> Matthew 13:31–35

Remarkable unseen growth is one of the points of today's liturgy. Paul and Apollos were fellow evangelizers and at one point Paul comments on their accomplishments: "I have planted, Apollos watered, but God gave the growth" (1 Cor 3:6). All of us like to see the fruit of our labor and are not averse to taking a certain credit. In the realm of the Spirit, human effort is present but it is God who produces the end result.

Today's parables point in the same direction. The very small and insignificant mustard seed shows an outstanding growth. Likewise it takes a small amount of yeast to leaven a large batch of dough. And none of this is due to human industry. So too in the realm of faith, there is often a very high level of acceptance. But just as the crops grow while the farmer sleeps, so too in the real of the Spirit.

Naturally we are happy when an important project comes to fruition. But the kingdom is the work of Christ, and we are pleased to be his collaborators. Of his first followers Francis of Assisi never said that he gathered them. His only comment was, "God gave me brothers."

Points to Ponder

> Collaborators in God's kingdom
> Recognizing the work of God
> Zeal for the kingdom

TUESDAY OF THE SEVENTEENTH WEEK IN ORDINARY TIME

Year I

> Exodus 33:7–11; 34:5b–9, 28
> Psalm 103:6–7, 8–9, 10–11, 12–13
> Matthew 13:36–43

It was in the meeting tent outside the camp that Moses conversed with Yahweh. As the Book of Exodus presents the case, it was on these occasions that Moses gained further insights into the nature of God.

The meetings were revelatory. In today's reading the Lord declares himself as patient and forgiving, "for the thousandth generation." This is a fundamental notion of God in the Judeo–Christian tradition. Yet punishment for wrongdoing, where there is not a contrite spirit, is clearly not overlooked. Punishment for sin is never absent from the Lord's sight.

People often conjecture about the presence of the weeds at the end of time. And it should be noted that the weeds are not only sinners but those who cause others to sin. Will the rejected be many or few? It is very hard and of little value for us to play the "numbers game."

What the scriptures speak about very clearly is accountability. God is loving and infinitely forgiving but is also not mocked.

Our time here is very limited. We all make mistakes, and that is understandable. But we should never succumb to a spirit of indifference in the most important undertaking of our lives.

Points to Ponder

God as forgiving and punishing
Accountability for our lives
Seeking forgiveness

Year II

Jeremiah 14:17–22
Psalm 79:8, 9, 11 and 13
Matthew 13:36–43

Jeremiah today looks out over a pillaged and beleaguered Judah. She has reaped the punishment so often predicted. The picture could have been different had the population so decided. But even if the country is faithless, God remains faithful. And so Jeremiah utters a heartfelt plea for forgiveness. It is futile to turn to "do-nothing gods." It is to the covenant that the prophet returns and asks the Lord to forget it not.

The history of Christianity has seen repeated examples of infidelity. The people of the new covenant disregarded their special status no less than the people of old. But forgiveness requested has been forgiveness attained. If we are contrite of heart, all wrongs can be righted. The prophets never failed to turn to the Lord after punishment.

One of the clearest signs of contrition is our willingness to forgive others or to ask for forgiveness. In fact the New Testament uses this as a yardstick to measure God's forgiveness. We have all suffered hurts. But a magnanimous spirit rises above them. As we ask God's forgiveness, let us never forget to extend our own.

Points to Ponder

The fall of Judah and divine punishment
The prayer for forgiveness
Forgiving others

WEDNESDAY OF THE SEVENTEENTH WEEK IN ORDINARY TIME

Year I

Exodus 34:29–35
Psalm 99:5, 6, 7, 9
Matthew 13:44–46

We all know people who talk very little about their faith but whose whole demeanor reflects its importance in their lives. This is the transformative power of faith. This quality brings to mind the reflection of God that shone forth in the face of Moses. Moses' encounters with God had a lasting effect upon him. His face became so brilliant that he had to keep it veiled; the veil was removed whenever he entered the tent again to consult the Lord.

The story gives us pause and the opportunity to ask what effect my faith is having on my life or the life of others. We may be well versed in church teaching, even learned scholars, but if faith does not ignite a fire within us, it may be quite ineffective. Do we become enthused when others come to the faith? Are we willing to take the time to work patiently and at length with someone dealing with a major problem?

Sometimes we are called to give until it hurts. Years ago a pastor in lower Manhattan was known for never having refused a request for money. When asked, at one point, if he realized how many times he had been taken advantage of, his answer was simple. "No, I don't. But I know that God is not going to ask me about that." What was known to all his friends and acquaintances was that his face shone like Moses'.

Points to Ponder

The glow of Christian virtue
Giving beyond measure
Our relationship with God: transformative?

Year II

> Jeremiah 15:10, 16–21
> Psalm 59:2–3, 4, 10–11, 17, 18
> Matthew 13:44–46

There have to be days when we ask ourselves, "Is it all worth it?" Discouragement and doubt enter every life at some point. Is it really the treasure hidden in the field? The pearl of great price? In our less troubled moments, we can say, "Yes," when we consider what God has done for us.

Salvation is not something we have to go and seek. It comes to us in the inestimable gift of a God made man. Paul says very clearly that faith is not something we attain. It is extended by God to us. Who can stand in the presence of such love and not be grateful? We want to buy the field; we want to treasure the pearl.

We want to pray often that we not become lukewarm. There is too much at stake, and the gift only shows our own unworthiness.

Lord, stir up my faith in a spirit of gratitude. I want the field and the treasure, as well as the priceless pearl. Why? Because it is a gift for which you have paid dearly. Of that I can never lose sight.

Points to Ponder

> Taking faith for granted
> The price God has paid for us
> Praying for an increase of faith

THURSDAY OF THE SEVENTEENTH WEEK IN ORDINARY TIME

Year I

> Exodus 40:16–21, 34–38
> Psalm 84:3, 4, 5–6a and 8a, 11
> Matthew 13:47–53

The completion of the dwelling has singular importance, for it was the locus of Yahweh's unique presence. The ark was the throne of his presence; it was separated by a curtain from the rest of the dwelling. The cloud representing the *shekinah* or glory of the Lord hovered over the dwelling, and only when it lifted did the Hebrews move on. Within the ark were placed the commandments of the law. When the temple was constructed, the ark was located in the Most Holy Place.

God was never missing from the life of his people. The same is true in the Christian era. Christ promises his followers that he will be with them always until the end of time. He remains with us in word and sacrament, especially in the great gift of the Eucharist. By reason of the gift of the Spirit, he remains present in all of us as well, a presence that is especially accented when we gather as an assembly of worship.

St. Teresa of Avila, who suffered for years from spiritual aridity, once asked the Lord where he was when she felt so desolate. His answer was, "Right in the center of your heart." Let us never feel abandonment, for even in our darkest moments, Christ is with us.

Points to Ponder

Sacred space
The presence of Israel's God
Christ's presence in our lives

Year II

Jeremiah 18:1–6
Psalm 146:1b–2, 3–4, 5–6ab
Matthew 13:47–53

Once again Matthew includes a parable that speaks of the coexistence of good and evil, the worthy and the unworthy, within the community of believers. He further goes on to say that the community will contain new things and old, new departures as well as tradition. Like Israel, we too are like clay in the potter's hands. He can fashion and mold us as he would. Of course, we are free to turn out well or badly, to be embraced or rejected. There are those in the

Christian community who have separated themselves from the potter. Also, as the net is cast, some fish are good; others are not.

But we should never lose sight of the efficacy of prayer. Christ speaks of sheep who have strayed, yet have found their way home. Remorse and contrition are not that unusual. Evil ways can be left behind. If we keep the wanderers in our hearts and prayers, good things may yet appear.

Points to Ponder

> Clay in the potter's hands
> Fashioned according to God's will
> Open to conversion

FRIDAY OF THE SEVENTEENTH WEEK IN ORDINARY TIME

Year I

> Leviticus 23:1, 4–11, 15–16, 27, 34b–37
> Psalm 81:3–4, 5–6, 10–11ab
> Matthew 13:54–58

Three of Israel's major feasts are cited in today's first reading: Passover-Unleavened Bread, the Day of Atonement, and the feast of Booths. The first recalls the redemption of God's people from the slavery of Egypt; the second was the annual day of prayer for forgiveness of sin; and the third a feast of thanksgiving for the fruit of the harvest.

We are reminded that this threefold approach to God is paralleled in our Catholic liturgical life. Our Passover is celebrated in our Holy Week Triduum and Easter; our atonement in the Lenten season; and thanksgiving in every Eucharist that is offered. And it represents an excellent summary of our Christian experience. We are redeemed by the blood of the Lamb of God, the Son of the eternal Father. Our failings are repeatedly forgiven by an all-good and merciful God. And our life is one of gratitude for all that God has done for us.

Christ, our deliverer and Savior, we are grateful for our new life in you and for the forgiveness of our sins. Make of our lives a continual hymn of gratitude.

Points to Ponder

> Celebrating the paschal mystery
> Repentance for sin
> Prayer of thanks

Year II

> Jeremiah 26:1–9
> Psalm 69:5, 8–10, 14
> Matthew 13:54–58

Both Jesus and Jeremiah were prophets who were not honored in their own country. Although the people were amazed at Jesus' learning and insight, he was such a "local boy" that he could not be taken seriously. Jeremiah's message was so threatening with reference to the temple and the city that it seemed sacrilegious and out of place. The best solution was to be rid of the prophet.

In many ways we are not much different. We settle into a particular way of thinking and make what we hear conform to that. We see acts of violence perpetrated against innocent people. When we wage a war we see only one side and fail to see the hurt that may be present in the opposition. We sometimes exploit the natural resources of poorer countries and then fail to understand their resentment.

Let us try to have an open and understanding spirit. The law of averages tells us that there are times when we will be right and times when we will be wrong. At least we want to try to comprehend what others are saying. It is surprising to see how much we can change and learn from others.

Points to Ponder

> Opposition to Jeremiah
> Jesus as the "local boy"
> A willingness to learn and to change

SATURDAY OF THE SEVENTEENTH WEEK IN ORDINARY TIME

Leviticus 25:1, 8–17
Psalm 67:2–3, 5, 7–8
Matthew 14:1–12

Land and life—two basic goods that are addressed in today's readings. The fiftieth or Jubilee year was one in which private property on lease or loan reverted to its original owner. It was seen as a matter of basic justice, and personal property was not permanently alienated. The right to ownership of personal property has long been championed in the Judeo-Christian tradition.

Any political or economic system that denies people the right to property has not long endured. But this is not a right without limits. We have a right to what we need, not the right to accumulate property as desired.

Wars have been fought against the tyranny of denying the right of ownership, as well as against landowners who overran the poor to have more for personal gain. The right to private property is not limitless.

That John the Baptist should lose his life under such tawdry conditions only adds to the pain and insult. Herod was moved to take his life because of the insistence of a dancing stepdaughter and her scheming mother. It all takes place in the context of Herod's birthday party.

Excesses in food and drink can produce great tragedy. The one whom Jesus thought of as the greatest ever born of women died because of a woman's whim, with no serious charge brought against him. A lack of discretion often accompanies excessive consumption of alcohol. It is one of those cases where forewarned is forearmed.

Points to Ponder

Limits on the right to private property
Scheming to silence a prophetic voice
Moderation in food and drink

Year II

> Jeremiah 26:11–16, 24
> Psalm 69:15–16, 30–31, 33–34
> Matthew 14:1–12

It is encouraging to read accounts of the prophet's voice being heeded. Such is the case in Jeremiah's warning to the princes and the people.

But it is equally sad to read, in today's Gospel, the account of the Baptist's death to satisfy a perverse whim. It is true that it is not always easy to verify a prophet. But even when one might be inauthentic, the prophet should not be silenced. Jeremiah's word was verified; his call to conversion could have resulted in the people and country being saved. But instead of paying attention to his message, his opponents latched on to words that sounded treasonous. Simple attachment to the temple of the Lord would not bring deliverance; a life of fidelity to God would.

John was beheaded because he told Herod that the king's marital relationship was immoral. Herod knew that the people revered John and therefore would not have him killed. But Herodias, his wife, proved to be the schemer and brought about his death.

Duplicity in our lives should be avoided at all cost. Any form of double dealing or behind-the-scenes manipulation is unchristian. Let us be attentive to voices that differ from our own thinking, even when we may not be in agreement. And above all, let our words be honest and straightforward.

Points to Ponder

> Listening to the divergent voice
> Uprightness in moral decisions
> Respect for the other person.

MONDAY OF THE EIGHTEENTH WEEK IN ORDINARY TIME

Year I

Numbers 11:4b–15
Psalm 81:12–13, 14–15, 16–17
Matthew 14:13–21

When people are hungry we often see an unpleasant side of their character. The Hebrews in the desert were given manna. But they quickly tired of that and longed for the food that was theirs in Egypt. Moses' patience was exhausted, as he felt that he could no longer carry this burden alone. He would rather face death than continue to support such an obstinate people.

The people who followed Jesus also found themselves at one point without food. In his compassion, Jesus provides enough for the crowd to eat, with nothing more at his disposal than five loaves of bread and a few fish.

The narrative contains a strong eucharistic imprint as Jesus blesses, breaks, and gives. In other words, the account cannot be separated from its eucharistic implications.

We too are often anxious and dissatisfied in life and, like the Hebrews, are inclined to forget the goodness of a providential God. Jesus is the bread from heaven who continually provides for us in many ways, not the least of which is in the Eucharist. The common elements of daily life become the body and blood of the Lord. Our anxieties pale in insignificance before the goodness of the Lord.

Points to Ponder

Our grumbling and murmuring
Jesus satisfies our hunger
The Eucharist and our journey of life

Year II

Jeremiah 28:1–17
Psalm 119:29, 43, 79, 80, 95, 102
Matthew 14:13–21

Hananiah was a prophet who told the people what they wanted to hear. A quick end to exile, an imminent return to their homeland, restoration of the temple property. Jeremiah upbraids him and predicts his death for misleading the people. The length of time for the Hebrews to bear the yoke of Nebuchadnezzar, King of Babylon, remains undetermined. To minister in the name of the Lord remains a very sacred call.

In Matthew's account of the miraculous provision of food, there is an interesting note. After blessing and breaking the bread, Jesus gives it to the disciples to distribute. It is Matthew who shows special deference to the disciples and highlights their ministerial role. Jesus appears to them in Galilee after his resurrection and commissions them to carry his message to the world.

In today's church, new forms of ministry have appeared, with the laity accorded new roles. These come to the fore in every Sunday Mass we attend. This is as it should be but carries with it its own responsibilities. A coherent Christian life, a reverence for the sacred, and a deep sense of faith. Ministers are commissioned by Christ in what must always be seen as a sacred trust.

Points to Ponder

The prophecy that pleases
Ministers of the Eucharist
Willingness to respond to the Church's call

TUESDAY OF THE EIGHTEENTH WEEK IN ORDINARY TIME

Year I

Numbers 12:1–13
Psalm 51:3–4, 5–6ab, 6cd–7, 12–13
Matthew 14:22–36

In today's readings we see the effects of a lack of faith. As the sea becomes rougher and Jesus is sighted, Peter is told to leave the boat and walk to Jesus on the water. He begins steadily enough, but in the face of the strong wind, he wavers and begins to sink. It was for arguing and complaining against Moses that Aaron and Miriam are faulted and Miriam is struck with leprosy.

It is all too easy to strike a position by which our faith remains largely undisturbed, unchallenged. We follow a contented middle way of comfortable belief, not walking on water, perhaps, but at least not sinking. We must continually strive to strengthen our faith.

Why not participate in one of the many forms of apostolate that are present in the church today, all valid expressions of faith? We should work to help the faith of others. And then there is the added responsibility of educating our children in the faith. This is not something we can simply turn over to religious educators. The values of faith have to appear in our own lives; parents are the first to form children as Christians.

It is faith that saves, says St. Paul, and it is a vibrant and lively faith of which he speaks. Jesus speaks of it often and explicitly states the role it plays in the healings that he performs. We seldom reflect on faith in our lives when, in fact, our constant prayer should be, "Lord, increase my faith!"

Points to Ponder

> The faith to deal with a complaining spirit
> Walking in faith over the troubled water
> Ministry as an expression of faith

Year II

> Jeremiah 30:1–2, 12–15, 18–22
> Psalm 102:16–18, 19–21, 29 and 22–23
> Matthew 14:22–36

There were many times in the Old Testament when Yahweh threatened his people with punishment. But he relented. In today's Gospel, Peter steps out boldly on the water to meet the Master but soon begins to sink. Christ's extended hand saves him from drowning. Then there is the sinful woman of the Gospels whose accusers wanted to stone. Scarcely able to speak in her shame, she receives forgiveness from Jesus without reproach.

Jeremiah today sees a sinful Israel. Struck in her sinfulness and crying out in her wounds, Israel senses deeply her alienation. But Yahweh pledges a rebuilding and resettlement, a city on a hill and a splendid palace, with songs of laughter and of praise. It is a new and restored Jerusalem, a place where forgiveness has been assured.

We have all been guilty of sin, some more serious than others. But those sins, once as red as scarlet, are now white as snow. The saddest thing is to slink away and wallow in our guilt. It takes no more than an act of sorrow. What was true in Jeremiah's time is equally true today.

Lord, forgive me a repentant sinner.

Points to Ponder

> Attitudes of intransigence
> Christ's helping hand in times of distress

WEDNESDAY OF THE EIGHTEENTH WEEK IN ORDINARY TIME

Year I

> Numbers 30:1–2, 12–14:1, 26a–29a, 34–35
> Psalm 106:6–7ab, 13–14, 21–22, 23
> Matthew 15:21–28

The scouts who were sent ahead by Moses to reconnoiter the land of Canaan were successful in overriding the proposal of Caleb that the land be taken. They convinced the people that they were no match for the race of giants that occupied the land. For their refusal to comply with Yahweh's wish, they pay a dear price: their generation will not enter the land.

The Israelites were obstinate in opposing God's will. The Canaanite woman in the Gospel is also a persistent figure. But her persistence results in her turning the mind of Jesus in her favor.

Because of her determination, she turned the Lord to her side. It is important to note that in Matthew's Gospel the earthly ministry of Jesus was restricted to the land of the Jews. Here a pagan Canaanite woman ventures into Jewish territory to make her plea. Jesus at first rebuffs her—with a form of verbal sparring—then, recognizing her great faith, agrees to her request.

St. Monica prayed for years for the conversion of her son Augustine, and her prayer was ultimately answered. Persistence can be a sign of deep faith. And it may be asked of any of us. The Israelites were obstinate; the Canaanite woman was persistent. The two stories illustrate well the difference.

Points to Ponder

> Sin as obstinacy to God's will
> Constancy as consistent compliance to God's will
> Persistence in prayer

Year II

> Jeremiah 31:1–7
> Jeremiah 31:10, 11–12ab, 13
> Matthew 15:21–28

Jeremiah excels in poetic imagery, especially in those sections that speak of Israel's restoration. The country would one day stand out among the nations as the favored of God, a love that was there from the beginning. The faithful remnant of a faithless people would ultimately triumph.

In Matthew's Gospel, Jesus has come primarily for the people of Israel. But even in that Gospel the non-Jew is not forgotten. The account of the Canaanite woman is a case in point. One stands in amazement at her determination. She had undoubtedly heard of Jesus and had decided to approach him at all costs. She enters the land of the Jews, a foreign woman in an alien culture. She was not only a woman; she was a nonbeliever in a world that did not look with favor on Gentile people. In the interests of her daughter, she is not about to be dissuaded. When Jesus first refuses her request in proverbial form, she responds to him in a similar fashion.

The Canaanite woman was a person of uncommon faith. The narrative is very clear on that point. And it is that faith that brings Jesus to accede to her request. Much of the Western world today champions reason over faith. Governments consider faith obsolete. Religious practice, prayer, and observance are dismissed as medieval holdovers. Those who do believe must not waver in their conviction. Every time that faith has been challenged in history, it returns with greater vigor.

Points to Ponder

The Lord's forgiveness of Israel
The persistence of the Canaanite woman
Faith the cornerstone of our life

THURSDAY OF THE EIGHTEENTH WEEK IN ORDINARY TIME

Year I

Numbers 20:1–13
Psalm 95:1–2, 6–7, 8–9
Matthew 16:13–23

It was at Meribah that the Israelites' lament about lack of sustenance was met by the Lord with water from the rock. But in giving themselves a place of prominence in the event and not emphasizing God's providence, Moses and Aaron will not be permitted entrance into the land of promise.

In Peter's profession of faith in Jesus at Caesarea Philippi is the fullest depiction of this in the three Synoptic Gospels. The other two accounts may represent an earlier tradition, while Matthew presents a full post-Easter expression of faith in the full divinity of Jesus. He is recognized not only as the Christ Messiah or promised one of Israel, but as the true Son of the living God. It is upon the believing Peter that primacy among the apostles is conferred, including the power to retain or absolve sin, and the keys admitting entrance to the kingdom. As the narrative continues, however, Jesus described his different type of messiahship in terms of suffering and death, and Peter's attempt to discount such an assertion meets with a sharp rebuff from his Master.

After the apostles had reached a point of confessing Jesus to be the Messiah, the king of promise for God's people, it was not easy for them to hear his prediction of suffering and death. But such is the great Christian paradox. We are assured a life in God and the total forgiveness of sins. But it has come at a dear price, the saving death of God's Son. And it reminds us that our life, too, is a path to God through hardship and pain. The task in life is to bring the two together. *Per aspera ad astra*. "Through trials to the stars."

Points to Ponder

> Belief in Jesus as Messiah and God's Son
> The pain that led to salvation
> Our own life of "cross and crown"

Year II

> Jeremiah 31:31–34
> Psalm 51:12–13, 14–15, 18–19
> Matthew 16:13–23

There are few passages in the Old Testament that speak as clearly to the Christian believer as today's passage from Jeremiah. If there is one theme that links the two Testaments, it is that of covenant, the bond between God and his people. It is the prophet Jeremiah who predicts in the clearest terms that a new covenant will be established at a future date.

Unlike the covenant of old, the new bond will be written not on stone tablets but on the human heart, pointing to a deeply personal relationship with God. By reason of God's action in human lives, the new relationship will be direct and immediate. It will mean the total remission of sin. "I will be their God, and they shall be my people." One cannot read this passage without being reminded of Christ's words over the cup at the Last Supper: "This cup…is the new covenant in my blood " (Luke 22:20).

Peter wanted to profess Christ as Messiah and God's Son but found the prediction of suffering and death unacceptable. But there could be no other way. The greatest proof of God's love was Calvary, and it was there that the new covenant of the heart was established. Jesus is recognized as Lord and Son of God with his resurrection and the conferring of the Holy Spirit. But the resurrection had to be preceded by a saving death. The new covenant embraces both the death and rising of Jesus.

Today's scripture reminds us that we are indeed a kingdom of priests, a holy people.

Points to Ponder

> Jeremiah's new covenant
> Peter's profession of faith
> Christians people of the new covenant

FRIDAY OF THE EIGHTEENTH WEEK IN ORDINARY TIME

Year I

> Deuteronomy 4:32–40
> Psalm 77:12–13, 14–15, 16 and 21
> Matthew 16:24–28

The exhortations to love and adore Yahweh in the Book of Deuteronomy are both stirring and filled with a lyric quality. Indeed, what people had ever heard the voice of their god? Our God is one who has drawn near to us, lifted us out of bondage, and brought us to the land he promised. Deuteronomy is strong on motivation. In view of God's goodness, he must be our only God, and his commandments and statutes must be observed.

Matthew today transposes the discussion to another level. In the Christian life, there is no glory without the cross; there is no life without a death. Who of us can deny that the self is always standing in the way of good intention? We tend to want to satisfy our desires and give them priority, but it cannot be that way. We are continually faced with human need, with coming to the aid of another. The Christian must stand ready at every turn to die to personal interest and generously give of self to God and others.

The return of Christ in glory will be the time of retribution. Verse 28 cannot refer to the evangelist's contemporaries; it most likely refers to the inauguration of the kingdom with Christ's death and resurrection. But the injunction is clear enough. There is no easy way to glory, even though it may be accomplished joyfully and willingly. Our life is a challenge—let us embrace it.

Points to Ponder

> God's initiative on our behalf
> Examples of dying to self
> Ways in which we gain a life

Year II

> Nahum 2:1, 3; 3:1–3, 6–7
> Deuteronomy 32:35cd–36ab, 39abcd, 41
> Matthew 16:24–28

The prophets are masters at showing both sides of the coin. Yes, Israel has paid a dear price for its wanton disregard of Yahweh's will. But it is not the end of the plan. "Good tidings" are announced by Nahum: the restoration of Jacob, the end of invasion, and the punishment of invaders. And what will become of the dreaded Assyrians? God's wrath will fall upon its charging cavalry, the bearers of death and destruction. And Nineveh will be without mourners. As an empire, she cast a long shadow; now she will receive her just dessert.

The Christian life too has its light and shadows. It requires a dying and a rising, from which there is no escape. God did not have to become man to achieve redemption; there are other paths he could have chosen. But if we were to be convinced of his unparalleled love, it had to take a striking form.

And then Jesus reminds us that it can be no different for us. No two Christians endure the same denial of self. But without showing preference to the needs of others and of giving God his due, then life is not lost. But when there is a death to self, the new life gives joy and satisfaction and leads to an eternity of love.

Points to Ponder

> The permanence of God's love
> The response to God's love
> Dying and rising in daily life

SATURDAY OF THE EIGHTEENTH WEEK IN ORDINARY TIME

Year I

> Deuteronomy 6:4–13
> Psalm 18:2–3a, 3bc–4, 47 and 51
> Matthew 17:14–20

The Deuteronomy reading today contains the primary profession of faith for the Jewish people. Known as the great *Shema* ("Hear, O Israel"), it emphasizes primarily the exclusive hegemony of Yahweh over the Hebrew people; to him alone belongs total adherence in love and worship. Of equal importance is the observance of his commandments and statutes. This God, the Lord of heaven and earth and all that they contain, has chosen this people as his own for his own inscrutable reasons. This belief, Israel is to hold at the center of its life in a spirit of deepest gratitude.

When questioned as to the first and greatest commandment, Jesus cites the *Shema*, adding to it a single verse from Leviticus that speaks of the love of neighbor as well. Therefore, in the Christian tradition as well, this remains the cornerstone precept; it summarizes the entire Christian ethic.

In every instance, regardless of what the precept may be, observance points to love; it is the only response worthy of the creator-redeemer God.

Jesus' annoyance in today's Gospel is not with the father of the possessed boy but rather with the disciples for their lack of faith. Our failures in life usually point in the same direction. We are afraid to launch out into uncharted waters because we are afraid. We want to hoard food in our barns because of the possible dangers of tomorrow. If we truly believe as the great *Shema* enjoins, the Lord will not disappoint.

Points to Ponder

The *Shema*: a comprehensive prayer
Jesus and the *Shema*
Examples of our lack of faith

Year II

Habakkuk 1:12—2:4
Psalm 9:8–9, 10–11, 12–13
Matthew 17:14–20

There is a tendency to quote frequently a few well-known verses of minor prophets like Habakkuk. Such is the case with the final verse in today's reading from the prophet. The conduct of human beings is so often reprehensible; people exploit others for their own gain. People worship their own industry and eliminate others without mercy. In response, the Lord advises the prophet to consign the prophetic vision to writing. "The righteous live by their faith."

The vision contains a timeless truth. We err if we think that evil will last forever or never be brought to justice. Wherever there is deceit and the absence of integrity, clear boundaries will be set up. Evildoing will meet its recompense. On the other hand, where there is a just person, life is assured. It is faith that determines the just person's conduct. It is the good that ultimately triumphs.

Jesus in the Gospel today assures us that faith can move mountains.

If the disciples believe strongly enough, anything is possible. Goodness sometimes emerges in unexpected forms. Just when we believe that affluent countries think too little of the poor and diseased people of the world, important industrialists turn over funds from their earnings—at times in the billions of dollars—to alleviate the world's pain. We are distressed at evil, but we must never dismiss the good.

Points to Ponder

> Evil's presence in the world
> The ultimate triumph of good
> A justice that leads to life

MONDAY OF THE NINETEENTH WEEK IN ORDINARY TIME

Year I

> Deuteronomy 10:12–22
> Psalm 147:12–13, 14–15, 19–20
> Matthew 17:22–27

It seems that we never escape the question of taxes—neither in modern or biblical times. The temple tax was imposed on all Jewish males of a certain age. Peter's affirmative answer to his questioners clearly shows that he expected Jesus to comply with the tax law. But Jesus introduces an interesting question. Roman law drew heavily on foreigners to meet the tax debt. Evidently much less was asked of its own citizens. When it came to the temple, Jesus was a son in the Father's house, not a foreigner. Therefore, he and his disciples were exempt from the tax. But in order to prevent scandal, he decides to comply, in a miraculous fashion.

The reign of God stands above any human government. Its authority is not divided. The state has its own duties and an income that has to be supplied by the citizenry. The temple had restorations and maintenance to be concerned with. It is obviously the beneficiaries who must pay. But for Jesus it is a secondary and irrelevant question.

Today there is much justifiable debate about the justice of taxation. There are instances when the working class carries the heaviest burden, with benefits often given to the wealthier classes. As Christians we are dutiful citizens who are willing to do our share. But justice often demands that we raise our voice in protest to elected officials when there is a disproportionate weight placed upon people who already carry too heavy a burden.

Points to Ponder

> Christ as a subject of taxation
> Christ's willingness to comply
> Citizens as taxpayers

Year II

> Ezekiel 1:2–5, 24–28c
> Psalm 148:1–2, 11–12, 13, 14
> Matthew 17:22–27

Ezekiel's inaugural vision is both vivid and puzzling. The throne, the firmament, and the four winged creatures are integral to what is seen, but decoding the vision in its entirety is not an easy task. What is clear, however, is the notion of mobility, a God who is as much at home by the river Chobar in Babylon as in the land of the Israelites. This will be a key feature of the prophet's message: the universality of God's presence and reign.

The question of Jesus' paying a tax strikes us as being quite irrelevant, considering his status as God's unique Son. Jesus' concern is with the reign of God, which rises above any human state or government.

And yet he accedes to the request in order not to offend or give scandal. In his epistle to Corinth, Paul admits that as a Christian there are many practices of Jesus law from which he was now exempt. And yet if his neglect of the law were to give scandal, he would not do it.

There are many practices that were ours at one time and are no longer part of our lives. There is a custom among practitioners of some religions to remove their shoes on entering a sacred space. We would and should do the same out of respect for another's belief. Freedom is important in our lives, but to sacrifice freedom to avoid scandal or misunderstanding can be a genuine expression of virtue.

Points to Ponder

> The universality of God's reign
> Respect for another's belief
> Sacrificing freedom for a greater good

TUESDAY OF THE NINETEENTH WEEK IN ORDINARY TIME

Year I

> Deuteronomy 31:1–8
> Deuteronomy 32:3–4ab, 7, 8, 9 and 12
> Matthew 18:1–5, 10, 12–14

An interesting contrast appears in today's two readings. Moses turns aside from his position of leadership to entrust Joshua with the task of bringing the Israelites into the land that had been promised them. Joshua had many of the traits of Moses: leadership skills and strong religious faith as well as military ability. He is clearly the Lord's choice, and Moses has no hesitancy in entrusting the leadership position to him.

Yet in the reign of Jesus, where does greatness lie? In child-like humility. In the spirit of total dependence on God and the realization that he alone is great. There is nothing said about learning or the ability to lead, or even about profound spiritual insight. To receive the lowly one is to receive Christ. To care as much about the one follower who strays as the ninety-nine who do not. To recover the weak brings incomparable joy.

We are all inclined to claim our heroes in life, including in the Christian life. But the Gospels give us pause. It is not the great achievers who are applauded, nor those who are entrusted with positions of authority. It is the humble person for whom God has an unquestionable priority. The one for whom the Eucharist is a daily must, the one who shows great concern for a needy neighbor. We needed a Joshua to reach the land of promise. But we need another type for the reign of God to flourish.

Points to Ponder

> Moses' completed task
> The role of Joshua
> Humility, the cornerstone of the Christian life
> Concern for those who have strayed

Year II

> Ezekiel 2:8—3:4
> Psalm 119:14, 24, 72, 103, 111, 131
> Matthew 18:1–5, 10, 12–14

In eating the scroll that had been handed to him, Ezekiel fulfills the Lord's command. The message that he was to preach to the people was one of lamentation and woe. But in eating it, it tasted sweet even though its message was a dire one. The prophet had completed the task that had been set before him. Yahweh is determined to settle accounts with the evildoer.

But it is the picture of recovering the sinner that dominates in the New Testament. One may wonder about the wisdom of leaving ninety-nine unprotected sheep alone and going in search of one. Or of the woman who celebrates the finding of a small coin with an open house. Or the forgiving father who utters not a word of reproach to the son who returns after squandering his inheritance.

Our ways are not the Lord's ways. God does not measure out forgiveness. His forgiveness is boundless. There is no one who can say that he or she is beyond the pale of forgiveness. The Lord may have to condemn the adamant sinner. But his greatest joy is to invite us back into his love.

Points to Ponder

> God's word: sweet to taste
> God wills conversion
> The sinner's return to God

WEDNESDAY OF THE NINETEENTH WEEK IN ORDINARY TIME

Year I

Deuteronomy 34:1–12
Psalm 66:1–3a, 5 and 8, 16–17
Matthew 18:15–20

Moses died at a very old age and was buried in Moab without ever entering the land of promise. He was unquestionably the greatest of the prophets, the man who had led his people to freedom, remained with them through their desert experience, and brought them to the point of entering the land that the Lord had promised. He will remain always the striking image of obedience and fidelity.

The church, early on, had to deal with problems of rejection and infidelity. Drawing on Old Testament precedent, today's Gospel sets forth the norms that are to be followed. In the matter of a personal offense of some gravity, the person offended is to take the initiative at reconciliation. If this meets with success, the matter is closed. Where the offender remains obstinate, witnesses are to be called to attempt to change the person's attitude. This failing, the local church is to be advised. Failure to heed even the church results in excommunication. The decision of the church in this matter is reinforced by God himself.

Within the church, certain actions incur automatic excommunication. But a trial to determine serious guilt and obstinacy is rare. Of far greater concern is what is referred to as "silent apostasy," or a turning away from the church on one's terms without any public stance being taken. This is serious as a rejection of the church in a grave matter and seriously harms one's spiritual life. We approach the dissident person with kindness and understanding. It is far better to win a person over than to act with harshness or reproof. Our motive must always be a deep appreciation of the church as a source of life and direction and the good of the person involved.

Points to Ponder

> The faith-filled figure of Moses
> Seeking reconciliation
> Encouraging a return to the church

Year II

> Ezekiel 9:1–7; 10:18–22
> Psalm 113:1–2, 3–4, 5–6
> Matthew 18:15–20

Punishment for the sinful Israelites was to be definitive and widespread. Only those marked were to be spared, the faithful ones who lamented the widespread abandonment of the Lord. This is accompanied by the glory of the Lord leaving the temple area and carried aloft by the cherubim. It is a picture of desolation and immense loss.

In the church, serious effort is made to save everyone who is in danger of exclusion. On both a personal and communal level, there are obstinate and hostile souls. Their failure to be in accord with the church merits exclusion and excommunication. But this is to be a last measure, taken only after the utilization of established means to solve the problem have been exhausted.

Most of us wince at the thought of any widespread elimination of people. Part of that is due to the fact that in our lifetime we have seen more than enough extermination of people, most of them innocent of any wrongdoing. We remain deeply attached to the parable of the lost sheep, the lost coin, and the lost son. We want to do all that we can before any censure, automatic or imposed, falls upon someone. Yet, in the Gospel today, the steps are clearly outlined, to make contrition possible.

Lord, touch the hearts of serious wrongdoers. And give us a deep sense of concern for their spiritual well-being.

Points to Ponder

> God's punishment in the Old Testament
> Forgiveness: a central theme in the New Testament
> Understanding excommunication as a last resort

THURSDAY OF THE NINETEENTH WEEK IN ORDINARY TIME

Year I

Josh 3:7–10a, 11, 13–17
Psalm 114:1–2, 3–4, 5–6
Matthew 18:21—19:1

It is the faithful Yahweh who is strikingly present as the Book of Joshua opens. A people that had shown itself repeatedly ungrateful and self-willed reaches the land that the Lord had promised long ago. Despite the Israelites' repeated efforts to reverse the tide of salvation history by longing for the comforts of Egypt, Yahweh's plan is realized, as the crossing of the Jordan River makes clear. There is no mistaking the echoes of the exodus as the waters part once again for the people's passage.

Nowhere is God's faithfulness as present as in the forgiveness of sins. To Peter's question as to how often forgiveness is to be extended, Jesus' answer is "endlessly" ("seventy times seven" is a way of saying this). This is not easy to accept especially in the face of repeated offenses. The parable illustrates the moral well. The king remitted the debt of his servant in its entirety. But the servant, faced by a much smaller debt incurred by one of his peers, is merciless in his demand for payment.

"Forgive us our sins as we forgive those who sin against us." This is the prayer we utter daily. But are we truthful in our words? If we are resentful and do not forgive others, we are asking God to use the same measuring stick with us. The message is clear. Divine mercy reaches us in abundance provided that our own forgiveness is always forthcoming.

Points to Ponder

Parallels: crossing the Red Sea and the Jordan
The parable: forgiveness extended and forgiveness denied
Harboring resentment, dislike, and negative attitudes

Year II

Ezekiel 12:1–12
Psalm 78:56–57, 58–59, 61–62
Matthew 18:21—19:1

In the performance of his prophetic action, Ezekiel clearly announces the punishment of God upon his obstinate people. In the daytime he is to prepare his baggage, then at night dig a hole through the city wall and go off in the darkness. Punishment in terms of capture and deportation was now inevitable for the Hebrew people. It was a sobering lesson indeed.

A similar price is demanded by the servant of the parable, who is merciless in his demand for repayment. In modern times, the payment of a debt, even an insignificant one, seldom takes into consideration the circumstances of the debtor. The king in today's parable is equally exacting with his servant debtor until he is made aware of the man's financial problems. Then the debt is forgiven in its entirety.

We sometimes have debtors who are slow to repay. We must be patient. And let us be hesitant about demanding our "pound of flesh" without considering the circumstances of the debtor. But above all, let us be mindful of our all forgiving Father who time after time has remitted all our debts without question.

This teaching comes into play when considering the death penalty. Regardless of what the crime may have been, to demand the life of the criminal is to resort to a type of murderous conduct. Conversion is always a possibility, and when it occurs God has made a gain. There are no limits to forgiveness. Let us pray for an expansive heart and to realize that pardon is at the heart of Jesus' mission in the world.

Points to Ponder

The prophetic action of Ezekiel
The lesson of forgiveness
Reflection on the death penalty

FRIDAY OF THE NINETEENTH WEEK IN ORDINARY TIME

Year I

Joshua 24:1–13
Psalm 136:1–3, 16–18, 21–22 and 24
Matthew 19:3–12

Jesus' teaching on divorce goes back to Genesis itself and shows little room for exceptions. Moses allowed divorce and remarriage under certain circumstances, but Jesus rescinds the Mosaic teaching.

In New Testament teaching, marriage is definitive and its dissolution rescinded. Matthew does allow of one exception over that of the other Synoptics. Divorce was permitted in the case of *porneia* (Geek for "lewd conduct"), but we are left to conjecture as to what exactly is meant, perhaps some form of illicit union. The basic teaching is clear. Jesus wishes to restore marriage to its status as a lifelong commitment.

As to the disciples' comment that, if such be the case, it would be better not to marry, Jesus responds that celibacy is indeed a commendable state when undertaken in the interests of the kingdom of God.

In today's reading from Joshua, the Hebrews are reminded of all that Yahweh had done for them, from the time of Abraham to the present. The demands that God makes of us in the matter of marriage also spring from his love and concern. There is no denying the fact that divorce in today's culture is a great scourge, a veritable destroyer of family values. We are wrong in seeing the church's teaching on marriage as too narrow. This is a teaching that comes from Christ himself.

Points to Ponder

Marriage as indissoluble
Divorce in modern society
Celibacy for the kingdom of God

Year II

> Ezekiel 16:1–15, 60, 63
> Isaiah 12:2–3, 4bcd, 5–6
> Matthew 19:3–12

It is a stirring picture of Israel's youth and adolescence that is depicted in today's reading from Ezekiel. Born of pagan parentage, with the coming of Moses and Aaron, Israel was the recipient of God's favor. This continued until the land of Canaan became hers. All of this made Israel's later rejection of Yahweh in covenant betrayal truly lamentable.

Today's Gospel centers on the marriage commitment and its indissoluble character. The same teaching is repeated in Mark and Luke.

This is a teaching that comes not from the church but from Christ himself. The church has very little latitude in a matter that is as explicit as this is in the New Testament. Considering our very high divorce rate, one wonders how seriously this teaching is taken. The widespread breakup of marriage casts a dark cloud over society today. The church has to take very seriously marriage preparation. What was true of old is equally true today: the family is the keystone of society.

Points to Ponder

> God's abiding love for is people
> Attitudes toward marriage today
> Preparation for marriage

SATURDAY OF THE NINETEENTH WEEK IN ORDINARY TIME

Year I

> Josh 24:14–29
> Psalm 16:1–2a and 5, 7–8, 11
> Matthew 19:13–15

As Joshua prepares to renew the covenant between God and the people, he must first ascertain the will of the people. Experience had taught some bitter lessons. Will the people abide by the terms of the covenant and give their undivided loyalty to Yahweh alone? Will they abandon forever the gods of Egypt or those of the people in the land they now occupied? The response of the people is unanimous and clearly in the affirmative. As was the custom in treaty making, the large stone remains a permanent witness to the commitment made.

In the Gospel today Christ receives the children, who stand as a prototype of those who will inhabit the kingdom of heaven. In what sense?

Children are utterly dependent on their guardians; they do not take an independent stand. Like the people renewing the covenant at Shechem, the citizens of heaven are childlike in their total adherence to God. We live in an era of complexity, and the human personality often reflects that complexity. How often we are forced to wonder about what a person really intends. Transparency is a sterling quality that is often missing in our daily life.

We pray for the trust and confidence, the uncomplicated dedication and love, the assurance and trust of a child.

Points to Ponder

> Renewing our dedication to the covenant
> Living in a childlike spirit
> God as a loving Father

Year II

> Ezekiel 18:1–10, 13b, 30–32
> Psalm 51:12–13, 14–15, 18–19
> Matthew 19:13–15

Solidarity in guilt was a strong belief in ancient Hebrew society. Simply stated, it meant that guilt could be hereditary; one could pay for the sins of their forebears, without personal guilt on their part. Ezekiel makes it clear that this belief is at an end. The sour taste visited on the children because their father had eaten sour grapes is an assumption that will no longer have meaning. If a person lives a virtuous life and is upright in his conduct, he shall surely live. If that person fathers a son who follows a path of sin, death or separation from God will surely be his lot.

The child is sinless and thus finds a special place in Jesus' heart. The disciples were annoyed at parents' bringing their children to Jesus in what they see as an intrusive manner. Not so with Christ. Children represent the citizens of the kingdom. Candid, direct, uncomplicated, and totally trusting, young children are the model of faith.

Points to Ponder

> Development in thought regarding guilt
> The trust of the child
> God as the loving Father

MONDAY OF THE TWENTIETH WEEK IN ORDINARY TIME

Year I

> Judges 2:11–19
> Psalm 106:34–35, 36–37, 39–40, 43ab and 44
> Matthew 19:16–22

Today's passage from Judges gives a summary of the sad tales that will be recounted in the book as a whole. There was a lack of constancy in Israel's efforts to remain faithful. As the book indicates, the people would fall into idolatry. They were punished by God. Efforts were made at repentance. Finally a judge would arise and deliver them. But shortly thereafter the whole process would repeat itself. This is a book with very interesting personalities, but is a sad testimony to Israel's failures. With one notable exception, the judges were not magistrates but heroic individuals who "judged Israel" in the sense of giving expression to Yahweh's judgment on behalf of Israel.

The young man who approaches Jesus in regard to eternal life was undoubtedly well intentioned. He had been faithful in observing the Ten Commandments, but it was his wealth that stood between him and eternal life. Jesus invites him to divest himself of his riches and then follow him.

But the man's attachment to his possessions proved to be too much, and he walks away. It is one of the few instances in the New Testament where Jesus' invitation was refused.

The call is not for everyone to divest himself of his holdings. It is not the possessions but the attachment that is the problem. It does mean that if there is something standing between the individual and his goal, whatever it may be, it must be sacrificed in the interests of God's kingdom. Here we can speak only in generalities—it may be a person, an occupation, or something that we treasure. If it stands between us and the concerns of God, it must go.

Lord, give us a love for you that will never be diminished by passing interests. You are the one good, the only good, the good that is at the center of my life.

Points to Ponder

The role of the judges
The commandments and eternal life
Fleeting goods versus the one eternal good

Year II

Ezekiel 24:15–23
Deuteronomy 32:18–19, 20, 21
Matthew 19:16–22

The prophetic action called for in today's reading is unusual, and perhaps hard to comprehend. The wife of the prophet dies. He is told to forego all the customary signs of mourning. This is to be a foretaste of the people's response to the desecration of the temple and the massacre of many of the citizens still living in the country. This is to be seen as the people's just deserts for their abandonment of Yahweh. It will be a loss without mourning or the customary signs of grief. It was so difficult for Israel to learn its lesson. Repeatedly the people's conduct led to disaster. And here the prophet is told to act it out.

The Gospel today is also a story of refusal. The young man prefers his riches to the company of the Lord. But how similar this is to our own conduct? What is sin but a refusal of Christ in the interests of something else? It is vitally important for our sense of Christian values to be sharpened, to be vitally alive to God's will, not to be taken by surprise.

But there is one important difference. When we fail, God is always willing to forgive. To return to the Lord is the story of conversion, and we are told of the joy in heaven that accompanies such a step. Our mistakes in life are numerous and regrettable. But our homecoming is a moment of joy. Let us never become discouraged.

Points to Ponder

God's fidelity to an unfaithful Israel
Sorrow for sin
The joy of reconciliation

TUESDAY OF THE TWENTIETH WEEK IN ORDINARY TIME

Year I

Judges 6:11–24a
Psalm 85:9, 11–12, 13–14
Matthew 19:23–30

Gideon did not see himself or his family as worthy of God's selection to defend Israel. Before undertaking the task of defeating the Midianites, he asks the angel of the Lord for a sign. When fire consumes the offering he brings, he realizes that the Lord has intervened in his life.

In the New Testament it is not insignificance that is an obstacle to engagement in God's will. In fact, as the story of Gideon illustrates in its own way, there are other criteria at work in God's plan. Jesus today makes it clear to his disciples that riches can easily stand in the way of responding to God's invitation. Indeed, it is extremely difficult to give oneself to the reign of God while storing up treasures of this world's goods. And what of the disciples who have surrendered all in following Jesus? They will sit in judgment of the twelve tribes of Israel. In fact, all who give themselves entirely to the name of Jesus will be adequately provided for and will inherit eternal life.

Is there then no hope for the rich? Indeed, there is. What seems to be humanly impossible is possible for God. We need but think of the wealthy people who are on our calendar of saints—Elizabeth of Hungary, Catherine Drexel, Catherine McAulcy. Not only were they wealthy, they launched important religious traditions. But when all is said and done, we have nothing to regret if we have little of what this world has to offer. Our inheritance still remains intact.

Points to Ponder

> Gideon's hesitation
> Riches and the reign of God
> Selfishness as an obstacle to God's plan

Year II

> Ezekiel 28:1–10
> Deuteronomy 32:26–27ab, 27cd–28, 30, 35cd–36ab
> Matthew 19:23–30

Our two readings today are antitheses. The first reading on the wealthy prince of Tyre is a clear illustration of what unlimited wealth can effect; the Gospel, on the other hand, deals with the true values that are indispensable in the kingdom of God. The Phoenician city of Tyre, located on the Mediterranean coast, was wealthy and affluent, in great measure due to its geography, which was ideal for trade.

Ezekiel utters a diatribe against the prince of Tyre, who will be duly punished for making himself the equal of a god. He prides himself on his wisdom and clairvoyance, his coffers filled with gold and silver, his thirst for unlimited wealth. The day of destruction will be adequate proof that he is human and not divine. He will suffer the death of the uncircumcised. The prince, of course, is not an individual person but rather stands for the country as a whole; the passage is a classical expression on the dangers of wealth.

Jesus' words in the Gospel today make perfect sense in the light of Ezekiel's prophecy. Riches can be and frequently are an entrapment, a major obstacle to a life lived in God. The reading makes it clear that the obstacle is not insurmountable, but it serves as a sound warning. But for those who have left all for the sake of Christ's name, there will be provision made, even in this life, and eternal life is assured. There is ample testimony to the truth of Christ's promise in the lives of those who have given themselves to the Lord unreservedly in Christian ministry.

Points to Ponder

> Inequality: the wealth and poverty of nations
> Poverty for the reign of God
> The last will be first

WEDNESDAY OF THE TWENTIETH WEEK IN ORDINARY TIME

Year I

> Judges 9:6–15
> Psalm 21:2–3, 4–5, 6–7
> Matthew 20:1–16

Kingship was not introduced in Israel without a struggle. While it is true that kings ruled over the neighboring countries, its presence among the Hebrews was initially seen as an interference into the authority and power that belonged only to Yahweh. The event that brought Abimelech to power over the people of Shechem proved to be an unfortunate step; this local king did not rule for long and finally met a tragic end. Jotham in today's reading decries the rise of Abimelech and sees him as the "bramble" king, that is, the least desirable of all.

God's generosity should never be the source of envy within the Christian community. A just recompense is given to the faithful who have labored the long day. But there will be some who enter only at a late hour, and their reward will be as great. But if the Lord chooses to be generous, why should he be taken to task? This is the main point of the parable of the laborers hired at different times of the day.

It took a considerable period of time for the Hebrews to adjust themselves to the idea of an earthly king. We at times find problems with the "admissions policy" of the church. Some people live a public life that is clearly at odds with Christian values; sometimes it is scandalous as well. But we never know the person's sentiments when life comes to an end. Genuine sorrow and conversion take very little time to actualize. Whether it be church and state issues or end-of-life issues, answers are not always apparent and immediate.

As we search for answers, it is well to remember that discretion is often the better part of valor.

Points to Ponder

Our first allegiance: God or civil authority?
Examples of God's generosity
The deathbed conversion

Year II

Ezekiel 34:1–11
Psalm 23:1–3a, 3b–4, 5, 6
Matthew 20:1–16

Ministry in the church is an honored position; it is especially the case for priestly ministry. But it is also a matter of serious responsibility. Ezekiel's prophecy regarding the sheep and the shepherds merits pause and reflection. The goodness of God can also cause surprise, as the parable of today's Gospel makes evident. As we lend ourselves to the task before us, we pray for the grace to be nonjudgmental.

Israel was not well served by its priests. The prophetic word that came to Ezekiel registers great displeasure with God's representatives in the priestly office. They are busy taking care of themselves instead of the faithful. They lord it over others, take wool and milk from the sheep, and leave them unprotected from a type of predator. The result is that their mission will be revoked, and God himself will become the shepherd. We cannot rest easy with the fact that modern times have seen so many instances of sexual and financial abuse in the ranks of the clergy. It calls for repentance, care for those who have been injured, and a careful assessment of vocations to the priestly ministry.

It does strike us as being unfair for all the laborers to receive equal pay, even those who were hired late in the day. But, on the other hand, the wage agreed upon was the one received. Therefore the master cannot be accused of being unjust. When someone experiences religious conversion, even late in life, there is joy in heaven, says the Lord. Do our own hearts resonate with joy? It may well be that some profound experience has brought about the change. God welcomes the person at any hour, and our joy too should be full.

Points to Ponder

> The responsibility of the clergy
> The deathbed conversion
> Conversion: "joy in heaven"

THURSDAY OF THE TWENTIETH WEEK IN ORDINARY TIME

Year I

> Judges 11:29–39a
> Psalm 40:5, 7–8a, 8b–9, 10
> Matthew 22:1–14

In Matthew's Gospel, the Jewish people have priority in the ministry of Jesus. They are represented by the first category of people who make excuses for not attending the wedding feast.

After their failure to respond positively, the broader Gentile world is invited and soon fill the hall. All are welcome, but the king, upon entering, finds a man not properly attired and orders him expelled. The universalism of Jesus' mission is underscored, but, at the same time, there are certain spiritual dispositions that every Christian must possess. When these are missing, exclusion is the result.

In the reading from Judges, Jephtah had made a vow and was held to it. His daughter was the first to meet him upon his return from battle and thus was the one to be sacrificed. The story strikes us as brutal, and in fact, in later Hebrew culture, human sacrifice was forbidden. But here there is a vow involved that could not be dismissed.

Commitment is pertinent to both readings. Those who enter the Christian community do so realizing what that entails. In the minds of many today, that commitment is not taken seriously. While avoiding the extremes of Jephtah, we could use a measure of his seriousness. Christianity is not simply a peg on which we hang our coat. It is a matter of God, his Christ, and our eternity. Today's readings call us to renew our resolve.

Points to Ponder

> The seriousness of a vow
> Conversion: entering the wedding feast
> The spiritual dispositions of being a Christian

Year II

> Ezekiel 36:23–28
> Psalm 51:12–13, 14–15, 18–19
> Matthew 22:1–14

Faith ultimately is a matter of the heart, not simply feast days and rituals. Like Jeremiah, Ezekiel speaks of a new era wherein the Lord will renew the religious spirit within us. The law will not be written on stone tablets but on the flesh of the human heart. Cleansed of our impurities, we will respond to God from inner conviction and with a true sense of personal purpose. Religion, to be authentic, must go beyond externals and emanate from the very core of our being.

Many of the people in today's parable saw the wedding invitation as simply another calendar event, not a divine calling to be taken with the utmost seriousness. While not as guilty as those who refused, the improperly clothed guest lacks a true appreciation of what God is offering. The lesson should strike us as being particularly meaningful.

The fact that we are identified as Christian or Catholic says very little in and of itself. But we all know what it means to take faith seriously. We have met it in people many times. The kind word, availability, service to others, as well as love of the Eucharist.

With these values in place, we are properly dressed for the wedding. We will never be embarrassed by being improperly clothed. We have received that new Spirit within us, the first gift of the risen Christ.

Points to Ponder

> Religious faith: stone tablets or a new heart
> Excuses: God's interests will come later
> The wedding feast: being properly attired

FRIDAY OF THE TWENTIETH WEEK IN ORDINARY TIME

Year I

> Ruth 1:1, 3–6, 14b–16, 22
> Psalm 146:5–6ab, 6c–7, 8–9a, 9bc–10
> Matthew 22:34–40

The Book of Ruth, only four chapters in length, is one of the Bible's most charming. It has a calm and engaging domesticity, telling the story of one of David's ancestors. Ruth, a Moabite girl of non-Jewish origin, marries the son of Naomi. After ten years of marriage, Ruth's husband dies, as did her brother-in-law and, at an earlier time, her father-in-law, Naomi's husband. Urged by

Naomi to join her sister-in-law in returning to her own country, Ruth, realizing that Naomi is now quite alone, refuses to leave and so remains with the widowed in-law. "Do not press me to leave you or to turn back from following you! Where you go, I will go; where you lodge, I will lodge; your people shall be my people, and your God my God." It is a beautiful expression of generous love.

As Christ gives us the Great Commandment as the summation of the Christian spirit, Ruth stands out as an example even though she lived almost a millennium before Christ. The neighbor whom she loved was her own mother-in-law. In comedy fare today, relatives are often belittled, especially in-laws. They are the butt of jokes. To live in Italy is to realize the respect that is had for relatives. They are frequent guests at Sunday dinner; for children, in-laws are part of the extended family.

The story of Ruth is simply an account of what the love of neighbor means. Ruth was not about to return home and leave her widowed mother-in-law alone. It is a touching story of self-giving and makes of Ruth a worthy forerunner of David. If charity begins at home, our relatives should not be overlooked.

Points to Ponder

> Strengthening family ties
> Ruth as a convert to the Hebrew faith
> Sacrificing personal interests for others

Year II

> Ezekiel 37:1–14
> Psalm 107:2–3, 4–5, 6–7, 8–9
> Matthew 22:34–40

Ezekiel and the dry bones. This is not an account of a personal resurrection. The symbolism of this famous passage is one of a resurrected Israel after the time of its punishment is over. Not only do the bones reassemble, but God's Spirit takes possession of them. Life has come to the beloved people once again.

There is a genius to Christianity. Any faith that can be summarized in one short quotation drawing on two precepts of the

Old Testament compels us to sit up and take notice. The teaching is clear: the Lord our God stands always at the center of our life and receives our unqualified allegiance. But in the words of the presbyter John, how can we love God whom we do not see if we do not love our neighbor whom we do see? Therefore, love of God and neighbor are inseparable. For the Jews, a neighbor was a fellow Israelite. For the Christian, as is made clear in the Good Samarian story, my neighbor is anyone in need.

The dry bones image is often used in reference to our personal final engagement in God. Ours is a blessed future. But it must be rooted in love.

Every day of our life is a preparation day, a time when we give to God our unqualified love and to our neighbor the extended hand of friendship.

Points to Ponder

The symbolism of the dry bones
The juncture of love of God and neighbor
The great command: our pledge of future glory

SATURDAY OF THE TWENTIETH WEEK IN ORDINARY TIME

Year I

Ruth 2:1–3, 8–11; 4:13–17
Psalm 128:1b–2, 3, 4, 5
Matthew 23:1–12

Both Naomi and Ruth are rewarded for their fidelity with Ruth's child, born of her marriage with Boaz, Naomi's relative. The child was Obed, David's grandfather. Naomi is congratulated by the neighboring women; she now has an heir whom she nurses. The story ends with recognition of Ruth, who had taken Naomi to her heart and had now provided her with an heir.

As strong and warm as human relations are, the Gospel tells us that they are secondary to our being members of God's family.

The text excoriates the religious leaders of the day who were masters at placing heavy burdens on others. Their teaching may be valid; their conduct is not. The titles accorded them were common and well known: rabbi, father, and teacher. Among the disciples of Jesus, titles such as these are to be avoided since they divert attention from the singular leader of the new era, the heavenly Father. It is he who teaches and forms us in the faith and therefore the only one to be called rabbi, teacher, or father. It is understood that we are speaking of titles within the Christian community, not in family relations or academic situations.

Spiritual leadership often disappoints. This may be due to a human lack of gifts or a failure to respond in a suitable manner. The fact is that, in the order of faith, it is God who instructs and inspire us. This is the God of the scriptures, the God of the sacraments, the God who directs our lives. To canonize human leadership is to overlook the fact that it is the Lord who has planted the seed of faith in us, which he cultivates and nourishes.

Points to Ponder

> Ruth's motherhood and the law of God
> Compromising God's position in our lives
> Titles of honor within the Christian community

Year II

> Ezekiel 43:1–7ab
> Psalm 85:9ab and 10, 11–12, 13–14
> Matthew 23:1–12

Authentic worship in Israel could not be imagined without the temple. From the time of Solomon it had been sacred as the unique dwelling place of the Lord. Accordingly, Ezekiel's end-time vision contains the return of the Lord and his taking possession of the temple once again. The vision is reminiscent of Ezekiel's inaugural vision at the river Chebar in its awesome power and majesty. With a people now committed to fidelity, Yahweh's presence is seen as one that will last forever.

Christianity has never had a central location of cult. As Christ himself indicates in John's Gospel, this is a new relationship with God that is not tied to a particular place. It is a worship in spirit and truth. Baptism infuses us with the Spirit of God and establishes us as members of God's household—sons and daughters. It is a question of God with us and in us.

This being the case, the Lord becomes our enlightenment and instructor. Today's Gospel advises us against giving to humans titles and functions that belong properly to God. The evangelist speaks, of course, in the context of Christian community and not of the same titles that are used in family life or other social contexts. One is our rabbi, father, and teacher. It is the Lord who instructs and builds us up in the true Christian spirit. It is to this growth in Christ that we are dedicated and in which we mature as believers.

Points to Ponder

> The temple as the center of Hebrew cult
> Worship in spirit and in truth
> Both in our understanding of the faith

MONDAY OF THE TWENTY-FIRST WEEK IN ORDINARY TIME

Year I

> 1 Thessalonians 1:1–5, 8b–10
> Psalm 149:1b–2, 3–4, 5–6a and 9b
> Matthew 23:13–22

Exchanging the lesser for the greater. Confusing the lesser and the greater. These are two ideas that emerge from today's readings. Paul is full of praise for the Thessalonians because of their faith, their openness, and their acceptance of the word of God. In all of this, they have exchanged the lesser for the greater in going from idols to the service of the living God. Jesus finds fault with the Pharisees for their misplaced values in seeing the gold of the temple as more sacred than the temple itself, and the gift on the altar as being of greater value than the altar itself.

We should not reduce our faith life to some sort of bank transaction. Rather our faith is a grateful response to an all-loving God. Some people will receive communion only from a priest, not a eucharistic minister. Others will avoid the Mass in the vernacular at all cost and travel great distances to attend the Latin Mass.

Such hang-ups can make us blind to the real values that remain uncompromised.

In religion, as in many things in life, we can lose sight of the forest for the trees. We can tend to make secondary considerations primary, even to the point of contention. Our faith, at every turn, should contribute to our joy. We don't want to make a bargaining partner of God.

Points to Ponder

The privilege of adoring the living God
Distinguishing the primary from the secondary in our
    faith life
Living in expectation of the end-time

Year II

2 Thessalonians 1:1–5, 11–12
Psalm 96:1–2a, 2b–3, 4–5
Matthew 23:13–22

In his Second Letter to Thessalonica, Paul again congratulates the church there for its constancy in faith and mutual love. The grace they have received has a twofold benefit. "The name of our Lord Jesus Christ may be glorified in you, and you in him." This two-way benefit of the Spirit merits our consideration.

Christ is glorified in us when our lives become conformed to his will. When virtue and goodness become so much part of our life that, with Paul, we can say that we no longer live in Christ but that he lives in us. The real test of faith is when Christ comes so much to life in us that we become the living portrait of his teaching. Gandhi is said to have remarked that his respect for the teaching of Christ was profound; the disappointment came in the failure of his followers to live his teaching.

And, in addition, we are glorified in him when we become part of his total offering to the Father. We are the beneficiaries of God's redemptive love. We are not only heirs of the kingdom; we are part of the household of God. As recipients of the Spirit that binds Father and Son together as one, we too cry out, "Abba." With Christ our brother, we acknowledge the Father as ours. In this way we are glorified in Christ.

Christ in us and we in Christ. It is an inestimable blessing.

Keep us ever mindful, Lord.

Points to Ponder

Christ in us: to mirror Christ
We in Christ: part of God's family
The Spirit as life

TUESDAY OF THE TWENTY-FIRST WEEK IN ORDINARY TIME

Year I

1 Thessalonians 2:1–8
Psalm 139:1–3, 4–6
Matthew 23:23–26

Hypocrisy under any circumstances is an unwelcome trait; when found in religious conduct, even more so. Jesus decries various aspects of the comportment of religious leaders. They observe minutiae of the law while overlooking the major precepts. In paying tithes of the field to the temple, they admit the most insignificant garden plants (mint, dill, cumin) while neglecting major issues as judgment, mercy, and fidelity. They are taken up with externals (the outside of the cup), while failing to clean the inside of the cup (plunder and self-indulgence). All of this leads to a disregard for what God truly asks while emphasizing matters of purely secondary importance.

How different was the conduct of Paul. He and his companions had been entrusted with the gospel, and this they delivered without flattery, greed, or a desire for praise. So deep was his affection for the people that he wanted to share not only the gospel but his very self. For this reason Paul made himself one with his congregation wherever he went.

Ministers of the gospel must be continually alert. It is the truth of Jesus Christ that they preach and not their own interests. Temporalities have their place, but to spend excessive amounts of time preaching about parish needs, income problems, our debts is a betrayal of the good news. Sunday preaching is a solemn obligation. There is no other moment of our week when we have the attention of such a large segment of our community. It is the word of God that is to be preached.

Points to Ponder

Undue concern about the outside of the cup
Addressing with courage our serious issues
The importance of the Sunday homily

Year II

2 Thessalonians 2:1–3a, 14–17
Psalm 96:10, 11–12, 13
Matthew 23:23–26

The earliest writings of the New Testament clearly express the belief that the return of Christ was expected soon.

Our reading today from Thessalonians shows that the question had caused some consternation among the believers there. Paul makes a disclaimer of any indication from him that the day is near. He simply encourages them to stand firm in their belief that they will share in the glory of Christ, holding fast to what they have been taught. He further prays that they will be strengthened by God in word and deed.

It is not difficult to get caught up in the minutiae of our belief, as did the religious leaders of Jesus' day. There are any number of major issues to which we give little attention. In preparing for the sacrament of reconciliation, people repeatedly return to the Ten Commandments. Fundamentally this is an Old Testament ethic that has its validity but does not stand at the center of the Christian life. We should not fail to examine our conscience in light of the Sermon on the Mount.

Did we extend ourselves to someone in need? Are we guilty of lust in our hearts? Did we remain unmoved at a request or did we go the extra mile? In our prayer for forgiveness we ask to be pardoned for what we have done and also what we have failed to do. Our failure to respond positively may truly mark our weakness as Christians.

Points to Ponder

> Belief in the return of Christ
> The proper Christian response
> Looking at what we have failed to do

WEDNESDAY OF THE TWENTY-FIRST WEEK IN ORDINARY TIME

Year I

> 1 Thessalonians 2:9–13
> Psalm 139:7–8, 9–10, 11–12ab
> Matthew 23:27–32

Stronger words than these regarding the scribes and Pharisees are not found in Jesus' teaching. Today they are likened to tombs of the dead, externally maintained in the best condition but internally a place of bones and decay. Religious leaders maintained all the signs of correctness but in their hearts were far from God. There is a word of warning there. It is quite possible for any of us to fall into ungodly habits that we can justify in our own minds. At the same time we can retain all the externals of a pious life while our hearts remain distant from God.

Quite different is the teaching of Paul today. While among the Thessalonians he had worked tirelessly to proclaim the gospel of God without being a burden to them. He likens himself to the father of a family, encouraging and exhorting them to walk in a way worthy of God's call. And he now gives thanks to God that they received the message, not as the word of men, but as the word of God. Paul speaks with utter candor because there is nothing to hide. His life is an open book before God and humans.

Let us pray that in all we do a spirit of openness may be present. Our life here is to be lived in a spirit of faith with no agenda other than that to which God has called us. Over the filth of betrayal the enemies of Jesus wore the garments of uprightness. The gospel we profess is not a human teaching but that of the living God.

Points to Ponder

> A faith that masks hypocrisy
> Working tirelessly for the concerns of God
> Hearing the prophets' words today

Year II

> 2 Thessalonians 3:6–10, 16–18
> Psalm 128:1–2, 4–5
> Matthew 23:27–32

What exactly Paul refers to as disorderly conduct is not clear, but if the context is any key then it would point to laziness and an unwillingness "to carry one's load." Paul did not want to be a burden on the young community, and therefore he worked arduously to provide for himself and never asked for anything from the community.

It happens in life that some people are continually dependent on others for their needs, and the word *work* finds little resonance in their lives. They have never found their own way and have no desire to do so.

Unfortunately there are those who encourage such listlessness by providing for the needs of such people. Whether it be simply lack of motivation or some sort of mental illness, there are people who pass from childhood to adulthood and never leave home.

A work ethic is a commendable part of one's character. It provides for self and family but should never become the controlling factor in life. Rest and relaxation are essential ingredients of the good life. We want to be active and productive and not those who are unhealthily dependent on others. To fail to carry our burden in life is what Paul would designate "disorderly conduct." It falls short of what a Christian is called to be.

Points to Ponder

Sloth as a vice
Being productively talented
Encouraging a listless life

THURSDAY OF THE TWENTY-FIRST WEEK IN ORDINARY TIME

Year I

1 Thessalonians 3:7–13
Psalm 90:3–5a, 12–13, 14 and 17
Matthew 24:42–51

Be alert! This admonition appears repeatedly in the New Testament, encouraging preparedness in light of the expected return of Christ. Most modern Christians apply it to our present life and its unknown termination, which is a second coming in its own way. Paul has been repeatedly reassured about the faith of the Thessalonians. His one desire is to make the journey to see them; in the meantime they are in his prayers that they may increase and that their love for one another may grow ever stronger.

In speaking of the end-time, Jesus in today's Gospel encourages his followers to remain attentive. Who would be careless if he knew his house was going to be broken into? In view of the uncertainty of the hour of the Lord's return, we too must be cautious and alert. The faithful servant is the one who provides for the household's needs; the master upon his return will give him even more responsibility. The servant, who in view of the master's delayed return, mistreats the members of the household will pay dearly for his misconduct.

The warning should not lead to anxiety. If every day we are trying to serve the Lord in whatever we have to do, then we are living in a state of preparedness. To become careless and indifferent about life's greatest challenge is what we are warned against.

Points to Ponder

Strength derived from the believing community
Alertness in fulfilling our daily tasks
Flesh over spirit: dulling our conscience

Year II

1 Corinthians 1:1–9
Psalm 145:2–3, 4–5, 6–7
Matthew 24:42–51

Paul begins his Letter to Corinth by clearly stating his position and call as an apostle. This Paul does repeatedly since he sees the rank as apostle as deriving from a commission by the risen Christ, even though he had not been with Christ during his earthly ministry. He then addresses the Corinthians as the "sanctified," called out of the world to be a holy people together with all those who profess their faith in the lordship of Christ.

To realize the extent to which we have been gifted by God is to be imbued with the desire to avoid sin at all cost. To cast away a precious heritage for false and passing values is a great tragedy. To share fellowship with Christ is to belong to the household of God and with Christ to address God as "Abba," Father. To live in Christ is to be irreproachable when the day of reckoning comes.

Lord, renew and strengthen your Spirit within me today. Let my life of faith be a song of gratitude for your goodness. May every day prepare me for that life of glory to which you call me.

Points to Ponder

Paul as an apostle
Baptism as our sanctification
Living in God's household

FRIDAY OF THE TWENTY-FIRST WEEK IN ORDINARY TIME

Year I

1 Thessalonians 4:1–8
Psalm 97:1 and 2b, 5–6, 10, 11–12
Matthew 25:1–13

It's not sufficient to talk the talk; we also have to walk the walk. The parable reminds us to be prepared for an unspecified delay in the Lord's coming. It's not enough to say, "Everything's okay. We belong to the club." The five foolish virgins are excluded because they did not bring sufficient oil to provide for their lamps in the case of a long delay. The lesson is clear. We can never let our guard down.

The coming of Christ in our life often comes at an unexpected moment. A couple looks forward to retirement. No sooner does it come than death takes the wife or husband unexpectedly.

Paul today speaks of an area where vigilance comes into play.

It is the question of marriage. The decision to enter upon the married state should be sober and judicious, not controlled by passion or lustful considerations. Preparedness means that in every step we take in life we look at it in the light of the gospel.

Discerning the Lord's will in our undertakings is to carry sufficient oil in our lamps.

Preparedness is a distinctive mark of our recent popes. To a man they worked to discharge the duties of office through great physical trials, when it was evidently difficult for them to walk or speak. Only when confined to bed to await the end did they surrender themselves to the inevitable. It is the lesson of the virgins come to life anew.

Points to Ponder

> Are we prepared for whatever tomorrow may hold?
> The frequent suddenness of the final call
> Marriage as a sober and major step in life

Year II

> 1 Corinthians 1:17–25
> Psalm 33:1–2, 4–5, 10–11
> Matthew 25:1–13

Christ is the power and wisdom of God. This is Paul's teaching today, and yet he admits its human irony. A crucified God flies in the face of human expectations. The Jews looked for convincing signs, and the Greeks, in their philosophical bent, looked for wisdom. Jesus on the cross looked unconvincing on both counts. The sign was only one of weakness to the Jews and foolishness to the Gentile. But in fact the outcome was just the opposite. To those who are being saved, there is power in the cross and wisdom in a God who is willing to die to save us.

Over the centuries we have come to appreciate that power and wisdom. But if we place ourselves in the first century, we can appreciate the human obstacles that had to be overcome in accepting the Christian message. There was the added fact that the Jews for whom he had principally come had not accepted him, while the Gentiles in ever-greater numbers are embracing the message.

Fortunately we are the beneficiaries of that great act of God. May our lamps burn bright with a supply of oil that does not run short. Daily let us renew our commitment to the God who has first loved us.

Points to Ponder

> The cross as God's power and wisdom
> The foolishness and stumbling block for unbelievers
> The oil of fidelity and preparedness for the Lord's coming

SATURDAY OF THE TWENTY-FIRST WEEK IN ORDINARY TIME

Year I

1 Thessalonians 4:9–11
Psalm 98:1, 7–8, 9
Matthew 25:14–30

Paul exhorts the Thessalonians to be faithful in three specific areas: a life of peace and tranquility, noninterference in the affairs of others, and an industrious way of life. These are all issues he addressed in the course of the epistle. The Gospel today picks up on the third area of Paul's teaching: to apply oneself to the daily task.

The man left home after giving determined sums of money to three of his servants. The first two traded with the amount they received and doubled the original sum. The third showed no sense of industry but simply buried his in the ground. The first two are commended by the master upon in his return, and the third is reprimanded and rejected. We are all gifted by God with certain abilities. They are not to be left idle but put to use, especially in the interests of the kingdom of God.

We all know people who have been blessed with ability, and yet they never succeed in actualizing their talents. This is seen within the church as well. Good lectors are vitally important at Mass in order that God's word be well spoken and understood. Some people have excellent speaking voices but they do not step forward in order to read at liturgy. There are many ways in which church needs can be filled by members of the congregation, but so often people are hesitant to step forward.

Every gift is to be cherished; every talent put to use. The lawyer, the professor, and the doctor have need of the plumber, the electrician, and the grocer. It is not the superiority of the gifts that count; it is the way that they are utilized. It is hard to look back on a life that has not been productive. We want to put those talents to use.

Points to Ponder

> Being at peace with neighbor
> Recognizing and channeling our gifts
> Talents at the service of the church

Year II

> 1 Corinthians 1:26–31
> Psalm 33:12–13, 18–19, 20–21
> Matthew 25:14–30

Paul reminds the Corinthians that they now have worth as members of Christ's body. But this is no reason for them to boast, since it is all gift; the only possible boast can be in Christ Jesus. This is the great paradox. God did not turn initially to nobility and wealth. Rather he chose the weak and the insignificant in order to shame the wise.

This complements our Gospel today. The gifts that we have are all God-given, and they should not be buried. We use them not to impress or to feel superior. By the same token, it is not an act of humility to claim that we are not gifted. If there are accomplishments in our life, we recognize them and speak of them. It is not vanity to admit one's accomplishments. It does mean that we don't want to develop airs of superiority. There is in this world of ours a wonderful blend of gifts, a concert of gifts and talents. For all of this we should feel a real indebtedness, with jealousy to be avoided at all costs.

Let us give praise to God for Jesus Christ in whom we now live. He is our righteousness. He is our sanctification. He is our redemption. For all that he means we are grateful, and any boasting that is done will be done in him.

Points to Ponder

> Gratitude to God for our gifts
> Honest recognition of our talents
> The avoidance of jealous criticism

MONDAY OF THE TWENTY-SECOND WEEK IN ORDINARY TIME

Year I

> 1 Thessalonians 4:13–18
> Psalm 96:1 and 3, 4–5, 11–12, 13
> Luke 4:16–30

There is a note of consternation in both readings today. The Thessalonians expected the imminent return of the Lord in glory. Not only did this not occur, but some of the faithful were dying before the return. The people of Nazareth, while impressed with Jesus' insights, wanted him to perform the wonders there that he had performed elsewhere. In reply, Jesus cites two examples from the Old Testament in which the prophets' wonders had been performed not for their fellow Israelites but for foreigners.

The passage from Isaiah that Jesus read in the synagogue speaks of Yahweh's definitive action in the world as alleviating the pain of the unfortunate. Good news for the poor, freedom for captives, and sight for the blind. In fact, the miracles of Jesus are never done for display, but only in the interest of rendering assistance. But even at that, Jesus states that no prophet wins acceptance in his home town.

How true it is. When we want to make an important point or shed light on a major controversy, we look for a celebrated speaker from out of town. And, all too often, we recognize that the same point could have been made just as effectively by someone close at hand. In addition, when a prophetic voice is raised by someone close at hand, it is often not taken seriously.

The truth, when spoken honestly and candidly, does not have to be varnished. Let our conscience be our guide. If the speaker has the truth on his side, the speaker's origins make no difference. Let the truth be our guide. And it is the truth that will set us free.

Points to Ponder

Jesus' mission to the unfortunate
Listening for the truth from any quarter
The meaning of the Second Coming

Year II

1 Corinthians 2:1–5
Psalm 119:97, 98, 99, 100, 101, 102
Luke 4:16–30

Jesus was a local boy from Nazareth! And as is cited else-where in the New Testament, "Can anything good come out of Nazareth?" (cf. John 1:46). There were no scriptural hopes connected with Nazareth; it was simply an unimpressive town on a major trade route. But God's ways are not our ways. It is the small and insignificant things out of which God's will is realized. This is verified repeatedly in the prominent persons of the New Testament.

This is also the clear message that Paul sets forth today. It was not with words of wisdom that Paul addressed the people of Corinth. Rather it was with fear and trembling that he preached to them, not with the power of rhetoric, but with a single topic, Jesus Christ crucified. It was evident then that whatever was accomplished was solely the work of God. Paul did not do the persuading; the Spirit did. It was the power of God that was at work.

Experience often bears this out. Good is derived from something we say or preach that we considered very unimpressive. Great saints have taught more by their lives than by their words. One dedicated pastor lacked eloquence in every way and yet people hung on his words. One parishioner made the simple observation about him: "That man really believes."

Points to Ponder

The simple language of salvation
Conviction over rhetoric
Jesus' unimpressive origins

TUESDAY OF THE TWENTY-SECOND WEEK IN ORDINARY TIME

Year I

> 1 Thessalonians 5:1–6, 9–11
> Psalm 27:1, 4, 13–14
> Luke 4:31–37

We are children of the light! Paul designates the believers as such, and in so doing he addresses us. Discussion in Thessalonica centered on the season and time of the Lord's return. Paul sees this as useless talk; it is something we simply do not know. At any rate, Paul says, the second coming will be unannounced; it will come like a thief in the night. But the believers have nothing to fear, since they do not belong to the night. They are daytime people, basking in the light. We are not destined for wrath but for salvation in Christ Jesus. Therefore, we must take pains to stay alert and fully awake.

Christ had no part in darkness. Listen to the question the demon puts to him as they confront each other. Literally it is, "What have you to do with us?" Meaning, "What do we have in common?" The answer, of course, is "Nothing." Satan belongs to the realm of evil and darkness, and therefore between the demon and Jesus there is no commonality. Jesus meets him only to expel him from the possessed man's life.

In today's world we have more than our share of darkness. Theft, murder, greed, sexual promiscuity—the list goes on and on. But we know that we are called to better things, fully attainable if we remain in Christ. Word and sacrament keep us in the light. We must keep a stiff upper lip. We are children of light who have no fear.

Points to Ponder

> The significance of the baptismal candle
> Darkness as a symbol of evil
> Jesus as the holy one of God: the demon's recognition

Year II

1 Corinthians 2:10b–16
Psalm 145:8–9, 10–11, 12–13ab, 13cd–14
Luke 4:31–37

"What have you to do with us?" asks the demon of Jesus. In other words, "What do we have in common?" The broadest chasm separates Jesus from evil. The powers of evil will never understand him, but he has authority and power over them. Who can ever fully understand God except God himself? The same can be said of us. Nobody understands us fully; we alone delve into the mysteries of our heart. The same is true of God.

One of the great treasures of the Christian is the extent to which we do understand God. This is what we call "revelation." We know there is one God in three persons. We know that in his love for the world, God became man and offered himself in death. We know that God remains with us in the church, in word and sacrament. We know, as well, that we share God's Spirit and now belong to the household of God. These are all the deep things of God. For the nonbeliever, says Paul, it is foolishness, incomprehensible. Only those who live in the Spirit can judge it properly.

Lord keep us free from the demons that would destroy us! We thank you for the knowledge of yourself that you have shared with us. Let us never be trapped by temporal allurements, which belong to the realm of darkness. As the apostle teaches, we know that we have the mind of Christ.

Points to Ponder

Our self-knowledge
God's self-knowledge
God's self-knowledge shared with us

WEDNESDAY OF THE TWENTY-SECOND WEEK IN ORDINARY TIME

Year I

Colossians 1:1–8
Psalm 52:10, 11
Luke 4:38–44

It is easy to read about the illness of Peter's mother-in-law without realizing it has something to teach us. It follows the very succinct pattern of the miracle story form: a description of the illness, the action of Jesus, and the result of his action. The woman in the story suffers from a high fever. Jesus rebukes the fever, and the woman gets up to serve them. But it also reminds us of our responsibility in response to God's goodness to us. We are called to serve.

In many modern parishes, volunteerism is a way of life. It flows from that sense of love about which Paul speaks today to the Colossians. Service, or *diakonia*, was a hallmark of the church from its inception. It is the clearest and simplest way for love to be manifest. It may take many different forms: parish outreach to the poor, communion calls for the sick, coaching athletics, presence to the bereaved at a time of grief. In addition, for the liturgy, we need servers, lectors, and eucharistic ministers.

To see church as only a place where we are served falls far short of the mark. We have been healed of our fever at various times. But have we gotten up to serve? That is the critical question. If I have not done so, let me look at the ministries of my parish to determine how my own willingness to serve might best be realized.

Points to Ponder

Jesus' response to need
Our call to serve
Matching our talents and church needs

Year II

> 1 Corinthians 3:1–9
> Psalm 33:12–13, 14–15, 20–21
> Luke 4:38–44

Early in his first epistle to Corinth, Paul deals with one of the community's clear problems. It centers on rivalry and a form of hero worship. Groups were championing their own apostolic heroes: Paul, who had first preached to them; Apollos, whose rhetoric and speaking ability are noted in the New Testament; and Peter, who was first among the apostles.

Paul makes it clear: If that is the route you want to follow, then count me out. Paul may have planted the seed, Apollos may have cultivated it, but it was God alone who made it grow. It is not right to attribute to human beings what is clearly the work of God. The people are God's field; the missionaries are collaborators of God in caring for the field. It is an important perspective to maintain. Like Christ in today's Gospel, Paul did not want to bask in the light of spiritual accomplishment.

It is normal to recognize the gifts of priests and ministers who serve. But the parish is not great because of them; nor do they make virtue more visible. They are collaborators of the Lord (and that is no small matter). The principal work is God's, to whose name belong honor and glory.

Points to Ponder

> Ministry as collaboration with the Lord
> The danger of hero worship
> The Lord gives growth

THURSDAY OF THE TWENTY-SECOND WEEK IN ORDINARY TIME

Year I

> Colossians 1:9–14
> Psalm 98:2–3ab, 3cd–4, 5–6
> Luke 5:1–11

Conversion in its broadest sense means turning from an absence of faith to a belief in Christ, and it is no small thing. The scriptures clearly see it as the work of God, although human beings may well play a part as his instruments. This is the meaning behind the large catch of fish that the apostles make in today's Gospel. It had not been a good night for fishing; with the coming of daylight they had nothing to show for their effort.

Jesus advises them to cast their nets once again, and the catch fills two boats.

Recognizing that their success was wholly the work of the Lord, Peter can only admit his own sinfulness. They are then informed that in the future they will bring people to the faith.

The act of conversion requires grace, and the source of grace is God himself. Paul today speaks of God's role in conversion. "He has rescued us from the power of darkness and transferred us into the kingdom of his beloved Son." The human agents in this work naturally feel a sense of accomplishment, but this movement of Spirit must be attributed to God. It is a movement of grace for which we are undoubtedly grateful. But it is clearly a work of God.

When someone dear to us has wandered far from the faith, our prayer should be incessant. Augustine's mother prayed for years for the conversion of her son. What strikes us as being unlikely or impossible is not so for God. As pastoral experience shows us, there is unspeakable joy when the faith is embraced. Prayer can accomplish what human effort cannot. The fruitless night of fishing became a morning of unexpected joy, through the power of Jesus.

Points to Ponder

Grace and conversion
From darkness to the light of the kingdom
Perseverance in prayer

Year II

1 Corinthians 3:18–23
Psalm 24:1bc–2, 3–4ab, 5–6
Luke 5:1–11

Today's reading from Corinthians contains one of the strongest Christocentric statements of the New Testament. Paul begins by diminishing in value the wisdom of this world, quoting texts that indicate that such wisdom leads to vanity. It is in being foolish that the Christian comes to the true wisdom. That wisdom convinces one not to make boasts or elicit plaudits about any human being. For you do not belong to them—whether it be Paul, Apollos, or Kephas. As ministers of the gospel, they belong to you. The same is true of the whole created order, since it is you who stand at the pinnacle of creation and the summit of the order of grace. All things belong to you, you then are Christ's, and Christ belongs to God.

This is a succinct summary of the theology of the body of Christ. We all stand as members of that one body of which Christ is the head. We then can boast of nothing except of Christ. The whole order of redemption is for our good, and it places us in a unique position in the created order. And it is Christ who stands as our mediator with the Father.

How foolish it is for us to be envious of others. How lacking in faith for us to champion others' heroes. In the goodness of God's love, we have been transported out of darkness into his wondrous light. And it is all the work of Christ alone, acting at the Father's behest. Redeemed by the Son and drawn by the Father, we are members of God's household. Continuing in that relationship, our destiny is assured.

Points to Ponder

> The foolishness of faith
> We belong to Christ
> Christ belongs to God

FRIDAY OF THE TWENTY-SECOND WEEK IN ORDINARY TIME

Year I

> Colossians 1:15–20
> Psalm 100:1b–2, 3, 4, 5
> Luke 5:33–39

The celebrated hymn of Colossians, read today, was in all likelihood taken from the early Christian liturgy and incorporated by Paul in his epistle. It centers on the primacy of Christ in three distinct ways. He first of all has a primacy in all of creation. He stands with God from all eternity and is the blueprint in and through whom all things are brought into being. All things are created through him and for him. In the order of redemption, he is the head of the body, which is the church. We are all members of that one body, which draws its life from him who is the head. Finally, he is the first to rise from the dead and therefore is the prototype of what we are called to be. Through the blood of his cross he has reconciled the whole of creation, not solely humankind, to God.

This is the new wine about which Jesus speaks in the gospel. It cannot be placed in the old wineskins of the former covenant and its precepts.

We are a new creation with a new and unique relationship to God in Christ. This gives us a newfound liberty to be inspired by the human concerns that are present to us each day. While fasting is never excluded, its fixed times and season are not pivotal to the new life in God.

The hymn speaks to us of cosmic redemption. The whole of creation has been redeemed. By the blood of the cross all things have been reconciled. Concern for our environment and the preservation of the beauty and order that surround us are deeply Christian concerns.

Christ, then, is central to us who share in his redemption. He is also the guide and moderator of our daily life as the head of the body. Through him also we are related to the whole of creation as part of the universe that has been touched by redemption.

Points to Ponder

Christ the eternal blueprint of creation
Christ the head of the body
Christ and the redemption of the universe

Year II

> 1 Corinthians 4:1–5
> Psalm 37:3–4, 5–6, 27–28, 39–40
> Luke 5:33–39

Paul recognizes his call to be a servant and steward of the Lord. The quality of his response to that call will be judged by God alone and by no human agency. Paul is not conscious of any major failing, but he is not acquitted on that score. The Lord in his time will be the judge, at which time even that which is hidden will be brought to light. It is when the motives of the heart are made known that praise from God will be accorded.

The disciples of Jesus were not known for observance of the fasts, as were the disciples of John and the Pharisees. While not neglected in Jesus' teaching, fasting was not accorded a lion's share of his ethic. Perhaps he was avoiding the often-empty observance of the letter of the law against which the prophets inveighed. The Christian ethic was a way of life, not a determined program. In the new covenant, the covenant of the heart, everyone will know from his heart the right and wrong way to respond. The supreme law of love of neighbor cannot be programmed; it must come from the heart.

The Christian life is not a question of schedules and procedures. It is a response determined by circumstances, not personal convenience. It goes the extra mile, gives the new coat, and cares for the injured traveler on the road. It is a life of compassion and concern, not easy but very fulfilling.

Points to Ponder

> "Judgment is mine," says the Lord
> Christianity: a program or a way of life?
> Giving without counting the cost

SATURDAY OF THE TWENTY-SECOND WEEK IN ORDINARY TIME

Year I

> Colossians 1:21–23
> Psalm 54:3–4, 6 and 8
> Luke 6:1–5

Paul's injunction to the Colossians today can well be applied to all of us. We were initially alienated from God, but through the death of Christ we have been reconciled in order to be presented holy, without blemish, and irreproachable before him. We need but persevere in the faith, well grounded and not slipping away from the hope of the gospel. It is this latter injunction that causes us concern. In the midst of so many secular, even pagan, values today, it is not easy to remain firmly grounded. We all know people, sometimes those close to us, who have abandoned the faith.

That the apostles were plucking and eating some of the grain on the Sabbath strikes us as being very irrelevant. Jesus engages in a little casuistry in citing the example of David taking the bread from the sanctuary on the Sabbath. Then he cites the main reason for the dispensation from the law, something his opponents would never accept. Jesus was lord of the Sabbath.

Jesus was not concerned about minutiae. As Paul states so clearly, what is important is to stay in the friendship of Christ. It is not that easily lost. Some people will confess missing Mass on a Sunday when there were perfectly valid reasons for doing so. A mature Christian knows when sin is present and when it is not. It makes little sense for us to wrestle with our conscience over non-issues. Ours is a gracious God, not a taskmaster.

Points to Ponder

> The crucified Christ and our new life
> Mature decision making
> Jesus as Lord of the Sabbath

Year II

1 Corinthians 4:6b–15
Psalm 145:17–18, 19–20, 21
Luke 6:1–16

In Corinth there were evidently problems of the human ego. The question of the inflated ego led to one person's being championed over another. But when all is said and done, everything they had was gift. People began to brag about their accomplishments. The apostles continued to work incessantly as ministers of the gospel, often ridiculed and seen as fools; at the same time, there were those in Corinth who exalted themselves.

Paul writes to them as their father in Christ; it is a paternal admonition.

Self-esteem is something that we all cherish. But when this leads to self-adulation, we are wandering from true Christian humility. Christ rejected the request of James and John for places of honor in his kingdom. For anyone to be first, he must be the servant of all. It is the last who will be first. This is not an easy lesson to learn, but it is at the heart of the gospel.

It is not surprising that Jesus showed little interest in the apostles' plucking grain on the Sabbath. His concerns went far beyond that. When we are tempted to place ourselves on a pedestal, let us remember the apostles, who went hungry and thirsty while they followed Christ. It remains a great and noble thing to give oneself entirely for the cause of Christ, even if it escapes human notice.

Points to Ponder

True greatness: recognition by the Lord
The dangers of pride
Admonition and Christian concern

MONDAY OF THE TWENTY-THIRD WEEK IN ORDINARY TIME

Year I

> Colossians 1:24—2:3
> Psalm 62:6–7, 9
> Luke 6:6–11

How can anything be lacking in the sufferings of Christ? His work of redemption was complete in itself and was effected once and for all. But the application of Christ's work is ongoing and will not be complete until the end of time, when Christ presents the church to the Father. Therefore, in the sufferings of his ministry, Paul helps to bring to completion the work of the Lord and therefore, in that sense, fills up what is lacking in the afflictions of Christ.

When his opponents object to Christ healing on the Sabbath, Jesus raises a fundamental question. Is it lawful to do good on the Sabbath rather than do evil? There is no response. Hence, Jesus proceeds to heal the man with the withered hand. To exclude the performance of a good deed on the Sabbath flies in the face of divine teaching.

We can apply the teaching of Colossians here as well. When through our efforts within the church, the lot of other human beings is bettered, the saving work of Christ is enhanced. When we grow weary in the service of the Lord, the work of redemption is carried forward. Christ healed on the Sabbath. We also may do his work on the Sabbath and thus carry forth the suffering of Christ for the sake of his body, the church.

Points to Ponder

> The lack in the afflictions of Christ
> To do good on the Sabbath
> Our apostolic efforts and the sufferings of Christ

Year II

1 Corinthians 5:1–8
Psalm 5:5–6, 7, 12
Luke 6:6–11

Paul today deals with two problems present in Corinth. The first is a case of incest; the second, the question of boasting. He unquestionably sees the man living with his stepmother as a grave matter. The man should be excluded from the community; in fact, his conduct has already excluded him. Thus excluded, he is handed over to Satan so that his flesh may be subdued in order that his spirit may live.

Boasting was part of a former life. And like a little yeast in a batch of dough, boasting can affect the whole spiritual life. As baptized in Christ, the Corinthians are a new batch of dough, the unleavened bread of sincerity and truth. This is the state appropriate to the Christian. To revert to conduct of the past is the betrayal of a new birthright.

Excommunication is a harsh penalty and, although rarely pronounced today, can easily offend our sensibilities. But its positive side deserves a hearing. Its ultimate objective is salvific, the desire of the church to bring about a change in a person's life and to avoid a sense of indifference.

When Jesus healed on the Sabbath, he was not demeaning Sabbath observance. But he was acting in accordance with a greater good.

Points to Ponder

Attitudes toward public immorality
Sinful conduct: a reverting to un-Christian ways
The meaning of Sabbath observance today

TUESDAY OF THE TWENTY-THIRD WEEK IN ORDINARY TIME

Year I

Colossians 2:6–15
Psalm 145:1b–2, 8–9, 10–11
Luke 6:12–19

Today's first reading from Colossians spells out the benefits of Christian baptism. In Christ dwells the fullness of the deity. By being incorporated into him, we are circumcised with a circumcision not of the flesh but one in the Spirit. When we were dead by reason of our transgressions, in our state of uncircumcision, we were buried with him in baptism and thence brought to life. And what did that mean? All of our transgressions were obliterated. The handwriting that had been against us was nailed to the cross, rendering powerless the evil powers that had been aligned against us.

This is what Christian freedom means. We are no longer the slaves of sin nor subject to a law that was powerless to save. We are now free to do the good that God inspires, as long as we walk in Christ, rooted in him, established in the faith, and abounding in thanksgiving.

Our lives should make a difference. Our conduct should be an inspiration. Some time back, five Amish children in Pennsylvania were killed in a school classroom by a crazed citizen of the town. What was the response? Profound grief, of course. But also a common sense of forgiveness for the crime's perpetrator and a common ministration to his family. This was what Christ asked of them. Uncommon, yes, but deeply Christian as well.

Points to Ponder

The meaning of baptism
My life in Christ and Christ in me
Our sins, nailed to the cross

Year II

> 1 Corinthians 6:1–11
> Psalm 149:1b–2, 3–4, 5–6a and 9b
> Luke 6:12–19

In Luke's Gospel, before every major moment or decision in his life, Jesus is at prayer. This is seen in today's Gospel prior to his selection of the apostles. One often notes this in our time as well. There are people in every community who would never make a major decision without bringing it before the Lord in prayer. This is a living and vibrant faith.

People came from all regions to be cured by Jesus. To have contact with him was to feel power go forth from him. This was but a foretaste of the power of faith that he would share with his followers after the resurrection.

It is little wonder that Paul finds fault with the Corinthians for bringing their lawsuits before civil courts. Jesus himself was clear enough in speaking of settlements out of court. Certainly there are people within the community who can settle matters. To make evil public only begets more evil. And Paul reminds the community that adherents to evil of any kind have no part in the kingdom of God.

Today there are lawsuits brought against Christians, even members of the clergy, because of violations of the civil law. This is partly because we do not live in a distinctly Christian society. There are wrongs that must be righted by civil courts. But it is still difficult to see Christians going to court against one another. It is always preferable to settle minor cases out of court when such is possible.

Points to Ponder

> Prayer in decision making
> The power of faith
> Settling disagreements among Christians

WEDNESDAY OF THE TWENTY-THIRD WEEK IN ORDINARY TIME

Year I

Colossians 3:1–11
Psalm 145:2–3, 10–11, 12–13ab
Luke 6:20–26

Comfort in adversity! The Beatitudes in Luke speak to people who find themselves in adverse situations in life: the poor, the hungry, the grieving, the excluded, the demeaned. Situations in this life are not definitive; the future offers the opposite of these deprivations. Therefore, take courage and continue to walk in the way of the Lord.

Paul speaks in today's reading of the old and new way of living. There is the way of "earthly" immorality. By our baptism we have been raised with Christ, and thus our thoughts should be centered on the things that are above, not the things of earth. Therefore impurity, passion, greed, obscenities, and anger are to be put to death. They are mere relics of the past. We have taken off the image of the old creature and put on the image of the Creator. Old distinctions now fade: race, nationality, social status. Now we are formed in the likeness of Christ who is all and in all.

It is quite possible for people to live on a small income with scarcely enough to feed and clothe a family and, at the same time, live a life in harmony with God's will. They do not live with their hearts attached to this world, and their values are very much in place. They know what it is to suffer, but their peace no one can take from them. The Santal—tribal peoples of northern India—are certainly poor and needy. They live in their single-room mud houses, and yet their joy and hospitality are invariably noted. They live at peace, cultivate a piece of land, and love their Christian faith. They are the privileged ones of the gospel.

Points to Ponder

The Lucan Beatitudes: the burdens of life
The values of those who have risen with Christ
Living the image of Christ

Year II

> 1 Corinthians 7:25–31
> Psalm 45:11–12, 14–15, 16–17
> Luke 6:20–26

In view of the expected return of Christ, Paul tells the Corinthians not to be unduly concerned about marriage. He speaks not from the teaching of Christ but from his own insight. If one is married, then remain so. If one has no wife, then don't look for one. If those without a spouse decide to take one, they do not sin, but there will be trials and difficulties ahead.

Paul saw the advantage of celibacy in the service of the kingdom from his own experience. He would not hesitate to advise it, but this is a matter he leaves to personal choice. In the Western church today, celibacy remains mandatory for the clergy, and it has many positive values. But it is a discipline that could change. Many feel today that it should be optional. That day may well come. What is of paramount importance is the ministry itself, which is essential to the church's life.

Luke's Beatitudes list some of the categories of people to whom ministry is directed. They are the suffering ones, the *anawim* of God. They are the people to whom we can never say, "I don't have time." The consolation and help that we bring is a foretaste of the joy of the kingdom that will one day be theirs.

Points to Ponder

> Marriage as a holy state in life
> Celibacy and ministry
> Ministry as the indispensable value

THURSDAY OF THE TWENTY-THIRD WEEK IN ORDINARY TIME

Year I

> Colossians 3:12–17
> Psalm 150:1b–2, 3–4, 5–6
> Luke 6:27–38

Many of the injunctions found in Matthew's Sermon on the Mount are found here in Luke. We are told in very concrete terms what the love of enemies means. Blessings for curses, prayers for mistreatment, good cheek for injured cheek, tunic for cloak. To love those who love us is common even among nonbelievers. To lend money and expect repayment has no virtue attached at all. In short, do good because it is the right thing to do, without expecting anything in return. In addition, be nonjudgmental and forgiving. God will repay you in even greater measure.

Paul tells the Colossians what it means to walk in the Lord's way. Realize that you are loved by Christ; this means compassion, kindness, humility, patience, and, in a special way, forgiveness (as the Lord has forgiven you). It means, above all, to be clothed in love, which is the keystone of all perfection. This will mean a sharing in the peace that Christ brings. It means gratitude expressed in hymns and songs. And, thus enveloped by Christ, every act of the day becomes a prayer of thanks to God the Father through Christ, his Son.

Before such a program of action, we would have to admit that we all fall short. But we must never give up. There is always an area that calls for improvement. Meditation on the gospel ethic is not meant to lead to discouragement. God understands our weakness. But it does mean that we are not content with the status quo. There is always that someone out there with whom we should make peace. There is that family whose monthly income is below the subsistence level. There is always some stab of conscience. Today's reflection may just lead us to do something about it.

Points to Ponder

Our shortcomings in the way of holiness
Forgiveness as we have been forgiven
Hostility in my life

Year II

1 Corinthians 8:1b–7, 11–13
Psalm 139:1b–3, 13–14ab, 23–24
Luke 6:27–38

Can scandal, or bad example, be given when there is no objective reason for it? Paul feels that such can be the case. In the matter of food offered to "idols" or "false gods" (a common occurrence in the pagan Greco-Roman world), some Christians will realize that since these gods don't actually exist there is no sin in eating food that has been offered to them. But there may be other Christians with very sensitive consciences who still regard this as a sinful practice. So to eat such food in their presence may scandalize them and should be avoided for that reason. Therefore Paul would be willing to swear off meat entirely, if eating it would ever lead another into sin.

Paul argues always from the primacy of love. Even if conduct is objectively proper and not scandalous, he will avoid if it brings another to sin (at least subjectively). This is but another example of love carrying one beyond the law, about which the Gospel today has much to say. In the face of evil conduct (hostility, mistreatment, hatred), the Christian is called upon to respond with love.

Admittedly, this is not the ordinary way of acting. But the Christian way of acting is not the customary human response. I will do nothing that may cause my neighbor to sin. That is not an easy directive. But as Cardinal Suhard put it years ago, "We are to live our lives in such a way that they would make no sense if God did not exist" (*Growth or Decline*, Notre Dame: 1951).

Points to Ponder

Scandal and its consequences
Objective and subjective sin
Christianity and going beyond the law

FRIDAY OF THE TWENTY-THIRD WEEK IN ORDINARY TIME

Year I

1 Timothy 1:1–2, 12–14
Psalm 16:1b–2a and 5, 7–8, 11
Luke 6:39–42

Moral values have become an important feature of the American political scene in recent years. Some of it has come from the conservative right wing and some of it with a general dissatisfaction with the lack of concern for traditional values in modern Western life. Thus in this modern secular society, one candidate for public office does not hesitate to conclude a campaign speech with the request, "Please pray for me." Another distributes a card with his picture on one side and the Ten Commandments on the other.

Our Gospel today has something to say to politicians or anyone responsible for moral leadership. One must make sure his or her plate is clean before exhorting others to finish their meals. We have had all too many examples of people in public life, as well as church life, who were anxious to remove the splinter from their neighbor's eye while neglecting the wooden beam in their own. This was as true of some of the religious leaders in Jesus' time as it is today. In our very public times, it is very difficult to keep skeletons hidden in the closet.

Paul's letter to Timothy today finds the apostle admitting his past sinfulness—blasphemy, persecution, arrogance. But the grace of God was received in abundance and brought about a complete change of life. We share that same faith and love in Christ Jesus, and our lives are to reflect it.

Before correcting others, we always profit by some soul searching to see if our own lives are in order.

Points to Ponder

> Importance of the examination of conscience
> Value of fraternal correction
> Honesty in admitting past guilt

Year II

> 1 Corinthians 9:16–19, 22b–27
> Psalm 84:3, 4, 5–6, 12
> Luke 6:39–42

Paul is not about to boast because he has faithfully preached the gospel. In doing it willingly, he is compensated; if unwillingly, he still does it free of charge. In other words, he makes himself a slave to all in order to win at least some for Christ. Every athlete who runs wants to attain the prize. For this the athlete willingly subjects his or her body to a training regime.

We are in training, not for a perishable crown, but one that is imperishable. Paul, perhaps more than others, strains lest in preaching to others he should be disqualified.

Sometimes in reading the New Testament we lose sight of its excitement and enthusiasm. We go through chapter after chapter, some of us even writing about it, but it is all done in a matter-of-fact way. We forget that it is not a textbook to be memorized but a way of life to be lived. It calls for a spirited commitment and a regime of self-discipline. The Gospel today reminds us that it is often easier to find fault with others than with ourselves. We must be honest with ourselves and with others.

We are runners in a great race that is more than worth the effort.

Our dedication is there, but it may get a little cold at times. It is then that we should stand back and take a hard look, to renew our dedication and enthusiasm. Above all, let us be certain that our words and commitment are in correspondence with our life.

Points to Ponder

> The athletic image
> Maintaining our enthusiasm for the message
> The importance of self-discipline

SATURDAY OF THE TWENTY-THIRD WEEK IN ORDINARY TIME

Year I

> 1 Timothy 1:15–17
> Psalm 113:1b–2, 3–4, 5 and 6–7
> Luke 6:43–49

The greater the sinner, the greater the patience and mercy of God. That is the message of Paul to Timothy. Of sinners, he (Paul) was the foremost, and therefore in him the mercy of God is most evident. But now the good tree that he has become must bear good fruit. And good fruit means a solid foundation. That is today's Gospel message. There can be no doubt that Paul's life change was astounding. He had been a well-known persecutor of the early church. He was on the Damascus road for that very purpose. As Acts of the Apostles describes God's intervention in his life, it is a visible, earth-shaking experience in which there is a brief conversation between Christ and the future apostle. His powerful leadership in the growth and outreach of early Christianity has won him the title of Christianity's second founder. His letters, read now for centuries, bespeak an incredible insight into the meaning of Christ's mission.

In today's Gospel, Jesus indicates the importance of rootedness in the faith. A superficial embrace of Christ's teaching will not hold up under duress. This means not only a practice of the faith but also an ongoing understanding of its meaning. With the great strides that were made in theology and scripture studies in the twentieth century, it is clear that religious education cannot end with the sacrament of confirmation.

With a sense of dedication and commitment, we shall certainly bear fruit. In this way we become the salt of the earth and the light of the world. Spiritual values take on a greater importance in our lives. It is what faith is all about.

Points to Ponder

> From great sinner to great lover
> A deep-rooted faith
> Withstanding assaults on faith

Year II

> 1 Corinthians 10:14–22
> Psalm 116:12–13, 17–18
> Luke 6:43–49

Paul further advises the Corinthians to avoid idolatry, especially in matters of worship. Our sacrifice is not mere symbolism. The bread that we take from the altar is truly the body of Christ; the cup of which we drink is truly his blood. We all eat of the one loaf, and thus though we are many, we are one in partaking of the one loaf. There can be no sharing in the one sacrifice of Christ and the pagan sacrifices offered to idols, which Paul sees as being offered to "demons." There can be no compatibility between sacrifices offered to God and those offered to demons.

We are hardly likely to be involved in demon worship in our times. But when we surrender so much to secular values in living for this world and what it has to offer, when we build a house without a foundation, we become implicitly idolatrous. We cannot carry water on two shoulders. Built on a firm foundation, we are united in the one bread with the one body.

When Hurricane Katrina hit the Gulf Coast, many homes collapsed entirely. We were reminded that many of our citizens live in poverty conditions that are hard to reconcile with an affluent country.

But the collapse of a weak faith is equally devastating. A solid foundation is our only assurance, and a deep love of the Eucharist is the sign of a solid foundation.

Points to Ponder

> One bread, one body
> Idolatry in today's world
> A eucharistic spirituality

MONDAY OF THE TWENTY-FOURTH WEEK IN ORDINARY TIME

Year I

> 1 Timothy 2:1–8
> Psalm 28:2, 7, 8–9
> Luke 7:1–10

There are a number of admirable qualities that appear in the life of the pagan centurion in today's Gospel. He is concerned about his seriously ill servant; he has shown himself sensitive to the needs of the occupied Jews; he does not hesitate to make a request of Jesus; he is conscious of the ritual impurity Jesus would contact in entering his house. But above all there is his faith recognition of Jesus' power over impending death.

The centurion lives out what the Letter to Timothy says explicitly.

There is but one God and one mediator between God and man: Christ Jesus, himself human, who gave himself as ransom for all.

Jesus commends the centurion in one of the Gospels' strongest expressions of praise. Nowhere in Israel had he found such faith. We may well ask ourselves whether we show similar concern for needy people who play secondary roles in our lives. Our faith tells us that Christ is present to us in all circumstances. But how often do we consider our own unworthiness? God's grace has been lavished upon us; it is all gift. But we sometimes act as if it is all due to us. The centurion knew what it meant to give orders and get an immediate response. But he was not about to ask the same of Jesus.

We certainly want to pray and pray unceasingly, at the same time realizing our own unworthiness.

How often do we say a prayer of thanks for petitions granted? Blessed be the Lord for he has heard my prayer.

Points to Ponder

> Praying with confidence
> Mindfulness of our unworthiness
> Requesting in faith

Year II

> 1 Corinthians 11:17–26, 33
> Psalm 40:7–8a, 8b–9, 10, 17
> Luke 7:1–10

In addressing the Corinthians, Paul recalls the eucharistic formula that by the mid-first century had become a centerpiece of Christian prayer life. Since in the early church the Eucharist was celebrated with a community dinner, the apostle sees that there is a protocol to be observed. Some people were eating their own meals ahead of others, with the result that some had little or nothing and others had more than enough. Paul insists that they wait for one another with a sense of respect.

The reason that Paul gives is found in the words and action of Jesus. "This is my body that is for you....This cup is the new covenant in my blood." This is not simply a memorial of Christ's death. It brings to life anew the new covenant of the Spirit that Christ has effected through his sacrificial death. It bespeaks generosity, concern, and deep love. Jesus commends the centurion in today's Gospel because of his faith and his respect.

As a community centered in the Eucharist, we are called to be well mannered and considerate. In a parish we approach the altar together week after week. Respect and good conduct are necessary. In receiving the Eucharist, we should avoid haste and act with devotion. After Mass, it is commendable to spend some time together with the other parishioners. It is a good time to learn who in our parish or community may need assistance. The Eucharist extends itself into our daily lives, beyond the walls of the physical church.

Points to Ponder

> The Eucharist and a new covenant
> The Eucharist and concern for others
> The Eucharist and the elimination of parish factions

TUESDAY OF THE TWENTY-FOURTH WEEK IN ORDINARY TIME

Year I

> 1 Timothy 3:1–13
> Psalm 101:1b–2ab, 2cd–3ab, 5, 6
> Luke 7:11–17

The qualities of leadership in the early church are clearly specified in the pastoral epistles. Bishops were not understood in the same way as they are in the modern church. They acted as overseers for the overall conduct of the local church's life. Deacons assisted with pastoral duties within the church. They were to be men above reproach, responsible in the management of their own families, who enjoyed a good reputation within the church and the broader community. They could be married only one time.

The church has long insisted on basic qualification in those called to ministry. In the main, this has been successful; in some cases, less so. But there is no doubt that a dignified and worthy comportment enhances the cause of Christ. Where there is a lack of good conduct, the church suffers. Authorities are called to be self-controlled, kindly, gentle, and generous.

There is a lesson to be learned in Jesus' conduct in today's Gospel. His heart went out to the widow who was burying her son. Without being asked, he takes the initiative and restores the young man's life. It is often said that there is nothing more difficult than for a parent to bury a child. Jesus, it would seem, understood this well. At least, his action reflects a very deep compassion and sensitivity.

Points to Ponder

> Proper comportment in church ministry
> Jesus' initiative at Nain
> The role of the New Testament "bishop"

Year II

> 1 Corinthians 12:12–14, 27–31a
> Psalm 100:1b–2, 3, 4, 5
> Luke 7:11–17

In the spiritual order the church is a living organism. St. Paul sees it as a body composed of many parts, with Christ as the head. In addition we have been given certain functions to perform, no two of which are the same, yet all contribute to the well-being of the whole. There is no reason for jealousy, since we all benefit from each of the functions. The greater gift for which we should strive is developed in the next chapter of the letter: the gift of love. No gift surpasses that, and it is capable of being shared by all of us.

Jesus gives little heed to the many gifts that will come to represent the church. Although he would not deny their importance, it is the virtue of love to which he points repeatedly. This is evident as he comes upon the woman burying her son in today's Gospel. Without being asked, he notes the widow's grief and moves in the direction of alleviating her pain. Not a word is spoken. Jesus restores the son to his mother; the crowd is amazed. Jesus continues on his way.

How frequent it is that we meet human need. It may be severe depression, lack of money or food, a devastating illness, unemployment—misfortune comes in many forms. We may well feel inadequate in such circumstances. But there is usually something we can do. A Christian does not walk away from someone who is suffering. The greatest gift is love, and all of us can extend that.

Points to Ponder

> The many functions in the body of Christ
> The supreme gift of love
> Jesus' immediate response to the grieving widow

WEDNESDAY OF THE TWENTY-FOURTH WEEK IN ORDINARY TIME

Year I

1 Timothy 3:14–16
Psalm 111:1–2, 3–4, 5–6
Luke 7:31–35

The children sitting in the marketplace find their playmates unresponsive to any suggestion. The crowds listening to Jesus are the same. They find reasons at every turn for remaining uncommitted. John the Baptist fasted from food and wine and was accused of being possessed by a demon. Jesus came eating and drinking and was accused of being a glutton and a drunkard. Where there is an unwillingness to act, any excuse will do.

There are moments in life when resolute action is called for, and we may offer very weak reasons for not acting. There are times when we know that our children are following a very dangerous path. But rather than suffer their rejection, we do nothing. We lose sight of the very serious pledge we have made before God to act in keeping with our responsibility.

Our commitment to Christ calls us to action, not passivity. The quotation from Timothy today (1 Tim 3:16) summarizes Jesus' life and ministry, especially his glorification; in a very expressive way. He came among us in the flesh, a true human being. In his resurrection he is vindicated in his life and teaching. Now glorified, he is seen by angels, preached to the Gentiles, and beloved in as the universal savior. Christ was always the total "Yes" to God.

His decisiveness is what we are called to live.

Points to Ponder

Evading commitment
Christ's unqualified "Yes" to God
The dangers of vacillation

Year II

> 1 Corinthians 12:31—13:13
> Psalm 33:2–3, 4–5, 12 and 22
> Luke 7:31–35

Today's reading from Corinthians is one of the New Testament's most cherished chapters. Couples preparing for marriage often select it for their wedding ceremony. Speaking in the epistle of the various gifts and charisms present in the church, Paul saves his strongest praise for love.

If one enjoys the other gifts (eloquence, prophecy, faith, and self-sacrifice) but lacks charity, it counts for nothing. What are love's characteristics? Patience, kindness, transparency, consideration, and understanding. Other gifts will come to an end when they will no longer be of use. Certain gifts are needed now because of our imperfections. But as my knowledge in faith grows, I realize that I will know God more fully. Finally, faith will give way to vision; hope, to actuality; but love will never vanish. Therefore, it has a primacy among all the gifts and virtues.

Unfortunately, in earlier textbooks on theology, charity was not given the primacy accorded it in the scriptures. This is not the case in most moral theology courses taught today. In treatises on chastity in the past, even the slightest infraction was treated with solemn gravity, while violations of charity were considered to be of secondary importance, if that. Fortunately in our time we have a different perspective.

Charity is the virtue that explains the whole Christ event. Let us pray that we always see it with the eyes of Paul.

Points to Ponder

> Love in relation to the other gifts
> Love as the virtue that never dies
> The invitation to dance and to weep

THURSDAY OF THE TWENTY-FOURTH WEEK IN ORDINARY TIME

Year I

> 1 Timothy 4:12–14
> Psalm 111:7–8, 9, 10
> Luke 7:36–50

Timothy is reminded today to stir up the grace of God that he received at the inauguration of his ministry. It is excellent advice. We have all experienced the outpouring of God's love at various sacramental moments of our life. That initial experience is kept alive through renewal and rededication. It's not sufficient to put it on "automatic pilot"; we need moments of conscious reengagement.

Because the sinful woman of Luke's Gospel had experienced such profound forgiveness, her gratitude was unbounded. "Her sins, which were many, have been forgiven; hence she has shown great love." The woman was not embarrassed; she does not hesitate to show her gratitude, even in a public setting. Her faith was great in Jesus, who was able to forgive her sins.

One of the reasons why the woman's conduct seems so incongruous today is that we in many cases have lost the sense of sin. Reconciliation of a sinner with God is one of the most touching aspects of ministry. There is such a sense of relief as a huge burden is lifted.

We need forgiveness. We have received it at various times in our lives. Christ's consoling words have reached us as well. *Your sins are forgiven*. God holds no grudges and does not demand an accounting. It is simply a "Welcome home." With the psalmist today, we can rejoice in the greatness of the Lord's works.

Points to Ponder

> Renewing our faith commitment
> Gratitude for sins forgiven
> Retaining a sense of sin

Year II

1 Corinthians 15:1–11
Psalm 118:1b–2, 16ab–17, 28
Luke 7:36–50

Paul today recalls the *kerygma* or basic teaching of the church in which the Corinthians have been instructed. What is our core belief? What is the fundamental word that has been preached? That Christ died for our sins and was buried. That he rose on the third day and appeared to Peter, the Twelve, James, and the other apostles, and finally to Paul. It was on the basis of the acceptance of these basic truths that baptism was administered. Only after baptism was there further instruction in the teaching (*didache*) of Jesus. It is good for all of us from time to time to return to the fundamentals of faith. No other doctrine supersedes these.

Paul is reminded of his own unworthiness. He had persecuted the followers of Jesus. But he recognizes that the grace of God in life has not been in vain. He has not been ineffective, and this not due to his own merit. It is the grace that he has received that has been operative. His preaching and his audience's reception of the preaching has been realized through the goodness of God.

Paul is enthusiastic about his conversion. The sinful woman of today's Gospel performed her act of love because she was deeply grateful. We too have received the gracious Word and have been forgiven all our failings. He died to bring us home.

Points to Ponder

Reflecting on the church's earliest proclamation
Paul's unworthiness
The sinful woman's gratitude

FRIDAY OF THE TWENTY-FOURTH WEEK IN ORDINARY TIME

Year I

> 1 Timothy 6:2c–12
> Psalm 49:6–7, 8–10, 17–18, 19–20
> Luke 8:1–3

As Jesus continues his preaching mission, he is accompanied by the Twelve and by a number of women, three of whom are mentioned by name. It is somewhat surprising to have women as part of an itinerant mission. They proved very helpful, however, in providing for the needs of Christ and his apostles.

This brings us to a merited consideration of the role that women play in the life of the church. Today it is safe to say that the institution would not be able to function without them. And this was true in the past as well. Women religious were responsible for the education of the young. It was due to the competence with which this was done that the Catholic Church was built on such a firm foundation in this country. Today women are involved in almost all areas of parochial life. These include religious education, the social ministries, presence to the bereaved, and eucharistic ministry. Their unfailing presence to spiritual need in so many forms is reason for deep gratitude.

Timothy today is advised to avoid discord and greed at all cost. If our basic needs are provided for, we should be grateful and content. Christians are called to a positive way of life, and the pursuit of virtue is paramount. It is eternal life to which we have been called. Therefore, lay hold of it with uncompromising faith.

Points to Ponder

> The role of women in the church
> Building on the positive
> Avoiding the divisive

Year II

> 1 Corinthians 15:12–20
> Psalm 17:1bcd, 6–7, 8b and 15
> Luke 8:1–3

The problems facing the church in Corinth were not few in number. Some people were questioning the resurrection from the dead. This was a question in Jesus' ministry as well, with the Jewish Sadducees excluding any belief in a resurrection. Paul's response is very much *ad hominem*.

Belief in Christ's resurrection was an essential feature of Christian belief. Not only did it have apologetic importance; it was the risen Christ who was the life giver, with the gift of the Holy Spirit being the first fruit of the resurrection. The presence of the Holy Spirit was concomitant with the forgiveness of sins. The conclusion, then, is clear enough. If Christ is not risen, then our faith is in vain and our sins remain.

What form will the resurrection take? That is difficult to say. We do know that it means that we will be participants in the end-time happiness and that we will be united with Christ. Paul himself admits that he cannot describe a resurrected body. It is as different from the present moment as the oak is from the acorn. But there is a continuity between the present and future life. We have that on the word of Christ.

Points to Ponder

> The meaning of resurrection faith
> Continuity between the present and future life
> The relation between the Holy Spirit and the forgiveness
> of sin

SATURDAY OF THE TWENTY-FOURTH WEEK IN ORDINARY TIME

Year I

> 1 Timothy 6:13–16
> Psalm 100:1b–2, 3, 4, 5
> Luke 8:4–15

Parables were oblique ways of communicating a truth. They were intended to be illustrative, but since they involved comparisons and figures of speech, they could be misunderstood. It is this latter ignorance that the evangelists highlight in the crowds' failure to understand. Today's parable is a classic and fits responses to the faith as well in our time as in the time of Jesus.

The seed is the word of God. The various types of soil represent people's response to the word. The seed that fell on the path has no effect whatever. It is simply lost. This represents those hearers who register no response at all. The rocky ground is the hearer with no roots. These people believe only for a time and then quickly forget. The seed among thorns represents those who are so taken with the pleasures of this world that they abandon the word. The seed in rich soil are the hearers who cultivate and embrace the word and, through their perseverance, bear fruit.

Our own experience points up the reality of the parable. Some people register no interest at all; some accept the message for a while; others mean well, but passing interests eventually take over. It is all too easy to fall into one or other of these categories. Finally there are those who cultivate the word and grow in their appreciation of it. We pray and we trust that we are and will remain the good soil that provides for the word unto eternal life.

The Letter to Timothy today prays that he remain firm in the teaching of Jesus until the end. Perseverance is a grace for which we should pray. Left to our own resources, our convictions may waver. We too can become entrapped in other concerns. We pray frequently that we may remain faithful, the good soil that remains fertile unto eternal life.

Points to Ponder

> Responses to the word today
> Cultivating the word of God
> The grace of perseverance

Year II

> 1 Corinthians 15:35–37, 42–49
> Psalm 56:10c–12, 13–14
> Luke 8:4–15

The differences between the present body and that of the future are considerable. Paul gives some attention to this question in today's reading. Trying to speak of the present and the future is a question of apples and oranges. The present body must die before the new body can emerge. What is here corruptible is raised incorruptible; the dishonorable becomes glorious; the natural becomes spiritual. Just as we are all children of the first Adam, so we become children of the second Adam, a life-giving spirit.

There are many things about the future that we believe but cannot visualize. Some things we must leave to God. He brought us into this world, which, with all of its problems, is a wonder that we would not have imagined. So too for the future. We had best leave it in the hands of God, without pressing too hard for answers.

For the present, today's Gospel calls us to be the fertile ground that will embrace the word through to the finish. The seed has been sown in our hearts. We want to turn away from coldness and indifference. As to the future, let us leave it in the hands of God. We believe that we shall be with Christ and those we love. That alone makes it worth the effort.

Points to Ponder

> Speaking of a resurrection
> Certainties about the future
> Seed in the fertile soil

MONDAY OF THE TWENTY-FIFTH WEEK IN ORDINARY TIME

Year I

> Ezra 1:1–6
> Psalm 126:1b–2ab, 2cd–3, 4–5, 6
> Luke 8:16–18

The postexilic personalities Ezra and Nehemiah were responsible for the religious and political restoration of Judah. It was the Persian king Cyrus who had mandated the return of the Jews to their homeland and the rebuilding of the temple. It was a moment of true elation for the Jews, who had suffered so much at the hands of pagan rulers. Cyrus's decree provided for the return of the Jews and encouraged the people among whom they had lived to assist them with provisions for their return. It was a moment of great hope for a people who had too long lived in a foreign land, separated from the dwelling place of their God and deprived of the worship that was Yahweh's due.

It was because of their own conduct, not the design of God, that the Jews had been punished with spiritual deprivation. It is clear from the Old Testament teaching that their religious dedication was to serve as a magnet for the nations of the earth.

Jesus in the Gospel directs his followers to be shining lights that others (especially the Gentiles of Luke's thought) may be moved to embrace the gospel. Christianity is not an esoteric religion destined only for the enlightened. Rather it is destined for all people, and its authenticity is to be seen in the faith of its adherents. If one shares the truth generously, one's faith will be increased. But if one is miserly about the faith he has, the loss will embrace even the little that he has.

The truth of our belief is to shine forth in our lives. St. Francis sent his followers to preach the gospel "with words, if necessary." If we are truly enraptured by the person of Jesus, such light will inevitably appear in our lives. May the joy that is ours because of what God has done for us shine before others. It is the person of Jesus who comes to life in us. And that remains our greatest form of witness.

Points to Ponder

Israel's sinfulness and God's fidelity
The light of faith shining in our lives
The value of who we are rather than what we say

Year II

Proverbs 3:27–34
Psalm 15:2–3a, 3bc–4ab, 5
Luke 8:16–18

The Bible's Wisdom literature offers practical advice for everyday situations. In today's reading the lender is advised not to delay in providing for the need of another. If the donor or the lender can provide at once, then this should be done—without procrastination. Plotting against another, quarreling, and envy have no place in the life of the upright person. It is on the upright whom God's blessing descends; it is the humble whom he loves.

The teaching of the Lord does not leave us confused. Yet we still make bad choices. How often today we see the result of bad decisions: people in public life brought to justice after a long period of wrongdoing. Some people will always take the chance. But evildoing brings unhappiness and failure in the long run.

But the Gospel today places in strong relief the power of good. Both good and light attract; darkness repels. Christ expects us to carry him forward. In effect, he tells us, Where your feet go, I can go. Where your eyes see, I can see. Where your ears hear, I can hear. That is what it means to be the light of the world. It is the mission to which each of us is called.

Points to Ponder

Proverbs' practical wisdom
Human choices: good or evil
The light on the lampstand

TUESDAY OF THE TWENTY-FIFTH WEEK IN ORDINARY TIME

Year I

> Ezra 6:7–8, 12b, 14–20
> Psalm 122:1–2, 3–4ab, 4cd–5
> Luke 8:19–21

Both the scriptures and tradition attest to the fact that Jesus was raised in a God-fearing family characterized by love and respect. When the subject of his human family comes up in his ministry, however, Jesus invariably raises the discussion to another level. Jesus was not simply another man who became someone of note. He was born with a mission, given by God himself, and that always held the priority in his life. In today's Gospel we are reminded that the true kin of Jesus are those who hear God's word and act on it.

With that fuller understanding of the Christian message, we know that with baptism we enjoy a new and fuller life, the life of the Spirit. This is the life that unites Christ and the Father and is now shared with us. We thus become members of the heavenly household that entitles us to know Christ as our brother and God as Father ("Abba"). In today's Gospel, then, Christ lays claim on us. We are truly mother, brother, and sister to him.

The extraordinary cooperation of the Persian authorities, as well as the Jewish elders and prophets, in the rebuilding of the temple is highlighted in today's reading from Ezra. It was the dawn of a new spiritual era for Israel, one that unfortunately was to become less impressive with the passing of time. Our family relationship with Christ has more significance than the rebuilt temple. Do we succeed in keeping it front and center in our lives?

Points to Ponder

> International help in rebuilding the temple
> The true family members of Jesus
> Jesus' human family: subordination not disdain

Year II

Proverbs 21:1–6, 10–13
Psalm 119:1, 27, 30, 34, 35, 44
Luke 8:19–21

Proverbs highlights the choices of the wicked and those of the good. Proper conduct has more value than the execution of ritual. Pride and arrogance lead to ruin. Diligence and care reap benefits; haste leads to loss. The proud and haughty person proceeds with little care for his neighbor. He who shows no concern for the cry of the poor will one day be unheard himself.

Transposed to a slightly higher key, the conduct of the just person as found in the Wisdom literature is also that of the true family of Christ, highlighted in today's Gospel. The brother and sister of Christ work for the good of their neighbor, avoid arrogance and pride, are sensitive to the needs of the poor. We can all profit by the Old Testament ethic and, as we read the books of Wisdom, make our own examination of conscience.

Today's Gospel carries us back to another Lucan narrative (in chapter 2), the loss of Jesus for three days during the family visit to Jerusalem. Jesus remains respectful of Mary and Joseph but also emphasizes the priority to be given to his Father's concerns. There are times in our own lives when the concerns of God take precedence over the best of human interests.

Points to Ponder

Reading Proverbs with a Christian heart
Arrogance: the antithesis of Christian morality
The loss in Jerusalem and the priority of the Father's
  concerns

WEDNESDAY OF THE TWENTY-FIFTH WEEK IN ORDINARY TIME

Year I

Ezra 9:5–9
Tobit 13:2, 3–4a, 4befghn, 7–8
Luke 9:1–6

Two features of God's concern with humanity appear in today's readings. The first is his forgiveness of Israel as seen in Ezra's powerful prayer of gratitude. The second is the Lucan account of Jesus' commission of the Twelve to proclaim God's kingdom and to cure disease everywhere.

The prayer of Ezra is divided into two parts. The first deals with the punishment visited upon God's people because of their wicked deeds. This has meant defeat and destruction at the hands of foreigners over many years: "to the sword, to captivity, to plundering, and to utter shame." But finally, mercy was attained. The remnant has returned home and the temple restored. The good will of the kings of Persia has rested upon them. When Jerusalem and the temple are restored, hope for the future is restored. Through it all, God has remained faithful to his people.

The fidelity of God as evidenced in Jesus is even more pronounced. Jesus shares his power over demons and diseases with the Twelve. He sends them forth to proclaim the good news everywhere. They are to travel light, unencumbered by nonessentials. In any given town, they are to remain in the house where they are offered hospitality. If they are rejected, they are to shake the dust from their feet and move on. The narrative is in line with a clear Lucan theme: God's concern for all people.

The Jewish people have a long history of God's concern about their sin. In their repentance, they recognize their guilt and God's abiding fidelity. This love and concern, as seen in Jesus, now goes out, in very concrete terms, to embrace all people. This universal love reminds us of God's inclusiveness and the need to avoid attitudes that exclude any group of people from that love.

Points to Ponder

Ezra's recognition of Israel's guilt
The freedom of few possessions
The urgency of God's call

Year II

Proverbs 30:5–9
Psalm 119:29, 72, 89, 101, 104, 163
Luke 9:1–6

The author of Proverbs draws on a very interesting maxim that no doubt enjoyed common coinage in his culture. He asks God for neither poverty nor riches. In want, he may steal and thus profane the name of God.

With riches, he may become complacent and even question his need of God. He asks only that his basic needs be met. The request is a good one. We don't value poverty for its own sake. We see its value only in relationship to our freedom to draw closer to God. With a positive goal in mind, turning aside from material concerns has meaning. Otherwise, it is a negative pursuit.

In today's Gospel, Jesus is not introducing religious poverty. He is speaking of a mission that has such importance that it is worth every sacrifice. We all, even those who have taken a vow of poverty, have a tendency to acquire too much. If the concerns of the gospel have priority in our lives, that will serve to deter us from becoming entrenched in that which is passing away.

We strive to be obedient to the Lord because, like the psalmist, we have chosen the way of truth. With the highway well marked, the chances of our getting lost are greatly reduced. Let us keep our attention riveted on the goal that is ours.

Points to Ponder

Neither wealth nor poverty; a simple sufficiency
Placing the gospel at the center of life
The dangers of wealth and God's kingdom

THURSDAY OF THE TWENTY-FIFTH WEEK IN ORDINARY TIME

Year I

Haggai 1:1–8
Psalm 149:1b–2, 3–4, 5–6a and 9b
Luke 9:7–9

Today's readings register Yahweh's displeasure with his people and Herod's curiosity about Jesus. Haggai sees unfortunate delays in the reconstruction of the temple. People are ready to settle in their own new homes at the same time that the house of the Lord lies in ruins. Yahweh speaks through the prophet, telling them to get about the task of rebuilding without delay.

Herod had heard much about Jesus and was anxious to see him. Rumor had it that he was John raised from the dead or perhaps Elijah returned. Herod had executed John; he was certain of John's death. His curiosity will be only partially satisfied. At the time of his trial, Jesus will be sent to Herod by Pilate. But in the present of the Tetrarch, Jesus utters not a word.

Procrastination and curiosity are two weaknesses to which we can all fall prey. Many times a task will face us, and we delay unduly in addressing the issue. It is very often simply a question of self-discipline. Our sense of responsibility needs to be fine-tuned. This is especially true in our spiritual challenges. Many times undue delays affect other people as well and therefore can point to a lack of charity. In the matter of curiosity, these are frequently issues that do not touch us personally. The Internet can feed an unbridled curiosity and lead us into areas that are clearly contrary to our moral standards.

We may say that these are minor issues that have no major importance. But they are building blocks needed for a worthy structure.

The old saying goes, "Trifles make perfection, but perfection is no trifle."

Points to Ponder

> Delays in religious responsibility
> Undue curiosity about others
> Using time well

Year II

> Ecclesiastes 1:2–11
> Psalm 90:3–4, 5–6, 12–13, 14 and 17bc
> Luke 9:7–9

Ecclesiastes (or Qoheleth, as it is commonly known today) is not a very uplifting book. The author maintains that the big questions in life remain unanswered. One can do no better than to continue with one's daily pursuits, confident that God will see him through, but not struggling to understand the divine plan. There is an endless repetition in life, cycles that remain the same, and humanity's unending desire to make sense of it all. All of this is vanity (or a wisp of smoke), provoking desires that will never be satisfied. With "nothing new under the sun," one can only continue on the path set before her.

Herod's burning curiosity to see Jesus is due to the rumors that have spread about him. Some claim that Jesus is the Baptist returned to life. But the Baptist was the man that Herod himself had executed. Was he Elijah or one of the prophets? Herod wanted to question him. This desire to see Jesus will be fulfilled partially at the time of Jesus' trial. Pilate has Christ sent to Herod, but in the presence of Herod Jesus does not utter a word.

Herod's designs come to nothing. There are times when idle speculation gets us nowhere, and there is a certain truth in Qoheleth. There are many things in life that remain unanswered questions. All of us have experienced those moments. Some things we must simply leave in the hands of God, trusting fully in his wisdom and goodness.

Points to Ponder

> Unanswered questions in life
> Unbridled curiosity
> Trust in the wisdom of God

FRIDAY OF THE TWENTY-FIFTH WEEK IN ORDINARY TIME

Year I

Haggai 2:1–9
Psalm 43:1, 2, 3, 4
Luke 9:18–22

The striking profession of faith in Jesus that Peter makes is different than its Matthean counterpart. As is typical of Luke, it occurs while Jesus is at prayer. When Jesus asks the disciples how people are identifying him, their answers are varied: John the Baptist, Elijah, one of the prophets. When asked about his own view, Peter answers, "The Messiah."

Peter identifies Jesus as the promised Messiah, the one sent from God to deliver his people from further devastation. Peter does not go as far as Matthew in identifying him as the Son of God, but it is still a quantum leap forward. Of course, there were problems with seeing Christ as only the anointed (*Christos* in Greek). The term could take on too political a sense, seeing Christ as a human liberator sent to deliver an oppressed people. But the truth is that, in a very distinct sense, he was the Messiah of Israel.

Our first reading today continues the hope-filled prophecy of Haggai. He continues to speak of the reconstruction of the temple and assures his people that its future glory will surpass that of the past. But the greatest gift to be given God's people will be that of peace, a freedom from warfare and hostility, and most especially a harmonious relationship with God.

The day will come when the temple will receive Christ himself, the anointed one, he who is the authentic temple of God, the temple in which God dwells uniquely.

Points to Ponder

Jesus identified as the Messiah
The splendor of the reconstructed temple
Jesus as the final temple of God

Year II

> Ecclesiastes 3:1–11
> Psalm 144:1b and 2abc, 3–4
> Luke 9:18–22

Today's reading from Qoheleth is the famous song of the seasons. There is an appointed time for everything under the sun—planting and reaping, birth and death, war and peace. This is an endless cycle from which no one escapes. Human beings would love to break through all of this, but to no avail. The large plan remains unfathomable. With all its beauty, this song of the seasons is not written from an optimistic point of view.

Peter's profession of faith in Jesus is, on the other hand, a remarkable breakthrough. While his contemporaries may speculate about the identity of Jesus, Peter cuts through it all. He recognizes Christ as the Messiah, the anointed one, the promised one destined to deliver his people from bondage and oppression. In Luke this is not a recognition of Jesus as divine, but it is an important step forward in the faith life of the apostles. Jesus loses no time in seeking their confidence in this matter and then immediately sets things awry in speaking of his forthcoming suffering.

The plan of God in the case of Jesus was clarified only with the giving of the Spirit with his resurrection. And that revealed plan of God has been at the center of the Christian life through two thousand years. With Qoheleth there are still many things in life we do not understand; but those things that are of the greatest moment have been made known to us in knowing God and in knowing Christ whom God has sent.

Points to Ponder

> Qoheleth and his endless cycles
> The futility of the search for meaning
> The redemptive plan of God in Christ

SATURDAY OF THE TWENTY-FIFTH WEEK IN ORDINARY TIME

Year I

Zechariah 2:5–9, 14–15a
Jeremiah 31:10, 11–12ab, 13
Luke 9:43b–45

The special concern of Yahweh for Jerusalem appears again in the prophet Zechariah. It is not difficult for us to understand the deep affection that the city holds for the fervent Jew in our times. Here the prophet predicts a peaceful return for its people who will dwell peacefully in its midst; God himself will be its protective wall of fire. The prophet almost cries in seeing that, even though the city's inhabitants were repeatedly unfaithful, God's fidelity remained.

Once again Jesus in today's Gospel speaks of his impending betrayal. The disciples, who by this time have come to recognize him as the Messiah, cannot accept the idea of a suffering Messiah. Indeed, at that time its meaning was hidden from them. Only as events unfolded, and with the Spirit's help, would they come to a better understanding.

Jerusalem was rebuilt because of God's fidelity. Jesus was handed over to death because of God's redemptive love. There are many events in our lives today that remain incomprehensible. Yet we remain convinced that their sense will eventually become clear. Unlike some of the Mesopotamian gods, ours is not a God of caprice or deception. But his ways are not our ways. As we look back on our long religious history, we are in a better position to evaluate events. God is ultimately truth and love. Even with our questions, of that we can be assured.

Points to Ponder

God's love of Jerusalem
The disciples' incomprehension
Making sense of events in faith

Year II

> Ecclesiastes 11:9—12:8
> Psalm 90:3–4, 5–6, 12–13, 14 and 17
> Luke 9:43b–45

Ecclesiastes today outlines the stages of life as well as their unchangeable character. The young are advised to enjoy their youth and to ward off grief from their hearts. They are fleeting days and should be enjoyed while they last. For the days will come that bring no pleasure. They will be days of clouds and darkness. There will be no song and laughter. Man goes to his lasting home; the silver chord is snapped, and the golden bowl broken. Man's dust returns to the earth; the life breath returns to God who gave it. The cycle never ends, nor will it ever be broken. Everything is vanity or a wisp of smoke.

The difference between Qoheleth and Luke is the latter's strong afterlife belief. This is something that the Hebrew sage did not enjoy. The moments in life simply come to an end, and there they stay. Jesus' assurance that he will be handed over to death was puzzling to his hearers but not terminal. Jesus was on mission from the Father and would return there. To all who put their trust in him, a final return to God is also promised. In many ways, Qoheleth is a prophet of doom; yet hope is the overriding theme of the Gospels.

Qoheleth is important to read if only to realize that here we have no lasting home. When we read of Jesus impending death, we realize at once that this is the avenue of our hope. Even in the midst of anxiety and difficulty, we are not downcast. If we remain faithful, he remains faithful.

Of that there can be no doubt.

Points to Ponder

> The endless cycles of Qoheleth
> Hope through Jesus' death
> The lesson of Qoheleth

MONDAY OF THE TWENTY-SIXTH WEEK IN ORDINARY TIME

Year I

> Zechariah 8:1–8
> Psalm 102:16–18, 19–21, 29 and 22–23
> Luke 9:46–50

Zechariah is a prophet of exceptional imagery. Yahweh again speaks of his return to Jerusalem, the holy mountain, the faithful city. He then presents a picture of heart-warming domesticity. Anyone who has visited an Italian town can readily identify with the scene presented. There is the village piazza surrounded by benches. There on a bright afternoon the elderly gather, with canes and walkers, for a neighborly chat. The children, of course, occupy the center of the piazza, filling it with laughter and merriment. It is a picture that one never forgets. This is the restored Jerusalem that the prophet presents. "They shall be my people and I will be their God."

Children also play a part in the teaching of Jesus today. He has little time for lofty ambition. He looks for the sentiments of a child—dependent, uncomplicated, candid. Children want to be loved simply for who they are. To receive the child or anyone of similar sentiments is to receive both Christ and the Father.

Erudition in the service of God is always good to encounter. But the kingdom is not built on learning, but rather on simplicity and goodness and a simple and direct love of God. Many saints of the church had great minds, but intelligence was not the key to their sanctity. Let us pray for that simplicity that characterizes the children playing in the town square, as well as those of any age who turn lovingly to Christ.

Points to Ponder

> The spiritual qualities of a child
> The child's openness to faith
> Acquiring a childlike spirit

Year II

Job 1:6–22
Psalm 17:1bcd, 2–3, 6–7
Luke 9:46–50

Today we begin our readings from the Book of Job, one of the classics of world literature. Job is a wealthy landowner, a God-fearing man who had received many blessings. In his conversation with Satan (here the tester, not the devil), God prides himself on Job's upright character. But Satan argues that if the man were to lose all that he possesses, he would quickly turn to blasphemy. Satan is allowed to put him to the test. Job soon loses property and family. But still he gives glory to God. Yet this will lead to the heart of the book's thesis: Why is it that the just suffer?

Jesus himself leaves some questions unanswered. But he is eminently clear on the qualities required to be part of the kingdom. The simplicity of the child is called for. It is that open spirit to God and his designs that should characterize the lives of all of us. The child has no complicated questions; the child operates on a spirit of trust. It is that which is asked of us.

Jesus adds another observation that can be of help to us. The fact that someone was casting out demons in Jesus' name drew no reaction from the Master. It was the demon that Jesus had problems with, not the exorcist. The exorcist was doing a good thing. In our world today, there are churches and organizations doing very good things. They care for the sick, feed the hungry, find homes for children. They are doing the work of the Lord, for which we are grateful. They are not against us; therefore they are for us.

Points to Ponder

The question of the suffering just person
Faith and the spirit of the child
Cooperation among the churches

TUESDAY OF THE TWENTY-SIXTH WEEK IN ORDINARY TIME

Year I

> Zechariah 8:20–23
> Psalm 87:1b–3, 4–5, 6–7
> Luke 9:51–56

At this point in Luke's Gospel, Jesus sets his sights on Jerusalem as he begins the journey that will lead to his death and resurrection. The company is not afforded a welcome in a Samaritan village because they are headed for Jerusalem. The anger at this rebuff by Jesus' disciples finds no echo in the Master himself. Their willingness to see the village destroyed sprang from a lengthy period of hostility between Jews and Samaritans. But as early Christianity spread in the region, Samaria became a center of belief.

So convinced is Zechariah of the universal appeal of Judaism that he envisions the Jewish population being inundated by peoples of other nations who attach themselves to the Jewish believers in coming to seek the Lord in Jerusalem. Hebrew universalism does not involve proselytizing on the part of the Jews; it is wholly the work of God.

Jesus does not disdain people of other beliefs. In fact, in a number of cases, he commends their sincerity and uprightness. While not all people share our faith, we are convinced that they are God's children and are in no way excluded from his love. If we can share our faith with them, we are glad to do so. Certainly we want to bring them before the Lord in prayer. To speak of other believers with disdain is alien to our spirit.

Points to Ponder

> Old Testament universalism
> The tolerance of Jesus
> Our respect for other faiths

Year II

> Job 3:1–3, 11–17, 20–23
> Psalm 88:2–3, 4–5, 6, 7–8
> Luke 9:51–56

Having suffered the loss of his family and property and left with no satisfactory explanation, Job laments his very birth. Why could he not have been as one of those infants who die before they see the light of day? He could then have slept with the kings and princes of this world, the place where the weary are at rest. Life holds nothing for him. Unlike the Job of the first chapter, who never questioned God's decision, we now meet the Job of the heart of the book, who is very much taken with the question *Why*.

The Lucan Jesus today begins his journey to Jerusalem, the city where his mission on earth will reach its fulfillment. He is not dismayed by the hostility of the Samaritan village. His universal mission militates against negative attitudes from whatever quarter. During his ministry, he demonstrates a positive attitude toward the Samaritans, and the early church will make inroads in that part of the region.

Two different mind-sets appear in today's readings. That of Job is one of despondency. He sees no rhyme or reason for his great loss and therefore can only lament his birth. Discouragement and depression are all too characteristic of our own times. This leads to people giving up on life.

Although Jesus' journey will entail betrayal and death, it will end in triumph. Therefore he willingly sets about the task before him.

Encouragement and optimism are important ingredients of the Christian life.

Even with all its difficulties and challenges, the Christian life leads to victory. That we should never forget.

Points to Ponder

> Dealing with depression
> Optimism in the Christian life
> Our personal journey to Jerusalem

WEDNESDAY OF THE TWENTY-SIXTH WEEK IN ORDINARY TIME

Year I

Nehemiah 2:1–8
Psalm 137:1–2, 3, 4–5, 6
Luke 9:57–62

There is an urgency about the following of Christ that gives it exceptional priority. That is the point of today's Gospel. One need not press the seeming harshness of the reply to the legitimate requests. When it comes to the kingdom of God and its proclamation, there are no fringe benefits; it is a life of hardship. It will ultimately take precedence over family concerns in its demands. Discipleship, when one is serious about it, is clearly uncompromising and demanding.

In medieval times, church life often meant privilege and comfort. Francis of Assisi was not interested in luxury. He set about to take the Gospels with the utmost seriousness in a literal following of Jesus. For him it proved to be a life of joy, but it certainly was not one of ease. In modern times, we want too much to have it our way. We are willing to comply, but we don't want to feel the pinch. But in some way we have to go beyond the merely acceptable.

Nehemiah worked in the service of a very amenable king. Today politics is frequently seen as a less than honorable profession. To maintain political office, it is said, moral compromises have to be made. Perhaps. Some people will say it always happens. Others would say, "Sometimes, yes; sometimes, no." Artaxerxes showed a genuine interest in the welfare of Nehemiah, as did Cyrus in the well-being of the Jewish people. The less than perfect are found in every profession, but that does not invalidate the profession as such. Postexilic Israel met friends and sympathizers in high places, and their praises are sung in the scriptures.

Points to Ponder

> The priority of the kingdom of God
> Faith and sacrifice
> Virtue in civil authority

Year II

> Job 9:1–12, 14–16
> Psalm 88:10bc–11, 12–13, 14–15
> Luke 9:57–62

In his dealings with God, Job goes back and forth. In today's reading, he believes that no one can be justified in contending against the Lord. Given God's majesty and power, it is true to say that no one can withstand him. He commands the whole of the universe, and it obeys. He can be taken to task for nothing that he does. In the presence of the greatness of God, Job was dwarfed into insignificance.

This makes Jesus' Gospel demands, read today, even more significant.

The God revealed in Jesus is the God who comes close to us, who understands our weakness, who heals our infirmities, and who forgives our wrongdoing. Jesus was capable of powerful acts, but his miracles are performed only for the benefit of others. The God-Man Jesus wants only to draw close to us and to enable us. That is a far cry from the Yahweh before whom Job trembles.

Why does the just person suffer? The Book of Job wrestles with the problem and concludes by leaving the question in the mystery of God. We still have problems today. But at least the suffering of Jesus gives us insight.

Suffering can be redemptive. It opened the door to eternity for all of us. It can therefore play a role in our lives as well in bringing us closer to the One who has gone before us.

Points to Ponder

> Job and the majesty of God
> Christ as the man for others
> Suffering in union with Christ

THURSDAY OF THE TWENTY-SIXTH WEEK IN ORDINARY TIME

Year I

Nehemiah 8:1–4a, 5–6, 7b–12
Psalm 19:8, 9, 10, 11
Luke 10:1–12

As the book of the law of Moses was read aloud in the presence of all the people, at the time of Jerusalem's reconstruction when Nehemiah was the governor and Ezra the high priest, a turning point in the history of the Jews was reached. After centuries of destruction and deportation, they were once again at home. If they were to remain faithful, God's protection was assured. The occasion was celebrated with choice foods and wines, with food generously shared with those who were unprepared. It was a day holy to our Lord. We can only imagine the great joy that was present to this war-weary people.

The mission of the seventy-two disciples was also celebratory in character. They were announcing the arrival of God's kingdom. They were to travel light, not encumbered by needless possessions. They were to remain in the house that gave them initial hospitality as they proclaimed their message of hope. If any town rejected them, it was rejecting God himself. The disciples were to have no further dealings with it, symbolically indicated by shaking the village dust off their feet.

Eating and dinking has always been seen as part of religious feasting in the Judeo–Christian tradition. To share food is to promote the life of another and therefore has a sacred character. Unfortunately in our time eating is largely functional. Meals are taken on the run, determined by scheduled events and hardly open to the life-sharing implications long associated with eating. We do well to recapture some of this significance by reclaiming time at the table where a true spirit of family can be enjoyed.

Points to Ponder

Jewish commitment to the Mosaic covenant
Traveling light with the good news of the covenant
The symbolism of meal sharing

Year II

Job 19:21–27
Psalm 27:7–8a, 8b–9abc, 13–14
Luke 10:1–12

If the original Hebrew of this text read as smoothly as later translators have rendered it, we would be at a distinct advantage. The fact is that verses 25–27 have become hopelessly corrupt in the course of the text's transmission, and early translations into other languages do not agree among themselves. The most that we can say is that Job envisions some eventual form of vindication wherein his integrity would be established. The three friends who accompany him throughout the narrative have only added to his grief, upholding the side of God, thus implying Job's guilt.

The disciples are sent out to announce the kingdom—seventy-two in number, or pairs of thirty-six. St. Gregory saw the journeying of pairs as illustrative of the law of charity, since love of neighbor implies at least two.

They are to pray that more emissaries will be provided by the Master, since the work is immense and the workers few in number.

We too are in our time much engaged in asking the Master for more laborers. But we must also draw on the pool that is already present. Those of us who have worked in preparing permanent deacons can attest to the fact that, especially in recent times, the quality of candidates is rich indeed. Many of these men would be excellent priests. It is a possibility that the church should weigh well.

In one sense, all of us are harvesters called to live the message authentically, and to announce the good news with our lives. Frequently converts ascribe their embrace of the faith to the example of a friend or coworker. We should never lose sight of the power of good example.

Points to Ponder

Why do just people suffer?
Harvesters traveling in pairs
The source of future harvesters

FRIDAY OF THE TWENTY-SIXTH WEEK IN ORDINARY TIME

Year I

Baruch 1:15–22
Psalm 79:1b–2, 3–5, 8, 9
Luke 10:13–16

There are few passages in the Old Testament that summarize Israel's failings as graphically and as well as this short summary from Baruch. Israel had been given more than enough advance warning. From the time of their departure from Egypt to the time of the exile, the will of God on their behalf had been made very clear. And yet what had been their choice? From top to bottom—kings, rulers, priests, prophets, as well as the citizenry as a whole—all disregarded God's precepts and followed their own whims. They had been guilty of idolatry and all manner of evil in God's sight. Now they can only cry out with the psalmist, "Help us, O God of our salvation, for the glory of your name."

And what is to be said of the responses that Jesus received in a number of his own cities? If the wonders that he performed had been done in pagan cities (Tyre and Sidon), they would long before have repented. Even Capernaum, in his home region, will be drawn to the dark of the underworld. The final injunction, heard before, does not fit well in context. But its truth is unassailable. To reject the disciple is to reject Christ, and to reject Christ is to reject the Father.

We receive many warnings in life. They sometimes come from friends or family, from our own physical makeup, from faith or conscience. But in the attraction of the moment, warnings may be disregarded. In very short order, we may turn our backs on everything we have learned. With Peter, we may well say now,

"Not I, Lord." But beware, lest we fall. Our house must be built on solid ground to withstand the onslaught. Pray the Lord to steel us against the day of battle.

Points to Ponder

Disregard for the law of God
Attentive to the signs
Spiritual advantages: the word and church

Year II

Job 38:1, 12–21; 40:3–5
Psalm 139:1–3, 7–8, 9–10, 13–14ab
Luke 10:13–16

Throughout the book, Job was accused and taunted by his three friends as he unwaveringly claimed innocence. In the final chapters of the book, God himself appears, with answers that prove to be less than satisfactory. God is not about to deal with a problem as great as suffering on a one-on-one basis. There are many mysteries in life that defy human explanation. The Lord presents some of them in today's reading; they extend from light to darkness, morning to night, the depths of the sea, death itself. Does Job have any answer for all of this? If not, why does God owe Job an explanation? Embarrassed and demoralized, Job can only regret that he had ever spoken.

Far more reprehensible are the citizens of Jesus' time who heard the call of salvation and disregarded it. That they were excluded from God's favor is more understandable. To reject God is far worse than to question him. But even there we can make no final judgment in God's disposition of wrong-minded people. But it is fair warning. We have more than ample opportunity to know what God wants of us. We have opportunities and graces that enable us to respond. Every day is a grace.

The problem of why the just suffer remains a mystery. Whether through famine, war, or natural calamity, hundred of thousands of innocent people die. And we often ask, Why does calamity so often strike the world's poorest? There are many mysteries in life that we cannot resolve. But they stand together with the overwhelming evidence of the order in the universe, the details that make human life possible, the many factors that point to the divine direction of the world and life. The point is that faith touches the unknown.

Points to Ponder

> Trust in the fidelity of God
> Faith and the unknown
> The rejection of Christ

SATURDAY OF THE TWENTY-SIXTH WEEK IN ORDINARY TIME

Year I

> Baruch 4:5–12, 27–29
> Psalm 69:33–35, 36–37
> Luke 10:17–24

Israel's punishment was medicinal, not terminal. That is the clear message of today's reading from Baruch. When they sacrificed "to no gods" and abandoned the God who had delivered them, Israelites angered and provoked the Lord. But they need not fear. If they will but turn to the Lord in a true spirit of repentance, all will be forgiven and their homeland will be restored.

The disciples in today's Gospel are overwhelmed by the fact that they can now cast out devils. But Christ reminds them that there are greater things than that; their greatest joy is that their names are inscribed in heaven. Christ then gives thanks for the little people. It is not the learned and wise who are open to the kingdom, but the childlike, those who are humble before the Lord. It is they who are privy to the mysteries of God, shared with the Son by the Father and by the Son with those whom he chooses.

Like the disciples, we too should rejoice, because the truths of God have been shared with us. There were many sterling figures who lived before Christ and yearned for "the day of the

Lord." It was a privilege not given to them. We can be very thoughtless about the great truths that have been shared with us. As Baruch reminds the Israelites, forgiveness can be theirs for the asking. We too are reminded that gratitude to God for his revelation to us is wholly in order.

Points to Ponder

Forgiveness
Spiritual power
Knowledge of God: a gift

Year II

Job 42:1–3, 5–6, 12–17
Psalm 119:66, 71, 75, 91, 125, 130
Luke 10:17–24

The epilogue to Job ties in with the prologue and constitutes a complete story in itself. Job is tested by Satan, loses all his earthly possession, still blesses the Lord, and receives back in possessions and family more than he had to start with. The explanation is satisfactory but is something of which Job was ignorant during the lengthy dialogue that constitutes the heart of the book. If we look only at the beginning and end of the book, we can say that the innocent Job suffered because he was tested. But the larger question still remains unanswered. Why is it that so many innocent people in this world suffer without apparent reason?

We, like the disciples, have ample reason to rejoice. So much that was not known to the ancients has been revealed to us. The Son of God as reconciler, the God life in the Spirit, the church, the Gospels, the sacraments.

And yet we still struggle with faith questions. There are issues that remain unanswered. And with Job we can only place them in the hands of a God who moves in ways that are at times incomprehensible to us.

Job, for the most part, had a blessed life. But at the heart of the book that bears his name, he struggled with his faith. There are times in our own life when we must do the same. We should not be disconcerted. It is a strong faith that asks the deeper questions.

Points to Ponder

> The Job of the prologue and epilogue
> The questioning Job
> The human struggle with faith

MONDAY OF THE TWENTY-SEVENTH WEEK IN ORDINARY TIME

Year I

> Jonah 1:1—2:1–2, 11
> Psalm 2:3, 4, 5, 8
> Luke 10:25–37

Today we begin our readings from the Book of Jonah. This short book of four chapters is an extended parable, underscoring God's concern for foreign peoples, well beyond the confines of Jewish identity. Commanded by God to preach to the people of Nineveh, the capital of Assyria, urging them to leave their wickedness behind, Jonah refuses to obey and heads for the seaport and a ship that will carry him far from Nineveh's shores. Once on board, the ship is beset by a serious tempest that does not abate until Jonah realizes that the storm may well have been caused by his own disobedience. He urges the mariners to cast him overboard, at which point he finds himself entrapped in the belly of a giant fish. He is finally discharged by the fish in the region of the hated Nineveh.

In the Gospel today we are treated to one of Jesus' most celebrated and beloved parables, that of the Good Samaritan. Following up on Jesus' pivotal teaching, on the love of neighbor, the questioner asks, "Who is my neighbor?" The familiar story finds the unfortunate traveler beset and beaten by robbers and left to die. Two religious personalities do not approach him; believing him to be dead, they feared the ritual impurity they would incur in having contact with a corpse. It was only a member of a despised sect, a Samaritan, who gave the man attention and provided for his welfare and recovery.

What is interesting is the way in which Jesus responds to the questioner. The original query "Who is my neighbor?" is answered differently by Jesus: Who was neighbor to the robber's victim? The parable answers both question. One's neighbor is anyone in need. The one who proved to be a neighbor was a Samaritan, a member of a group with whom a pious Jew had no contact. So the parable highlights concern for any needy person and also stresses inclusiveness; goodness can proceed from any quarter. Virtue is not limited by race or social background.

Jonah sees Yahweh concerned about the pagan Ninevites. The Lucan Jesus teaches us to see our neighbor in the events of every day and also realize that good example may come from any quarter, even from the despised Samaria. The scriptures present us with very broad horizons, to which we must remain alert.

Points to Ponder

> The obstinate Jonah
> Who then is my neighbor?
> Who proved himself to be a neighbor?

Year II

> Galatians 1:6–12
> Psalm 111:1b–2, 7–8, 9 and 10c
> Luke 10:25–37

Paul's Letter to the Galatians is introduced today. It is a bold and forthright presentation of the Christian message, in language that is at times strong and eye-opening. The apostle loses no time in addressing one of the letter's major claims. Certain members of the Christian faith are attempting to distort the gospel that Paul had preached by introducing different practices and norms. Who those people are will become evident later in the letter. Here Paul excludes their authenticity. In fact, anyone preaching a gospel different from that which he had preached is simply accursed. He says that because he preached a gospel not received or taught by human agents. It came to him as a revelation of Jesus Christ. Any attempts to alter or dilute it are in clear opposition to God's revelation.

The Samaritans were not in communion with the Jews. Their relations were marked by clear hostility. But in the Gospels, in more than one instance, the Samaritans are presented in a positive light. Today's parable is one of the most beloved in the whole of the New Testament. The history of the church points out the inroads that Christianity in its earliest years made among the Samaritans.

There are two lessons that emerge in today's scripture. The first is never to exclude anyone from God's love, which is universal and all-embracing. The church should be in the forefront of this all-inclusive love. The second lesson is to respect the sacredness of God's revelation. There are many things within the church that are not essential to faith and can change. But other matters that touch the very heart of our belief cannot change but must remain as the teaching of God himself. It is an important distinction to make; lack of clarity can easily lead to discord and disagreement.

Points to Ponder

> Paul and the revelation of God himself
> Jews and Samaritans: the lesson
> Our neighbor: anyone in need

TUESDAY OF THE TWENTY-SEVENTH WEEK IN ORDINARY TIME

Year I

> Jonah 3:1–10
> Psalm 130:1b–2, 3–4ab, 7–8
> Luke 10:38–42

The lesson to be learned from the Jonah story, like any authentic parable, is singular and in this case clear at a first reading. God has concern for all people, even a one-time enemy. At his reluctant preaching, all the people, from greatest to least, repent of their sins and don sackcloth, the symbol of repentance. The king orders a strict fast from food and drink for all the people, with the hope that God will turn from his threatened punishment.

The family of Martha, Mary, and Lazarus were evidently close to Jesus. He will visit them again on the occasion of Lazarus's death. Mary is intent on listening to Jesus, while Martha is busy attending to the needs of their special guest. The Lord is unquestionably appreciative of Martha's concerns in providing for his needs. But the meditative Mary is involved in a more important pursuit, that of listening to and weighing the word of Christ.

The task of preparing the Sunday homily is a sacred one. It is ten minutes of the week in which people are in tune and receptive to the word of God. The homily is a sacred trust. As the story of Jonas goes, the Ninevites are open to and receptive of the call of the prophet. The same should be true of us. Our failings become clear to us from the word of God, which like a sword cuts to the quick and can result in a complete change of heart.

Jesus promised not to leave us orphans. He calls us to a deeper love, to a sense of sorrow for sin, to conversion, and our rightful place in the kingdom. The response is ours. Let us pray that we harden not our hearts.

Points to Ponder

> The Ninevites and the call of God
> With Mary, listening to Jesus
> Our personal response to the word

Year II

> Galatians 1:13–24
> Psalm 139:1b–3, 13–14ab, 14c–15
> Luke 10:38–42

In the detailed description of his calling, Paul insists that his is not merely a human vocation. For years he had been an enemy of the church, which he persecuted relentlessly. He was schooled in Judaism much beyond his peers. All of this up until the time when the God who had called from before his birth revealed his Son to Paul and directed him to proclaim him among the Gentiles. Without any human consultation, Paul began his work. Only after three years had passed did he go to Jerusalem to confer with Peter and James. He continued his Gentile mission and was known in Judea only by name as the one who now preaches the faith he tried to destroy.

In the Gospel today we are faced with contemplation (Mary) and action (Martha). The former has greater importance, but both are necessary. Paul is a happy combination of the two. His intense life of prayer linked him with the Lord and the various churches where his evangelizing efforts had been felt. He wanted only to know and experience Christ in the power of the resurrection and to join in Christ's sufferings. His active life carried him through much of Asia Minor, where he preached and worked for his own livelihood.

In our times, there is far more Martha in our lives than there is Mary.

Paul reminds us that without Christ crucified at the heart of our ministry our life lacks focus. Prayer is important for all of us. In times past when I rode the commuter train regularly into the city, I always kept my rosary at hand so that I would use the time with profit. One night a well-dressed young businessman was seated across the aisle from me, praying his beads. I was immediately reminded of what I wanted to do but found I had left my rosary at home. I did the best I could, but before deboarding, I thanked the gentleman for the reminder he had given me. For both of us it was a positive experience.

Points to Ponder

Total conversion in Paul's life
The necessity of a Martha
Love for the life of prayer

WEDNESDAY OF THE TWENTY-SEVENTH WEEK IN ORDINARY TIME

Year I

Jonah 4:1–11
Psalm 86:3–4, 5–6, 9–10
Luke 11:1–4

Today's readings join the end of the Jonah story and the Lucan version of the Lord's Prayer. Jonah is a very hapless fellow. He is angry at Yahweh for saving the Ninevites. And he is upset about every subsequent turn of events in his life. He has preached repentance to the Ninevites, and they have turned to the Lord. Then he complains when a plant God causes to grow to shelter him from the sun withers and fades after only a day. Yahweh's rejoinder is a classic. He observes that Jonah is upset by the loss of a gourd plant. But how much more strongly should God feel about the loss of 120,000 Ninevites?

The Lucan version of the Lord's Prayer has two petitions that look to God and three that look to us here on the human scene. In praying for God's name to be hallowed, we pray that it be reverenced and sanctified. We then pray that his kingdom, that era of justice and especially concern for the poor, be inaugurated. The final three petitions ask for our daily sustenance, a deep spirit of forgiveness akin to that by which God forgives, and a deliverance from the end-time battle between good and evil that was part of Israelite eschatology.

Jonah ends with a clear sign of God's forgiveness. God's thoughts are not our thoughts. When it comes to our enemies in our time, for whatever reason, our only petition should be forgiveness. Forgive our enemies who have turned on us; forgive us who have turned on them. Jonah failed to grasp the lesson.

May the same not be said of us.

Points to Ponder

Yahweh and the Ninevites
Forgiveness and the Lord's Prayer
God's concern for all people

Year II

Galatians 2:1–2, 7–14
Psalm 117:1bc, 2
Luke 11:1–4

Paul makes no apology for his belief that Christians were free from the Jewish law. He himself had excellent Jewish credentials, born and raised a Jew, educated well beyond his peers, an opponent of the Christians even to the point of persecution. But called from birth by God, he realized that God's Son had been revealed to him and that he was sent to proclaim him to the Gentiles. He went up to Jerusalem and conferred with Peter and James. He was completely confirmed in his mission. The question of the Jewish law for the Gentiles had been resolved.

And yet Peter, when he came to Antioch, ate freely with the Gentile Christians. But when Jewish Christians came from Jerusalem, Peter pulled back and would not eat with the Gentile Christians. For Paul this was pure hypocrisy, and he did not hesitate to confront Peter about it directly. In the midst of conflict, Paul asks Peter, How can we ask Gentiles to live as Jews?

We no longer live under the Jewish law. But does that mean that we are lax and indifferent? The Christian ethos goes far beyond the law in calling us to be perfect as is our heavenly Father. Its demands are great. In the love of God and neighbor, we are called to go beyond the law. We go wherever charity calls us. The fact is that the Jewish law has been supplanted by the law of love.

Points to Ponder

Paul and the law
Peter's equivocation
The Christian ethic and the law

THURSDAY OF THE TWENTY-SEVENTH WEEK IN ORDINARY TIME

Year I

> Malachi 3:13–20b
> Psalm 1:1–2, 3, 4 and 6
> Luke 11:5–13

"That was the answer to a prayer."

"I have been praying for this for years."

"Fortunately God said 'No' to my request."

We have all heard comments like these. We also know how often people ask for our prayers, and they do so with great confidence in the power of prayer. The short story Jesus tells in today's Gospel emphasizes the importance of persistence in prayer. Jesus in no way downgrades the prayer of petition; it is clearly commendable and an indication of our dependence on the giver of all good gifts.

Prayer is closely connected with God being our Father. A child's request of his father is received favorably. Therefore we should approach God full of confidence. Yes, there are times when we later realize that what we asked was not in our best interest. The outcome is not always certain, but the prayerful posture is always in order.

We seldom hear the *Dies Irae*, the sequence of the funeral Mass. It is a classic but perhaps a little too descriptive in treating the final lot of the just and the unjust. It has been immortalized also in Verdi's *Requiem Mass*. But the truth is that it says no more than did the prophets themselves. Malachi today speaks of the final deliverance of the just and the punishment of evildoers. Even if the imagery need not be pressed, we cannot forget that there is justice in God, and the pursuit of evil differs greatly from the pursuit of good.

Let us be vigilant in our prayer, bringing our intentions willingly before our Father. Let us also remember that evildoing will receive its just desserts. We should be vigilant in our pursuit of good and persevering in our prayer.

Points to Ponder

> The value of the prayer of petition
> Perseverance in prayer
> Context of prayer: "Father knows best"

Year II

> Galatians 3:1–5
> Luke 1:69–70, 71–72, 73–75
> Luke 11:5–13

Paul's anger in Galatians at times almost sears the pages. There are members of the community who want to incorporate the Jewish law into their belief. For Paul, this is nothing short of sacrilegious. He asks them to stop and reflect. Did they receive the Spirit from faith in what he preached or from the works of the law? Paul finds their move senseless. For Paul, it is faith in the salvific work of Christ that makes us holy, not any work of our own, as good as it may be.

The Gospel today reminds us that our God is a good and loving Father. Precisely because he is so good, we should be dutiful in carrying out his will and confident in expressing our needs. To place the law between God and the believer would mean that we must work to attain his favor. Such is not the case. We are loved simply because we are.

Paul rightly asks, What brought faith to Galatia—the word that was preached or works of the law? It was the faith that was preached, of course. What counts is not the things that we do but rather our faith in the One who has done the work for us.

Points to Ponder

> The faith that saves
> The role of works
> Perseverance in prayer

FRIDAY OF THE TWENTY-SEVENTH WEEK IN ORDINARY TIME

Year I

Joel 1:13–15; 2:1–2
Psalm 9:2–3, 6 and 16, 8–9
Luke 11:15–26

Joel paints a very grim picture of the day of the Lord. Priests and temple attendants are in sackcloth in a temple where offering is no longer made. Darkness and punishment for the population is the order of the day, as retribution descends upon a people who for years have wandered far from their founding objective.

No greater insult could be hurled at Jesus than to accuse him of being an agent of Beelzebul, the prince of demons. This was nothing less than labeling good as evil. Jesus responds by presenting a dilemma. If he works for Beelzebul and at the same time works against him, how can Satan's kingdom remain? But if Jesus works as an agent of God, then God's kingdom is at hand.

Further insight into the problem of evil is attached at this point. It is good to be prepared and strongly fortified. But if a stronger one than the defendant appears, the defendant may well be overcome. Moreover, it is not wise to be overconfident. If your house is now well kept and in good condition, the unclean spirit may well return, this time with a coterie of companions. Then the situation will be worse than ever.

Beelzebul appears in many forms, and they prove to be very attractive. Today's Gospel reminds us that we dare not be overconfident.

We are still fully human and may easily fall prey to evil designs. One may feel that his lofty objectives protect him or his service as a minister of the altar. But we have too many examples of serious falls to believe that anyone is exempt. Each day we pledge ourselves anew to our objective and then pray for God's help to remain faithful. Of ourselves we are weak and profitless servants, but we can do all things in him who strengthens us.

Points to Ponder

> God's intolerance of evil
> The danger of overconfidence
> A daily prayer for fidelity

Year II

> Galatians 3:7–14
> Psalm 111:1b–2, 3–4, 5–6
> Luke 11:15–26

Who are the true descendants of Abraham? This is the question that Paul raises in today's reading from Galatians. The answer, of course, is those who have faith. In fact, Abraham was told that all the nations of the earth would be blessed in him. This means those who have faith, as Abraham did, not those who attempt to obey the law. In fact, those subject to the law are under a curse. Scripture teaches that those who have faith shall live. Faith and law are at counter-purposes; justification comes from one or the other.

The curse reserved for the law observer has been assumed by Christ himself. Now the faith of Abraham may be extended to the nations. It is this faith that saves through the gift of the Spirit.

Paul worked tirelessly in promoting faith in Christ Jesus as the sole cause of salvation. To promote circumcision or any precept of the law was to detract from the saving work of Christ. And for Paul that was nothing short of blasphemy. Works in the Christian life proceed from faith; it is the justified person who works in charity. Works do not lead to faith or bring about justice.

The Gospel today reminds us that temptation still remains our lot. Our justification must be highly prized, which means that we must be on guard. The forces of evil still try to overtake us.

Points to Ponder

> Paul and the faith of Abraham
> The curse of the law
> Dealing with evil

SATURDAY OF THE TWENTY-SEVENTH WEEK IN ORDINARY TIME

Year I

> Joel 4:12–21
> Psalm 97:1–2, 5–6, 11–12
> Luke 11:27–28

From a purely human perspective, the woman's praise of Jesus' mother in today's Gospel gives Christ an ideal opportunity to speak of his mother's virtues. But the Gospels repeatedly show that Jesus extols another form of relationship comprised of those who accept and live the word of God. Given the right setting, Christ would certainly have extolled the virtues of his mother. But the mission given him by the Father far surpassed his human ties. He was the end-time prophet sent to announce the advent of the reign of God. Therefore, whenever in the gospel his attention is drawn to his human family, he immediately indicates that the family that matters is the community of believers.

This teaching is further confirmed by the "life in Christ" teaching. The risen Christ is endowed by the Father with that life-giving Spirit that makes us part of God's family. This new life force makes us brothers and sisters of Christ and children of the one Abba (Father). This relationship with Christ goes far beyond human procreation and is essentially connected with the mission of Jesus.

Our reading from Joel today highlights Judah and Jerusalem. So often taken to task by the prophets for its faithlessness and betrayal, Judah sees its enemies punished for their violence, while she retains her privileged position.

It is an interesting note. Judah, so frequently chastened for her own infidelity, in the end sees God still faithful to his initial promises. It verifies the word of scripture: although we may be unfaithful, he remains ever faithful.

In remaining faithful to God's word and living it, Christ calls us blessed. Great good fortune is our spiritual birthright.

Points to Ponder

> Judah freed from destruction
> Mary: mother or model of fidelity
> Christ and his human family

Year II

> Galatians 3:22–29
> Psalm 105:2–3, 4–5, 6–7
> Luke 11:27–28

If we are now free of the law, what role does it play? For the Jews it was the disciplinarian leading to the freedom of faith. The law restricted and confined the Jew, setting limits within which he was held, until he was brought to Christ and the freedom that he conveys. Those who have been baptized have been clothed with Christ. This investiture eliminates all other distinctions. There is now no inequality between Jew and Greek, slave and free person, male and female. We are now one in Christ Jesus and as believers the true children of Abraham.

Human parentage means little in comparison with being one with the Lord in faith. That is the clear teaching of today's Gospel. It is one thing to be redeemed in the blood of the Savior. It is quite another to share in his life, to be Spirit-filled, to be a member of the household of God. Our faith is not a question of duty or precepts. It is a matter of gratitude. We have not only been drawn out of darkness; we have been bathed in light, bound together in a family of love.

Mary's virtues are also sung in the scriptures. God looked on her lowliness; future generations will call her blessed. She too recognizes that it is all due to God's goodness. It was he who is mighty who has done great things for her. While none of us will ever be seen in the same light as Mary, that same goodness of God has been showered on us and brought us into a new level of life.

Points to Ponder

> The role of the Jewish law
> Faith and freedom
> Equality in Christ

MONDAY OF THE TWENTY-EIGHTH WEEK IN ORDINARY TIME

Year I

> Romans 1:1–7
> Psalm 98:1bcde, 2–3ab, 3cd–4
> Luke 11:29–32

Today we begin a series of readings from Paul's Letter to the Romans. Paul identifies himself as both a slave to the interests of Christ Jesus as well as an apostle, one called and set aside for the spread of the gospel. He then presents the two features of the incarnation that are essential to the understanding of Christ. Jesus was Son of God in the flesh, a descendant of David. While always God's Son, his became an effective Sonship only with his resurrection from the dead, when the power that was his through the Holy Spirit, conferred with the resurrection, led to the faith conviction that he is God's Son and fully experienced as such. Christ is now recognized as Son and Lord. As Paul teaches elsewhere, no one can say Jesus is Lord except in the Holy Spirit. With this full recognition of Christ as Son and Lord, Paul is commissioned to bring this truth to the Gentile world, for the Gentiles too are called to this "obedience of faith." The Romans are part of this company of belief, called to belong to Jesus Christ.

But as the gospel points out, the message of Christ himself did not fall on eager ears. In earlier times the queen of the South came a great distance to hear Solomon. She will arise at the time of judgment and condemn the hard-hearted people of Christ's generation, for they were host to one greater than Solomon. The Ninevites converted at the preaching of Jonah; they too will condemn the present generation. There is no reason to ask for a sign, since the sign has already been given.

We who have been called to the obedience of faith want to accept in full the teaching of Jesus. It is not always easy to accept what Christ asks of us. But we have accepted the obedience of faith and, in view of all that God has done for us, we want to respond with the "gratitude of faith," in the full realization that here is One greater than Solomon.

Points to Ponder

> Son of God in power
> Christ and the Spirit of holiness
> The sign of Jonah

Year II

> Galatians 4:22–24, 26–27, 31—5:1
> Psalm 113:1b–2, 3–4, 5a and 6–7
> Luke 11:29–32

Slavery made a slow exit from human history. It played a part in American life until the nineteenth century, and there are still parts of the world in our time that live in social oppression. It certainly played a part in Israelite life. In today's reading Paul takes up the story of Sarah and Hagar. The former was the free woman, the latter a slave girl. But Paul turns the account on its head. And the key players take on exactly the opposite roles.

There are two covenants involved, one from Mount Sinai, the other from Jerusalem, from above. The Christian is a child of the heavenly covenant, a child of the free woman, a child of the Abraham of faith.

We err indeed if we believe that we have been born into a religion of rules and regulations. We have been born into a community of faith, confident that God has acted on our behalf in his Son. Once a part of that community, we give expression to our gratitude in conduct that renders God's glory and respects the dignity and worth of every human being. This is the meaning of being a child of the free woman.

Points to Ponder

> The two sons of Abraham
> The covenant of law and the covenant of freedom
> The One greater than Jonah

TUESDAY OF THE TWENTY-EIGHTH WEEK IN ORDINARY TIME

Year I

> Romans 1:16–25
> Psalm 19:2–3, 4–5
> Luke 11:37–41

The knowledge of God revealed by creation leads to a belief in the creator. This is not the same as the faith that Paul proclaims and that is salvific. But it is still salutary. And Paul faults those pagans who instead of seeing the qualities of God reflected in the created order turned their backs and followed their vain pursuits with images of mortal men or other creatures. The final result was their embrace of impurities and lusts and the basest types of human conduct.

Jesus in today's Gospel takes issue with another type of improper conduct: formalism or externalism. This is the type of conduct that is much taken up with the correct externals but gives scant attention to internal moral dispositions. If the Pharisees were as concerned with the needs of the poor as they were with ritual purity, their lives would have been much different.

The truth of the matter is we are inclined to become overly attached to creatures and not enough concerned with the Creator. The passing values of this world claim our attention exorbitantly. We often forget that what is in vogue today is passé tomorrow. Yet God's concern for us is everlasting. As far as externals go, that may be all the farther we can see. When was the last time we as a family had a good discussion about our moral values? It is quite a good idea and is capable of producing very good results.

Points to Ponder

> The wonders of God in creation
> Undue concern about religious externals
> Sharing our moral values

Year II

Galatians 5:1–6
Psalm 119:41, 43, 44, 45, 47, 48
Luke 11:37–41

If we have been set free from the law, says Paul, there can be no returning to it again. Water cannot be carried on two shoulders. If some Galatians return to circumcision, then they are bound to the whole law and they no longer belong to Christ. In following this path they hope to find justification. But the fact is that justice comes only through faith in the Spirit, and therein lies our hope. Neither the presence nor the absence of circumcision counts for anything; only faith works through love.

Faith working through love. Here Paul discloses what it means to believe. It cannot be divorced from love of God and neighbor. Faith without love is a dead faith, as James states in his epistle.

The Gospel reminds us that to be absorbed in the externals of faith is another form of emptiness. It is quite possible for one to be a strong supporter of the church in a financial way and still be involved in forms of corruption in business or politics, practices completely at odds with his faith commitment. There are people who have left well-paying jobs because they were asked to compromise their consciences through inflated expense accounts or other irregularities.

We walk assisted by the strength of the Spirit. Our evil inclinations need not rule the day. Let us walk the way of truth and integrity. Let us be grateful to God who dwells within us and manifests himself in the nature that surrounds us. God is a friend and Father who manifests himself in so many ways in our lives. Indeed, we are a blessed people.

Points to Ponder

God known through faith and not the law
A faith that works through love
Faith and our internal dispositions

WEDNESDAY OF THE TWENTY-EIGHTH WEEK IN ORDINARY TIME

Year I

> Romans 2:1–11
> Psalm 62:2–3, 6–7, 9
> Luke 11:42–46

Two categories of sinful people appear in today's readings. First, there are those who have no difficulty judging others but fail to look into themselves. This is set forth by Paul in Romans. The second are those who are masters in articulating the law but pay scant attention to its major teachings and its call to love God.

There are those who sit in judgment of the conduct of others, yet fail to see that they are guilty of the same conduct that they condemn. Do these people believe that they will escape judgment? The kindness and patience of God has been theirs and should have led to repentance. To continue on this path will only incur the wrath of God on the day of judgment for all, Jew or Greek, without exception. For God is not partial.

The Pharisees permit tithing on every species of garden herb. But what about love of God? The Lucan Jesus does not show displeasure with concern for the less significant items, as long as the major issues are not overlooked. To walk over graves was to incur ritual impurity. The teaching and life of the Pharisees was to lead people unwittingly into wrongdoing. They had no difficulty in imposing burdens on others but never showed the compassion to assist those who were burdened.

Religious leadership has serious responsibilities. Leaders in the community are called to live with integrity whatever they ask of others. Social outreach should be part of the mission of every parish so that the needs of the poor may be met. Where burdens are heavy and can be lightened, they should be.

Years ago a pastor in New York's lower Manhattan, known for his charity, could not recall a time when someone in need was turned away from his door. When he was asked if he had any idea how many times his charity had been abused, his answer was simple. "No, I don't know. But God is not going to ask me about that!"

Points to Ponder

Judge not and you will not be judged
Undue concern about minutiae
Lightening the burdens of others

Year II

Galatians 5:18–25
Psalm 1:1–2, 3, 4 and 6
Luke 11:42–46

For Paul, the law has a purpose as an antidote to sin where there is immorality, licentiousness, jealousy, orgies, dissension, jealousy, and the like. Where such obtains, the law can regulate such conduct, but none of it has anything to do with the reign of God. But the conduct of those who live in the Spirit is of a different order: love, joy, kindness, gentleness, and self-control. Here the law has no place. Against such things there is no law.

If we belong to Christ, the flesh has been crucified with its passions and desires. To walk in the Spirit is to walk with God toward a destiny with God forever. This is the great message of hope that the preacher is called to articulate. It is small wonder that the Lucan Jesus in the Gospel was concerned about the absence in his time of a message of hope. Both the Pharisees and the scholars of the law were much too concerned with secondary matters and signs of status. It is easy to understand his frustration. This is a far cry from the message that he came to bring.

When we examine our conscience, we spend an inordinate amount of time on issues that belong to the era of the law. How much time do we devote to the good that we are called to espouse? How far are we willing to go in extending ourselves? In being truly people of the Spirit? If most of our time is spent in evaluating ourselves in the light of the commandments, we act as people of the former covenant instead of the freed people of the new dispensation.

Points to Ponder

The function of the law
The lawless life in the Spirit
The Christian examination of conscience

THURSDAY OF THE TWENTY-EIGHTH WEEK IN ORDINARY TIME

Year I

Romans 3:21–30
Psalm 130:1b–2, 3–4, 5–6ab
Luke 11:47–54

The law, good in itself, had proven ineffective in bringing about justification. Incapable of being observed in all its detail, it had led to nothing but frustration. But now God's righteousness or fidelity to his promises has been realized in the justification that comes to Gentile and Jew alike through faith in the redemption in Jesus Christ. Sins of former days, committed with God's patient forbearance, are now remitted through faith in Christ Jesus. All of this is accomplished apart from the law, since this is the God of the Gentiles as well as the Jews. Both the circumcised and uncircumcised are justified because of his universal love. Since this is all gift, there is no room for boasting.

In continuing his reproach of the Jewish leaders, the Lucan Jesus accuses them of building memorials to the prophets whom their fathers had killed. These acts of violence continued to the present in the persecution of both prophets as well as apostles of the Christian era. The end result is the present culpability for the death of all the prophets from Abel, the first to die, to Zechariah, the last prophet to be mentioned in the Hebrew Bible.

And with the dawn of the era of Christ, the scholars of the law not only refused to enter but prevented others from doing so. Hostility toward Jesus arises after these accusations. In speaking of the ineffectiveness of the law, Paul has alienated his former co-religionists. In speaking out, Jesus points to the continued wrongdoing of the Jewish leadership. There are times when all of us are called to take a stand. It is not an easy thing to do. But if principles for which we stand suffer attack, we have no other choice.

Points to Ponder

Justification through faith: a matchless gift
A faith that embraces all: Jew and Gentile
Standing for principle

Year II

Ephesians 1:1–10
Psalm 98:1, 2–3ab, 3cd–4, 5–6
Luke 11:47–54

The first ten verses of the Letter to the Ephesians are rich in Pauline theology. Three words stand out very vividly: *mystery*, *redemption*, and *adoption*. The *mystery* of God consistently in Paul's thought is the plan of salvation in God's Son that was concealed from eternity and revealed only in these final days. *Redemption* means the acquisition of humanity from the throes of sin "by the blood of Christ." But redemption does not signify simply moving from a state of alienation to one of favor. It means "adoption." Through the gift of the Spirit, the living bond between Christ and the Father, we are made part of that life, not by nature as was true of Christ, but by adoption. Christ becomes brother and God becomes "Abba" (Father). Finally, since all of creation has been touched by Christ's saving blood, the ultimate part of the mystery of God means that all things are summed up in Christ in heaven and on earth.

This is as complete a summary of the work of God in Christ as we will find in the New Testament. It aptly points to the extent to which we have been favored. When we are encouraged to walk in the Spirit, we are moved by the realization of what this mystery entails and the extent to which God has loved us. To sin seriously is to turn our backs on this goodness and to walk in another direction.

The Lucan Jesus today reminds the Jewish leaders that they have taken away the "key of knowledge." Not only have they not entered, but they have deprived others of entry as well. Our time in this life is limited indeed; let us use it with the gratitude of members of God's household.

Points to Ponder

The mystery of God
Redemption in his blood
Adoption in God's family

FRIDAY OF THE TWENTY-EIGHTH WEEK IN ORDINARY TIME

Year I

Romans 4:1–8
Psalm 32:1b–2, 5, 11
Luke 12:1–7

Jesus today speaks of the age of God's reign as an era of light. Nothing is concealed, and whatever is done in secret is brought to light. Persecutions will occur. But it is not the death of the body that is to be feared; it is the death of body and soul that represents an irreparable loss. But we must not live in fear. Nothing is lost to God's sight, not even the fate of the sparrows sold in the market-place. And we have a worth much greater than many sparrows.

Paul insists that Abraham is the father of those who believe. As Genesis states, it was because he believed that he was declared righteous. This was not done because he did good things; it was conceded solely on the basis of his faith.

It is often argued that faith and trust are two different things and should not be confused. This is true, but trust is a component of faith. Our trust is present because we believe. As the Gospel teaches us today, our faith rests in a God who is trustworthy. Hardships will inevitably come our way. But before God our lives are very precious. Let us live in confidence that we will not be abandoned.

Points to Ponder

> The righteousness of Abraham
> Trust as a component of our faith
> Nothing hidden; nothing secret

Year II

> Ephesians 1:11–14
> Psalm 33:1–2, 4–5, 12–13
> Luke 12:1–7

Ephesians speaks today of the manner in which God's plan is being realized among the believers. They first have heard the word of truth, "the gospel of your salvation." In their baptism, they were sealed with the promised Holy Spirit, "the first installment of our inheritance." They are in progress toward final redemption "to the praise of his glory." All of this is accomplished in Christ the Lord.

One of the great moments of the Easter vigil is the baptism of the catechumens. One can see the joy of their newfound faith in their faces. For them this moment so often signifies a great step forward in life; they prize something we so often take for granted. They are spoken of in the liturgy as "the elect."

It is at times such as these that we understand the teaching of today's Gospel. In our calling we know that we are of an inestimable worth. Baptism convinces us of that. Hypocrisy is rejected in the teaching of Christ. We cannot claim openness and live a secret. Our life is destined to become an open book. This calls for transparency in all that we do.

Points to Ponder

> Baptism as the first installment of our inheritance
> The Easter Vigil as a teaching moment
> The importance of transparency

SATURDAY OF THE TWENTY-EIGHTH WEEK IN ORDINARY TIME

Year I

Romans 4:13, 16–18
Psalm 105:6–7, 8–9, 42–43
Luke 12:8–12

What is the sin against the Holy Spirit? It can only be determined by context, and the context in Luke is not very helpful. The meaning can be derived from the other Gospels where it also appears. To sin against the Holy Spirit would be to attribute the work of God to evil or to call light darkness. This would be the total rejection of God's saving plan. Jesus assures us that when we are called for an accounting of our faith in a public forum, we need not worry about what our defense will be. The assistance of the Holy Spirit is assured.

Again Paul summarizes his position on the faith of Abraham. That faith was a gift, not something earned. The descendants of Abraham, then, are those who believe as he did. He was told that he would be the father of many nations, even in his advanced years. He believed, hoping against hope. It is important for us to return to this fundamental teaching repeatedly in life. We will be saved because we have been gifted.

Therefore, to acknowledge Christ before others wins his acknowledgment before the heavenly court. On the human scene, a failure to profess him can be forgiven while blasphemy against the Holy Spirit cannot. The content of the faith profession will be provided by God himself. Through it all, his word is with us: "Do not worry."

Points to Ponder

The sin against the Spirit
Abraham, father of many nations
The Lord provides our defense

Year II

Ephesians 1:15–23
Psalm 8:2–3ab, 4–5, 6–7
Luke 12:8–12

In this passage from Ephesians, Paul speaks of the post-Easter Christ. God raised him from the dead and seated him at his right hand far above every category of being in the heavenly court. He gave him the preeminent name of "Lord," the title proper to Yahweh alone. All of creation is made subject to him, and finally he is made head of the church, which is his body. Christ then has become the summation of all things because not only humanity but all things have been touched by redemption.

It is this theology that regulates our thinking on the environment and the nature that surrounds our life. The degradation of our universe, often done in the name of progress, has reached alarming proportions.

Global warming is not simply hypothesis. It has been clearly established. Unless we are prepared to do something about it, life on this planet will be severely affected within the present century. Ecology has become a pronounced moral concern that, if not affecting us, will seriously affect our children.

Jesus in the Gospel commends us for confessing him before others.

A faith concern for our environment is one of the ways in which he can be confessed. There is a lesson here that directly concerns the school and the home. Let us open our hearts and our minds to those activists who are seriously trying to enlighten our consciences on a matter of primary importance.

Points to Ponder

Christ's preeminence in the universe
Christianity and ecology
Jesus Christ as Lord

MONDAY OF THE TWENTY-NINTH WEEK IN ORDINARY TIME

Year I

Romans 4:20–25
Luke 1:69–70, 71–72, 73–75
Luke 12:13–21

Many of the parables of Jesus, coming from a diverse time and culture, need some explanation. Today's is one that clearly does not. Its meaning is immediately evident and its truth borne out by experience.

Jesus is asked to settle an inheritance dispute. Wisely he refrains from any involvement but does give an injunction against greed.

The account is of the man who did everything to prepare for a relaxed retirement by multiplying his holdings and increasing his storage space. But then suddenly his life comes to an end, and all these preparations passed to someone else's hands. The story may be old, but the situation is as relevant as today. It seems so frequent that people who have prepared for a comfortable retirement are suddenly taken from our midst. Certainly it is not always a case of abundant holdings, nor is it always a question of greed. But it is a fact of life.

Paul today reminds us of our greatest treasure. We have been credited with justice—the most important reality of our life—because of our faith in the One who died and rose again in order that our sins be blotted out and that we be sealed in the Holy Spirit. This is our inheritance, over which there can be no dispute. As for whatever possessions may be ours in life, we cannot take them with us.

Points to Ponder

We have here no lasting home
The treasure of being righteous before God
Family disputes over inheritance

Year II

Ephesians 2:1–10
Psalm 100:1b–2, 3, 4ab, 4c–5
Luke 12:13–21

Our psalm today speaks of God's steadfast love, which endures forever. If these were the sentiments of an Old Testament believer, how much more do these words resound in the Christian heart? Paul speaks of his pre-Christian life and that of his fellow Christians. This was a life lived in the darkness of sin, subject to ethereal powers. Dominated by desires of the flesh, we were, says Paul, "children of wrath," destined for destruction. But God in his great mercy has raised us up with Christ as Exhibit A of his boundless grace in Christ Jesus. By that grace we have been saved through faith.

When we read this in conjunction with today's Gospel, in our hearts we know that there are better things in life than barns filled with grain. The trouble is that we don't always act that way. If we had an estate in the Hamptons or a yacht that took us on a tour each year, they would be overshadowed by that great gift of new life in Christ Jesus.

Our hearts are lifted up by philanthropists who use their fortunes on behalf of the less fortunate. With their millions they are fighting our most devastating diseases and giving hope to the desperately poor.

They are not waiting for some future date to make their bequests but acting now. This is a lesson from today's scripture. Yes, wealth is to be shared.

Points to Ponder

Using our goods for others
The danger of wealth
God's greatest gift: our faith

TUESDAY OF THE TWENTY-NINTH WEEK IN ORDINARY TIME

Year I

Romans 5:12, 15b, 17–19, 20b–21
Psalm 40:7–8a, 8b–9, 10, 17
Luke 12:35–38

Today's reading from Romans is the classical contrast between the disintegration inherited from Adam and the reintegration that comes from Christ. The one man, Adam, introduced sin to the world; with sin came death. Death passed to every human being in as much as all sinned. Through one man's sin, all inherited condemnation, since they in turn ratified by their own conduct the sin of the first man. The conclusion is a tragic one; because one man disobeyed, all then have become sinners, and sin has reigned in death.

Yet, in this dire situation, God's remedy was already at hand. In the coming of Jesus the damage inflicted by Adam is overcome, and in abundance. The gift of Christ is justification and life; humanity is acquitted of its sinfulness. If disobedience brought death and tragedy, so through the obedience of one man, justification has come to the many. Where sin may have proliferated, now grace is more than abundant. Sin brought death; grace has brought justification and life eternal in Jesus Christ our Lord.

Now what God asks of us is vigilance. We do not know when the master will return from the wedding. He may come at the first, second, or third watch. When he finds his servants alert and waiting, he will render them able service. In other words, the faithful will be received into glory.

The lesson is clear. We have been immensely favored. Death has been overcome. We now live in the Spirit.

Points to Ponder

The tragedy of Adam
The victory in Christ
Christian alertness

Year II

Ephesians 2:12–22
Psalm 85:9ab–10, 11–12, 13–14
Luke 12:35–38

In a former age, Jew and Gentile were separated by a wall of hostility. But Ephesians today highlights the reconciling work of Christ. Before, the Gentiles were alienated from Israel, strangers to the promise, without hope and without God. But now in the blood of Christ, the wall of enmity has crumbled. He has abolished the law in which Jews placed their hope so that he might bring Jew and Gentile together in one body of which he is the head. His message was one of peace—both to the Gentiles who were far off and to the Jews who were near at hand.

The Gospel today encourages us to be vigilant, not in an atmosphere of anxiety and fear, but as family members who anxiously await the arrival of their brother, with whom they will dine as brothers and sisters at the Lord's heavenly table.

Points to Ponder

The wall of hostility destroyed
The body of Christ
Christian vigilance

WEDNESDAY OF THE TWENTY-NINTH WEEK IN ORDINARY TIME

Year I

Romans 6:12–18
Psalm 124:1b–3, 4–6, 7–8
Luke 12:39–48

Sinfulness or Christian stewardship? In our present circumstances, it is always possible to revert to a state of sin by letting it reign over our bodies and surrendering to the body's desires. However, since we have been raised from death to new life, our bodies are ruled by grace to perform works of righteousness. Since we are no longer under the law but under grace, our conduct should correspond to this new reality. We are now slaves to the one we obey. There are only two choices: to sin, which leads to death, or to follow God, which leads to righteousness. The latter is the choice that we have made.

In terms of responsibility, we are now stewards of the things of God. Before going away on a trip, the master of an estate entrusts his steward with certain tasks, hoping he will work hard. But if the steward abuses the servants of the house while the master is away, then the master will punish him severely when he comes home. An interesting note of lesser guilt is introduced at this point. If the servant is ignorant of the master's will and acts inappropriately, he will receive a lighter punishment. The point of the parable: where much has been entrusted, much will be required.

In our times, the moral failures of those entrusted with responsibility in the church has caused great scandal. But much is expected of religious leaders precisely because it is *grace*, not sin, to which they profess their obedience. They also profess to be responsive to the needs of the Christian community. It is a sacred trust. Negligence only diminishes credibility.

Points to Ponder

> The obedience of grace
> Stewardship within the church
> Moral failure in stewardship

Year II

> Ephesians 3:2–12
> Isaiah 12:2–3, 4bcd, 5–6
> Luke 12:39–48

Paul takes up once again this mystery of God that has been concealed from the ages and made known only in these final days in a special revelation made to the apostle. At the heart of this revelation is the realization that the Gentiles are now partners with the Jews. They are members of the same body and copartners of the gospel message in Christ Jesus.

The Gospel today speaks at length of Christian stewardship. Paul realizes that, by God's grace, he, the very least of all the holy ones, was given the charge of bringing this message to the Gentile world. This was the eternal purpose of God, which has now been actualized in the redemptive mission of Christ himself. Through faith in Christ, Paul has found boldness of speech and confidence of access in his proclamation of this great message.

We know from his own writings that Paul experienced many trials in his proclamation of the good news. And yet it was with boundless energy that he continued his mission. We can only pray that in the discharge of our own stewardship we will remain faithful and that the Master upon his return will find us joyfully continuing our mission. The prophet exhorts us today to make known the great deeds of God among all the nations. To proclaim the word is a great challenge and a great joy.

Points to Ponder

> The mystery that is hidden from the ages
> The mystery in which two become one
> Faithful stewardship

THURSDAY OF THE TWENTY-NINTH WEEK IN ORDINARY TIME

Year I

> Romans 6:19–23
> Psalm 1:1–2, 3, 4 and 6
> Luke 12:49–53

A New Testament idea is that Christ came as an agent of peace. But the Gospel reading today seems to claim just the opposite. Christ asserts that he has come to establish not peace but division. How are we to understand this claim? Certainly, Christ's message is one of peace; that is clear in his teaching in its entirety.

Love stands at the very heart of his message. But it is in the reception of the message that discord lies. In the acceptance or rejection of his teaching, families will be torn asunder. Father against son, daughter against mother, in-laws against each other. This is not the desire of Christ, nor does it reflect his teaching. But his message is capable of causing deep cleavage within a family. In that sense, Christ has brought division.

Paul again exhorts the Romans to turn their bodies away from sin and impurity; they should become now slaves of righteousness for sanctification. When they were slaves of sin, they reaped its harvest, which is death. But on this new and better track, they are slaves of God in a sanctification that leads to eternal life. In summary, sin pays wages, and that is death. On God's side there are no wages since nothing is earned. It is the gift of God that is eternal life in Christ Jesus our Lord.

In our dealings with God there are no bargaining chips since everything is pure gift for which we can only be grateful. That gift, however, can continue to cause strife and division even within a family. Parents suffer greatly when children walk away from their faith. Or it may be that a child embraces the faith while parents remain apart or perhaps even hostile. We must always try to overcome hostilities. We reject the sin and love the sinner. That remains always the Christian response.

Points to Ponder

> Sin pays wages
> Life in Christ is gift
> Christ as a source of division

Year II

> Ephesians 3:14–21
> Psalm 33:1–2, 4–5, 11–12, 18–19
> Luke 12:49–53

In his prayer to the Father, Paul prays that the community be "strengthened...with power." The power is that of the Holy Spirit. He prays that their hearts may be Christ's dwelling place and that they be rooted and grounded in love. To the one who is able to accomplish far more than we imagine, he prays that our love and knowledge of Christ may ever more abound in order that the fullness, which is God himself, may be ours. May the God who is capable of realizing far more than we even imagine manifest his glory in the church and in Christ.

Paul's prayer goes to the Father who shares his glory with the Son and the church. Our liturgical prayer is directed to the Father in and through his Son or the intercession of the saints. It is the Father who is the source of all good.

Our Gospel today reminds us that our faith can also be a source of division. The early church experienced sharp separations over the acceptance of the faith. It sometimes happens today, especially in the political field, that religion is used as a weapon. Our beliefs can be stated openly but always with civility. Our sincerity should never boil over into arrogance.

Points to Ponder

> Prayer directed to God the Father
> Stating our beliefs in charity
> Prayer as growth in love

FRIDAY OF THE TWENTY-NINTH WEEK IN ORDINARY TIME

Year I

> Romans 7:18–25a
> Psalm 119:66, 68, 76, 77, 93, 94
> Luke 12:54–59

In today's passage from Romans, Paul presents the contrast between the unregenerated person and the one who has experienced redemption in Christ. Even with the unregenerated person, there is an inner desire for good, but the possibility of achieving it is absent. That which the person would do, he does not do. Sin has taken possession of the person's life; the law of sin prevails over the law of the mind. In his desperation, the person cries out for deliverance from his slavery to his mortal body. And, "thanks be to God," the solution has been found in "Jesus Christ our Lord."

The Gospel reminds us of how willing we are to read the signs of the times. The meteorologist on the evening news gives us a five-day forecast of the weather with a high degree of accuracy. Before taking a trip we investigate the roads and their traffic level to determine the best route. Why should we fail to carefully consider all the aspects of our moral choices in life? With our new life in Christ, sin is no longer inevitable. We begin from a position of strength and are well equipped to meet any challenge.

The Lucan Jesus in speaking of litigation advises his followers to settle out of court. Court proceedings can be long and expensive. And if acrimonious enough, one may well end up the loser. Therefore, it is far better to settle the matter beforehand, especially in light of the fact that Christians should be able to settle differences among themselves rather than appearing before civil magistrates.

Points to Ponder

> The freedom that comes with the Christ life
> Recognizing the strength that is ours
> Settling out of court

Year II

> Ephesians 4:1–6
> Psalm 24:1–2, 3–4ab, 5–6
> Luke 12:54–59

The call to unity in Ephesians is one of its most stirring passages. The unity will find expression in a bond of peace. A hostile or divided Christian community flies in the face of our basic affirmations. We have been baptized into the one body of Christ, under the headship of the one Lord. There is only one baptism, one faith that we profess, and one God and Father of us all.

The ecumenical efforts of the church today are of paramount importance. A divided Christianity is a sin and a scandal. It clearly stands in opposition to the expressed will of Christ. We should take seriously the summons we have received, especially from the Second Vatican Council, to work and pray together with other Christians and to be supportive of important dialogue with other churches. With Christ we pray that they all may be one.

This is what it means to read the signs of the times, as the Gospel today exhorts us. Christian unity is not an optional idea.

Ecumenism should be a vital part of any pastoral work. It may take different forms, such as joint prayer services, or joint blessings of the palms on Palm Sunday. Ecumenism requires creativity and an open spirit.

Points to Ponder

> The one body of Christ
> The single baptism
> Parish ecumenical endeavors

SATURDAY OF THE TWENTY-NINTH WEEK IN ORDINARY TIME

Year I

> Romans 8:1–11
> Psalm 24:1b–2, 3–4ab, 5–6
> Luke 13:1–9

The great human tragedy is to die without repentance. That is the lesson of today's Gospel. To sin seriously is one thing; to persist in sinfulness is another. It is this latter that the Lord warns against. But his teaching is balanced by his great patience. The man who came to the fig tree for three years is willing to wait another year before destroying the tree. This he does to give the gardener time to cultivate the tree.

Paul today points out our reason for joy in having been touched by God's saving grace. The law of sin and death now has no place in our lives, we who now live the law of the Spirit in Christ Jesus. For the law of sin, enclosed in the flesh, has been condemned and rendered powerless that its righteous decrees might be fulfilled in us who live now, not in flesh, but in the Spirit. The great hope lives in us. If the Spirit who raised Jesus from the dead now dwells in us, life will be given to our mortal bodies as well.

This great message of life and hope is one of joy and consolation. Our life, not unlike Paul's, brings its share of sorrow and disappointment. But to read Paul's message and to believe in it enables us to cope with any trial.

And the message of the gospel teaches us never to lose hope in our prayers for anyone. The patience of Christ is without measure. *Sursum corda!* Lift up your hearts!

Points to Ponder

> The patience of God
> The law of righteousness
> The basic joy of Christianity

Year II

> Ephesians 4:7–16
> Psalm 122:1–2, 3–4ab, 4cd–5
> Luke 13:1–9

Like any human body, the body of Christ is in the process of growth and development. Ours is not simply a static insertion into the whole Christ. Paul addresses this question in today's first reading. Christ has ascended on high to give gifts to humanity. This means that he first descended in mortal flesh to dwell in our midst. But now, in his glorified state, he makes provision for the church endowing it with the various ministries. There are apostles, evangelists, pastors, and teachers whose function it is to build up the body of Christ to attain full Christian maturity. Thus we pass from a childlike immaturity, easily deceived and misled, to that fuller knowledge of Christ in love and truth. With every part of the body performing its proper function, there is an ongoing growth into full maturity.

We err indeed if we see ministry in the church identified only with the ordained. Paul never speaks of ministry in that way.

There are a variety of ministries, all of which contribute to the building up of the one body. One of the beauties of the church since Vatican II has been a recapturing of that ministerial diversity. We see it on the altar during the liturgy, in the ministry to the sick and the homebound, to the bereaved at the time of death. All of this in conjunction with the more traditional ministry of education and formation.

The question is real for anyone of us today. What gift may I have to offer my church today? None of us excels in everything; each of us has some particular area of contribution. There is room for everyone. I must give it some thought and see where it may lead. The man in the Gospel showed patience in waiting for the fig tree to yield fruit. God is no less patient with us.

Points to Ponder

Growth within: the one body
From childhood to adulthood in the Spirit
My contribution to ministry

MONDAY OF THE THIRTIETH WEEK IN ORDINARY TIME

Year I

Romans 8:12–17
Psalm 68:2 and 4, 6–7ab, 20–21
Luke 13:10–17

The woman whom Jesus heals in today's Gospel suffered from a crippling disease that for eighteen years made it impossible for her to stand up straight. Without even a request on her part, Jesus moves immediately to cure her. With his touch, her posture is restored. We cannot help but applaud his action. But the opposition is, as always, close at hand. The leader of the synagogue complained that to perform a cure on the Sabbath was inexcusable. Jesus cites a parallel example. Farmers do not hesitate to provide for their livestock on the Sabbath. It is perfectly logical to think that a person so badly crippled should be freed from her distress on the Sabbath. The crowd enthusiastically endorses Jesus, while his legalistic adversaries are humiliated.

Paul today remains with his Spirit/flesh antithesis. Just as the woman in the Gospel was enslaved to evil for eighteen years, so too those who give themselves over to the flesh are the slaves of sin and are destined for death. But we have been liberated and now live in the Spirit as adopted daughters and sons of God. We are adopted children of the Father God and joint heirs with Christ. If we suffer with him, we shall be glorified with him.

When we witness the good that Jesus accomplished during his life, we too become annoyed with the legalistic claims of his opponents. But we can take it one step farther. When we consider all the good that Christ has done for us, it seems absurd for us to revert to worn-out patterns of sin. We no more desire to revert to slavery than the woman wanted to be enslaved to her illness. Let us stay the course as we walk the glory road with Christ. To apply the words of the psalmist today, the Lord "leads out the prisoners to prosperity."

Points to Ponder

The unrestricted time for doing good
Our liberation from evil in Christ
Heirs of God; co-heirs with Christ

Year II

Ephesians 4:32—5:8
Psalm 1:1–2, 3, 4 and 6
Luke 13:10–17

Borderline conduct! Paul today is not speaking to unbelievers but to the community of faith. He is clearly advising them against compromising their commitment by dabbling in the type of conduct that they should abhor. It is charity, compassion, and forgiveness that are to be the mainstays of their daily lives. Immorality, impurity, and greed should not even be part of their conversation. Since they are a people of thanksgiving to God for benefits received, this posture should dominate their comportment. They are to live as children of light.

There is real wisdom here. Even though we would not want to betray our inheritance in Christ, there are moments in all our lives, especially in conversations with others, when we treat virtue lightly and indulge in conversations that are in no way helpful. It is not always easy to maintain our sense of values in what we say. The more we engage in talk of immoral conduct, the greater is the danger. In this regard we should be especially mindful of the good name of other people and not damage it by our remarks, which, even though truthful, may still be hurtful.

In today's Gospel Jesus acts on behalf of the deformed woman before being asked. It is that type of response we would all like to have in the face of difficult situations. We may pray with the psalmist today to be like the trees planted near running water, which yield abundant fruit in due season.

Points to Ponder

> Avoiding hurtful conversation
> Respecting the good name of others
> Taking the initiative for good

TUESDAY OF THE THIRTIETH WEEK IN ORDINARY TIME

Year I

> Romans 8:18–25
> Psalm 126:1b–2ab, 2cd–3, 4–5, 6
> Luke 13:18–21

We live in an interim stage—not only ourselves but the whole of creation with us. Just as sin brought consequences for humanity, so too creation itself was affected by sin in the world. Corruption has tainted the universe as a whole, subjected to it by the One who inflicted the punishment. And just as we who now enjoy the first fruits of redemption look forward to its completion, so too does the universe. The universe itself is destined to share in the final glory of God's children. This is part of what we term "cosmic redemption," the belief that all of the universe has been touched by redemption and therefore enjoys a sacred character. We now wait for what we do not see, and we wait with patient endurance.

The parables of today's Gospel are meant to console followers of Christ who have seen the small beginning. The small mustard seed when it comes to full growth is a large bush visited frequently by the birds of the air. So too a small amount of yeast produces a large quantity of leavened dough.

The single point is being made. From insignificant beginnings great things come forth. So too will it be in the kingdom of God.

A God-of-the-earth theology is more relevant in our times than ever before. Global warming is a reality that we ignore to our own grave detriment. Unlimited consumption, with its ceaseless exploitation of natural resources and its total disregard for waste, will certainly affect the lives of our children and their children. God will not condone human destruction of the natural world he created.

This is a serious threat to the universe that shares in our redemption. Any step that we can take to move our government to action or to conserve on a local level has become a moral imperative. We cannot forget that the kingdom of God embraces the world in which we live, and its preservation is part of our faith expression.

Points to Ponder

> The fall and corruption in the universe
> Cosmic redemption
> The growth of the kingdom

Year II

> Ephesians 5:21–33
> Psalm 128:1–2, 3, 4–5
> Luke 13:18–21

Today's passage from Ephesians is often seen as disregarding the equal dignity of the woman in marriage. But that fails to take account of the passage as a whole. There is indeed a subordination present, but it is mutual, equally binding on both parties. Humility and lowliness are part of the Christian ethic as a whole and are therefore applicable to both man and woman in marriage. If the wife is told to be submissive to the husband as the church is to Christ, by the same token the husband is told to love the wife as does Christ the church. And on Christ's part, that love carried him even to death for the sake of his beloved. In Paul's teaching there is no sparing the husband. Mutual love is always humble on both sides.

From small beginnings come great things. The kingdom of God in full growth will indeed be impressive. In our present state, we await the full expression of God's reign. Our interim efforts on behalf of the church should look toward unity and docility. There is no issue faced by our sister churches today that is not in some way present in our Catholic ranks as well. Prayer and dialogue are necessary as we serenely ask for God's guidance.

Many marriages fail because of a lack of mutual submission. Husband and wife must listen to each other and together seek solutions to common problems. There is an inestimable witness given by the marriage that lasts for many years. It shows a willingness to find common solutions and to be patient in the face of human weakness. This is the way in which Christ deals with his church.

Points to Ponder

> Mutual submission in marriage
> The Christ-church image
> The growth of the kingdom

WEDNESDAY OF THE THIRTIETH WEEK IN ORDINARY TIME

Year I

> Romans 8:26–30
> Psalm 13:4–5, 6
> Luke 13:22–30

The entire process of justification is planned by God. At the same time, there is no privileged class before him. This message comes home clearly in today's readings. Jesus, on his way to Jerusalem, preaches to the villagers on the way. Asked if only a few people will be saved, he does not answer the question. He only recommends the narrow door. Free admission will not be granted on the basis of familiarity or ethnicity. This is the Jesus who will ultimately be rejected by his own people. When the final sort takes place, they will not be able to claim table fellowship or hometown company as the key to admission. These people were opponents of his message. Not only will they be on the outside looking in, but they will see foreigners from the four corners of the earth join the patriarchs and prophets in the kingdom of God.

Paul reminds us that our own place within the church is not a question of chance. Foreknown, predestined, confirmed, justified, and glorified, God has led us along the way. We can only rejoice in his goodness, just as we recognize that we too must enter by the narrow gate. We always remain free, and that means we can move away from God's plan.

Points to Ponder

Heartfelt response to God: the key to salvation
God's call to each of us
The disregard of God's love

Year II

Ephesians 6:1–9
Psalm 145:10–11, 12–13ab, 13cd–14
Luke 13:22–30

As Ephesians today counsels various segments of society, we can both nod in agreement and wince a bit. To the family counsel, especially in an era when there is insufficient discipline, we give ready consent. Children should be appreciative and submissive. Obedience to parents is as old as the Decalogue. By the same token, parents should be caring and not overbearing, providing a type of training and instruction that reflects the goodness of God.

We are forced to wonder why slavery had such a long leash in the history of Christianity. Today we consider the practice abhorrent, marked by an incredible lack of respect for human dignity. In the United States its demise did not occur until the mid-nineteenth century, and its relics lasted for a century longer. Paul recognizes the right to have slaves but encourages slaves and masters to be mindful of their relationship to Christ and argues against any form of ill treatment.

Our Gospel today reminds us that privilege and status play no part in the reign of God. It is a matter of the heart and gratitude to God. Since charity begins at home, we can ask ourselves how well our home reflects the harmony of the holy family of Nazareth. Our faith flows into everything we do, and the influence of our home life is unparalleled.

Points to Ponder

> The influence of family love
> Slavery as an institution
> Entering by the narrow gate

THURSDAY OF THE THIRTIETH WEEK IN ORDINARY TIME

Year I

> Romans 8:31b–39
> Psalm 109:21–22, 26–27, 30–31
> Luke 13:31–35

Jesus' moving lament over a hostile and unresponsive Jerusalem is found within a context that speaks of Herod's designs on Jesus' life. Jesus certainly will fulfill the plan of God at the appointed time. In the meantime, spoken figuratively in terms of a series of days, he must continue his ministry of healing and consolation. When the appointed time comes, he, like the prophets before him, will die in Jerusalem. But now he can only regret the fact that Jerusalem remains unresponsive to his message. The people will soon be deprived of their religious leaders; Christ himself will not be seen again until the time of his solemn entry into the city.

Paul today illustrates the lot of the elect, the life that his readers are currently experiencing. Their present lot is privileged and their future assured. He argues that if God loved us enough to send his Son to die for us, he will certainly not deprive us of faith's final outcome. That incomparable love of God for us is fully actualized in Christ Jesus our Lord. Nothing can possibly separate us from that love, neither human trials (anguish, distress, persecution, famine, nakedness, or peril), nor life or death, past or future, heavenly powers, heights or depths. The love of God in Jesus breaks through every barrier and gives us the greatest confidence.

There is nothing more distressing than indifference in the face of such love. Jerusalem was in direct contact with the work of God in Jesus and yet remained cold. The great tragedy of our times is the fall-off in religious practice, the ever-increasing number of people who live for the present moment. To turn our backs on God's love in Jesus makes Jesus' lament over Jerusalem applicable to us. What is called for is a new evangelization, a renewed appreciation of our faith.

Points to Ponder

> Overcoming hardness of heart
> Paul's description of the love of Christ
> A new evangelization

Year II

> Ephesians 6:10–20
> Psalm 144:1b, 2, 9–10
> Luke 13:31–35

The author of Ephesians uses military imagery to describe the Christian state of preparedness to deal with the present conflict. The struggle is not with human powers but the full array of evil. This includes supernatural powers and the evil rulers of the present time.

Only with the armor of God are we able to cope. Our loins must be girded in the truth; righteousness as our breastplate. Our feet, well shod in footwear suitable for preachers of the gospel of peace. We bear the helmet of our salvation; our sword, the word of God. In addition, our prayers must go up for the whole community and for Paul to have a boldness of speech to proclaim the gospel, for which he is currently an ambassador in chains.

With the apostle, we too pray for the courage to speak. The ministry of Jesus was characterized by the compassion and understanding of today's Gospel. But he also spoke unhesitatingly the gospel of conversion in the presence of hardness of heart. Conviction does not back off in the face of hostility. We must always speak the truth in love. Religious leaders in Jerusalem refused his call to conversion. They were then left to reap the results of their hostility.

Compassion and understanding are not to be confused with a laissez-faire attitude. We show the greatest love for another when we speak the truth in love. Our words may sometimes hurt as they prod the conscience. But they are only spoken because we care. If the wayward person sees our genuine concern, our words may prove fruitful indeed.

Points to Ponder

Our need for moral strength
Boldness is speaking the "gospel of peace"
Jesus' concern for Jerusalem

FRIDAY OF THE THIRTIETH WEEK IN ORDINARY TIME

Year I

Romans 9:1–5
Psalm 147:12–13, 14–15, 19–20
Luke 14:1–6

Our Jewish friends do not share with us our faith in Jesus Christ, and that is something we regret. But there are many things we do share with them. Paul lists a number of these as he begins that section of Romans wherein he speaks of his hope for his former co-religionists. They are "Israelites," adopted children of God. They have the covenants, the law, the prescribed worship, and the patriarchs. Jesus Christ in his human nature was born a Jew. This alone should prompt us to avoid all anti-Semitic ideas or expressions.

Jesus did not feel himself bound to many of the traditions of Judaism. When the man with dropsy appears before him in today's Gospel, he does not hesitate to heal him on the Sabbath. The law of charity is paramount. If some accident were to befall a family member or even their livestock on the Sabbath, his Jewish listeners would not hesitate to act.

After Jesus heals the man, his opponents remain silent.

We have legitimate differences with our Jewish neighbors. But they are not barriers to respect and friendship. Paul says that he could even endure being set aside by Christ for the sake of his Jewish brothers and sisters. In our society we have far too much polarization and negativity. As Christians we have to begin with the fact that Christ destroyed barriers. Why should we rebuild them?

Points to Ponder

> My sentiments toward the Jewish people
> Jesus' attitude toward Jewish prescriptions
> Paul's pain over Jewish separation

Year II

> Philippians 1:1–11
> Psalm 111:1–2, 3–4, 5–6
> Luke 14:1–6

Today we begin our readings from Paul's letter to the people of Philippi, a community very close to his heart. In his introduction, he gives thanks to God for them. It is a friendship rooted in faith. Paul sees the Philippians as partners of the gospel, sharers with him of the message of salvation. He prays that the work begun in them will continue to grow until the day of the Lord. These Christians are with him partners, whether in his present imprisonment or in defense of the gospel.

Paul prays as well that they will continue to grow in their knowledge and understanding of the message, that they may grow in the Spirit, that they may present themselves pure and blameless for the day of Christ.

The onlookers in today's Gospel are silent in the face of Jesus' compassion. They do not answer the question he poses. Animosity finds speech difficult, whereas love is multifaceted in its expression. In speaking of his love for the Philippians, Paul gives different reasons and takes different approaches. Peace and harmony are signs of Christian love.

Points to Ponder

> Our partners of the gospel
> Growth in the Spirit
> Hostility and the Christian spirit

SATURDAY OF THE THIRTIETH WEEK IN ORDINARY TIME

Year I

> Romans 11:1–2a, 11–12, 25–29
> Psalm 94:12–13a, 14–15, 17–18
> Luke 14:1, 7–11

What prospects remain for Israel, the people beloved by God?

Paul takes up this question in chapters 9—11 of Romans. Clearly God has not rejected his people. Paul himself was a Hebrew, a descendant of Abraham, of the tribe of Benjamin. He has come to the fuller truth, as will Israel eventually.

How then to explain their present situation. The Jews have stumbled on the way, and that is to the Gentiles' benefit. Through the Jews' opposition and obstinacy, salvation in Christ has passed to the Gentiles. But the state of the Jews is a temporary situation. If the few Jews who have converted is an enrichment for the Gentiles, how much more will the full number be?

We are not to gloat over this setback. Israel, too, now is an inimical stand toward the gospel. Yet their call is irrevocable. They are beloved because of the patriarchs. They too will enter the kingdom.

Jesus, in today's Gospel, is invited to the house of a prominent Pharisee for dinner. Since there were a number of invited guests and (needless to say) no place cards, Jesus tells a parable regarding honor seeking. The setting is a dinner invitation, but the application is much broader. It is a word against honor seeking, social climbing, or whatever expression best grasps the point. Let us be content with our state in life; then when an honor or a promotion comes, it is not because we advanced our own cause. It is simply due to recognition. Self-promotion is personal aggrandizement and unworthy of the Christian. When the humble person is raised up, we realize that this is the order of God's preference.

Points to Ponder

> The place of the Jews in the Christian life
> The danger of self-promotion
> The humble are raised up

Year II

> Philippians 1:18b–26
> Psalm 42:2, 3, 5cdef
> Luke 14:1, 7–11

In his imprisonment Paul is faced with a real dilemma. What is to be preferred: life or death? For his part Paul would rather die and be with Christ. The affirmation is an important one because it recognizes a "being with Christ" after death and before the second coming. Yet as far as the earthly community is concerned, it is better that he live and be of service to them. They will be able to boast in Christ Jesus all the more if he returns to them. He feels confident that he will live on for their benefit.

Today's Gospel message is clear in Paul's case. He does not seek to advance himself. He sees himself solely as the servant of

Jesus Christ. His preference is to die and be with Christ. But, if on the other hand, if Christ calls him to further ministry, he is just as content. Why is it in life that we think that every decision must come from us? When an important decision to be made is placed before the Lord, circumstances point out the direction to be followed. We think we are masters of our own fate, but often the facts show otherwise.

Most of us live with the inevitability of death but don't really yearn for it. Sometimes the ethical arguments for the prolongation of human life in the face of death-inducing circumstances lose sight of the fact that we are made for death, with the outcome being positive and not negative. We have all met people who were content and peaceful in the face of approaching death. They say that time has run out, and they will be happy when the call comes. That reflects a deeply Christian spirit, which we pray will be ours.

Points to Ponder

Paul's dilemma: life or death
To live is to serve
Waiting for the call

MONDAY OF THE THIRTY-FIRST WEEK IN ORDINARY TIME

Year I

Romans 11:29–36
Psalm 69:30–31, 33–34, 36
Luke 14:12–14

O felix culpa! "O happy fault!" Misfortune can be turned into good. It was through the disobedience of the Jews that the message of salvation went to the Gentiles. The Jews have persisted in their disobedience, even after mercy has been shown to the Gentiles. But mercy is also in store for the Jews. God had allowed the Gentiles at an earlier time to live in disobedience, and now the Jews in order that mercy might be showered upon all. Indeed, the ways of God are shrouded in mystery.

We are all aware of deathbed conversions, of a turning to the Lord only in the terminal phase of life. It is but another example of the mercy of God. For this we should praise God whose love reaches the just and the unjust.

In today's Gospel Christ suggests that the dinner invitation should be extended, not to close relatives and friends, but to the unwanted—the crippled, the lame, and the blind. There is no indication as to whether the invitation will be appreciated or not. The fact is that these are the people with whom God is particularly concerned. His mercy reaches the most unwanted people of the earth.

Points to Ponder

God's mercy for Jew and Gentile
Invitations for the noninvited
Seeking the disenfranchised

Year II

Philippians 2:1–4
Psalm 131:1bcde, 2, 3
Luke 14:12–14

In these few verses from Philippians, Paul underscores the importance of concern for others. We are inclined so often to act out of self-interest and vainglory, when what really matters is to see others as more important than ourselves and their concerns as more important than our own. Why is this such an important part of the Christian ethic? Because this is precisely the way God has dealt with us. If God lived only for himself, our redemption would not have entered the picture. It was because his love for us was so deep that he gave of himself without counting the cost.

The same lesson applies in Jesus' counsel on the dinner invitations. Do not invite the people who are always invited; rather go after those who do not know what it means to be invited. There is no personal gain for the host. It is simply a matter of concern and generosity. That, in a few words, is the heart of Christianity.

It makes one think of Operation Safety Net. A young doctor a prominent hospital in a large city draws on young volunteers to seek out and care for the homeless, the people who live under bridges and simply try to survive from day to day. The organization provides medical attention as well as food and clothing. There is no personal gain for the doctor; he does it simply because it is the right thing to do.

We do not live in a godless age. Examples of this type can be multiplied. They are simply examples of that living for others about which today's scriptures speak. It simply verifies the saying that it is more blessed to give than to receive—and more satisfying.

Points to Ponder

> Acting out of concern for others
> Examples of generous self-giving
> Contributions of time and energy

TUESDAY OF THE THIRTY-FIRST WEEK IN ORDINARY TIME

Year I

> Romans 12:5–16ab
> Psalm 131:1bcde, 2, 3
> Luke 14:15–24

Jesus' parables repeatedly register his disappointment in the poor response of his own people to his announcement of the kingdom's inauguration. In today's account, when told that the dinner was prepared, all the invited guests make excuses for their inability to attend. The enraged host then orders that the outcasts of the community be invited—the poor, the crippled, the blind, and the lame—from the streets and alleys of the town. With that done, there is still room for guests. The servants are then sent to the countryside—the highways and the hedgerows—in order to fill the dining halls. The last two categories include the imperfect Jews from within the town and the Gentiles who are not part of the community.

We are now members of that elect community because of the Jews' default. In Paul's language today, we have become members of his body. Within that body, there are different functions to perform—prophecy, teaching, ministry, to mention a few—all of which are to be exercised with love and concern.

Paul goes on to speak of characteristics that typify the guests at the banquet. Cling to the good and hate what is evil. Honor, zeal, and joy are essential to all that is done. Bless those who hate you, rejoice with the joyful, and weep with the sorrowing. Respect one another and associate with the lowly.

The emphasis on human civility and the domestic virtues is not unwarranted. There are more hurts inflicted through the careless word than we can estimate. They may not be major insults, but they are unworthy of a caring community. We are, after all, grateful guests at the banquet table, and our daily conduct should reflect it.

Points to Ponder

> The acceptance of the Gentiles
> Contributing to the body of Christ
> Respect for others

Year II

> Philippians 2:5–11
> Psalm 22:26b–27, 28–30ab, 30e, 31–32
> Luke 14:15–24

The reading from Philippians today is the celebrated hymn, which in view of its highly structured form seems to have been a hymn of the early church, taken over and slightly adapted by Paul in his letter. The hymn begins on the highest level of the Godhead, as it exhorts Christians to mirror the humility of Jesus in their own lives.

Christ was from time eternal equal to God, but he did not embrace the trappings of divinity, even the title "Lord." Instead he moved in an opposite direction, coming among us in human form as a slave of the Lord. In his humility he embraced full humanity, obedient to death, and (in the only phrase probably added to the hymn by Paul himself) even to death on a cross. Because of this spirit of submission, God has now lifted him on high, with all of creation (heaven, earth, and "under the earth") now bending the knee and confessing him as Lord to the glory of God.

The hymn is one of Christianity's finest and is rich in early church theology. Its recognizes the preexistent Christ, with the acclaiming of his Lordship coming only after his death and resurrection. The salvific character of his death is implied, as well as the universal effects of redemption.

The Gospel today sees all of us as gathered together for the Messianic feast. What this means is understood when we read the Philippians' hymn. We have been bought at a great price!

Points to Ponder

The eternity of Christ
Redemption and the humility of God
The Lordship of Christ

WEDNESDAY OF THE THIRTY-FIRST WEEK IN ORDINARY TIME

Year I

Romans 13:8–10
Psalm 112:1b–2, 4–5, 9
Luke 14:25–33

When Jesus speaks of "hating" family members and one's own life, he is using a typical form of exaggeration in the interests of emphasis. We know well that any form of hatred of others is excluded in Christ's ethic. What is true is that the pain of separation will be part of the disciple's adherence to Jesus. It is as inescapable as is cross bearing. In discipleship one must persevere and stay the course. Therefore, it pays to weigh the likely consequences before undertaking the task. It is much the same as constructing a tower or waging a war. Without preliminary planning, one may easily find oneself unequal to the task of successful completion.

Paul can readily say that love is the fulfillment of the law. Christ himself has placed love as the foremost of the commandments. The commandments of the Decalogue—against, for example, adultery, murder, or theft—are all rooted in love of neighbor. In short, if one places the love of neighbor at the center of one's life, other elements of true Christian living will follow.

It is unfortunate that we attach gravity to many sins but brush violations of charity off as being insignificant. There is no virtue that the scriptures treat that even approximates the importance of love. When we think of the harm that is done and the pain inflicted by unkind speech and action, we realize that such actions carry considerable weight. In building our tower or waging our war, an ongoing and patient assessment is always necessary.

Points to Ponder

> The love of Christ surpasses any human love
> Perseverance to the end
> Love as the fulfillment of the law

Year II

> Philippians 2:12–18
> Psalm 27:1, 4, 13–14
> Luke 14:25–33

The single boast that Paul will have on the "day of Christ" will be the "word of life" that continues to shine forth in the lives of the Philippians. He asks them to be mindful of the fact that it is God who is working out his good pleasure in them. He insists that they be marked with the spirit of charity, acting without grumbling or questioning, even though the world that surrounds them is a crooked and perverse generation.

To undertake the Christian life is a lifetime commitment. Thus, as today's Gospel indicates, it is to be well weighed beforehand. Discipleship means cross bearing; it is something from which the Christian cannot shy away. In our times, for example, people are often faced with the care of an aging parent. As time goes on, the cross becomes heavier and the parent less compliant. Many caregivers continue to bear the cross because they never forget the debt of gratitude owed to parents who were with them through childhood to adulthood. It is this thought that gives them the strength to persevere.

In all of this, Paul calls for the obedience of faith. The Philippians have long been obedient to what he asked, whether he was present or absent.

We have to ask ourselves today whether or not we have that same obedience of faith. We should be grateful if, as the years pass, we are still committed to God's will. Moments of discouragement there have been, but our ingrained sense of gratitude has kept us on course. Persevere to the end!

Points to Ponder

> Let your light show in the world
> Bearing the cross with patience
> The obedience of faith

THURSDAY OF THE THIRTY-FIRST WEEK IN ORDINARY TIME

Year I

> Romans 14:7–12
> Psalm 27:1bcde, 4, 13–14
> Luke 15:1–10

The fifteenth chapter of Luke is rich in setting forth God's concern for the sinner who has strayed from the path. It contains three parables (the lost sheep, the lost coin, and the lost son), the first two of which appear in today's Gospel. It may be a little hard for us to imagine leaving a large flock of sheep in the desert to go in search of one that was lost, or to think of a woman, even one of modest means, who does a thorough house cleaning to find one coin and then holds an open house to celebrate its discovery.

The parables are meant to illustrate God's concern for a single person who has wandered from the truth. With the person's conversion to the Lord, there is not solely human joy but also a happiness that resounds in heaven. Any person involved in pastoral ministry recognizes the joy of conversion. If it occurs through the sacrament of reconciliation, it is evident that a heavy burden as been lifted, and the homecoming is deeply appreciated. The Gospel today tells us that this joy is echoed in heaven.

Whether alive or dead, says Paul today, we belong to the Lord. We shall all be held accountable for our actions. For this reason, there is nothing to be gained by judging others. We will have our own accounting to make when we stand before God. When we read the parables of discovery or forgiveness, we are reminded of how much we are loved. We may have wandered in life, but once back in our Father's house, we may feel confident about the future.

Points to Ponder

Lost and found
Heaven's joy at conversion
Being nonjudgmental

Year II

Philippians 3:3–8a
Psalm 105:2–3, 4–5, 6–7
Luke 15:1–10

If anyone could boast of credentials, it was Paul. Circumcised on the eighth day, he was a member of the tribe of Benjamin, a Pharisee deeply devoted to the law, a persecutor of the church. But now he counts all of that as loss; he has attained the great good of knowing Jesus Christ our Lord. That knowledge of Christ is not merely cerebral; it is a lived experience.

Paul could certainly understand the joy of today's Gospel. In his conversion, the goodness of God had touched him. He was the sheep brought home, the coin that was found. He was first known by the Christians as the one who had persecuted the church, and initially they may not have been convinced of his conversion. He counts everything from his past as loss in view of the great good of knowing the Lord.

Converts to Christianity so often register their deep appreciation for the faith that is now theirs. Unfortunately many of us seem to take it all for granted, something of a birthright inherited from our parents. But the fact is that we are deeply privileged, called out of darkness into God's wondrous love. There are no limits to God's love; nor should there be any to our sense of gratitude.

Points to Ponder

Paul's Jewish credentials
The only reality: to know Christ Jesus
The sheep, the coin, and God's concern

FRIDAY OF THE THIRTY-FIRST WEEK IN ORDINARY TIME

Year I

Romans 14:7–21
Psalm 98:1, 2–3ab, 3cd–4
Luke 16:1–8

Most of us would consider the steward's conduct reprehensible in defrauding his master in order to ingratiate himself with his master's debtors. Even if it may be the case that the steward was simply eliminating his own commission, in accord with what we now know after examining financial transactions of the time, the reader is not advised of such a procedure, and we are left to deal with the story as it stands.

The parable is not intended to deal with every feature of the steward's conduct. The point is that in the face of a crisis he acted decisively to provide for his future. Whether or not his action was morally appropriate is not the point of the parable. The master commends him, not for his honesty but for his ready decisiveness to avoid greater damage.

Would that all were as prudent and ready to act in the interests of the reign of God as was the steward to protect his own interests.

After extending words of counsel to the Romans, Paul defends his action on the basis of the gospel. The only objective Paul has in mind is to bring the Gentile world into obedience to Christ. Whatever is accomplished is done by the Spirit of God. This has carried him from Jerusalem through much of the Greco-Roman world always in the spirit of the gospel.

The Gospel today reminds us that we should be as decisive as was the steward in the interests of God and the gospel. Procrastination usually spells inaction. A laissez-faire attitude does not spell progress. We are engaged in the world's greatest drama as key players, not walk-ons. That calls for enthusiasm and spirit!

Points to Ponder

> The action of the steward
> The response of the master
> Acting for the gospel

Year II

> Phil 3:17—4:1
> Psalm 122:1–2, 3–4ab, 4cd–5
> Luke 16:1–8

Paul reminds his hearers today to be on guard. There are people who are enemies of the cross of Christ. They are lost in selfish and evil concerns, eating and drinking to excess, engaging in sexual misconduct. They are destined for destruction. But we are citizens of the heavenly country, from where we expect our

Savior to return. He will transform our mortality into immortality, conferring on us the glorification that is now his. And what must our posture be? Stand firm in the Lord!

We too live in the midst of what is in many ways an evil generation.

We must avoid being seduced and losing sight of our goal. The Gospel today reminds us of the importance of decisive action in the face of danger. Passivity in the face of danger can easily lead to corruption. The steward reduced the cost of payment to his master in order to be on friendly terms with the debtors.

Financial burdens can weigh heavily in people's lives. Every time that we can extend a helping hand, the burden is lightened. Even if we cannot do a great deal, life is made a bit easier. Money in itself is not "filthy." It becomes that through passivity and greed. Our treasure is above, in a place that is beyond corruption. There we can amass a fortune by using the things of this world for the well-being of others.

Points to Ponder

> Citizens of another realm
> Using the Mammon of iniquity to make friends
> Helping others in financial straits

SATURDAY OF THE THIRTY-FIRST WEEK IN ORDINARY TIME

Year I

> Romans 16:3–9, 16, 22–27
> Psalm 145:2–3, 4–5, 10–11
> Luke 16:9–15

Today's Gospel contains a series of sayings regarding the proper use of material goods. Wealth is characteristically disparaged ("Mammon"), but disciples can use it for worthy purposes, especially helping the needy. Correctness in handling small responsibilities bodes well for similar conduct in dealing with matters of greater importance. One cannot serve both God and "filthy lucre." One's allegiance lies with one or the other. These sayings reflect the very distant relationship between Christianity and commerce. Money making, for whatever good it may serve, is seen as a dangerous engagement. It is difficult, although not impossible, to emerge unscathed.

Paul concludes his letter to Rome with a series of greetings to friends. Some are unknown to us, but Prisca and Aquila have appeared elsewhere. They were Jewish Christians expelled from Rome by Claudius. Paul got to know them in Corinth, and they accompanied him to Ephesus. They were evidently of great service to him. Paul's scribe, Tertius, adds his personal greetings. The apostle prays that they will be strengthened in their faith and the proclamation of the gospel, a gospel destined for the nation that unites Jew and Gentile in the mystery of salvation.

The conclusion to this letter is interesting; it points up the friendships that Paul made in the course of his life as a Christian. He is too often seen as so single-minded and determined that human friendships had little significance. His writings themselves dismiss such a position, as he openly speaks of the love and concern he has for the churches. In his conclusion to Romans, he greets numerous friends. Friendship is one of life's greatest gifts, and Paul centers it all in the Lordship of Jesus.

Points to Ponder

> The proper use of wealth
> The dangers of wealth
> Paul's friends and coworkers

Year II

> Philippians 4:10–19
> Psalm 112:1b–2, 5–6, 8a and 9
> Luke 16:9–15

Today we have an interesting juxtaposition of texts. Jesus in the Gospel speaks of the proper use of material goods, while Paul speaks of the concrete ways in which the Philippians have responded to his needs in a material way. For his part, Paul knows what it means to live in humble circumstances as well as what it means to have abundance. Paul finds himself self-sufficient in either set of circumstances. Christ strengthens and empowers him in any situation, but he is still grateful to the Philippians for being mindful of him. He is happy not so much for himself but for the benefits that will accrue to the community. Now he prays that the riches of Christ will be theirs in abundance.

To use money for a worthy cause is commended by Christ in today's Gospel. In our own times we have seen philanthropists contribute billions of dollars to eradicate disease and poverty in poor parts of the world. This is something that deserves commendation and is wholly in accord with Christian belief. Outsourcing work to poor countries of the world where labor is cheap and employees here find themselves without a job is quite another matter. Is the latter a case of serving God? Or Mammon?

Points to Ponder

> The charity of Philippi
> Examples of generosity with wealth
> Serving Mammon at the expense of people

MONDAY OF THE THIRTY-SECOND WEEK IN ORDINARY TIME

Year I

> Wisdom 1:1–7
> Psalm 139:1b–3, 4–6, 7–8, 9–10
> Luke 17:1–6

Writing in Egypt in the first century before Christ, the author of Wisdom was more than familiar with Greek speculation and the pursuit of philosophical wisdom. He champions wisdom of a different sort, that which is imparted in the Jewish scriptures and offers true enlightenment to the discerning soul. This book is written in Greek and is not part of the Hebrew Bible.

The author argues today that true wisdom never enters where evil dwells. It opposes deceit and injustice. The author's advice to the believer is to seek justice in goodness and integrity of heart. True wisdom is to be found in the revealed will of God; to follow after it will bring true happiness and peace of mind.

The Gospel today realizes that sin will appear with a certain inevitability but predicts dire consequences for the one through whom it arrives. It is a serious and grave offense for one person to lead another into sin. However, where sin does occur and repentance follows, forgiveness should always be granted, even when there are multiple occurrences. Faith alone makes this understandable, but where faith is strong, all things are possible.

It may well be that we do not often understand our faith as true wisdom. It may make little sense to some (a stumbling block to Jews and foolishness to Gentiles); to us who are being saved it is the great wisdom of God.

Points to Ponder

> Wisdom as different from intelligence
> The seriousness of leading another to sin
> Faith makes all things possible

Year II

> Titus 1:1–9
> Psalm 24:1b–2, 3–4ab, 5–6
> Luke 17:1–6

Titus was Paul's emissary of the faith on the island of Crete. The apostle sets forth the criteria for an authentic Christian leader in the community. Any future leader of the community must himself be beyond reproach, only married once, with a believing household, not marred by licentiousness or a spirit of rebellion. Those who are arrogant, aggressive, or greedy should not be considered. An elder in the church should be welcoming, holy, and self-controlled.

It may come as a surprise to some to know that not all leaders in the church are so blessed. An unwelcoming spirit has distanced more than one person from the church. A harsh comment or argumentative spirit is alien to what we profess. There was a woman who lost her husband at an early age. His funeral Mass was scheduled for 10 a.m. on a very snowy morning. The funeral cortege was further delayed by a passing train. The priest waited five minutes and then began the Mass. When the mourners finally arrived, the Mass was half over. The wife of the deceased left the church for many years and only in her later years returned. Sad to say, there have been other similar stories.

Today's Gospel speaks severely of those who would lead others into sin. This can be done in blatant or subtle ways. It is not easy for one to bear oneself always in the best possible form. But it is vitally important, as this morning's reading makes clear, that kindness and approachability be important marks of our faith.

Points to Ponder

> The qualities of a church leader
> Ways of leading others to sin
> Serving with the mind of Christ

TUESDAY OF THE THIRTY-SECOND WEEK IN ORDINARY TIME

Year I

> Wisdom 2:23—3:9
> Psalm 34:2–3, 16–17, 18–19
> Luke 17:7–10

The belief in personal immortality developed late in Hebrew thought. The Book of Wisdom from the first century BC is its clearest expression. God created humans for "incorruption,...the image of his own eternity." For those who have lived a just life, there is great blessing in store. In the time of the final visitation, they will shine brightly and even judge nations. The faithful shall abide with God forever.

Still, the Gospel today reminds us that all of this is gift. We can make no claims on God. Even when we carry out whatever is assigned to us, we have only done what we should. At dinner time, it is the responsibility of the hired servant to prepare and serve the meal, not to sit down and eat with the master. When we have accomplished in life whatever has been assigned, we have only done our duty.

This gives us pause. We are gifted with life and immorality, in addition, a redeeming God and a share in his life. This should be the source of our meditation and reflection. We are not only given a call to holiness; we are given the means to obtain it. In none of this can we say that we have been given our due, for none of it is due to us. Unless we see our calling in the light of gratitude, we will forever miss the point.

Points to Ponder

> Called to be immortal
> Responding to duty with gratitude
> Sunday Mass: a duty or a privilege?

Year II

> Titus 2:1–8, 11–14
> Psalm 37:3–4, 18 and 23, 27 and 29
> Luke 17:7–10

The Letter to Titus lists those domestic virtues that are conducive to a good home life and a strong Christian community. The older people have a special responsibility to reflect dignity and self-control and to be steeped in faith, hope, and endurance. In this way the word of God will not be discredited. The same ideals are to be held before younger men.

The reasoning behind such conduct lies in the order of salvation. The saving grace of God has appeared and has moved us away from godless and worldly ways and to live temperately and devoutly in expectation of our Savior Jesus Christ, who by his gracious will has delivered us from godlessness and immorality and cleansed us for himself, to be a people truly his own.

The Gospel today reminds us that we are doing simply what is expected of us in living a Christian life. It is not as if we had done something extraordinary for which God is rewarding us. No, it has all been done for us, and we receive it all as gift. The faithful servant lives the life of a grateful response to the God who has first loved him.

Points to Ponder

Maintaining a peaceful home
The importance of example
Virtue: a grateful response

WEDNESDAY OF THE THIRTY-SECOND WEEK IN ORDINARY TIME

Year I

Wisdom 6:1–11
Psalm 82:3–4, 6–7
Luke 17:11–19

Today's Gospel strikes at the very heart of the gospel message. To realize what God has done for us is to live a grateful response. The lepers first cry out to Jesus for a cure. He hears them and then tells them to present themselves before the priest. It was required in Israelite society that one who had been afflicted with leprosy or a skin disorder be quarantined and distanced from the community until a priest, after examination, pronounced the person cured. As the lepers leave Jesus' presence, they are cured of their illness. Only one of them returned to Jesus to thank him, and this man was a Samaritan, a member of that heterodox group of people from whom the Jews distanced themselves. Jesus commends the man's faith and sends him on his way.

The reading from Wisdom today is addressed to royalty and those who hold civil authority. They are told very clearly that they have no "blank check" but will be held to a serious account of the way they exercise authority. If they disregard the rule of law and the will of God, judgment will come quickly. Mercy will not be extended in the same way it is for the lowly person; those who are powerful will be put to the test. The authorities should be steeped in the law and observant of the holy precepts. If they do so, they will be respected and honored.

Violations of the principles of today's readings are met frequently enough in the course of our lives. We know people whose generosity and kindness have been repaid unkindly.

We have also seen people fall from great heights because they did not observe the very law that they were to uphold. It all proves the saying that virtue is its own reward. But above all, we should turn frequently to the prayer of thanksgiving. Like the leper, we too have been cured—and more than once—because of a forgiving and loving God.

Points to Ponder

> The pain of ingratitude
> Conscience and authority
> The prayer of thanksgiving

Year II

> Titus 3:1–7
> Psalm 23:1b–3a, 3bc–4, 5, 6
> Luke 17:11–19

Our reading from Titus today appears in part in our Christmas liturgy as a splendid expression of what the incarnation means. The Christians are advised to be submissive to civil authority and to be open to worthwhile enterprises. They are to be good citizens, always respectful of the rights of others and not given over to malicious or deceitful conduct. They are to remember that at a given time the kindness and love of God appeared in Christ our Savior. Not because of our righteousness, but solely because of his mercy, we have been saved through baptism and the gift of the Holy Spirit that has been poured out upon us.

Seen in the light of the Titus reading, the story of the lepers takes on even greater significance. The leper had no claim on Jesus.

It is interesting to see how favorably Samaritans are viewed in the Lucan Gospel. The early church evidently made considerable inroads among this "separate" people, and in Jesus' view they appear in a positive light. As in the epistle, the importance of gratitude takes on particular importance. Like the leper, we too have been favored far beyond anything deserved. And how often do we return thanks to the giver?

There is a thought in the Gospel also against excluding any people from our concern for reasons of nationality, ethnicity, or race. The work of Jesus centered on breaking down barriers, not constructing them. We certainly do not want to be Christians with a bias or prejudice. There is no people excluded from God's love.

Points to Ponder

Called because of God's mercy
The prayer of gratitude
The evil of bias or prejudice

THURSDAY OF THE THIRTY-SECOND WEEK IN ORDINARY TIME

Year I

Wisdom 7:22b–8:1
Psalm 119:89, 90, 91, 130, 135, 175
Luke 17:20–25

Jesus lived in a period of intense end-time expectation, with popular hope centered on the coming of the kingdom of God and the messiah. In his response to the Pharisees in today's Gospel, Jesus indicates that their anticipation that the kingdom of God will come at a specific point in the future is misplaced. Jesus' works and his teaching clearly indicate that the kingdom is already present in their midst. The closing verses may well have been directed to his own followers, who were anxious to see the Son of Man in his glory. That day will come, and Christ's glory will be fully evident. But first he must follow the path of suffering.

Wisdom in today's first reading is found primarily in God but also in the marvels of creation. Wisdom is pure and unsullied; no form of corruption is found in her. She enters the souls of humans and produces friends of God. Wisdom in the human order is the proper guiding of one's life in accordance with God's will. For the Jew, this was the law; for the Christian wisdom is the Spirit of Jesus himself.

Our belief is centered in the fact that the kingdom in its initial stage is present in our life. Baptism, the Eucharist, the scriptures are our expressions of the kingdom. And where do we find wisdom? In our formation in the faith. Sad to say, many of our young people today are instructed for the sacraments and nothing more. But to learn the message of Jesus and to live his life requires a deepening of our faith and a willingness to live a life in conformity with that wisdom that he imparts.

Points to Ponder

> The meaning of true wisdom
> The presence of the kingdom
> Growth in our understanding of the faith

Year II

> Philemon 7–20
> Psalm 146:7, 8–9a, 9bc–10
> Luke 17:20–25

Paul's Letter to Philemon is only one chapter in length. And its message is simple and direct. It concerns a former slave of Philemon, one Onesimus, who had become a Christian under Paul's guidance during his first Roman imprisonment. Philemon is now about to send Onesimus back to his master, whom he asks to receive his former slave as a brother in Christ. Paul speaks of the great assistance Onesimus had given him and how he would like to retain him but would not act without Philemon's concurrence. If Onesimus is guilty of any injustice or has debts to pay, Paul indicates that he himself will take care of reimbursement.

The short letter is one of affection and personal concern and gives us insight into another side of Paul's character.

His turning to Christ produced a deep sense of personhood and concern in Paul. In the Gospel today, Jesus speaks of the kingdom's presence among us. It was certainly present in the life and activity of Paul, the man who is frequently referred to as Christianity's second founder. He did not invent the message, but his life certainly confirmed it. It is important to remember that his writings antedate the four Gospels, and thus he is our first and earliest witness to the risen Christ. The letter to Philemon gives us insight into the warmth of his friendship, his very human concern for a fellow Christian no longer a slave but a brother.

Points to Ponder

Paul and Onesimus
The Bible and human friendship
Christian concern for others in need

FRIDAY OF THE THIRTY-SECOND WEEK IN ORDINARY TIME

Year I

Wisdom 13:1–9
Psalm 19:2–3, 4–5ab
Luke 17:26–37

The author of Wisdom lived in a highly intellectual and philosophical milieu. Alexandria in Egypt was the Athens of the East. Philosophers then, like scientists today, studied the natural world around them. In today's reading, the author of Wisdom argues that God is responsible for the material universe and all the wonders of nature. The power and beauty of the cosmos point to the God who is their Creator. But in their fascination with the visible realities of creation, humans have been distracted from discerning more about the One who is responsible for bringing the natural world into being. It is in this Creator God that we should seek ultimate truth.

The Pharisees in today's Gospel raise questions about the final days: How will the advent of those days be known? Christ's answer is that it will be sudden and unexpected, much like the days of the destruction in the time of Noah and the time of Sodom. But when those days come, one will either be prepared to meet them or not.

Most Christians today do not spend much time on questions of the "end of days" because they don't imagine they will be here to see them. There are some evangelical Christians who argue strongly that the final days are upon us. Some would argue that Palestine in its entirety must be returned to the Jews. For only when the land is theirs will the Lord return and the end of the world be here.

All of us have experienced at some point the fragility of our being. Tragic accidents, the wanton taking of life, the death of a young person. These are reminders of our real destiny and an encouragement to live each day as if it were our last. To contemplate beauty in the light of God himself, to see power in the light of the deity, the world about us as an expression of his goodness. "The heavens are telling the glory of God," says the psalmist, and we must be alert to that voice.

Points to Ponder

Philosophy and the search for God
The fragility of human life
Living each day consistently

Year II

2 John 4–9
Psalm 119:1, 2, 10, 11, 17, 18
Luke 17:26–37

Heterodoxy has affected the community to which the Second Letter of John is written. The author begins by encouraging those who continue to walk in the truth, observing the primary commandment of love. More disturbing, however, is the fact that there are some in the Christian community who are claiming that Christ did not really come as a man. This false idea may have been from the Gnostics or some group allied with them who saw anything material, including the human body, as evil. Their teaching, says the author, is clearly spurious. Many may call themselves progressive, but they have separated themselves from the truth and from God.

By the time of the Johannine literature, the belief in the early return of Christ had begun to recede. When there was a departure from the authentic teaching, this was more to the forefront. The community must retain its unity, that oneness for which Christ prayed in John's Gospel before he died.

What is common to today's first and second readings is a spirit of alertness. The Lord may call us at any time, and the community may become divided over particular issues. We must be seriously attentive to the word of God and conscious of the importance of retaining the unity of the community of faith.

Points to Ponder

Belief in the incarnation
Love: the great Christian witness
The acceptance of God's word

SATURDAY OF THE THIRTY-SECOND WEEK IN ORDINARY TIME

Year I

Wisdom 18:14–16; 19:6–9
Psalm 105:2–3, 36–37, 42–43
Luke 18:1–8

Wisdom was evident in the exodus of the Israelites from Egypt. Today's reading speaks of it in highly poetic terms. Deliverance was accomplished by God's word, which served as the conduit of his will.

It brought death to the Egyptians. Creation itself was made responsive to the needs of the fleeing Israelites; the Red Sea became a road to freedom. The now empowered people saw the hand of God and praised him for their deliverance.

The Gospel today encourages ceaseless prayer to God. The judge in the parable fears neither God nor man. He is repeatedly asked to render a judgment favorable to a persistent widow. He is not termed a just judge, and he grants her request only because she importunes him. Will not God, who is a just judge, act in favor of his chosen ones even more readily? Therefore, we are to continue in prayer. But the story ends on a questioning note. Will there still be faith on the earth when the Son of Man appears?

In the face of all that God has done on our behalf, we would like to believe that faith will perdure. Luke addresses the question because of a growing uncertainty in the community resulting from the delay in the Lord's return. The truth is, however, that faith does not always retain its sharp edge. Despite all the wonders that Israel experienced, their betrayal of God brought havoc upon them through the centuries. Persistent prayer is a sign of faith. We pray that we shall persevere and not grow weary.

Points to Ponder

>The exodus experience and Israelite faith
>Perseverance in prayer
>The prayer of petition

Year II

>3 John 5–8
>Psalm 112:1–2, 3–4, 5–6
>Luke 18:1–8

The author of this letter commends the disciple Gaius for his kindness and consideration to missionaries, especially those who are strangers. These Christians were preaching to pagan peoples from whom they accepted no payment. They bring Christ to a world that does not know him, and in supporting them the community of Gaius becomes "co-workers with the truth."

There are circumstances in life that prohibit an active engagement in ministry: age, illness, or some other situation. But there are always ways of lending support, especially providing financial means for others to continue their ministry. This makes one a coworker in what is being done and is seen as valuable in the ministry.

And the Gospel reminds us that prayer is always a valued form of assistance. Do we always realize how often someone asks for our prayers?

We invariably give our consent. But that means that we have a responsibility to carry through on the request and should not take it lightly. Mutual prayer is an integral part of the body of Christ, encouraged frequently in the scriptures. We should make a conscious effort to remember those who have asked for our prayers.

Points to Ponder

A missionary spirit
Assisting other Christians in their efforts
Remembrance at prayer

MONDAY OF THE THIRTY-THIRD WEEK IN ORDINARY TIME

Year I

1 Maccabees 1:10–15, 41–43, 54–57, 62–63
Psalm 119:53, 61, 134, 150, 155, 158
Luke 18: 35–43

This week we begin a series of readings from the Books of Maccabees. These books recount events from the period of Greek domination of Palestine. The heroism of the Maccabees resulted in a limited and short-lived period of freedom for the Israelites. However, it was a period in which the faith of the Jewish people was put to a very severe test. This was especially true during the reign of Antiochus Epiphanes in the second century BC.

Today's reading recounts some of the blasphemies inflicted upon the Jews by Antiochus. It was during his reign that the gymnasium, a purely pagan invention for athletics and entertainment, was introduced to Jewish culture. It helped to launch a period of serious immorality in the country. He further ordered that his own pagan religion should be the official cult. His order was accepted by the Gentiles and "many even from Israel." His greatest blasphemy was the construction of an altar to the Greek god Zeus within the Lord's temple ("a desolation of sacrilege"). Roadside altars to pagan gods were constructed throughout the country. Scrolls of the Jewish law were destroyed, and many devout Jews were put to death. The period of Antiochus proved to be one of the saddest in the history of the Hebrew nation.

Today's Gospel is of a very different cut. The blind man on the Jericho road cries out to Jesus for mercy. When silenced by the people, he cries out even louder. Jesus calls him and inquires about his request. It is his sight that he wants, and due to his great faith, he is healed. He sets about to follow Jesus.

There is no shortage of "cultural abominations" surrounding us today. Many have been blinded to the presence of God in our midst. Along with the Jericho blind man, in our very troubled times, we pray that we may continue to see.

Points to Ponder

Pagan attempts to eradicate Hebrew faith
Spiritual blindness
The compassion of Jesus

Year II

Revelation 1:1–4; 2:1–5
Psalm 1:1–2, 3, 4 and 6
Luke 18:35–43

This week we have a series of readings from the Book of Revelation. It comes to us from the end of the first century, during the persecution of the emperor Domitian (81–96 AD). We know little about the author other than his name. He is referred to as John of Patmos or John the Seer. He is distinguished from the apostles and cites nothing from the life of Jesus.

The book is famous for its symbolism. It looks forward to the imminent end–time and speaks of it in highly symbolic terms, most of which are derived from the Old Testament. Initially he receives a revealed message from the Lord directed to seven churches in Asia Minor. The churches are entrusted to seven angels, who are the recipients of the Seer's letters.

Christ is the speaker in the letters; he walks among the seven gold lampstands (the churches) as he sends his message. To the church of Ephesus he says much that is congratulatory. Its works are commendable; it excludes the wicked; its perseverance is more than evident. However, it appears that its initial zeal has diminished. It has fallen into serious error and is called to repentance. It must return to its original fervor.

The compassionate Christ in the Gospel goes out of his way to cure the persistent blind man. In gratitude the man follows Jesus.

Points to Ponder

> Christian understanding of the end–time
> The loss of initial fervor
> The cry of the blind man for mercy

TUESDAY OF THE THIRTY-THIRD WEEK IN ORDINARY TIME

Year I

> 2 Maccabees 6:18–31
> Psalm 3:2–3, 4–5, 6–7
> Luke 19:1–10

God's will or human respect? Both readings today speak of the primacy of God's will over the reaction of human beings. The wealthy Jewish tax collector Zacchaeus was anxious to see Jesus and so scurried up a sycamore tree. A Christian writer once remarked that there is no indication in the Gospels that Jesus ever laughed, but he probably did when he saw Zacchaeus up the tree.

Zacchaeus cared little about people's reaction and even hosted Christ at his home. And that day salvation came to his house.

Eleazar, an aging scribe, is set forth as an example of religious integrity in the first reading. His contemporaries were being forced to eat pork, in violation of Jewish practice. Friends of long standing urge him to bring his own meat; the onlookers would think he was eating pork. This then would save his life. Eleazar refuses to bend to such a ruse. Religious integrity meant more to him. He then refused to eat the meat and went to his death with a clear conscience.

It often happens that we bow to human respect rather than the demands of conscience. A person holding a very responsible position was once asked to pad his expense account to cover over illicit expenses incurred by other executives. He refused and was subsequently dropped as an employee. The decision was painful, but conscience triumphed over expediency. It is tempting to put principle aside and bow to pressure.

It is in such moments of truth that we learn where our principles really are.

Points to Ponder

> Zacchaeus and lack of concern for convention
> Eleazar, a striking example of integrity
> Avoiding compromises of principle

Year II

> Revelation 3:1–6, 14–22
> Psalm 15:2–3a, 3bc–4ab, 5
> Luke 19:1–10

Today's Revelation reading draws on the letter to the churches at Sardis and Laodicea. Conditions in Sardis are not at all positive. Its reputation for being alive in God is not accurate. In fact, it is quite dead. Thus, the call is to wake up and repent. This people does not know at what hour the Lord will come; therefore, alertness and sorrow for past sins is appropriate. In Laodicea, the picture is no brighter. The response there is simply lukewarm, neither hot nor cold. Affluence was Laodicea's downfall. The people believed they had everything and lacked for nothing. They needed to be clothed in the Spirit, with their shameful nakedness covered.

If Christ is listened to, his voice heard and the door opened, Christ will enter and dine with his host. With the proper response, the person will be enthroned, sharing in the victory of Christ himself.

This last was the lot of Zacchaeus in today's Gospel. Jesus recognizes his good will in climbing the sycamore and invites himself to dinner at the tax collector's home. When Zacchaeus indicates his will to correct his life and share his wealth with the poor, he is told that salvation has come to his house.

Points to Ponder

Lukewarmness in the faith
Zacchaeus's willingness to correct his life
Christ reproves and chastises those whom he loves

WEDNESDAY OF THE THIRTY-THIRD WEEK IN ORDINARY TIME

Year I

2 Maccabees 7:1, 20–31
Psalm 17:1bcd, 5–6, 8b and 15
Luke 19:11–28

Fidelity to God at all cost. An enterprising spirit in the reign of Christ. Our two readings today illustrate both of these ideas. The celebrated mother of seven sons in Maccabees stands at the center of this account of torture and death. At issue was whether or not they could be forced by the king to eat pork. All of the sons go to their death rather than violate God's law. In the case of the seventh son, the king promises him a lofty position, but, failing to get a favorable response, he asks the mother to intercede with her son. She feigns persuasion but actually encourages her son to remain steadfast. She argues that he will soon be with his Creator.

He too goes to his death. The account comes from the Hellenistic period, when defections among the Israelites were common.

In the Lucan parable, the utilization of gifts for the reign of Christ is underscored. The nobleman who went to a distant country to obtain his kingship may reflect a conflict over Herodian succession in Judea, or it may simply be the return of Christ to the Father after his death and resurrection. Each of the three servants is entrusted with a set amount of money to be used in trade. Upon his return, two of the servants report the financial gain they have made and are duly rewarded. The third, fearful of his master, simply preserved the single coin and done nothing with it. His conduct merits only condemnation.

Human respect often tempts us to bypass the dictates of the Lord in the interest of some human gain. But we must be steadfast. Faith is a matter of conviction, and conviction will always be tested.

To compromise our beliefs in order to achieve some human gain is an act of betrayal. The young son of the widow is prepared to die rather than violate the law of God. We are not tested to that extent. But to put God in second place even for lesser reasons is a serious failure. Similarly, the use of our gifts and talents in the interests of the kingdom is only right and just. Do I extend myself in the interests of the Christian community? Or am I completely absorbed in earthly concerns?

Points to Ponder

> Examples of betrayal of belief
> In what ministries of my parish am I involved?
> Are my energies in serving Mammon rather than God?

Year II

> Revelation 4:1–11
> Psalm 150:1b–2, 3–4, 5–6
> Luke 19:11–28

At this point in Revelation, the heavenly court becomes visible to the Seer. The throne becomes visible but there is no description of the one seated upon it. The occupant is God himself, who as Spirit, is not seen or described. What is visible is his crown, the symbol of royal authority. On twenty-four surrounding thrones are seated the twenty-four elders, representing the twelve tribes of Israel and the twelve apostles (thus embracing both covenants). Their crowns represent their heavenly royalty and the white garments, their fidelity. The seven torches represent the seven spirits of God, an extension of God himself who serve as his messengers.

The four living creatures draw on the imagery of Ezekiel 1. The images connected with each (lion, ox, eagle, and man) represent God's supremacy over all creation. The creatures are covered with eyes, front and back, representing God's oversight over all creation. A Jewish midrash on the four creatures tells us that "man is exalted among creatures; the eagle among birds, the ox among domestic animal, the lion among wild beasts; all of them have received dominion. Unceasingly they sing the praises of the Lord almighty, as do the twenty-four elders.

The heavenly court is taken up completely with the praise of God; whereas the earthly dimension of God's reign is concerned with the building up of the kingdom. This is the point of today's Gospel. God's work in this world is largely that of human agents. There is a distinctive role that each of us has to play. We cannot take our coin, wrap it up, and save it for a rainy day.

Points to Ponder

> Symbols that speak of heaven
> Liturgy: the earthly praise of God
> Extending the reign of God

THURSDAY OF THE THIRTY-THIRD WEEK IN ORDINARY TIME

Year I

> 1 Maccabees 2:15–29
> Psalm 50:1b–2, 5–6, 14–15
> Luke 19:41–44

The religious zeal of the Maccabees accounts for the narrative of their accomplishments found in the biblical books that carry their name. The pagan sacrifices offered in the city of Modein illustrate well the strong religious convictions of Matathias and his sons. They refuse to participate in the pagan rites. In reaction to this idolatry, Matathias kills a compromising Jew as well as the king's messenger. Then he and his sons flee into the mountainous country.

Many people in our time resent acts of killing such as those inflicted by Matathias and his sons. That is because the Christian conscience has matured in appreciation of nonviolence. This is the teaching of Jesus, but it must be remembered that Old Testament personalities did not enjoy that insight and believed that perpetrators of evil deserved the dire fruits of their action. Our opposition to violence arises from the response of Jesus, as well as the extent of war and killing in our own age.

Jerusalem, the holy city, was close to Jesus' heart, but it failed to recognize the time of its visitation. Jesus therefore predicts its end, which will come about in a few short decades. Religious privilege is no excuse for moral failure. From those to whom much has been given, much will be asked. As we cherish our faith, let us never take it for granted.

Points to Ponder

> The faith conviction of the Maccabees
> Violence and the Christian conscience
> Being responsive to God's will

Year II

> Revelation 5:1–10
> Psalm 149:1b–2, 3–4, 5–6a and 9b
> Luke 19:41–44

It is the Lamb in glory who stands at the center of today's heavenly apparition. The scroll that has been definitively sealed contains the plan of God for the future, but no one is found on the scene who is capable of opening the seals. This is reserved for

Christ alone, the "Lion...of Judah" and "the Root of David." The lamb image draws on the Passover lamb from the Book of Exodus. When the Lamb appears, he is superimposed upon the one seated on the throne, indicating the divinity of his nature. His seven eyes point to wisdom, his seven horns to power. As the Lamb receives the scroll from the throne, the elders and the four living creatures sing his praises.

The lamb that was slain continues to bear the evidence of his passion. By his blood he has purchased people of every nation for God. Members of Christ constitute royalty (a kingdom) and a worshiping community (priesthood).

In the Gospel today, Jerusalem, for centuries the dwelling place of God, is the object of Christ's lament. She failed to recognize her Lord and is destined for destruction. This contrasts sharply with the kingdom of the Lamb, where access is granted to those who accept him and believe. We are indeed a privileged people, the people for whom the Lamb was slain.

Points to Ponder

> The Lamb slain for us
> In what sense are we all priests?
> Jerusalem's lack of response

FRIDAY OF THE THIRTY-THIRD WEEK IN ORDINARY TIME

Year I

> 1 Maccabees 4:36–37, 52–59
> 1 Chronicles 29:10bcd, 11abc, 11d–12a, 12bcd
> Luke 19:45–48

Our first reading today recounts the rededication of the temple by Judas and his brothers, recalled today in the Jewish feast of Hanukkah. The temple had been desecrated with the blasphemies of Antiochus Epiphanes. Judas and his company constructed the altar of burnt sacrifices and offered sacrifice there according to the precepts of the law. On the anniversary date of defilement, rededication took place, with the participation of musicians as well as many public worshipers. For eight days following the dedication, the feast and work on the temple continued. It was decided that the feast should be solemnly celebrated each year to commemorate the end of the period of persecution and blasphemy.

Jesus shows his respect for the temple in today's Gospel with the ejection of vendors from the temple area. What had begun as a convenient space for visitors from other parts of the country to buy the necessities for the sacrifices that they were to offer had become a place of commerce.

The action is also an implicit Lucan acknowledgement that God does not dwell in houses made by human hands (Acts 7:1–53).

Christianity has always had churches of particular reverence, but never a single place of distinct, or obligatory, worship. The reason for this is clear from the Gospels. The risen Jesus is the locus of sacred worship; he is the unique tabernacle of the new dispensation. In addition, he now shares the Spirit with his followers, with the result that they too become temples of God. Or with the Johannine Jesus, we worship God not on Mount Gerizim nor in Jerusalem but in spirit and truth.

Points to Ponder

> The temple's importance in Israelite religion
> The temple of the new covenant
> Christian worship of God

Year II

> Revelation 10:8–11
> Psalm 119:14, 24, 72, 103, 111, 131
> Luke 19:45–48

John the Seer is told to go to the angel whose power extends to sea and to land and receive from him the small scroll. He does so and is told to take the scroll and eat it. He is then told that it will be sweet of taste but will turn sour in his stomach. This he does, and the results are those predicted.

As revelation, and therefore a message from God, the taste is sweet; but the message is one of destruction and devastation and therefore is sour in the stomach. But there are times when the word becomes the stab of conscience. It points out all too clearly where we fail or fall short. Then the word is sour. But medicine often has a sour taste. If scripture at times points out our weakness, let us take its message to heart. It is intended for our good.

Jesus' action in the temple in today's Gospel is not directed against use (sacrifice) but rather abuse. The legitimate sale of goods for sacrifice had resulted in commercial abuse, and Jesus moves against the vendors.

Moderation in the use of this world's goods is wholly in keeping with God's plan. When moderation becomes excess, moral equilibrium is lost and we become victimized.

Points to Ponder

God's revelation as "sweet in your mouth"
Moments in which the message is sour
Reverence in church

SATURDAY OF THE THIRTY-THIRD WEEK IN ORDINARY TIME

Year I

1 Maccabees 6:1–13
Psalm 9:2–3, 4 and 6, 16 and 19
Luke 20:27–40

King Antiochus lies dying with more than his share of regrets. His attempt to take the city of Elymais in Persia, with its reputed wealth, was unsuccessful when the forewarned populace rose up against him. While in Persia he learns of the Jewish revolt in Judah and their success in putting down his own forces. Stricken with fear and illness, he realizes that he is about to die. He regrets the havoc and sacrilege he caused in Judah. Now he must die in bitter grief in a foreign land.

The Jewish Sadducees did not believe in the resurrection of the dead. To test Jesus, they present him with a hypothesis that borders on the absurd. In Jewish practice, if a man died without offspring, his brother was to take his wife and raise up descendants for his brother. The case is one of seven brothers, all of whom die before a child is conceived. Finally the wife dies. Whose wife will she be at the resurrection? Jesus is not to be dawn into such casuistry. The life beyond, he insists, is of a completely different nature where marriage will no longer obtain but life will continue. Indeed God is invoked as the God of Abraham, Isaac, and Jacob. All point to the continued life of the patriarchs. Some of his opponents are impressed with his answer.

Antiochus was a man for whom we have little sympathy. But as he approaches death, he has deep remorse. That in itself is a sign of his moral posture. The truth is that many lives take unusual twists and turns. All of which means that we are never in a position to judge. Antiochus was a pagan military monarch who never had the moral compass that we possess. The Gospel reminds us that God's realm is much broader than our own. When it comes to anyone's final destiny, we can do no better than leave it in the hands of God.

Points to Ponder

> The remorse of Antiochus
> Marriage as a human institution
> Judgment is the Lord's

Year II

> Revelation 11:4–12
> Psalm 144:1, 2, 9–10
> Luke 20:27–40

The two witnesses of this passage are symbolically referred to as olive trees and lampstands, imagery drawn from the Book of Zechariah. Rather than being identified with any concrete individuals, they are best seen as sources of life and light before God. In the spirit of the prophets of old, they have the power to close the sky or to change water into blood. A period of desolation comes upon them with the emergence of the great beast, the symbol of evil, here synonymous with pagan Rome. The beast succeeds in conquering and killing the prophets, whose corpses are left exposed in the city of evil for three and a half days. The prophets are then restored to life and called to the heavenly realm.

The Sadducees in today's Gospel are guilty of too literal an interpretation of the scriptures. To understand the Book of Revelation we have to capture and interpret biblical symbols. What is clear from today's reading is that evil will have its day, but good will eventually triumph. The prophetic voice may be silenced for a while, but truth will eventually win out. We should never be discouraged to the extent that evil is seen as victorious. The scriptures consistently assure us that Christ will have the final word.

Points to Ponder

> Lampstands and olive trees: light and life
> The temporary triumph of evil
> The final victory: "Come up here!"

MONDAY OF THE THIRTY-FOURTH WEEK IN ORDINARY TIME

Year I

> Daniel 1:1–6, 8–20
> Psalm 3:52, 53, 54, 55, 56
> Luke 21:1–4

Two messages appear clearly in today's readings. Yahweh will triumph in spite of all the odds, and what is done with true personal sacrifice is pleasing to God. When Nebuchadnezzar sacked Jerusalem, he left the city in ruins and deported a large part of the population. In the Book of Daniel, written some three hundred years after the events it describes, the young Daniel, ever faithful to his Hebrew faith, is protected and rewarded by God for his unwavering conviction. Refusing to eat the food offered by the king and living on a vegetarian diet, Daniel and his three companions emerge healthier and more robust than the other young men who ate from the king's table.

Fidelity to religious principle is essential. Compromising on what we know is right is demoralizing from a human point of view. It is like the story of the man who, in his poverty, had to live on rice alone. A prosperous friend insisted that, if the man would learn to flatter the king, he would not have to live on rice. To which the poor man replied, "And if you would learn to like rice, you would not have to flatter the king."

For some people the easiest way to extend charity is to write a check. It is painless and unquestionably does good. But for others, financial means are minimal, and a financial offering represents a true sacrifice. Such was the case with the poor widow in today's Gospel. And Jesus goes out of his way to commend her charity, for what she offered represented true deprivation.

Points to Ponder

The strength that accompanies conviction
The giving that really hurts
Being satisfied with our state in life

Year II

Revelation 14:1–3, 4b–5
Psalm 24:1bc–2, 3–4ab, 5–6
Luke 21:1–4

The symbolic number of those who are saved is 144,000 (a multiple of twelve). They are adherents of both Christ and the Father. A new hymn is being sung in this heavenly setting, but only the followers of the Lamb are able to learn it. As true disciples, they follow the Lamb wherever he goes. This picture of blessedness precedes the account of the devastation that is to be inflicted subsequently.

As disciples of Christ, we are numbered among the elect today.

But do we follow the Lamb wherever he goes? There are certainly complex issues today for which there is no simple solution. But the basic truths that make us Christian are well known to us, and we must hold to them.

In today's Gospel story of the poor widow, we are given a clear teaching of what discipleship means. To have little and still find room for generosity is at the heart of our faith. Being a Christian certainly means more than simply avoiding serious sin. We must actively live out the teachings of the Sermon on the Mount.

Points to Ponder

Following the Lamb
Sacrificial giving
Living the Sermon on the Mount

TUESDAY OF THE THIRTY-FOURTH WEEK IN ORDINARY TIME

Year I

Daniel 2:31–45
Daniel 3:57, 58, 59, 60, 61
Luke 21:5–11

Many of the accounts in Daniel are legendary in character. The book comes to us from the time of Antiochus Epiphanes' reign (167–164 BC), even though the literary setting is the time of Nebuchadnezzar in the sixth century. Daniel interprets the vision of Nebuchadnezzar in terms of the kingdoms that extended from his time down to the time of the Hellenists: Babylon (gold), the Medes (silver), the Persian (bronze), and the Hellenists (iron). The last kingdom was divided between the Ptolemies and the Seleucids. The latter were persecuting the Jews at the time of the book's composition. The stone hewn from the mountain is the messianic kingdom; it will see the other kingdoms crumble and will be the only one to endure.

In the Gospel, Jesus speaks of other apocalyptic moments: the destruction of the temple and the coming of the kingdom. The former has already taken place when Luke's Gospel is written. Jesus does not specify the time of the final era and the consummation of all things. There will be wars and upheaval before the final time, as well as signs from the heavens. Christians must be ever alert.

The one clear message from today's readings is that better days are coming. As Christians we cannot live with a depressed spirit. The universe ultimately belongs to God, and while we may become impatient with his enduring patience, we have to believe that the final word will be his. We are often disturbed by the extent to which people are made to suffer and die at the hands of evil perpetrators. God's gift of free will can sometimes lead to dreadful consequences. Freedom often takes a frightful toll. But what the scriptures make very clear is that the end of history rests in God's hands.

Points to Ponder

> Daniel's prophecy: after the fact
> The uncertainty of the end-time
> God and the end of history

Year II

> Revelation 14:14–19
> Psalm 96:10, 11–12, 13
> Luke 21:5–11

The end-time is very much evident in this last week of Ordinary Time. In the vision of Revelation, the crowned Christ appears as the victor, but, bearing the sickle, he is also the judge. In his role as harvester, Christ is assisted by three angels, one of whom carries a sharp sickle. The angel with the sickle is ordered to harvest the ripe grapes. But the grapes harvested are thrown into the wine press of God's wrath. This moment before the end is clearly a time of judgment.

Judgment was also the lot of Jerusalem, which had not recognized the time of its visitation. Despite all its splendor, the temple was razed and not a stone was left upon a stone. It had all the features of an end-time experience, but Christ assures his listeners that more devastation is still to come.

We have our apocalypticists today, who are convinced that the end is approaching. Many of us are not that sure. But we are called to live our lives as if each day were the last. How often Paul issues the alert and tells us to wake from sleep. If we live a faith-filled life, we have no reason to fear. We affirm God's future in our liturgy: "Christ will come again." We say it, not in fear, but with trust and confidence.

Points to Ponder

The final harvest
The wine press of God's fury
The destruction of the temple; a Jewish turning point

WEDNESDAY OF THE THIRTY-FOURTH WEEK IN ORDINARY TIME

Year I

Daniel 5:1–6, 13–14, 16–17, 23–28
Daniel 3:62, 63, 64, 65, 66, 67
Luke 21:12–19

If you ever wondered where the expression "the handwriting on the wall" comes from, today you will have your answer. It all goes back to King Belshazzar's feast. After the wine had flowed much too freely and the drinking vessels were part of the plunder from the Jerusalem temple, the king sees a hand appear and begin to write on the wall. The Aramaic words were only three in number and were related to weights and monetary values. *Mene. Tekel. Peres.* Daniel's fame as a diviner makes him the likely choice to decode the message. *Mene* (to number); *Tekel* (to weigh), *Peres* (to divide). The news was not good for the king. God had numbered his days; he had been weighed on the scales and found wanting; his kingdom was about to be divided.

The mighty kingdom of Babylon was about to see its demise. Historically it was the Persians who overcame them; for the Hebrews it was the hand of God. Repeatedly in history, the story of the mighty who have fallen has been repeated. One would hope that the lesson has been learned by now. Nothing in history has a lasting character. The empires that lasted until the nineteenth century have passed from the scene.

The Gospel today throws into bold relief the One who is in command of history. Jesus today tells his followers that they will be persecuted for their belief, handed over to kings and governors, sometimes by members of their own family. They are not to worry about their defense; their wisdom will come from God. They will be saved though perseverance. In short, things may seem to be out of hand, but God is very much in control.

Points to Ponder

> The danger of being a superpower
> Rejection for the cause of Christ
> The importance of perseverance

Year II

> Revelation 15:1–4
> Psalm 98:1, 2–3ab, 7–8, 9
> Luke 21:12–19

There is in the Revelation vision today the preannouncement of the last tribulation, the seven last plagues. But first is the vision of the saved, those who had triumphed over the beast and won deliverance. They are standing on the sea of glass, the transparent waters typical of the heavenly realm. They are said to sing the song of Moses (Exod 15). It does not draw explicitly on the Exodus song, but it does combine themes from a number of hymns, forming an Old Testament collage that illustrates God's deliverance.

It is important to remember that many New Testament writings were written in the midst of early church persecution. What they show is an unquestionable faith in the power of Christ. The Gospel today speaks of the persecution that the early disciples faced. It speaks of a betrayal by others, even members of one's family. But perseverance will be rewarded.

This is all summed up in the psalm of the day. We are to rejoice unceasingly before God, "for he is coming to judge the earth."

Points to Ponder

No triumph without suffering
The meaning of "fear of the Lord"
Inspired by God to defend the faith

THURSDAY OF THE THIRTY-FOURTH WEEK IN ORDINARY TIME

Year I

Daniel 6: 12–28
Daniel 3:68, 69, 70, 71, 72, 73, 74
Luke 21:20–28

Today's first reading contains what is perhaps the most famous of the Daniel stories, his consignment to the lions' den. However, it is a tale fraught with historical difficulties. There is no Darius the Mede known to secular history. The Persians conquered the Medes, and Cyrus was the ruler who took both the Medes and the Babylonians. The character of Darius in this chapter is perhaps modeled on Darius the Persian of the sixth century.

The apocalyptic view of the author of Daniel repeatedly sees four successive kingdoms: Babylonians, Medes, Persians, and Greeks, all of which play a part in his end-time worldview.

Ignoring the king's mandate that no god is to be invoked by any citizen for thirty days, with all petitions being addressed to the king, Daniel ignores the decree and continues to invoke the God of Israel. Grieved that Daniel does not desist and faced with the irrevocable character of the decree, Darius places Daniel in the den of fierce lions, but God prevents the animals from doing him any harm. The king removes Daniel from the den and decrees that the God of Daniel be reverenced throughout the empire.

In Luke's end-time discourse, there is a notable divergence here. The fall of Jerusalem had been seen as part of the eschatological scene. By the time Luke's Gospel was written, Jerusalem was already destroyed and the end had not occurred. Hence, the fall of the city in this gospel is "de-eschatologized" and is simply placed in an historical setting. It is then followed by the end–time descriptions of the heavens, the seas, and the terrified population. But the elect should stand firm, for their redemption is close at hand.

While apocalyptic language is not always easy to understand, there is one over–arching message: the sovereignty of God. We really do not know what form the end of history will take, and, even less, the time of its occurrence. But we do know that God has an ultimate plan and that all unfolds according to his providence.

Points to Ponder

> The beginning and the end: the hand of God
> Human freedom and the right of worship
> Standing upright in the faith

Year II

> Revelation 18:1–2, 21–23; 19:1–3, 9a
> Psalm 100:1b–2, 3, 4, 5
> Luke 21:20–28

The end will not come before the downfall of the "great whore" Rome. The avenging angel sees this apocalyptic Babylon as a huge trash heap that has become a haven for demons and every unclean species of bird and beast. In her disgrace there will be no semblance of joy—no music, no art, no light, no marriage festivities. Her formerly lucrative mercantile ventures brought nothing but havoc to the nations.

With apocalyptic contrast, the heavenly choir sings of God's glory. He has eliminated the great whore and her corrupting spirit. The smoke of her dissolution will cease forever. It is the blessed who now enter for the wedding feast of the Lamb.

Luke's description of the end-time is less graphic. He is equally strong in stating that the time of its appearance is not known. But those who have been united to Christ and live in his Spirit should stand upright and hold their heads high, for their redemption is at hand.

Points to Ponder

The final destruction of evil: Egypt, Babylon, Rome
The wedding of the Lamb and the elect
Standing upright: the posture of the free person

FRIDAY OF THE THIRTY-FOURTH WEEK IN ORDINARY TIME

Year I

Daniel 7:2–14
Daniel 3:75, 76, 77, 78, 79, 80, 81
Luke 21:29–33

The four beasts of Daniel's dream, familiar to us by now, represent the four empires. The winged lion (Babylon), plucked wings (Kings Nebuchadnezzar and Belshazzar); the bear (the Medes); the leopard (the Persians); the beast with the horn (the Hellenists who gave rise to Antiochus Epiphanes). Offsetting this vision of destruction is the emergence of God himself (the Ancient One). All the kingdoms lose their dominion. Finally the Son of Man, the messianic figure, appears and is accorded full honors and an everlasting dominion.

Written in the second century BC, the book exemplifies the strong eschatological expectation that was present before the dawn of Christianity. The fact is that the reign of God appeared in a totally unexpected way, which many people found impossible to understand or accept. In today's Gospel, Jesus speaks of the time of the kingdom's emergence. When all the signs are present, just as the signs in nature point to the arrival of summer, so too the kingdom has signs of its forthcoming emergence. This is a kingdom that is present already in the person of Jesus. Perhaps we too yearn too much for the future without realizing what it means to be presently citizens of the kingdom. What a blessing! Jesus once said there was never a person born of woman greater than John the Baptist, but that the least in the kingdom of God is greater than he. That means each one of us.

Points to Ponder

> The end of evil
> The victory of the Son of Man
> The permanent character of the word of God

Year II

> Revelation 20:1–4, 11—21:2
> Psalm 84:3, 4, 5–6a and 8a
> Luke 21:29–33

As Revelation draws to a close, its imagery is heavenly in more ways than one. Without pressing the imagery, the main ideas are clear enough: the transformation of the world, the salvation of the just, and the punishment of the evildoer. The dragon or devil is shackled for a thousand years, after which he will be released for a short time. This book cannot be understood if taken literally, as is evident from the strong convictions that accompanied the dawn of the year 1000 AD. The millennium believers held that the thousand-year reign of the just with Christ would begin at that time.

The judgment scene features thrones, probably the twenty-four thrones intended for the saved Israel and the twelve apostles. Those who were martyred are the first to come forward. They had never betrayed Christ; they come to life and begin a thousand-year reign with him.

A second judgment is universal in character. All the dead emerge and are judged according to their deeds. Those whose names are not written in the book of life are condemned by the One seated on the great throne (at this point, perhaps the figures of God and Christ coalesce). The evildoers are consigned to the punishment of a second death. The closing is a scene of the heavenly Jerusalem, situated in a new heaven and a new earth. It is the bride of Christ, the dwelling placed of the elect.

Points to Ponder

Final separation of good and evil
Priority of the martyrs
Final era: transformation, not destruction

SATURDAY OF THE THIRTY-FOURTH WEEK IN ORDINARY TIME

Year I

Daniel 7:15–27
Daniel 3:82, 83, 84, 85, 86, 87
Luke 21:34–36

The reading from Daniel gives the prophet the meaning of the four beasts, with special attention given the aftermath of the fourth kingdom (especially the fourth horn), the reign of Antiochus, and the persecution of the Jews that transpired at the time of the book's composition. He was a blasphemer and was allowed to persecute the Jews for three and a half years (seven was number of "perfection"; half of that was a major evil). This is to be followed by the final triumph of the just—a kingdom with dominion over all others, everlasting, in total service to God.

The Lucan Jesus wants nothing more than that the Lord's disciples be part of that kingdom of God, ready and waiting for his return. Jesus prays that they will be unaffected by the tribulation that will precede the end. The key to victory remains vigilance and alertness.

In these readings, which have preceded the end of the liturgical year, the clear message has been "Watch and wait." It is clearly stated that although there will be havoc and chaos, the end belongs to the Lord. The universe is the Lord's, as is the life of each one of us. We have all made mistakes. Regrets must be part of our past. But with trust and confidence, we know that the God who has shown us so much love will not let us down in the final hour.

Points to Ponder

> The passing of the great empires
> The fidelity of God
> Trust and confidence in God

Year II

> Revelation 22:1–7
> Psalm 95:1–2, 3–5, 6–7ab
> Luke 21:34–36

The final picture of the heavenly city continues the story of God's generosity. The life-giving water issues from the throne of God and the Lamb; the tree of life produces fruit every month of the year. No semblance of evil will be found there. All of its citizens will worship God and the Lamb; the name of the Lamb will be inscribed on their foreheads. There will be no night nor any need for light from the sun or a lamp; God alone will be their light. The promise of the Lord is that he will come.

Yet all time is in the hands of the Lord. The message of today's Gospel envisions our being caught up in the events of daily life. There is the danger of carelessness, carousing, and anxiety. The only antidote is vigilance and prayer.

Many people have difficulty with reflections on the end of time. They wonder what it means to them, when it is their own mortality they deal with all the time. There is no problem in moving the end-time into a personal framework. The basic message remains always the same. "Christ will come again." It is a message that calls all of us to vigilance.

Points to Ponder

> The life-giving water
> The light of Christ
> My personal end-time

Also by Roland Faley
Published by Paulist Press

Apocalypse Then and Now

Biblical Profiles

Footprints on the Mountain

From Genesis to Apocalypse

The Mysteries of Light